Reforming Capitalism for the Common Good

Rather than surrender to the anarchy of the market, human intelligence should be used to buffer the hard edges of capitalism, improve society, enhance the quality of life, and reduce human suffering.

Vernon M. Briggs Jr., Institutional Economist

Reforming Capitalism for the Common Good

Essays in Institutional and Post-Keynesian Economics

Charles J. Whalen

Research Fellow, The Baldy Center for Law and Social Policy, University at Buffalo, Buffalo, NY, USA

Edward Elgar PUBLISHING

Cheltenham, UK • Northampton, MA, USA

Published by
Edward Elgar Publishing Limited
The Lypiatts
15 Lansdown Road
Cheltenham
Glos GL50 2JA
UK

Edward Elgar Publishing, Inc.
William Pratt House
9 Dewey Court
Northampton
Massachusetts 01060
USA

A catalogue record for this book
is available from the British Library

Library of Congress Control Number: 2022939117

This book is available electronically in the **Elgar**online
Economics subject collection
http://dx.doi.org/10.4337/9781803926292

Printed on elemental chlorine free (ECF)
recycled paper containing 30% Post-Consumer Waste

ISBN 978 1 80392 628 5 (cased)
ISBN 978 1 80392 629 2 (eBook)

Typeset by Sparks – www.sparkspublishing.com

Printed and bound in the USA

Contents

Acknowledgments

The author and publisher wish to thank the following publishers who have kindly given permission for use of copyrighted material.

Bard Journal of Social Sciences/Bard College for the article: "Economics must change: workforce insecurity and the need for a new political economy," *Bard Journal of Social Sciences* 5 (1–2), Summer 1996, 34–40.

Inderscience for the article: "Post-Keynesian economics: a pluralistic alternative to conventional economics," *International Journal of Pluralism and Economics Education* 7 (1), 2016, 22–38.

Labor and Employment Relations Association for the essay: "Economic insecurity and the problem-solving approach of John R. Commons," in P. Voos (ed.), *Industrial Relations Research Association Series: Proceedings of the Fiftieth Annual Meeting*, 1998, 320–327.

Levy Economics Institute of Bard College for the essay: "Economic policy for the real world," *Policy Note* No. 2010–1, July 2010, 1–5.

SAGE Publishing for the article "Social unionism in western New York: the case of the Economic Development Group," *Labor Studies Journal* 35 (4), December 2010, 540–565.

Springer Nature for the essays: "A Minsky perspective on the global recession of 2009," in D. Tavasci and J. Toporowski (eds.), *Minsky, Crisis and Development*, 2010, 106–126; and "Post-Keynesian institutionalism: past, present, and future," *Evolutionary and Institutional Economics Review* 17 (1), January 2020, 71–92.

Taylor & Francis Group for the articles: "Saving capitalism by making it good: the monetary economics of John R. Commons," *Journal of Economic Issues*, 27 (4), December 1993, 1155–1179; "Social security: a view from beyond the beltway" under the title "A nonexpert view of social security," *Challenge* 48 (4), July–August 2005, 5–10; "Full employment with liberty: John R. Commons's perspective and its continuing relevance," *Journal of Economic Issues* 44 (2), June 2010, 559–568; "John R. Commons and government as employer of last resort: three paths to a progressive right to work," *Journal of Economic Issues* 54 (2), June 2020, 428–435; "The 'middle way' of John R. Commons: pursuing reasonable value in the age of unreason," *Journal of Economic Issues* 54 (4), December 2020, 1161–1173; "Stabilizing the unstable economy: Minsky and Simons on business cycle theory and policy" under the title "Stabilizing the unstable economy: more on the Minsky-Simons connection," *Journal of Economic Issues*, 25 (3), September 1991, 739–763; "Budget amendment offers toxin, not tonic," *Challenge* 38 (3), May–June 1995, 50; "Destabilizing an unstable economy: the erosion of automatic stabilizers" (co-authored by Jeffrey Wenger) under the title "Destabilizing an unstable economy," *Challenge* 45 (6), November–December 2002, 70–92; "Money manager capitalism and the end of shared prosperity," *Journal of Economic Issues* 31 (2), June 1997, 517–525; "Integrating Schumpeter and Keynes: Hyman Minsky's theory of capitalist development," *Journal of Economic Issues* 35 (4), December 2001, 805–823; "Money manager capitalism: still here, but not quite as expected," *Journal of Economic Issues* 36 (2), June 2002, 401–406; "Minsky goes to Buffalo—and takes on the economics establishment," *Forum for Social Economics* 40 (2), July 2011, 273–280; "The post-Keynesian institutionalism of Wallace Peterson" under the title "Wallace C. Peterson: a post-Keynesian institutionalist," *Journal of Economic Issues* 50 (2), June 2016, 584–593; "Financialization and income inequality: a post-Keynesian institutionalist analysis" (co-authored by David A. Zalewski), *Journal of Economic Issues* 44 (3), September 2010, 757–777; and "Post-Keynesian institutionalism and the failure of neoliberalism" under the title "Post-Keynesian institutionalism and the failure of neoliberalism: returning realism to economics by highlighting economic insecurity as the flip side of financialization," *Journal of Economic Issues* 55 (2), June 2021, 469–476.

In addition, the author thanks Edward Elgar Publishing for permission to use the following copyrighted essays: "The institutional approach to political economy," in F. Foldvary (ed.), *Beyond Neoclassical Economics*, 1996, 83–99; "Sending jobs offshore from the United States: what are the consequences?" *European Journal of Economics and Economic Policies: Intervention* 2 (2), November 2005, 33–40; and "Human resources: the key to institutional economics after the Great Recession," in S. Kates (ed.), *The Global Financial Crisis: What Have We Learnt?* 2011, 204–217.

The author also thanks Alan Sturmer, Glen Atkinson, Jeffrey Wenger, David Zalewski, Vernon Briggs, Linda Whalen, Jack Reardon, and the Association for Evolutionary Economics, which produces the *Journal of Economic Issues*.

Foreword

Glen Atkinson

We live in times of instability. This is not new. Despite temporary respites which often lead us to think that we are living in a "new economy," reality demonstrates that our economy does not move smoothly from one equilibrium point to another and the consequences of instability can be severe. Mainstream economics has failed to grasp this reality. Charles Whalen advocates for a reconstruction of economics that understands instability and its causes.

Charles has been the leader in bringing institutional economics and post-Keynesian economics together. Post-Keynesian economics is not the Keynesian economics that countless students learned in the Paul Samuelson textbook and knock-offs of that book. John Maynard Keynes began the reconstruction of economics with an emphasis on uncertainty and the importance of stabilization. Throughout Charles's career, he has added to the reconstruction of economics. This book is a witness to his conscientious efforts to reach that ambitious goal.

This collection of the work of Charles demonstrates his knowledge and interests. Two of those interests are the well-being of workers and the economics of post-Keynesian institutionalism, a perspective that provides the foundation for his worker-oriented investigations. Today, as a result of Charles's efforts to reconstruct economics, there is a group of people who identify themselves as post-Keynesian institutionalists.

Charles brings to the effort to reconstruct economics not only a keen and well-versed understanding of economics but also the skills of a successful practitioner and communicator. His work as a journalist at *BusinessWeek*, consultant to labor unions, and macroeconomist with the Congressional Budget Office gives him insight into how business, labor, and government view the economy.

Charles leans heavily on John R. Commons and Hyman Minsky, and appreciates that both are linked to Keynes. In the mid-1920s, Keynes ([1925] 1932, p. 334) considered Commons "an eminent American economist" and "one of the first to recognize the nature of the economic transition amidst the early stages we are now living." In particular, Keynes gave credit to Commons for his understanding of three historical stages in the evolution of capitalism: the era of scarcity, which centered on handicraft production; the era of abundance, which centered on industrial production, and the era of stabilization, which resulted in the industrial stage of "banker capitalism."

The Commons–Keynes understanding of the economy as evolving through stages had its origin a century ago, but still underlies Minsky's analysis of the financial system and the work of Charles and other post-Keynesian institutionalists. Minsky's stages of economics are quite similar to Commons's stages, but Minsky had the chance to examine the continuing evolution of the economy over many more decades. For example, the Berle-Means finding (of the 1930s) that managers rather than owners ran the corporation, in an era Minsky called "managerial capitalism," was eventually rendered out of date in the "money manager" era of the 1980s and beyond. Over time, professional investment firms were established to manage the financial assets of not only the wealthy, but also ordinary workers with pensions. These firms demanded high returns and corporate managers lost their independence from stockholders, resulting in a focus on short-term corporate strategies. Finance began to rule corporate management.

In this new era, businesses need continuing debt financing instead of one-shot loans, but loans based on profit expectations are inherently risky. When economic expansion is slow, it becomes more difficult to refinance existing debt. This is Minsky's explanation, in brief, of his financial instability hypothesis, which describes a thrust to instability that is inherent in our contemporary economic system. To understand our current era, we must understand both its inherent instability and the contours of today's money manager capitalism. Whalen's work strives for just that.

The reconstruction of economics includes recognition of the abundance that created instability and the institutions which were developed to address it. Most often, institutional changes have been moves to secure scarcity. Mainstream economics textbooks begin with a statement that prices allocate scarce resources to their highest and best use. In the real world, however, abundance led to economic instability. Business executives were concerned about falling prices and bankers were concerned that their loans could not be paid back. Bankers responded by getting colleagues appointed to corporate boards and by working to prevent entry of new businesses into industries where they were exposed.

Another example of capitalism's evolution by means of institutional adjustment is provided by changing views on value, property, and competition. In 1890, when the US Supreme Court established exchange value rather than use value as the legal basis for valuing property, it also legalized intangible property. The shift was based on an extension of the Fourteenth Amendment, removing restraints on pursuing an occupation or holding property. However, as Commons ([1924] 1968, 17–18) observed in a detailed examination of Anglo-American law, it was quickly determined that "too much liberty of access on the part of would-be competitors is destructive of that exchange value. During the past three hundred years this excessive liberty has been restrained by the courts in the long line of cases going under the name of 'goodwill' or 'unfair competition.'"

Yet this is only part of the evidence that makes reconstruction of economics necessary. Charles understands the evidence, knows about the serious problems which call for reconstruction of economics, and has the qualities that contribute to this project. First, he is an excellent writer. Second, his knowledge of heterodox economics is broad and deep as the articles in this collection attest. Third, he has a vision of purpose which has inspired his work, whether his own or that done in collaboration with others. Let the reconstruction continue.

Meanwhile, as important as is that reconstruction, it remains only one portion of Charles's vision. Charles has a passion for improving workers' job opportunities and working conditions. He does not see employees as commodities or simply human resources. They have families and are citizens who make up a major part of our economic society. As their lives go, so does our society. However, against the backdrop of several successful state and local campaigns to increase minimum wages, and a continuing effort to do so nationwide through federal law, much of the media blames current inflation on rising wages. Many business commentators make wages sound like an invasion of locusts that ravage our stock buybacks.

Inflation has many causes. But a large contributing factor is that the coronavirus pandemic has disrupted fragile international supply chains, which are products of a globalization process driven by money manager capitalism's obsession with offshoring, outsourcing, and just-in-time production. For decades, those supply chains, designed in pursuit of profit over worker well-being, provided us with easy access to goods from low-wage countries. Now, after having lived off the wage "race to the bottom" for so long, consumers are paying a price for the existing shareholder-driven system and are being encouraged to blame inflation on workers, when the focus should be on the way globalization has been structured.

Of course, the problems with our current global economic system are not a reason to build a wall around our national economy. The United States is a vital part of the world economy. But we need to examine the consequences of changes in our institutions. Actual observation of the working of the economy is required, rather than just pulling shopworn concepts off the shelf. As Commons said, institutions matter. We also need to remember that institutions are not eternal, but are shaped by "working" rules, which means – as Charles stresses throughout this volume – that we need to continue to reform and reconstruct capitalism. After all, we are evolutionary economists.

REFERENCES

Commons, John R. (1924) 1968. *Legal Foundations of Capitalism*. Madison: University of Wisconsin Press.

Keynes, John Maynard. (1925) 1932. "Am I a Liberal?" Reprinted in *Essays in Persuasion*, 295–306. New York: Harcourt, Brace and Company.

PART I

Introduction

1. Reforming capitalism: economics at the crossroads of institutionalism and post-Keynesianism

This book presents selected essays on economic research conducted during a career of more than three decades.[1] The unifying thread is an effort to highlight economic challenges facing working families and shed light on how such challenges might be addressed through stakeholder engagement and constructive use of public policy. In short, the book aims at reforming capitalism for the common good.

Throughout the volume, economic activity is viewed from the crossroads of institutional and post-Keynesian economics. From that vantage point, economic outcomes are shaped by history, institutions, and expectations about an uncertain future. The chapters are also grounded in the premise that markets are not self-correcting, a key common element in the work of institutionalist founders such as Thorstein Veblen (1898) and John R. Commons (1925) as well as that of John Maynard Keynes (1935).

CAPITALISM AND THE COMMON GOOD

Following in the footsteps of Commons and Keynes, my orientation is toward socioeconomic reform. Like both Commons (1925; 1934a) and Keynes ([1926a] 1972; 1936), I focus on working toward a better-managed form of capitalism – through a process of identifying and correcting its most outstanding defects. As Commons (1934a, 143) explained, his aim was to "save capitalism by making it good."[2]

Hyman Minsky – an insightful post-Keynesian economist who appreciated the common ground of Commons and Keynes – had a similar reformist bent. Minsky (1986, 9–10) believed that capitalism is inherently flawed, owing to a tendency toward economic instability, but also that sensible institutions and policies can and should be used to "contain the thrust to instability." In addition, Minsky (1986, xiii) valued standing on the shoulders of giants such as Keynes to better understand economic life. While Keynes is an influence throughout this book, I stand most directly on the shoulders of Commons and Minsky.

Drawing on the work of Commons, Keynes, and Minsky, some important features of capitalism come into focus and are reflected in the chapters of this volume. One is that capitalism "is not a static or single concept" (Commons 1934b, 766). It has taken various forms over time; different varieties often coexist at the same time; and innumerable variants are possible. For example, as emphasized by Commons (1924; 1934b), collective action determines the nature of competition as well as the meaning of liberty and property.[3]

Another feature is that "capitalism" and "socialism" often blur in the real world – and what's most important "is for society to be democratic and humane" (Minsky 1985, 221).[4] Familiar with threats to democracy from both right-wing and left-wing authoritarianism, Commons, Keynes and Minsky saw a democratic, reformed capitalism as the best hope for humanity. Today, the struggle for genuine economic and political democracy – and against forces that favor plutocracy and autocracy – continues in the United States and around the world.

A third feature is the need for ongoing reform. Commons, Keynes and Minsky understood that pursuit of their reformist aim required commitment to an unending process, not enactment of a once-and-for-all economic fix. As socio-economic life evolves, new problems emerge and must be addressed. As Commons (1921; 1925, 692–693) argued, "There has not been and never will be an automatic harmony of [economic] interests… . If [any] harmony of interests is actually attained, it can be accomplished only…[by] dealing with each conflict as it arises, and settling it the best we know how" – which includes taking steps, whenever possible, to prevent the conflict from reoccurring.[5]

Commons, Keynes and Minsky drew attention to some of the most serious shortcomings of the advanced capitalist societies in which they lived. Of course, each gave special attention to unemployment (especially joblessness caused by business-cycle downturns) and extreme income inequality. But Commons went further to recognize the broader dimensions of worker economic insecurity, as did Minsky toward the end of his career.[6] In addition, Keynes ([1926b] 1972, 311) underscored the perennial challenge of combining economic efficiency, social justice, and individual liberty. The essays in this book focus heavily on unemployment and contemporary dimensions of worker insecurity, but attention is also given to inequality and the efficiency-justice-liberty nexus.

While advancing worker well-being was always a driving force in Commons's work, he consistently sought to place workers' interests in the context of promoting the common good.[7] That approach also underlies the chapters in this book. Pursuit of the common good is a vital, shared aspect of institutionalism and post-Keynesianism – as is the belief that defining, ensuring, and promoting it requires stakeholder engagement in public policy and other economic decision-making.[8] The constructive use of public policy is particularly important to institutionalist and post-Keynesian perspectives on the common good – especially collective action based on recognition that individual freedom *through* government is as essential as freedom *from* government.[9] As post-Keynesian institutionalist Charles K. Wilber (1991, 567) writes, the common good includes "a set of social conditions necessary for the realization of human dignity which transcend the arena of private exchange and contract."[10]

Pursuit of the common good aims to pay off over time for everyone individually, not just collectively. But institutionalists and post-Keynesians are not naïve: The resolution of socioeconomic problems usually comes, at least in the near term, with gains for some and losses for others – and those who stand to lose seldom take the prospect lightly.[11] Moreover, on the one hand there is the task of instituting meaningful stakeholder engagement, public policies that truly assist those in need, and other social conditions associated with human dignity. And on the other hand is the reality of unequal distribution of power, which often stands in the way of what needs to be done and gives coercion the upper hand over persuasion in dispute resolution. Thus, pursuit of the common good is rarely a matter of merely sketching out and publicizing a sensible policy agenda. Rather it is an ongoing struggle, not just in the world of ideas, but also in workplaces, communities, and, of course, the halls of government.

RECONSTRUCTING ECONOMICS

The ideas and research publications of academics do not change the world on their own, but they play a crucial role. As Keynes (1936, 383) wrote in the final chapter of *The General Theory of Employment, Interest and Money*, "The ideas of economists and political philosophers, both when they are right and when they are wrong, are more powerful than is commonly understood. Indeed, the world is ruled by little else." However, the problem in economics has long been that the old idea of self-regulating markets has remained at the heart of the professional mainstream, giving some ground to other ways of thinking in times of crisis, but usually only until memories of an emergency start to fade. As a result of its outlook, conventional economics often misses much of the economic distress that occurs in the real world; even worse, it tends to blame government (and labor unions) for the economic ills that do receive attention.[12]

In the early 1990s, I participated in a macroeconomic theory workshop that Hy Minsky organized at the Levy Economics Institute of Bard College. Describing his aims for the event, Minsky (1991, 4) wrote, "The perspective that underlies the work of this workshop is that to move policy it is necessary to move the discipline." A few years later, I served as a resident scholar at the Levy Institute, and it was during that residency that I wrote the first article in

Part II of this collection, Chapter 2 (published in 1996). It sketches several dimensions of rising worker insecurity in the United States since about 1970; explains how conventional economic theory blinds economists to this reality; and argues that a fundamental reconstruction of economics – grounded in history and institutional reality – is required to better deal with rising insecurity and other real-world economic problems.[13]

Following Chapter 2, the next two selections outline, in turn, institutionalism and post-Keynesianism, a pair of complementary alternatives to conventional economics. Chapter 3 (published in 1996) surveys the origins (in the work of Veblen, Commons, and others) and development of institutional economics, giving special attention to core preconceptions, key theories, and applications. It concludes with a discussion of challenges facing institutionalism, including the need to build bridges to post-Keynesian economics and other non-neoclassical schools of economic thought. Chapter 4 (published in 2016) surveys the post-Keynesian tradition, including its origins and various strands, fundamental preconceptions, and major findings. It also highlights the school's pluralistic features by looking first at the tradition as a whole and then at the economic outlook and policy views of Minsky.

THE INSTITUTIONALISM OF COMMONS

Part III explores the contemporary relevance of Commons's institutionalism. Chapter 5 (published in 1998) outlines problem solving as the foundation of his institutional approach to economics, giving special attention to workers' economic insecurity in the 1990s. Among the keys to Commons's problem-solving approach are investigations by researchers answerable to a diverse group of stakeholder representatives (such as an "administrative commission"), a focus on remedies that reinforce the common ground shared by competing economic interests and that might prevent a particular problem from reappearing, and an emphasis on identification and diffusion of best industrial practices.

Chapter 6 (published in 1993) examines Commons's contributions to monetary economics, which stem from viewing business cycles as the most important of all labor problems and aiming to "save capitalism by making it good." It shows that Common's perspective anticipates the post-Keynesian endogenous approach to money and that his profit-margin theory of cycles underscores institutionalism's compatibility with Keynes and post-Keynesianism.

Chapter 7 (published in 2005) presents the findings of a civic engagement project I organized (for the nonprofit, nonpartisan Interactivity Foundation) to explore alternatives and consequences regarding the future of retirement security in the United States. Broadly compatible with the sort of advisory committees favored by Commons to address economic problems, the project panel expressed deep concerns about the proposals of President George W. Bush's Commission to Strengthen Social Security (including the redirection of a portion of payroll taxes to individual retirement accounts) and revealed a sharp gap between the thinking of many federal policymakers and ordinary citizens. The panel's work stressed the need for – and value of – a thoughtful national discussion on public policies affecting retirement.

Chapter 8 (published in 2005) investigates, in the tradition of Commons's work on expanding labor markets, the magnitude of job offshoring from the United States as well as the types of occupations affected or "at risk." It describes offshoring's impact on enterprises, workers, and communities, and recommends steps – including expansion of federal trade adjustment assistance – to foster a more prosperous economy in the face of this trend.

Chapter 9 (published in 2010) traces a decade of union engagement in economic development within western New York, highlighting a case that echoes Commons's call for institutions that foster collaborative problem solving and community-wide consensus building. It also situates that case within the literature on labor studies and trade union history, areas of scholarship in which Commons conducted pathbreaking work that was integral to his institutional economics.[14]

The next two essays were written in response to the global financial crisis of 2007–2009. Chapter 10 (published in 2010) presents Commons's three-part strategy – addressing money, people, and politics – for curing joblessness while saving capitalism. It also underscores how Commons's insights extend beyond conventional Keynesian economics and remain relevant to contemporary economic downturns. Chapter 11 (published in 2011) surveys the emergence, evolution, and contemporary relevance of human resource economics, a policy-oriented research field championed by institutionalist Vernon Briggs and grounded in the work of Commons. The chapter argues that drawing on such work – which puts the attention of economics squarely on workers' capacities, contributions, and well-being – provides a useful starting point for institutionalist research in the aftermath of the Great Recession.

The final two essays of Part III are the most recent of the selections in this section (both were published in 2020). Chapter 12 identifies three arguments (legal, financial, and historical) in Commons's research that provide a case for government to hire the unemployed. It also highlights the contemporary relevance of those arguments (which draw attention to economic coercion, public works, and democracy) and concludes by maintaining that Common's writings offer a way to reclaim the "right to work" as a progressive cause.[15] Chapter 13, written against the backdrop of antidemocratic trends in the United States and abroad, builds on Commons's work to offer present-day proposals for protecting and strengthening American democracy, including ways to save judicial sovereignty and to bolster institutions consistent with the process of widespread stakeholder engagement that Commons called "collective democracy."

THE POST-KEYNESIANISM OF MINSKY

Part IV analyzes the US economy by standing on the shoulders of Minsky. Chapter 14 (published in 1991) outlines Minsky's perspective on business cycles, highlighting elements also found in the research of his University of Chicago professor, Henry Simons. It concludes that Minsky and Simons shared an endogenous view of cycles also held by Keynes and the institutionalists, suggesting that contemporary neoclassical cycle theories are an aberration from the historical mainstream in macroeconomics and that the work of Minsky provides a valuable starting point for revival of non-neoclassical cycle research.[16]

Chapter 15 (published in 1995) highlights – from a Minskyan perspective – several economic and political dangers of a proposed balanced budget amendment to the US Constitution, which received considerable attention in 1994 and early 1995 as the top item in the Republicans' Contract with America, but failed in the US Senate on March 2, 1995. Such an amendment (which these days is still proposed regularly by some members of Congress) would prohibit sensible fiscal policy action such as allowing federal budget deficits to adjust with economic conditions; it would also impede establishment of federal capital budgeting – and distract from robust public discussion of government's role in addressing socioeconomic challenges. This short essay summarizes a public policy brief that I wrote for the Levy Economics Institute in advance of House and Senate votes on the amendment (see Whalen 1995); the brief was distributed publicly before those votes as a working paper.[17]

Chapter 16 (co-authored by Jeffrey Wenger and published in 2002) explains the importance of the economy's built-in economic stabilizers (such as progressive taxes, unemployment insurance, minimum wages, and public income supports) and the risks their erosion poses for the American economy. It also draws on the work of Minsky to recommend policy action that would shore up the system's stabilizers – and explores why the US economy avoided a more serious downturn at the start of the new millennium despite the weakening of its stabilizers over several decades.[18]

The next three essays address the emergence and consequences of the shareholder-driven economy that Minsky called "money manager capitalism." Chapter 17 (published in 1997) traces the development of Minsky's ideas on the evolution of the US economic system after World War II; outlines his conception of the era of money manager capitalism (which emerged in the 1980s); and describes the connection between the rise of the present period and the end of the more broadly shared prosperity of the early postwar era. Chapter 18 (published in 2001) explains the purpose and essential elements of Minsky's theory of capitalist development, then applies that theory to the US economy, identifying several stages from merchant capitalism to money manager capitalism. It concludes by identifying possibilities for future research and by suggesting that Minsky's theory provides a vital way to inject greater attention to finance into contemporary institutionalism. Chapter 19 (published in 2002) demonstrates – in the wake of the collapse of the Internet-driven economic boom of the late 1990s – that Minsky's core insights about money manager capitalism remain relevant, despite several unexpected developments (including nearly a decade of technology-driven growth, which Barry Bluestone and Bennett Harrison attribute to public investments made prior to the era of money managers).

The final three essays in Part IV were written in the wake of the global financial crisis of 2007–2009. Chapter 20 (published in 2010) presents a Minskyan perspective on the far-reaching economic downturn triggered by that financial crisis. It highlights cyclical as well as structural aspects of the downturn (features that are perhaps best understood by drawing on the insight Minsky gained from Keynes and Schumpeter, respectively) and concludes by comparing Minsky's policy outlook with the recovery and reform initiatives actually pursued in response to the crisis. Chapter 21 (also published in 2010) offers a snapshot of economic challenges facing workers and their families in the wake of the Great Recession, emphasizing that the underlying problem is what Wallace Peterson called a "silent depression" – the accompanying "flip side" of the rise of Minsky's money manager capitalism. It also outlines a reform-oriented economic policy agenda, stressing the importance that Minsky placed on constructive public action. Chapter 22 (published in 2011) draws on Minsky's work not only to interpret the Great Recession and challenge his marginalization by mainstream economists, but also to shed light on the struggles of American workers and communities (such as Buffalo, New York) undergoing significant economic transformation and dislocation.

POST-KEYNESIAN INSTUTUTIONALISM

Part V closes the volume with four essays on the integration of institutional and post-Keynesian economics. Chapter 23 (published in 2020) documents the origins and development of post-Keynesian institutional economics, emphasizing the common ground long shared by many institutionalists and post-Keynesians. It also highlights the tradition's existing contributions and outlines directions for future research in areas ranging from microeconomic analysis to international economics.

Chapter 24 (published in 2016) assesses the pioneering post-Keynesian institutionalist contributions of Wallace Peterson (1921–2012) in three areas: foundations of economics (including attention to finance and economic power); analyses of the US economy (including research on the "silent depression"); and discussions of public policy (including infrastructure investment, active labor-market policies, and tax reform). It concludes by highlighting aspects of Peterson's work that remain relevant to the study of contemporary economic issues.

Chapter 25 (co-authored by David A. Zalewski and published in 2010) analyzes the link between financialization – a key feature of money manager capitalism – and increasing income inequality across a number of developed nations. It also demonstrates that the development of modern financial structures does not preclude the existence of egalitarian public policies that aim to reduce inequality.

Chapter 26 (published in 2021), the final essay, describes the various dimensions of US economic insecurity that have persisted for more than a generation, and explains how post-Keynesian institutionalism accounts for that insecurity as a consequence of the neoliberal pursuit of financialization. It also identifies several policy recommendations offered by post-Keynesian institutionalists, and stresses that the COVID-19 pandemic underscores the need for such policies.

LOOKING BACK – AND AHEAD

Reflecting on several decades of studying and writing about economics, economic problems, and public policy from a heterodox perspective, one might be tempted to feel discouraged. The economic mainstream remains enamored with models grounded in assumptions of hyper-rational expectations and continuously-clearing labor markets. Meanwhile, many of the same economic difficulties highlighted decades ago do not merely remain – they are even more serious today because they have been neglected and allowed to fester. And the situation is even worse when we recognize that democracy is currently in danger partly because demagogues have exploited the discontent associated with these economic problems.

But there has been some headway, even if much of the small progressive shift in thinking on economic analysis and policy over the past several decades can be attributed more to the march of real-world events than to the persuasive powers of unconventional economists within the academy.[19] Take, for example, the problems of economic insecurity and income inequality, which are now hard to ignore as contemporary issues. At the start of my career, institutionalist and post-Keynesian concerns about worker insecurity and the associated erosion of the US industrial base were dismissed by many economic advisers to Democrats as well as Republicans, and inequality research was largely in the shadows of the profession. Today, however, the Economic Policy Institute (founded by scholars with ties to institutionalism) and other think tanks highlight aspects of economic insecurity, and some of the world's most prominent economists (such as Emmanuel Saez and Thomas Piketty) study inequality.[20]

Moreover, institutionalists and post-Keynesians have made a difference. For instance, we offered vital analytical and policy insight in response to the global financial crisis and subsequent Great Recession – problems conventional economists never saw coming and dismissed as unimaginable. When that crisis hit, Minsky was featured on the cover of the *Wall Street Journal* (Lahart 2007), but he died more than a decade earlier, so it was up to those most familiar with Minsky's ideas to apply what we had learned and build on his intellectual foundation. To that end, we drew upon both his financial instability hypothesis and his theory of capitalist development (see, for example, Chapter 20). As it turns out, even conventional economists admitted that Minskyan insights proved more useful in the crisis than mainstream theory (Yellen 2009; Caballero 2010, 88).

There has also been considerable advance within institutionalism over the past several decades on at least two fronts: the economics of Commons, and the relationship between institutionalism and post-Keynesianism.[21] At the beginning of my career, institutionalism was heavily oriented toward the work of Veblen as interpreted by Clarence Ayres and his students; Commons was largely neglected among institutional economists. In addition, some prominent institutionalists argued that the economics of both Commons and the post-Keynesians were distinct from, and should remain independent of, modern institutionalism (see, for example, Gruchy 1987, 27–28, 147–153). Since that time, however, I've had the good fortune to live through, and contribute to, not only a resurgence of interest in the contemporary relevance of Commons, but also the emergence of a post-Keynesian institutionalism that appreciates the common ground (and underscores the compatibility) of the institutionalist and post-Keynesian traditions.

Looking ahead, there is much to be done by economists seeking to analyze real-world economic problems and reform capitalism for the common good – an aim that includes pursuit of a new, and more inclusive, era of broadly shared prosperity at home and abroad. Commons's insights remain relevant, and Minsky's theory of capitalist development provides an important analytical framework for our work, having already proven capable of generating cogent and integrative analyses of financialization, instability, inequality, insecurity, and industrial decline.[22] But much more is needed, especially in the face of mounting threats to democracy around the world and the existential threat of global warming – a problem that starkly underscores the need to temper and channel pursuit of near-term individual self-interest for the common good. I hope this book provides a starting point for such research and inspires others to join those already working at the crossroads of institutionalism and post-Keynesianism.[23]

NOTES

1. Over the course of my career, I've had the privilege to observe and analyze the economy from a variety of vantage points through work as a professor, workplace educator, consultant to labor unions, facilitator of business-labor partnerships, civic engagement coordinator, public policy researcher (Levy Economics Institute), journalist and editor (*BusinessWeek* and *Perspectives on Work*), and government economist (Congressional Budget Office). In 2014, I received the Outstanding Practitioner Award of the Labor and Employment Relations Association; in 2018, I served as president of the Association for Evolutionary Economics.
2. According to Kenneth H. Parsons (1985, 757), who edited Common's *The Economics of Collective Action* (Commons 1950), Commons devoted his career to understanding the US economy "in ways that could support [its] humanization and stabilization…, without, I should add, impairing the productivity of the system." For a comprehensive look at Commons's career and research, see Chasse (2017).
3. Also see Keynes ([1925] 1972; [1926a] 1972; [1925] 1981) and Minsky (1991, 10; 1993) on the evolution, varieties, and possible future directions of capitalism.
4. Minsky (1985, 221) writes: "As I see it, the socialism of [Oscar] Lange had more in common with the capitalism of [Henry] Simons than with the socialism of [Joseph] Stalin, and the capitalism of Simons had more in common with the socialism of Lange than with the capitalism of [Adolph] Hitler." In other words, we must look beyond labels—and focus on the values and institutions that shape socioeconomic life. Similarly, it is worth noting that Michael Harrington (1989), long one of the most prominent socialists in the United States, envisioned a socialist future that included markets and private property.
5. For a similar view of the need for continual reform, see Minsky (1986; 1993).
6. For the breadth of Commons's concern for worker insecurity, see Chasse (2017).
7. As Commons (1924, 325) recognized, many synonyms can be found for the "common good." For example, these include: "common interest," "public purpose," and "public welfare."
8. It is interesting to note that *The Times* of London concluded its obituary of Keynes as follows: "He was a humane man genuinely devoted to the cause of the common good" (reprinted in Harris 1947, xxii).
9. Consistent with the perspective on government described above is Commons's (1931, 648) definition of an institution: "collective action in control, liberation, and expansion of individual action." Commons's definition also hints at the unavoidable need for a balance of liberties in society, since all individual liberties impose corresponding duties on others (see also Commons 1924, 84–87).
10. For additional illustrative discussions on the notion of the common good in institutionalism, see Dugger (2010) and Tilman (2008); and for the same in post-Keynesianism, see Marangos (2000) and McKenna and Zannoni (1993).
11. As Deborah Figart (2017, 6) writes in an excellent book that highlights several recent cases of progressive institutional change (including the clashes and

mobilizations required to achieve them), advancing the public interest "may not benefit everyone."

12. Having grown up in a blue-collar family in the Northeastern part of the United States during the 1960s and 1970s, I've long been skeptical of conventional economics. The mainstream view of unemployment, inflation, minimum wages, plant closings, organized labor, and protective labor legislation (such as worker's compensation and unemployment insurance) seemed out of touch with the real world and the struggles of working families. In fact, my first academic article catalogued my concerns about standard economic theory. It began by quoting institutionalist Philip Klein: "In economics,…the paradigm is not the solution, it is the problem" (Whalen 1987a, 259).
13. While at the Levy Institute, I also collaborated with Minsky on a conference paper—published in the *Journal of Post Keynesian Economics* (Minsky and Whalen 1996)—highlighting emergence in the United States of what Minsky named "money manager capitalism."
14. I have written a few articles highlighting aspects of union efforts to address economic issues in western New York. For example, for an early examination, see Whalen (1987b); for a look through the lens of critical management studies, see Whalen (2007); and for an extended analysis that applies an interpretation of Commons's institutionalist research method, see Whalen (2011).
15. For an extended discussion of an institutionalist perspective of the "right to work" as a progressive cause, see my presidential address to the Association for Evolutionary Economics (Whalen 2019), which includes an examination of some specific policy proposals that address joblessness in the context of widespread US economic insecurity, a public-health crisis associated with the increased incidence of drug addiction, and the planetary emergency of global warming.
16. Chapter 14 was written as the second in a pair of articles comparing the business-cycle theory and policy views of Minsky and Simons. For the first article, which is summarized briefly in the second, see Whalen (1988).
17. A summary of my position on the balanced budget amendment proposal was also submitted to a hearing before the US House Judiciary Committee's Subcommittee on the Constitution on January 10, 1995. Owing to space constraints imposed on my original essay in *Challenge*, some financial-system aspects of a Minskyan perspective on the balanced budget amendment are not discussed in Chapter 15, though they do receive attention in Whalen (1995, 32–33). For Minsky's own statement on the proposed constitutional amendment, see Minsky (1995).
18. For a short article that contributed to fiscal policy discussion and action when the dot-com bubble burst at the start of millennium, see Whalen (2001). For a more recent stabilization proposal, written from the same overall economic perspective, see Zalewski and Whalen (2011).
19. Of course, institutionalist and post-Keynesian John Kenneth Galbraith (1958, 13) long ago told us that the march of events is usually more powerful than persuasion.
20. At the start of my career, institutionalist and post-Keynesian concerns about the nation's crumbling and outdated economic infrastructure were also ignored, but a $1.2 trillion infrastructure bill was passed by Congress as this introduction was being written (Lobosco and Luhby 2021).
21. Another area in which there has been considerable progress is the intersection of institutionalism and feminist scholarship. For an important early contribution, see Peterson and Brown (1994).

22. For an exploration of financialization, instability, inequality, insecurity, and industrial decline that extends beyond what is offered in this collection of essays, see Whalen (2020).
23. For a new collaboration that seeks to advance the concepts, theories, and analyses of post-Keynesian institutionalism, see Whalen (2022).

REFERENCES

Caballero, Ricardo J. 2010. "Macroeconomics after the Crisis: Time to Deal with the Pretense-of-Knowledge Syndrome." *Journal of Economic Perspectives* 24 (4): 85–102.

Chasse, John D. 2017. *A Worker's Economist: John R. Commons and His Legacy from Progressivism to the War on Poverty*. New York: Transaction Publishers.

Commons, John R. 1921. "Industrial Relations." In *Trade Unionism and Labor Problems, Second Series*, edited by John R. Commons, 1–16. Boston: Ginn and Company.

Commons, John R. 1924. *Legal Foundations of Capitalism*. New York: Macmillan.

Commons, John R. 1925. "Marx Today: Capitalism and Socialism." *The Atlantic Monthly* 136 (November 25): 682–693.

Commons, John R. 1931. "Institutional Economics." *American Economic Review* 21 (4): 648–657.

Commons, John R. 1934a. *Myself*. New York: Macmillan.

Commons, John R. 1934b. *Institutional Economics: Its Place in Political Economy*. New York: Macmillan.

Commons, John R. 1950. *The Economics of Collective Action*, edited by Kenneth H. Parsons. New York: Macmillan.

Dugger, William M. 2010. "Progressive Alternatives To Re-Regulation." *Journal of Economic Issues* 44 (2): 441–448.

Figart, Deborah M. 2017. *Stories of Progressive Institutional Change: Challenges to the Neoliberal Economy*. Cham, Switzerland: Palgrave Macmillan.

Galbraith, John Kenneth. 1958. *The Affluent Society*. Boston: Houghton Mifflin.

Gruchy, Allan G. 1987. *The Reconstruction of Economics: An Analysis of the Fundamentals of Institutional Economics*. Westport, Connecticut: Greenwood Press.

Harrington, Michael. 1989. *Socialism: Past and Future*. New York: Arcade.

Harris, Seymour Edwin. 1947. *The New Economics: Keynes' Influence on Economics and Public Policy*. New York: Alfred A. Knopf.

Keynes, John Maynard. (1925) 1972. "Am I a Liberal?" In *The Collected Writings of John Maynard Keynes, Volume 9*, 295–306. London: Macmillan.

Keynes, John Maynard. (1926a) 1972. "The End of Laissez-Faire." in *The Collected Writings of John Maynard Keynes, Volume 9*, 272–306. London: Macmillan.

Keynes, John Maynard. (1926b) 1972. "Liberalism and Labour." In *The Collected Writings of John Maynard Keynes, Volume 9*, 307–311. London: Macmillan.

Keynes, John Maynard. (1925) 1981. "The Economic Transition in England." In *The Collected Writings of John Maynard Keynes, Volume 19*, edited by Donald Moggridge, 434–442, London: Macmillan.

Keynes, John Maynard. 1935. "A Self-Adjusting Economic System?" *The New Republic* 82 (February 20): 35–37.

Keynes, John Maynard. 1936. *The General Theory of Employment, Interest and Money*. London: Macmillan.
Lahart, Justin. 2007. "In Time of Tumult, Obscure Economist Gains Currency." *Wall Street Journal*, August 18, A1.
Lobosco, Katie and Tami Luhby. 2021. "Here's What's in the Bipartisan Infrastructure Bill." CNN Politics. November 5. https://www.cnn.com/2021/07/28/politics/infrastructure-bill-explained/index.html. Accessed November 9, 2021.
Marangos, John. 2000. "A Post Keynesian View of Transition to Market Capitalism: Developing a Civilized Society." *Journal of Post Keynesian Economics* 23 (2): 301–311.
McKenna, Edward J. and Diane C. Zannoni. 1993. "Philosophical Foundations of Post Keynesian Economics." *Journal of Post Keynesian Economics* 15 (3): 395–407.
Minsky, Hyman P. 1985. "Beginnings." *Banca Nazionale Del Lavoro Quarterly Review* 38 (September): 211–221.
Minsky, Hyman P. 1986. *Stabilizing an Unstable Economy*. New Haven: Yale University Press.
Minsky, Hyman P. 1991. "The Transition to a Market Economy: Financial Options." Working Paper No. 66. Levy Economics Institute of Bard College, Annandale-on-Hudson, NY.
Minsky, Hyman P. 1993. "Schumpeter and Finance." In *Markets and Institutions in Economic Development*, edited by Salvatore Biasco, Alessandro Roncaglia and Michele Salvati, 103–115. New York: St. Martin's Press.
Minsky, Hyman P. 1995. "The Balanced Budget Amendment: A Time Bomb to Subvert American Prosperity." Hyman P. Minsky Archive. No. 50. https://digitalcommons.bard.edu/hm_archive/50. Accessed November 8, 2021.
Minsky, Hyman P. and Charles J. Whalen. 1996. "Economic Insecurity and the Institutional Prerequisites for Successful Capitalism." *Journal of Post Keynesian Economics* 19 (2): 155–170.
Parsons, Kenneth H. 1985. "John R. Commons: His Relevance to Contemporary Economics." *Journal of Economic Issues* 19 (3): 755–778.
Peterson, Janice and Doug Brown, editors. 1994. *The Economic Status of Women Under Capitalism: Institutional Economics and Feminist Theory*. Cheltenham, UK: Edward Elgar.
Tilman, Rick. 2008. "John R. Commons, the New Deal and the American Tradition of Empirical Collectivism." *Journal of Economic Issues* 42 (3): 823–851.
Veblen, Thorstein B. 1898. "Why Is Economics Not an Evolutionary Science?" *Quarterly Journal of Economics* 12 (4): 373–397.
Whalen, Charles J. 1987a. "A Reason to Look Beyond Neoclassical Economics: Some Major Shortcomings of Orthodox Theory." *Journal of Economic Issues* 21 (1): 259–280.
Whalen, Charles J. 1987b. "Consensus Mechanisms and Community Economic Development: The Buffalo Experience." *Journal of Economic Issues* 21 (2) 763–774.
Whalen, Charles J. 1988. "The Minsky-Simons Connection: A Neglected Thread in the History of Economic Thought." *Journal of Economic Issues* 22 (2): 533–544.
Whalen, Charles J. 1995. "Assessing the Constitutional Route to Federal Budget Balance." *Public Policy Brief*, No. 20. Levy Economics Institute of Bard College, Annandale-on-Hudson, NY.
Whalen, Charles J. 2001. "Give Taxpayers a $250 Rebate." *BusinessWeek*. February 19, 28.

Whalen, Charles J. 2007. "Union-Driven Economic Development Initiatives and Community Solidarity in Western New York." *Ephemera: Theory and Politics in Organization* 73 (3): 403–418.
Whalen, Charles J. 2011. "Union Engagement in Western New York Economic Development: An Institutional Analysis." *Advances in Industrial and Labor Relations, Volume 18*, edited by David Lewin, Bruce E. Kaufman, and Paul J. Gollan, 177–213. Bingley, UK: Emerald.
Whalen, Charles J. 2019. "Institutional Economics and Chock-Full Employment: Reclaiming the 'Right to Work' As a Cornerstone of Progressive Capitalism." *Journal of Economic Issues* 53 (2): 321–340.
Whalen, Charles J. 2020. "Understanding Financialization." In *Alternative Approaches to Economic Theory*, edited by Victor A. Beker, 185–206. London: Routledge.
Whalen, Charles J., editor. 2022. *A Modern Guide to Post-Keynesian Institutional Economics*. Cheltenham, UK: Edward Elgar.
Wilber, Charles K. 1991. "Roman Catholic Social Thought And Economic Theory: An Agenda For The Future." *Review of Social Economy* 49 (4): 566–577.
Yellen, Janet. 2009. "A Minsky Meltdown: Lessons for Central Bankers." *FRBSF Economic Letter* Number 2009–15. Federal Reserve Bank of San Francisco.
Zalewski, David A. and Charles J. Whalen. 2011. "Towards a More Rapid Recovery: Incorporating Subsidiarity into Macroeconomic Policy." In *Financial Instability and Economic Security after the Great Recession*, edited by Charles J. Whalen, 93–113. Cheltenham, UK: Edward Elgar.

PART II

Reconstructing economics

2. Economics must change: workforce insecurity and the need for a new political economy

Conventional measures indicate that the United States (U.S.) is experiencing strong economic performance. For most of the 1990s, overall national output and productivity have been growing steadily, while inflation and unemployment both have remained low. Also on the rise are corporate profits and stock values. And, as the current Administration is fond of reporting, over 8 million new jobs have been created since Bill Clinton became president.

Yet at the same time we hear stories of economic insecurity throughout the media. We also hear of polls suggesting that what John Kenneth Galbraith (1958) called "The Affluent Society" in the 1950s has given way to what might now be called "The Anxious Society" of the 1990s. This article explores workforce insecurity as a point of departure for a broader discussion of the nature of contemporary economic analysis. The analysis is structured around three questions:

1. Is there any substance to current concerns about U.S. economic insecurity – or is economic anxiety simply a product of reporters in search of doom, gloom, and public controversy?
2. How has the economics profession responded to this issue?
3. How must the discipline of economics change to become a better guide to real-world problems?[1]

WORKFORCE INSECURITY

The question of whether there is any substance to the problem of economic insecurity must be answered in the affirmative. The news media did not fabricate this issue in early 1996; it has been a matter of great concern for working families for some time. In 1993, Kevin Phillips argued that economic anxiety

Reprinted with permission from *Bard Journal of Social Sciences* 5 (1–2), Summer 1996, 34–40.

is the key to politics in the 1990s. According to a poll conducted by *U.S. News and World Report* in the fall of 1994, 57 percent of those surveyed stated that the American Dream is out of reach for most families. And in what the magazine called "*a major break from the nation's historic optimism*," more than two-thirds of the respondents indicated they expect their children will not live as well as they do (Roberts 1994).

There are at least eight trends contributing to the current economic anxiety:

- *Relentless downsizing* – Since 1978, America's largest 100 companies have reduced employment by 22 percent (Pennar 1996). Overall, more than one million U.S. workers have been laid off each year during the 1990s *(Economic Report of the President* 1996: 326). And this trend continues to the present: over 168,000 job cuts were announced in the first quarter of 1996 – a 74 percent increase from the first quarter of 1995 (Bloomberg Business News 1996). Today one in three American families fears job loss in the near future (Montague 1996; Herbert 1996).
- *Permanent job separation* – Unemployment in earlier decades was often cyclical and temporary. But jobs lost due to downsizing and restructuring are permanent and often come despite strong corporate earnings, as is the case with both AT&T and Mobil Corporation. Moreover, professional and managerial workers are no longer immune: these workers accounted for about one quarter of all layoffs in the 1991–1993 period, approximately double the share in the early 1980s (Montague 1996). For instance, of the 2,000 AT&T employees dismissed in January of this year, 60 percent were managers (Hanley 1996).
- *Longer job searches and sluggish job creation* – The average duration for a job search in 1995 was 2.5 months. A decade ago it took 1.5 months on average, in 1967 it was 2.5 *weeks (Economic Report* 1996: 326). We often hear about the eight million jobs created since early 1993, but the pace of job creation during the present recovery has been approximately 40 percent below the level of America's two previous expansions (Roach 1995).
- *Declining incomes* – According to a report by the U.S. Census Bureau, workers losing jobs recently have seen their wages drop an average of more than 20 percent upon regaining full-time employment (Zachary 1995). A 1994 Department of Labor study found that less than one of every three displaced workers returns to full-time employment with equal or higher pay (Montague 1996). Research by the Federal Reserve Bank of Chicago, meanwhile, indicates that many affected workers will never see a return to their previous income level. In particular, the Chicago Fed examined workers with approximately 10 years of experience who lost their jobs due to plant closings or downsizing – after 5 years these

workers were earning approximately 25 percent less than their pre-separation income (Jacobson et al. 1993).

- *Explosive growth in contingent work* – Both part-time and temporary positions have been growing much faster than the overall rate of job growth since 1970. In the period 1970–1990, total U.S. employment grew by less than 54 percent; but the number of persons working part-time yet preferring a full-time job rose 121 percent; and the number of temporary workers rose 210 percent (Callaghan and Hartmann 1991: 9). Jobs obtained through temporary-employment agencies such as Manpower, Incorporated – now the nation's second-largest employer – account for about 15 percent of all employment in the current economic recovery. In contrast, during the period 1982–1990, temporary agencies accounted for less than 5 percent of all jobs created *(Economic Report* 1995: 58).
- *Wage stagnation* – Perhaps the most striking aspect of the economic scene is the trend in the purchasing power of the average American. After adjustment for inflation, today's hourly wage gives the average American less purchasing power than the average U.S. worker had in 1965. Although families have responded by sending more members to work and having them work longer hours, real median family income has actually fallen more than five percent since 1989 *(Economic Report* 1996: 314, 330). In 1995, total worker compensation (wages plus benefits) grew at the lowest rate since this information was first collected in 1982. This rate just barely kept pace with inflation. In addition, last year both the Consumer Price Index and private-sector employment costs rose 2.8 percent (U.S. Department of Labor, *Employment Cost Index* 1996).
- *Rising inequality* – In the early post-World War II era, real annual income for most American families rose at about 2.5 percent a year; since 1973, however, income has been distributed more and more unequally. When U.S. families are ranked according to their incomes, the bottom 40 percent have seen their incomes fall since the mid-1970s and the middle 40 percent have seen their incomes stagnate. Sizable gains can be found only within the top 20 percent – with the most spectacular gains accruing to the wealthiest families (Cassidy 1995). In the mid-1970s, the average corporate chief executive (CEO) received 41 times the salary of the average U.S. worker; CEOs today receive incomes 225 times that of the average worker (Graef Crystal in Boroughs 1996: 47).
- *Increased moonlighting* – In 1985, 5.7 million Americans held two or more jobs; today the number is over 7.8 million. Research by Richard Freeman of Harvard University indicates that no other industrial nation approaches the U.S. when it comes to multiple job holdings (U.S.

Department of Labor, *The Employment Situation* 1996; Uchitelle 1994). President Clinton learned about this first-hand when a worker responded to his boast about job creation by stating: *"Don't tell me about the millions of new jobs created – I've got three of them and I'm not all that impressed."*[2]

THE POWER OF PRECONCEPTIONS

How have economists responded to the issue of economic insecurity? Most of those in the economics profession have denied that there is any problem. In part this is due to the disciplinary convention of separating microeconomics and macroeconomics into two distinct realms. But the problem goes much deeper – all the way to the fundamental preconceptions that underlie nearly all contemporary economic analysis.

The issues discussed above are national issues. As such, they might belong in the realm of macroeconomics. However, macroeconomic theory deals with aggregates but only with a few "key" aggregates – namely, output, employment, and inflation. As a result, the sources of insecurity are not captured by macro analysis.

But the problem is not merely that this insecurity is being missed. What conventional macroeconomists *can see* adds further evidence to the standard belief that all is well. The popular new approach to macroeconomics these days is known as New Classical Economics. A representative of the New Classicals is Robert Lucas of the University of Chicago, last year's Nobel Prize recipient. Lucas's economics provides what is known as a "general-equilibrium" account of business cycles; that is, the economy is believed to always be at full employment. In this model, public policy adds nothing to macroeconomic performance. Lucas's view results in an argument against activist fiscal policy – and a call for the stability and certainty that comes with monetarism (Lucas 1981).

The only macro approach that sees the possibility of a prolonged market failure is Keynesianism. But Keynesians – Robert Eisner of Northwestern, for example – see an economy where unemployment is the only real problem and where an overall fiscal stimulus is the solution. Thus, the only debate here is between those who think we can do better than the current unemployment level of 5.4 percent and those who fear that lower unemployment cannot be achieved without a high price in the form of inflation.

Microeconomics deals with a more diverse picture than macroeconomics, but it also sheds no real light on economic insecurity. According to the assumptions embedded in micro theory, market outcomes are products of free and rational choices. If there is a message here it is the same as that of New

Classical macro. The message reads: economic reality leads to efficiency, and what is efficient is good.

Not even development economics – a branch of international economics which was established to address what are inherently dynamic issues involving industrial transition – can offer much guidance on the matter of economic insecurity. For even here we are told that the only acceptable path to development is laissez-faire. All other paths are deemed either ineffective or inefficient (Amsden 1996, 250).

What now becomes clear is that a coherent set of preconceptions is driving all standard economic paradigms. One preconception states that the economy is self-regulating: it is in, or at least gravitating toward, a harmonious state of equilibrium. Another is that conventional theories have no room for analysis which involves time and the actual process of economic adjustment. All that can be said is that everything works out for the best in the long run; but there is still no reply to Keynes's observation that in the long run we are all dead. A third preconception is that economic institutions do not matter – economic behavior is reducible to individual choice, and individual choices make for the best of all possible worlds.

My conclusion about the centrality and pervasiveness of certain economic preconceptions is not novel. One component of it forms the core of Douglass North's 1993 Nobel lecture, in which he warns that standard economics does not account for the passage of time and that this can lead to poor – or even disastrous – policy advice (North 1994). A similar conclusion also lies at the center of a new book by Robert Heilbroner and William Milberg, *The Crisis of Vision in Modern Economic Thought*. According to Heilbroner and Milberg, conventional economists have sacrificed an ability to address real-world problems in order to construct elegant and highly mathematical theories. In particular, this pair stresses that mainstream theory is rooted in natural-law philosophy;[3] is isolated from time; is devoid of social content; and is leading economists to offer laissez-faire advice in nearly every situation (Heilbroner and Milberg 1996).

TOWARDS A MORE USEFUL ECONOMICS

To serve as a better guide to real-world problems, economics must undergo a fundamental change. In light of the power of economic preconceptions, change must begin with the definition of the discipline. Today economics is defined as the study of how humans seek to maximize gains (profit, income, satisfaction, etc.) in a world of scarcity. This definition inexorably leads to an incomplete view of reality.[4]

I would redefine economics as the science of *social provisioning*. As such, it would include the study of individual choice and markets, but it would also allow a look at the entire social landscape – markets, the state, the family, and all other institutions involved in resource use and allocation. In other words, I would return economics to the broader study of what was called "political economy" in the days before Alfred Marshall exerted his influence on the profession.

But my conception of political economy is not only more encompassing than the conventional view – it also rests on a foundation that is fundamentally *different* from that which supports standard theory. This foundation is pragmatic, process-oriented, and non-teleological. It is pragmatic in that political economy seeks to use realistic assumptions to explain actual events, rather than to use unrealistic assumptions in an exercise that is at best merely predictive and at worst merely hypothetical.[5] Political economy is process-oriented in that it emphasizes the importance of time progression and historical processes. And it is non-teleological in that the conventional idea of market self-regulation is rejected as is the Marxist notion of the self-destructive tendency of capitalism. Political economy recognizes that actual economic processes can tend in either direction depending upon existing institutional conditions.[6]

This redefinition of economics can be applied to any realm of inquiry – from the microeconomic to the global (as demonstrated in Whalen 1996). The economic insecurity discussed above comes most clearly into view when this redefinition is used as the foundation for a macro-analysis of structural change. A thumbnail sketch of this analysis is as follows.

In the wake of World War II, U.S. prosperity was generated by a set of economic structures, strategies, and practices that were complementary and mutually reinforcing. The economy was dominated by large and powerful enterprises which used techniques of mass-production to manufacture American goods primarily for domestic consumption. As these companies experienced productivity gains, workers were rewarded with rising incomes and steady employment. Strong consumer demand, combined with timely jolts of fiscal and monetary assistance from the federal government, kept firms profitable.

Over time, however, the economy was transformed by international competition and swift technological change. The result has been a rapidly-evolving world economy where sales, production, and finance have all become globalized. At the same time, developments in the financial world have led to the rise of institutional investors responsible for huge pension and money-market funds. These money managers have only one objective – maximization of short-term financial returns. In response to these various structural changes, corporations have stressed downsizing, outsourcing, and deunionization, while government has stressed deflationary macro policies and the deregulation of industry and trade.

According to this analysis, economic trends described in the first segment of this paper are the direct consequence of our nation's response to both economic evolution at home and the competitive challenges from abroad. The analysis also indicates that today's trends are not an entirely new development. From a political-economy perspective, an early sign of the emergence of the economy that now produces widespread insecurity was provided in the 1970s when foreign firms made significant inroads in apparel, steel, autos, and other manufacturing industries.[7]

CONCLUSION

This article has argued that workforce insecurity is a serious contemporary problem in America – one that is often overlooked by economists due to the misconceptions that underlie and shape their research. It has also maintained that economics must make a fundamental change if it is to be a better guide to real-world problems. In particular, I have suggested that economists need a new, historically and institutionally grounded *political economy.* To conclude, I will identify five implications of this proposed alternative:

1. Once the notion of a self-regulating economic system is rejected, researchers can no longer say that "laissez-faire" is, a priori, the best policy strategy. Indeed, since economic coordination and stabilization is seen as being achieved not by the regulating force of the price system but rather by institutional balance, one can conclude that structural economic problems often demand structural solutions (i.e., institutional adjustment). The key to success in today's global economy lies in how a nation organizes itself for economic activity. Capitalism may be the only accepted system, but it comes in multifarious varieties.
2. Economic security and economic progress are not necessarily incompatible. A central lesson of both the New Deal era and of the early post-World War II period is that security and progress can be complementary. This was true in the case of the postwar social contract that linked the interests of workers and firms, and it was also true in the case of U.S. agriculture in the New Deal period – when the stabilization of farm incomes ignited an advantageous dynamic by making it possible for farmers to invest in new technologies. While conventional economics focuses on static efficiency, political economy draws attention to the possibility of a more "dynamic" efficiency.[8]
3. Policy analysis must be grounded in history and institutional reality. In particular, political economy requires case studies and international comparisons of public policies. In fact, here economists might have a good

deal to learn from political scientists. Political excesses are an ever-present danger, but while public action can be excessive it can also be inadequate. Political economy can be particularly valuable if it helps with the identification and diffusion of the best existing policy practices.

4. While the public sector has always had a role in science and technology, it has a special role in this realm in the present era. In the past, natural resource endowments were pivotal in determining economic success. Today, however, economic success is determined by a nation's ability to compete in what Lester Thurow calls "brainpower" industries – industries such as microelectronics and biotechnology which can be located wherever the necessary talents are coordinated (Thurow 1996). Public action and public-private partnerships are often essential to achieve such coordination in a competitive environment oriented heavily towards short-term returns.
5. Finally, there is no "once-and-for-all" fix to economic problems. An economic system is an ever-evolving set of social institutions. Its operation requires social choices and its maintenance, like that of freedom, requires eternal vigilance. Standard economics missed our evolution into an "Anxious Society" because it treats the economy as a static natural system. Political economy can help correct this mistake.

NOTES

1. A version of this article was presented at a seminar of the political science department at the State University of New York, College at Brockport on April 11, 1996. The author thanks the participants for their comments.
2. This remark was first reported in 1995 and has since been mentioned by numerous journalists and administration officials.
3. According to natural-law philosophy, the world is governed by inherent tendencies and ultimate truths – in the case of economics, fundamental laws of supply and demand are believed to exert a tendency towards full-employment equilibrium.
4. For more on the narrowness of the conventional definition of economics, see Dugger (1996) and Myrdal (1973).
5. The use of unrealistic assumptions in standard economics is addressed in Caldwell (1982, 173–188) and Blaug (1980, 94–128).
6. A further discussion of this redefinition of economics and its implications can be found in Whalen (1992). A similar redefinition is at the core of Gruchy (1987).
7. A more detailed discussion of recent U.S. structural change and its implications for economic theory can be found in Whalen (1995).
8. Alternative conceptions of efficiency are discussed in Kuttner (1993). The "dynamic" efficiency mentioned here is analogous to what Kuttner calls "Schumpeterian" efficiency.

REFERENCES

Amsden, Alice H. "Late Industrialization: Can More Countries Make It?" *Political Economy for the 21st Century.* Ed., Charles J. Whalen. Armonk, NY: M.E. Sharpe, 1996.

Blaug, Mark. *The Methodology of Economics.* Cambridge, UK: Cambridge University Press, 1980.

Bloomberg Business News. "Planned Job Cuts Rise." *The New York Times.* April 9, 1996: D10.

Boroughs, Don L. "Winter of Discontent." *U.S. News & World Report.* January 22, 1996: 47–54.

Caldwell, Bruce. *Beyond Positivism: Economic Methodology in the Twentieth Century.* London: George Allen and Unwin, 1982.

Cassidy, John. "Who Killed the Middle Class?" *The New Yorker.* October 16, 1995: 113–124.

Dugger, William M. "Redefining Economics." *Political Economy far the 21st Century.* Ed., Charles J. Whalen. Armonk, NY: M.E. Sharpe, 1996.

Economic Report of the President. Washington, DC: U.S. Government Printing Office, 1996.

Economic Report of the President. Washington, DC: U.S. Government Printing Office, 1995.

Galbraith, John Kenneth. *The Affluent Society.* Boston: Houghton, Mifflin, 1958.

Gruchy, Allan G. *The Reconstruction of Economics.* Westport, CT: Greenwood Press, 1987.

Hanley, Robert. "Today, 2,000 Fewer AT&T Employees." *The New York Times.* January 21, 1996: B5.

Heilbroner, Robert, and William Milberg. *The Crisis of Vision in Modern Economic Thought.* New York: Cambridge University Press, 1996.

Herbert, Bob. "Separation Anxiety." *The New York Times.* January 19, 1996: A29.

Jacobson, Louis S., Robert J. LaLonde, and Daniel G. Sullivan. "Long-term Earnings Losses of High-Seniority Displaced Workers." *Economic Perspectives.* November–December, 1993: 2–20.

Kuttner, Robert. "Keynes, Schumpeter, and High-Growth Economics in the 1990s." paper presented at a conference of the Jerome Levy Economics Institute of Bard College, November 12, 1993.

Lucas, Robert E. *Studies in Business-Cycle Theory.* Cambridge, MA: MIT Press, 1981.

Montague, Bill. "Feeling the Squeeze of Downsizing." *USA Today.* February 19, 1996: Al.

Myrdal, Gunnar. *Against the Stream.* New York: Pantheon, 1973.

North, Douglass C. "Economic Performance Through Time." *American Economic Review.* June, 1984: 359–368.

Pennar, Karen. "Economic Anxiety." *Business Week.* March 11, 1996: 50–52.

Roach, Stephen. "Who Should Worry About the Economy?" *The New York Times.* June 16, 1995: A27.

Roberts, Steven V. "Why are We So Angry?" *U.S. News & World Report.* November 7, 1994: 30–36.

Thurow, Lester C. "Comparative Advantage, Factor-Price Equalization, Industrial Strategies and Trade Tactics." *Political Economy for the 21st Century.* Ed., Charles J. Whalen. Armonk, NY: M.E. Sharpe, 1996.

Uchitelle, Louis. "Moonlighting Plus: Three-Job Families Rising." *The New York Times.* August 16, 1994: Al.
U.S. Department of Labor. *Employment Cost Index – December 1995.* Washington, DC: Bureau of Labor Statistics, 1996.
U.S. Department of Labor. *The Employment Situation – February 1996.* Washington, DC: Bureau of Labor Statistics, 1996.
Whalen, Charles J., ed. *Political Economy far the 21st Century.* Armonk, NY: M.E. Sharpe, 1996.
Whalen, Charles J. "Structural Change and the Compulsive Shift to Institutional Analysis." *Institutional Economics and the Theory of Social Value.* Ed., Charles M.A. Clark. Boston: Kluwer Academic Press, 1995.
Whalen, Charles J. "Schools of Thought and Theories of the State." *The Stratified State.* Eds., William M. Dugger and William T. Waller. Armonk, NY: M.E. Sharpe, 1992.
Zachary, G. Pascal. "Census Bureau Confirms Eroding Wages." *The Wall Street Journal.* January 25, 1995: A2.

3. The institutional approach to political economy

Adam Smith saw political economy as a broad study of the many forces contributing to national wealth. Over the years, however, academics have narrowed 'political economy' to 'economics' – a discipline in which the mainstream confines its analyses to issues involving market allocation under conditions of scarcity. In contrast, institutionalists seek to retain a more expansive scope of analysis. Their approach yields theories and policy views that are often markedly different from those offered by neoclassical economics. The present chapter describes and discusses the institutional (or evolutionary) approach to political economy.[1]

ORIGINS AND DEVELOPMENT

The name 'institutional economics' is said to have been coined by Walton Hamilton in 1919. But the tradition's roots can be traced to at least the 19th century, when three influences contributed most significantly to the birth of institutionalism: the German 'historical school', American 'pragmatism' and Thorstein Veblen's writings on the preconceptions of economic science. After a brief explanation of these influences, six leading institutionalists are discussed.[2]

Influences

In the 1870s, Richard T. Ely and other American scholars were introduced to the historical school of political economy while studying in Germany. That school emphasized the interrelated and dynamic nature of reality; a need to ground theories in data obtained through empirical investigations; and attention to human institutions, social reform, and state economic-development activities. When the Americans returned home, many incorporated such views into their own writing and teaching. They were determined, writes Paul McNulty

Reprinted with permission from F. Foldvary (ed.), *Beyond Neoclassical Economics* (Edward Elgar, 1996), 83–99.

(1980, p. 131), to put new marrow into what they called the 'dry bones' of 'the old political economy' dominant in both England and the United States.

Another early influence on institutionalism was the creation of an American philosophical perspective called pragmatism. This perspective, outlined first by Charles Peirce and later by William James and John Dewey, views notions of absolute truth and teleology with skepticism. Instead, it emphasizes the element of uncertainty in human understanding. It also stresses the practical consequences of belief; pragmatists treat scientific investigation as an important step in the process of resolving practical problems, not merely as an intellectual exercise. Pragmatism provides institutionalism with both an epistemological foundation and a social philosophy.[3]

Veblen (1857–1929) was a student of both Ely and Peirce. His turn-of-the-century articles on economics revealed the discipline's methodological foundations. They also presented the case for what he called an 'evolutionary' science. In these works one finds many of the ingredients needed to establish an institutionalist approach to economics (see Veblen, 1919). Veblen's ideas are further developed in volumes including the following: *The Theory of the Leisure Class* (in which the phrase 'conspicuous consumption' first appears); *The Theory of Business Enterprise;* and *Absentee Ownership and Business Enterprise in Recent Times* (Veblen, 1967, 1904, and 1923).

Commons, Mitchell and Ayres

Central figures in the early development of institutionalism included John R. Commons, Wesley Mitchell and Clarence Ayres.[4] Like Veblen, Commons (1862–1945) was a student of Ely. In fact, Ely interested Commons in the labor field and later secured a post for him at the University of Wisconsin – a home base from which Commons launched a variety of industrial relations explorations and economic reform efforts (including those involving protective labor legislation, public-utility regulation, and price stabilization). Commons was also the first to write a book that attempted to explain institutionalist thinking (see Commons, 1934).

Commons's students did not grasp his theoretical formulations in the field of economics – formulations that sought both to give collective action 'its due place' in economic theory and to develop a 'volitional' alternative to the mechanistic theories of economic orthodoxy (Commons, 1934, p. 5; 1924, p. vii).[5] They understood clearly, however, that institutionalism should help resolve practical problems. As a result, while Commons's conceptual works have usually been ignored, most of his students and followers have remained united by an atheoretical notion of 'economics in action' (Witte, 1954, p. 132). As one Commons biographer wrote in reference to these institutionalists, 'The emphasis on public policy and practical economic problems [is] enough for them' (Harter, 1962, p. 206).[6]

Another early leader in the institutionalist movement was Mitchell (1874–1948). A student of Veblen – with a special interest in Veblen's distinction between 'industrial' and 'pecuniary' employments – Mitchell emphasized the role played by money in a capitalist economy.[7] In fact, he always intended to write a detailed and explicitly institutionalist treatise on what he called the 'money economy'. After some initial writing on this topic, however, Mitchell believed the project required additional research into business cycles. Although for many years he viewed the work on cycles as 'a special aspect' of his larger vision of a money economy, Mitchell gave the business cycle the bulk of his attention for the rest of his career (Dillard, 1987, pp. 1629–30).[8]

Despite failing to complete a book on the money economy, Mitchell contributed to institutionalist thinking in many ways: by writing essays on economic theory and the need for a historically-grounded science of human behavior (institutionalism) rather than an ahistorical science of price tendencies (economic orthodoxy) (Mitchell, 1937); by producing applied work on economic fluctuations (Mitchell, 1913); by creating the National Bureau of Economic Research (NBER) and establishing it as the premier US center for empirical investigation and statistical measurement in economics; and by developing a popular course on the history of economic thought (Mitchell, 1949). Over time, however, his concentration on economic statistics became so great that the NBER lost its institutionalist orientation. Today, in fact, that organization is controlled by neoclassical researchers – and Mitchell is known best not for interpreting facts but for collecting them.

Clarence Ayres (1891–1972) was introduced to the ideas of both Dewey and Veblen through studies in philosophy and economics at the University of Chicago. His interest in institutionalism grew as a result of working at Amherst College with Walton Hamilton (one of Veblen's students), and in the wake of discussions with Herbert Davenport (another student of Veblen) and Morris Copeland (an institutionalist influenced by Mitchell). His major attempt to explain and apply institutionalism – to the field of economic development – is found in *The Theory of Economic Progress*, a volume published while he served on the faculty at The University of Texas (Ayres, 1944).[9]

Unlike Commons and Mitchell, Ayres succeeded in transmitting a conceptual framework to subsequent generations of students. Many of today's leading institutionalists have studied with either Ayres or his students. In Austin, meanwhile, faculty members kept the Ayres tradition alive until the mid 1980s.[10]

Myrdal, Gruchy and Galbraith

Among more recent institutionalists, prominent contributors include Gunnar Myrdal, John Kenneth Galbraith and Allan G. Gruchy.[11] Myrdal (1898–1987) began his career in Sweden as a conventional monetary economist. While hints of his movement toward institutionalism are glimpsed in pioneering work on economic dynamics, Myrdal's conversion to institutional economics resulted primarily from his heavy involvement in policy matters at home and abroad.

Myrdal served, for example, as a member of the Swedish parliament; as his nation's minister of trade and commerce; and, in the wake of World War II, as executive secretary of the United Nations Economic Commission for Europe. He also conducted landmark studies on both race relations in America and the problems of developing nations (Myrdal, 1944, 1968). His efforts, which earned him the Nobel prize in 1974, led him to conclude that real-world problems require a holistic approach which looks beyond the conventional boundaries of economic science (Myrdal, 1973, 1978).

Gruchy (1906–90) founded two professional organizations designed to provide institutionalists with an opportunity to share and develop their ideas – the Association for Evolutionary Economics (sponsor of the *Journal of Economic Issues)* and the Association for Institutional Thought (sponsor of annual meetings held in conjunction with the Western Social Sciences Association). His scholarly contributions were in two areas – institutionalist thought and national economic policy. His work on economic thought led to three volumes that traced institutionalism from Veblen to the contributors of the late 1980s (Gruchy, 1947, 1972, 1987). His research on national economic policy stressed the need for policy guidance extending beyond Keynesian aggregate-demand management – and the value of lessons found in the experience of nations such as Norway and Sweden (Gruchy, 1977, 1984). As Dudley Dillard wrote shortly after Gruchy's death, both areas of research 'were intimately related in Allan's thinking' (Dillard, 1990, p. 668).

Galbraith (1908–) is perhaps the most prolific and widely-read economist of this century. Since publishing an article entitled 'Monopoly Power and Price Rigidities' in 1936 (Galbraith, 1936), he has focused much of his attention on pricing behavior, corporate power, and their implications for not only inflation and unemployment but also national wealth and human welfare.[12] Galbraith has also drawn special attention to the *cultural* sources and dimensions of economic activity. This is evident from the very title of *The Culture of Contentment* (Galbraith, 1992), but it is also clear from *A Short History of Financial Euphoria*, in which he examines the 'crowd psychology' that engenders recurrent episodes of speculative 'insanity' in financial markets (Galbraith, 1993).

PRECONCEPTIONS

Many critics have argued that institutionalists share only a rejection of economic orthodoxy. But what unites institutionalists is a common methodological foundation – a shared set of philosophical preconceptions. These preconceptions can be grouped into the following four categories: a conception of society; an image of the economic process; an approach to values; and a philosophy of science.[13]

Society and the Economy

The institutionalist conception of society is holistic in nature. In other words, social reality is viewed as a unified whole. Thus, institutionalist analyses – unlike those of the neoclassicals and traditional Marxists – cannot begin with the world neatly divided into 'economic' and 'noneconomic' realms. As Charles Wilber and Robert Harrison write, 'institutionalism's holistic theories are rooted in the belief that the social whole is not only greater than the sum of its parts but that the parts are so related that their functioning is conditioned by their interrelations' (Wilber and Harrison, 1978, p. 73).

Institutionalists also view society from a 'processual' perspective. This means they view social systems as dynamic, ever-developing entities, and are keenly aware of the fact that all social activity occurs in both historical time and an environment of uncertainty regarding the future. Their view contrasts sharply with the neoclassical emphasis on an 'equilibrium' state of rest.[14]

While most economists define economics as a study of the price mechanism and market transactions, institutionalists adopt a broader view. To evolutionary political economists, economics is a science of 'social provisioning' – one that must allow room for explorations of not only resource allocation but also the nature of both production and want creation.[15] According to this definition, markets represent only one type of human institution involved in provisioning. Institutionalists recognize that other institutions – including the state, the family, indeed culture in its totality – are also significant.[16]

Another difference between institutionalists and most other economists is that the former view economic systems as having no inherent tendency toward either self-regulation or self-destruction. Rather, evolutionary political economists see economic 'order' as a creation of the parties within a particular social system. As Gruchy writes, 'Actual economic systems exhibit cultural coherence, rather than the equilibrating forces of a mechanistic system' (Gruchy, 1987, p. 4).[17] For this reason, institutions and social processes considered to be noneconomic 'frictions' by neoclassicism are very often elements that warrant a prominent place in institutionalist analyses.[18]

Values and Science

Institutionalists consider the concept of value to be multifaceted. For example, depending on the problem, institutionalists might focus on use values, exchange values, individual values, or social values. In contrast, neoclasssicals and Marxists take a narrow view of value – their approaches emphasize market prices and labor exertion (rooted in the 'labor theory of value'), respectively.

Evolutionary political economists recognize that both their own judgments and those of public officials are important elements in public-policy analysis.

The neoclassical suggestion that economics can be value free is dismissed in favor of the position of Joan Robinson (1970, p. 122): 'An economist's attempt to be purely objective must necessarily be either self-deception or a device to deceive others. A candid writer will make his preconceptions clear and allow the reader to discount them if he does not accept them'.[19] Moreover, although institutionalists see much validity in the public-choice perspective on politicians, they also recognize its limitations and maintain that the state can also play a *creative* role in the economy by helping to expand individual liberty and shape community preferences and social institutions.[20]

The institutionalist philosophy of science, meanwhile, rests on a belief that economics should contribute to an understanding of actual processes of social provisioning. Institutionalists strive for theories with realistic assumptions, logical consistency and testable predictions, but they reject the neoclassical treatment of prediction as the preeminent goal of science. They also emphasize the importance of re-evaluating theories regularly, and the need for theories that help resolve real-world problems.[21]

Review

Institutionalists are united by a shared belief system – one that is holistic, processual, non-teleological and pragmatic. It is also problem-oriented and explicitly value-laden. This belief system provides a methodological foundation for institutionalist analyses. Examples of such analyses are considered in the next section.

APPLICATIONS

Methods, Tools and General Theories

The institutionalist methodology has been applied to a wide range of topics throughout the 20th century. In the course of their work, institutionalists have produced and employed a number of research methods, tools of analysis and theories. One method employed since the days of Veblen is that which presents a detailed description of economic behavior and/or institutional change. This work is often considered 'preliminary' in nature, a preamble to more 'serious' future scholarship. But it can *also* be work of considerable value. To neglect such research – as today's mainstream economists do often – is to increase significantly the risk that certain new features of the economy are overlooked (Lind, 1993, p. 9; Whalen, 1996a). Further, as Wassily Leontief reminds us, 'To keep the ... engine of our economy in good working order we must ... be acquainted with the details of its actual design' (Leontief, 1971, p. 7). Descriptive accounts can also be valuable if they provide new interpretations of familiar phenomena and processes.

While institutionalists from Veblen to Galbraith have made considerable contributions to political economy through description, others – such as Mitchell, Copeland, and Gerhard Colm – have been pioneers in the development and use of statistics and quantitative data.[22] Although most advanced statistical methods are currently developed by mainstream economists, institutionalists continue to engage in quantitative research.[23] Still other institutionalists, many with intellectual roots to Commons, have pioneered use of more 'qualitative' methods – including participant observation, comparative case studies, interviews and surveys.[24] These methods are used only rarely by neoclassical economists.[25]

Turning from research methods to tools of analysis, Veblen is again a prominent figure. Indeed, perhaps the most distinctive tool used by evolutionary political economists is the 'Veblenian dichotomy'. This device recognizes that human activities contain some elements that are 'instrumental' – involving actual causal sequences and relations – and others that are merely 'ceremonial' (see Waller, 1982). The dichotomy figures prominently in the work of Ayres and his followers, but it also appears in Mitchell's work in the form of his distinction between making goods and making money, and in Commons's writings as part of his analysis of transactions.

The Veblenian dichotomy is well-suited for use in general economic theories – theories not confined to time and place. Two theories of this sort that incorporate the dichotomy are Wendell Gordon's theory of economic development and Commons's theory of economic transactions. Gordon's theory of 'economic progress' involves the dynamic interaction of technology (instrumental), institutions (ceremonial), natural resources, and human biology (Gordon, 1980). Commons, meanwhile, viewed *transactions* – exchanges of ownership rights (not necessarily involving money) – as the fundamental units of economic life. His general theory of transactions interprets economic activity by giving equal weight to five interrelated factors that explain such exchanges: working rules (institutions), productivity (technology), scarcity, power and expectations (Commons, 1950). This framework incorporates insights from not only Veblen but also economic orthodoxy, Marxism and Austrian economists, respectively.[26]

Theories of a Particular Time and Place

After World War II, institutionalists devoted much attention to the structure of business institutions in the United States. Two important contributions here are Robert Averitt's *The Dual Economy* and John Kenneth Galbraith's *Economics and the Public Purpose* (Averitt, 1968; Galbraith, 1973). Instead of the competitive industrial system posited by neoclassical economists, both volumes described an economy with two very different types of firms. A few hundred large firms were described as being at this economy's 'center'. These corporations were guided by highly-trained technical experts and managers; had extensive resources and production capabilities (usually in key industries such as manufacturing, communications and finance); wielded a significant amount of economic power; and often coordinated activities with each other. On the economy's 'periphery', meanwhile, Averitt and Galbraith found literally millions of small, highly-competitive firms.

By adopting a dual-economy perspective and exploring the operations and interactions of the center and periphery, Averitt, Galbraith and other institutionalists (such as Eichner, 1976) sought a reconstruction of microeconomic theory as both an end in itself and as a more realistic foundation for macroeconomics. Much attention given to their 'new economics of microstructure' centered on the mark-up pricing behavior of the economy's powerful 'megacorps'.[27] But the institutionalists argued that even business activity in the periphery departed significantly from what is described in neoclassical analyses – primarily because corporate life in the periphery was conditioned by behavior in the center economy (see Galbraith, 1973). Attention to the problem of stagflation, a problem receiving much attention in the 1970s, offers an opportunity to both illustrate this last point and present an example of an institutionalist theory that focuses on a particular social problem.

Because neoclassicals (including monetarists *and* Keynesians) saw inflation and recession as inversely related, they had great difficulty explaining the stagflation phenomenon. The problem becomes entirely comprehensible, however, from a dual-economy perspective. The key is to understand what happens when traditional anti-inflation policies are implemented. According to institutionalists, center firms respond to such policies by reducing output and employment, not prices. In fact, some of these enterprises will even *raise* prices in an effort to stabilize revenues and profits (see Wachtel and Adelsheim, 1976) – a step that could cause public officials to intensify their anti-inflation activities. Firms in the periphery, meanwhile, cannot insulate themselves from the effects of state action. As a result, inflation fighting has a more profound and damaging impact on small firms than neoclassical economics would anticipate (Galbraith, 1973).

Since institutionalism recognizes the dynamic nature of economic life, institutionalists are continually re-evaluating and modifying their analyses of the dual economy (and the structure of the US economy in general) – especially in light of economic globalization and rapid technological developments (see Galbraith, 1989; Gruchy, 1987, chapter 5; Munkirs, 1985; Harrison, 1994; Harrison and Bluestone, 1988). But their processual perspective has also caused institutionalists to go beyond documenting change and to develop theories of *how* economic systems change over time. One example is their analysis of business cycles.

While neoclassicism asserts that capitalist systems are stable, institutionalism maintains that such economies – at least as structured in the major industrialized nations of the 20th century – are inherently prone to macroeconomic fluctuations. In particular, institutionalists argue that robust business earnings raise expectations about future earnings and cause bank loans and corporate-investment levels to increase. But while these loans and investment expenditures raise stock prices, employment and output levels (that is, they trigger a boom), they also produce fragile financial structures and push up production costs. Thus, the system eventually cannot support the accumulated debt. As a result, profits fall, bankruptcies occur, and loans, investment, employment and production levels are all reduced. In short, the result is a recession or depression that ends only when business expectations improve and investment levels once again begin to rise, due to either government intervention or a purely psychological change on the part of corporate managers.[28]

While a complete business cycle might involve five or ten years, other institutionalist theories of economic change involve a much longer time horizon. Commons's theory of capitalist development, for example, traces capitalism's history from the industrial revolution to a 20th-Century era he called 'banker capitalism' – a period of multinational corporations and huge investment institutions. Among the insights contained in this theory are the following: (a) that the ultimate conflict in capitalism is between the interests of consumers and producers; and (b) that economic conflicts often lead to political and legislative battles (Commons, 1934).

RECENT FINDINGS

A number of recent books have examined contemporary economic life from an institutionalist perspective. Among the most valuable are the following: William Dugger's (1989) *Corporate Hegemony;* Juliet Schor's (1991) *The Overworked American;* and Wallace Peterson's (1994) *The Silent Depression. Corporate Hegemony* describes how the corporation is coming to dominate every aspect of life in Western industrial societies. *The Overworked American* documents – and provides a non-neoclassical explanation of – a decline in US leisure both at work and in the home. *The Silent Depression* analyzes a downward trend in American wages, family income and productivity growth that began in the early 1970s and continues into the mid 1990s.

One new volume that adds a collection of essays – by Dugger, Frederic Lee, L. Randall Wray, Ray Marshall, Barry Bluestone, Lester Thurow, Brent McClintock, Alice Amsden and others – to the institutionalist literature is *Political*

Economy for the 21st Century (Whalen, 1996b). Some of its contributors explore perennial matters – such as the nature of resources, wants, and production/reproduction – while others orient their chapters toward problems that have developed only in the past few decades. A few of that book's findings are discussed here for the purpose of rounding out the present discussion of institutionalist applications.

According to Dugger, institutionalism offers a theory in which resources are not 'given' as in neoclassical economics. Instead, resources are 'functions of technological change, evolving property rights, and changing cultural norms'.[29] Similarly, he explains that *wants* are endogenous. He writes:

> Individual utility is not the causal factor in want creation and want satisfaction. The causal factors are external to the subjective preferences of the individual consumer because those preferences are learned, not inherent. Only such basics as hunger and thirst are inherent. A desire for potato chips and beer is learned.

To fill in the details of how advertising and salesmanship 'teach us what we want', Dugger says we must turn to Galbraith's theory of 'revised sequence'. According to this theory, our conventional notion of consumer sovereignty must be reconsidered in light of the fact that producers often create markets for products rather than create products in response to pre-existing consumer needs. Dugger adds that another institutionalist theory with insight into the want process is Veblen's theory of conspicuous consumption, a theory that emphasizes the struggle for invidious distinction that arises in pecuniary culture.

The production/reproduction process, meanwhile, is conceived by Dugger as one involving a wide range of social relations. Economic orthodoxy focuses only on production decisions within business enterprises ('the theory of the firm'); institutionalism considers additional factors including ownership of the means of production, workplace organization, the family, the state, and gender relations. While most mainstream economists view such matters as outside the scope of economics, Dugger stresses that institutionalists offers historically-grounded theories of each.[30]

Lee's focus is on corporate pricing. He emphasizes that price setting is a *social* process. That is, pricing is influenced by 'command' (the state) and 'custom' as well as competition. Lee's finding that product markets are 'social' markets dovetails with those of Wray and Marshall, who demonstrate that money and labor markets are also social markets.

Marshall also looks at recent global trends and stresses that there is ultimately only one path that will allow us to enhance US prosperity while competing in global markets – a path which requires that we compete on the basis of productivity, (product and process) innovation and product quality. Similar themes are developed by Barry Bluestone and Lester Thurow. Bluestone explores the structural roots of recent problems in US economic growth and distribution. These roots include a shift from manufacturing to services; a 'deunionization' of the workforce; an explosion of global trade and transnational capital mobility; a chronic US trade deficit; and increased immigration. Bluestone's conclusion is that structural problems require structural policies – especially in the realms of labor markets, manufacturing and trade. Thurow adds that the static, neoclassical theory of 'comparative advantage' is obsolete in the present era of 'brain-power' industries (such as microelectronics and biotechnology) – an era in which national advantage is determined primarily by strategic public- and private-sector decisions, not natural resources and tangible capital endowments.

Finally, both Brent McClintock and Alice Amsden offer contributions to institutionalist discussions of the international realm. McClintock provides evidence of the trend toward international trade and production; explains that this trend has generated significant economic and social dislocations in the United States; and argues that adapting to such developments will require both national adjustment policies (for workers and declining industries) and greater supranational governance. Amsden explains that the future success of newly-industrializing nations will depend heavily on their ability to learn from other countries and modify aspects of their own economic structure accordingly. The role of the state must be given special attention in this process of 'country model transfer' – analysts cannot be blinded by a doctrinal belief in laissez-faire; and they must look beyond the mere *existence* of government and focus instead on the *nature* of its activities.

CONCLUSION: CHALLENGES

The institutional approach to political economy cannot appeal to everyone. Many will always prefer the comfortable grooves and narrow scope of standard theory. Neoclassicism lends itself to mathematicization – a valuable objective in a discipline where formalism has often been not a secondary feature but 'a central programmatic aim' (Ingrao and Israel, 1990, p. 1). It also offers an optimistic view of economic activity (a world requiring little deviation from laissez-faire), and stands ready with a clear standard for use in evaluating that activity ('efficiency'). In contrast, institutionalism offers a far less tidy and comforting perspective. For example, institutionalism demands a constant re-examination of theories in light of real-world changes; insists that society drives the market, not the reverse; believes there are no neatly-defined 'economic' problems, just 'problems' (and, as Myrdal (1973, p. 142) stressed, 'they are all complex'); promises only a 'managed' – and temporary – economic equilibrium; reveals that efficiency is not only undermined by economic change but exists as just one possible measure of social well-being; stresses that state action can serve to both restrain and expand individual liberty; and recognizes that more government activity does not ensure an improved economy (what is important is the *nature*, not the level, of such activity).[31]

Nevertheless, institutionalists believe that their philosophical outlook (presented above) reflects reality more accurately than does the one found at the root of conventional theory. Institutionalist political economy does indeed raise new questions about theory and policy. But these questions, especially regarding the appropriate nature of public action in particular sectors and selected markets, are essential – how we answer them will influence the future shape of local, national and international economic life.

As institutionalism prepares for a second century, three challenges seem most in need of its attention. One is the development of theory. Veblen long ago stressed that evolutionary economics must offer a body of theory – theories that relate to our modern economy (Veblen, 1919, p. 58). Unfortunately, many contemporary institutionalists have been sidetracked by work on methodology and the history of economic thought.

Perhaps evolutionary political economists get sidetracked because numerous economics departments discourage – and sometimes even display hostility toward – institutionalist scholarship outside these two realms. But another part of the explanation may be that many institutionalists retreat into such work because they find life beyond conventional theory somewhat intimidating (especially when the challenges of a broad framework and time-consuming research methods collide with the heavy classroom responsibilities and limited resources found at colleges and universities most likely to employ such scholars). There is certainly a place for investigations into methodology and history of thought, but there is also – to paraphrase Veblen – a vast economic landscape in need of theoretical formulation. If institutionalism is to remain a viable academic tradition during the next century, and if it is to have more than an occasional and passing influence on public policy, institutionalists must find a way to devote more attention to theory construction and refinement in the years ahead.

A second challenge facing institutionalists is the need to build bridges to other non-neoclassical schools of economic thought. Institutionalists and Austrians have differing views on individualism and the role of the state, but they also agree on the importance of expectations and on the need for analyses that treat economic activity as a process in time. Institutionalists have even more in common with those in other heterodox traditions, including Marxism, Post Keynesianism, and the French 'regulation' school – especially in light of the recent emphasis on structural economic change that exists in the literature of each of these camps. The present is, therefore, a perfect time for institutionalists to interact with political economists of all varieties in an effort to synthesize their work wherever possible. This 'bridge building' will not only enrich individual traditions but it will also strengthen heterodoxy in relation to the neoclassical mainstream.

One relatively new area of inquiry that deserves the attention of institutionalists is feminist theory. Institutionalist preconceptions can serve as a useful methodological foundation for feminist analyses of androcentrism and patriarchy. Existing feminist scholarship, meanwhile, can alert institutionalists to issues that they should have been exploring for years. Two recent volumes – edited by Ferber and Nelson (1993) and Peterson and Brown (1994) – suggest that valuable collaborations across disciplines are possible in this realm.

A third challenge for institutionalism is that it must articulate a policy agenda capable of addressing the economic concerns of ordinary citizens. Institutionalists offered policies to stabilize the economy in the early decades of this century. They also pioneered work on incomes policies in the 1960s and early 1970s. In recent years, however, their agenda has often been unclear.

Since it is unlikely that the current laissez-faire path will provide a secure foundation for future prosperity and rising living standards, institutionalists must be prepared to offer a new strategy for dealing with contemporary problems.[32] This strategy must be able to evolve with changing conditions, but it must also be coherent. It should also give attention to issues of political control. Is it true, as William Greider (1992) and others suggest, that the interests of most Americans are not represented effectively in Washington? And if so, is there any type of political reform that can offer an improvement? An institutionalist agenda for the coming decade will need to address not only on the substance of policy but also the policy-making and electoral processes and the structure of government institutions.

The institutional approach to political economy has made important contributions to US economic thought and policy during the past century. Yet there is much work still to be done, especially since the present is an era of rapid technological, institutional and social change. The work will not be easy – but the most valuable human endeavors never are.

NOTES

1. The following provided helpful comments on an early draft of this chapter: Charles Clark, Janet Knoedler, Brent McClintock, Rick Tilman, and Linda Whalen.
2. Hamilton (1919) distinguishes 'institutional economics' from the 'value economics' of the neoclassical mainstream. He explains that while the latter focuses on prices and market values produced under competitive conditions, institutionalism casts a broader net and examines the various institutional structures and processes that explain the nature and extent of real-world economic order and human well-being. Institutionalism is sometimes called 'evolutionary' economics, a term that derives from Veblen (1919, pp. 56–81).

3. For a recent discussion of the influence of Peirce and other pragmatists upon the development of institutionalism, see Liebhafsky (1993).
4. In addition to Commons, Mitchell and Ayres, other important early institutionalists include Robert Hoxie, Walton Hamilton, Rexford Tugwell and Morris Copeland.
5. For evidence that students did not understand Commons's economic theorizing, see Commons (1934, p. 1) and Witte (1954, p. 132). It should be noted, however, that his theorizing on labor matters was much easier to follow. See, for example, Commons (1909); see also Kaufman (1993) for a discussion of Common's contributions to the interdisciplinary field of 'industrial relations'.
6. For evidence of a recent resurgence of interest in Commons's theoretical contributions to economics, see Ramstad (1986); Rutherford (1983); and Whalen (1993).
7. For Veblen's distinction between 'industrial and pecuniary employments', see his chapter with that title in Veblen (1919). In addition, it should be noted that Dewey was also one of Mitchell's professors.
8. Mitchell chose to accept a post at Columbia University in 1913 so he could move to New York and observe at first hand the financial center of the money economy (Dillard, 1987, p. 1630).
9. For a sketch of Ayres's career and discussion of his scholarship, see Breit and Culbertson (1976).
10. In the mid 1980s, The University of Texas did not replace a number of retiring institutionalists and instead sought to orient the department and its graduate program in a more conventional (neoclassical) direction.
11. A longer list of more recent institutionalists would include many others, including Robert Averitt, Dudley Dillard, William Dugger, Alfred Eichner, K. William Kapp, Ray Marshall, Anne Mayhew, John Munkirs and Wallace Peterson.
12. For an important trilogy by Galbraith, see *The Affluent Society; The New Industrial State*; and *Economics and the Public Purpose* (Galbraith, 1958, 1967, and 1973).
13. In this section I draw on earlier attempts to outline the methodology of institutionalism. See, for example, my chapter in Dugger and Waller (1992).
14. For a valuable recent discussion of the importance of considering time in economics, see North (1994).
15. 'Want creation' is important to institutionalists because they do not consider investigations into how individual or group objectives are determined (and modified) as studies that are outside the scope of economics. In addition, evolutionary political economists recognize that producers, workers and consumers are largely cultural products. An institutionalist interpretation of economic behavior must therefore inquire into the various cultural influences shaping that behavior.
16. Institutionalists also stress the importance of technology, both as a body of ideas that shapes social provisioning and as a process that contributes to the dynamic nature of society by providing an ever-changing knowledge base; see Gordon (1980) and Gruchy (1972).
17. As Yngve Ramstad (1985, p. 509) writes, evolutionary political economists maintain that 'institutional adjustment provides the balancing wheel of an economy'.
18. Some economists drawing attention to institutions in recent years are part of a movement known as the 'new institutional economics'. This group applies neoclassical concepts to explain institutional arrangements as 'efficient' outcomes of profit seeking and utility maximization. For more on the 'old' versus the 'new' institutionalism, see Dugger (1990).
19. For more on the role of valuations in economic analysis, see Myrdal (1968, chapter 1; 1983).

20. In contrast to the traditional neoclassical and Marxist views of the state – perspectives that see a corrective and protective entity, respectively – institutionalists look at the state as a creative agent (see Dugger and Waller, 1992).
21. For more on institutionalism's epistemology and pragmatic social philosophy, see Hill and Troub (1995).
22. For a discussion of Colm's work on national budgets, see Gruchy (1972); for Copeland's work on 'flow of funds' accounting, see Copeland (1952).
23. For examples or discussions of institutionalist research with a quantitative orientation, see Radzicki and Seville (1993); Hayden and Stephenson (1992); Peach and Nowotny (1992); Lower (1990); Seccareccia (1988); Eichner (1987); Hickerson (1983); and Bush (1983).
24. The word *qualitative* is in quotes in the text in recognition of the fact that such methods do not necessarily defy quantification.
25. For a classic study employing qualitative methods in the institutionalist tradition, see Doeringer and Piore (1971). While mainstream economics has narrowed the meaning of 'empirical' research to include only analyses using econometrics and other quantitative techniques, this work by Doeringer and Piore reflects the fact that institutionalism has retained the broader definition of that term – namely, work based on observation.
26. The expectational element in Commons's theory also anticipates a key ingredient in today's Post Keynesian economics.
27. The term 'megacorps' comes from Eichner (1976); the notion of a 'new economics of microstructure' is Averitt's (1 968, p. 200). Much of the work on mark-up pricing and related aspects of the aforementioned research on microeconomics can be traced to the studies of corporate behavior and administered pricing undertaken by Adolf Berle and Gardiner Means. See Berle and Means (1933) and Samuels and Medema (1990).
28. As indicated early in this chapter, Mitchell was a major institutionalist contributor in the realm of business cycles (see also Veblen, 1904). For more recent institutionalist discussions of cycles, see Dillard (1987), Peterson (1987) and Minsky (1986a). In addition to stressing the endogenous nature of cycles, this literature has drawn attention to an underlying long-term trend toward increasing financial fragility (see, for example, Minsky, 1986b). One final point: we should not be surprised that this topic serves as an important bridge between the institutionalist and Post Keynesian traditions. Keynes and the early institutionalists were well aware of their common interest in, and similar approach to, industrial fluctuations.
29. All passages quoted in the remainder of this section are located in Whalen (1996b).
30. For example, see Dugger and Waller (1 992) on the state; and Peterson and Brown (1994) on gender relations.
31. A recognition of the importance of the nature rather than just the level of economic activity is one reason why institutional political economists are interested in looking at the composition of government expenditures and in capital-budgeting proposals that draw a distinction between public consumption and public investment.
32. Robert Kuttner recently stated that the sentiment of most Americans could be expressed as follows: 'If the economy is doing so good, why am I feeling so bad?' Since institutionalists have always understood there is no inherent link between serviceability to the community and business gains, these political economists should be uniquely positioned to fashion an agenda that responds to the concerns of contemporary Americans.

REFERENCES

Averitt, Robert T. (1968), *The Dual Economy*, New York: W.W. Norton.

Ayres, Clarence (1944), *The Theory of Economic Progress*, Chapel Hill: University of North Carolina Press.

Berle, Adolf and Means, Gardiner (1933), *The Modern Corporation and Private Property*, New York: Macmillan.

Breit, William and Culbertson, William (1976), *Science and Ceremony*, Austin: University of Texas Press.

Bush, Paul (1983), 'An Exploration of the Structural Characteristics of a Veblen-Ayres-Foster Defined Institutional Domain', *Journal of Economic Issues*, **18** (March), 35–66.

Commons, John R. (1909), 'American Shoemakers, 1648–1895', *Quarterly Journal of Economics*, **24** (November), 39–84.

Commons, John R. (1 924), *Legal Foundations of Capitalism*, New York: Macmillan.

Commons, John R. (1934), *Institutional Economics*, New York: Macmillan.

Commons, John R. (1950), *The Economics of Collective Action*, New York: Macmillan.

Copeland, Morris (1952), *A Study of Moneyflows in the United States*, New York: National Bureau of Economic Research.

Dillard, Dudley (1987), 'Money as an Institution of Capitalism', *Journal of Economic Issues*, **21** (December), 1623–48.

Dillard, Dudley (1990), 'Allan G. Gruchy, 1906–1990: A Scholar's Life', *Journal of Economic Issues*, **24** (September), 663–72.

Doeringer, Peter and Piore, Michael (1971), *Internal Labor Markets and Manpower Analysis*, Lexington, MA: Heath.

Dugger, William (1989), *Corporate Hegemony*, Westport, CT: Greenwood Press.

Dugger, William (1990), 'The New Institutionalism: New But Not Institutionalist', *Journal of Economic Issues*, **24** (June), 423–32.

Dugger, William and Waller, William (eds) (1992), *The Stratified State*, Armonk, NY: M.E. Sharpe.

Eichner, Alfred (1976), *The Megacorp and Oligopoly*, New York: Cambridge University Press.

Eichner, Alfred (1987), 'Prices and Pricing', *Journal of Economic Issues*, **21** (December), 1555–85.

Ferber, Marianne and Nelson, Julie (eds), (1993) *Beyond Economic Man*, Chicago: University of Chicago Press.

Galbraith, John Kenneth (1936), 'Monopoly Power and Price Rigidities', *Quarterly Journal of Economics*, **51** (May), 456–75.

Galbraith, John Kenneth (1973), *Economics and the Public Purpose*, Boston: Houghton Mifflin.

Galbraith, John Kenneth (1992), *The Culture of Contentment*, Boston: Houghton Mifflin.

Galbraith, John Kenneth (1993), *A Short History of Financial Euphoria*, New York: Viking Penguin.

Galbraith, James Kenneth (1989), 'Trade and the Planning System', in Samuel Bowles, Richard Edwards and William Shepherd (eds), *Unconventional Wisdom*, Boston: Houghton Mifflin.

Gordon, Wendell (1980), *Institutional Economics: The Changing System*, Austin: University of Texas Press.

Greider, William (1992), *Who Will Tell the People*, New York: Simon and Schuster.

Gruchy, Allan (1947), *Modern Economic Thought*, New York: Prentice-Hall.

Gruchy, Allan (1972), *Contemporary Economic Thought*, Clifton, NJ: Augustus Kelley.

Gruchy, Allan (1977), *Comparative Economic Systems*, Boston: Houghton Mifflin.

Gruchy, Allan (1984), 'Uncertainty, Indicative Planning, and Industrial Policy', *Journal of Economic Issues*, **18** (March), 159–80.

Gruchy, Allan (1987), *The Reconstruction of Economics*, Westport, CT: Greenwood Press.

Hamilton, Walton (1919), 'The Institutional Approach to Economic Theory', *American Economic Review*, **9** (Supplement), 309–18.

Harrison, Bennett (1994), *Lean and Mean*, New York: Basic Books.

Harrison, Bennett and Bluestone, Berry (1988), *The Great U-Turn*, New York: Basic Books.

Harter, Lafayette (1962), *John R. Commons*, Corvallis: Oregon State University Press.

Hayden, F. Gregory and Stephenson, Kurt (1992), 'Overlap of Organizations: Corporate Transorganization and Veblen's Thesis on Higher Education', *Journal of Economic Issues*, **26** (March), 53–86.

Hickerson, Stephen (1983), 'Planning for Institutional Change in a Complex Environment', *Journal of Economic Issues*, **18** (September), 631–65.

Hill, Lewis and Troub, Roger (1995), 'Pragmatism as a Normative Theory of Social Value and Economic Ethics', in Charles Clark (ed.), *Institutional Economics and the Theory of Social Value*, Norwell, MA: Kluwer Academic Publishers.

Ingrao, Bruna and Israel, Giorgio (1990), *The Invisible Hand*, Cambridge: MIT Press.

Kaufman, Bruce E. (1993), *The Origins and Evolution of the Field of Industrial Relations in the United States*, Ithaca, NY: ILR Press.

Leontief, Wassily (1971), 'Theoretical Assumptions and Nonobserved Facts', *American Economic Review*, **61** (March), 1–7.

Liebhafsky, E. E. (1993), 'The Influence of Charles Sanders Peirce on Institutional Economics', *Journal of Economic Issues*, **28** (September), 741–54.

Lind, Hans (1993), 'The Myth of Institutionalist Method', *Journal of Economic Issues*, **27** (March), 1–17.

Lower, Milton (1990), 'A Type-of-Product System of National Accounts', *Journal of Economic Issues*, **24** (June), 371–80.

McNulty, Paul (1980), *The Origins and Development of Labor Economics*, Cambridge: MIT Press.

Minsky, Hyman (1986a), 'The Evolution of Financial Institutions and the Performance of the Economy', *Journal of Economic Issues*, **20** (June), 345–53.

Minsky, Hyman (1986b), *Stabilizing an Unstable Economy*, New Haven: Yale University Press.

Mitchell, Wesley (1913), *Business Cycles*, Berkeley: University of California Press.

Mitchell, Wesley (1937), *The Backward Art of Spending Money and Other Essays*, New York: McGraw-Hill.

Mitchell, Wesley (1949), *Types of Economic Theory*, 2 vols, New York: Augustus Kelley.

Munkirs, John R. (1985), *The Transformation of American Capitalism*, Armonk, NY: M.E. Sharpe.

Myrdal, Gunnar (1944), *An American Dilemma*, New York: Harper and Row.

Myrdal, Gunnar (1968), *Asian Drama*, New York: Pantheon.

Myrdal, Gunnar (1973), *Against the Stream*, New York: Pantheon.

Myrdal, Gunnar (1978), 'Institutional Economics', *Journal of Economic Issues*, **12** (December), 771–83.

Myrdal, Gunnar (1983 [1969]), *Objectivity in Social Research*, Middletown, CT: Wesleyan University Press.
North, Douglass (1994), 'Economic Performance Through Time', *American Economic Review*, **84** (June), 359–69.
Peach, James and Nowotny, Kenneth (1992), 'Sharecropping Chicago Style', *Journal of Economic Issues*, **26** (June), 365–72.
Peterson, Janice and Brown, Doug (1994), *The Economic Status of Women Under Capitalism*, Aldershot, UK: Edward Elgar.
Peterson, Wallace (1987), 'Macroeconomic Theory and Policy in an Institutionalist Perspective', *Journal of Economic Issues*, **21** (December), 1587–622.
Peterson, Wallace (1994), *The Silent Depression*, New York: W.W. Norton.
Radzicki, Michael and Seville, Donald (1993), 'An Institutional Dynamics Model of Sterling, Massachusetts', *Journal of Economic Issues*, **28** (June), 481–92.
Ramstad, Yngve (1985), 'Comments on Adams and Brock Paper', *Journal of Economic Issues*, **19** (June), 507–11.
Ramstad, Yngve (1986), 'A Pragmatist's Quest for Holistic Knowledge: The Scientific Methodology of John R. Commons', *Journal of Economic Issues*, **20** (December), 1067–106.
Robinson, Joan (1970), *Freedom and Necessity*, New York: Pantheon.
Rutherford, Malcolm (1983), 'John R. Commons's Institutional Economics', *Journal of Economic Issues*, **17** (September), 721–44.
Samuels, Warren and Medema, Stephen (1990), *Gardiner* C. *Means: Institutionalist and Post Keynesian*, Armonk, NY: M.E. Sharpe.
Schor, Juliet (1991), *The Overworked American*, New York: Basic Books.
Seccareccia, Mario (1988), 'Systemic Viability and Credit Crunches', *Journal of Economic Issues*, **22** (March), 49–78.
Veblen, Thorstein (1904), *The Theory of Business Enterprise*, New York: Charles Scribner's Sons.
Veblen, Thorstein (1919), *The Place of Science in Modern Civilisation and Other Essays*, New York: Viking Press.
Veblen, Thorstein (1923), *Absentee Ownership and Business Enterprise*, New York: B.W. Heubsch.
Veblen, Thorstein (1967 (1899)), *The Theory of the Leisure Class*, New York: Viking Press.
Wachtel, Howard and Adelsheim, Peter (1976), *The Inflationary Impact of Unemployment*, Washington, DC: US Government Printing Office.
Waller, William (1982), 'The Evolution of the Veblenian Dichotomy', *Journal of Economic Issues*, **16** (September), 757–71.
Whalen, Charles J. (1993), 'Saving Capitalism by Making It Good', *Journal of Economic Issues*, **27** (December), 1155–79.
Whalen, Charles J. (1996a), 'A Note on "The Myth of Institutionalist Method"', *Journal of Economic Issues*, **28** (September).
Whalen, Charles J. (ed.) (1996b), *Political Economy for the 21st Century*, Armonk, NY: M.E. Sharpe.
Wilber, Charles and Harrison, Robert (1978), 'The Methodological Basis of Institutional Economics', *Journal of Economic Issues*, **12** (March), 61–89.
Witte, Edwin (1954), 'Institutional Economics as Seen by an Institutional Economist', *Southern Economic Journal*, **21** (October), 131–40.

4. Post-Keynesian economics: a pluralistic alternative to conventional economics

INTRODUCTION

Post-Keynesian economics (PKE) grew out of dissatisfaction with conventional economics after World War II. Central to that postwar (conventional), economics was an interpretation of *The General Theory of Employment, Interest, and Money* (Keynes, 1936) that reconciled macroeconomics with neoclassical microeconomics, resulting in a body of theory referred to as the neoclassical (or neoclassical-Keynesian) synthesis. As an alternative, PKE produced analyses united by presuppositions that differed – and continue to differ – sharply from those underlying the mainstream literature.[1]

This article surveys the Post-Keynesian alternative to conventional economics and highlights its pluralistic features. The article begins by describing PKE's origins and strands, and by discussing the school's core presuppositions and some key findings. Then pluralistic features are identified, first by looking at the tradition as a whole and subsequently (to illustrate how pluralism can fuel a career of innovative scholarship) at the work of one prominent Post-Keynesian, Hyman P. Minsky. PKE does not have all the answers to important economic questions, but it warrants attention from those interested in bringing life back into economics after the global financial crisis of 2007 to 2009. Indeed, Minsky and other Post-Keynesians anticipated and warned of that crisis, while many conventional economists said it could not happen.[2]

Reprinted with permission from *International Journal of Pluralism and Economics Education* 7 (1), 2016, 22–38.

ORIGINS AND STRANDS OF PKE

PKE is not easy to pin down. It emerged as a body of thought in the 1970s, but its roots go back further.[3] Even those identifying themselves as Post-Keynesians sometimes worry publicly about whether PKE has enough coherence to be called a school of thought. In addition, the literature is full of disagreements about who and what should bear the PKE label [see, for example, Lavoie, (2014), pp.42–47].

Much of PKE originated from attempts to rescue the full significance of *The General Theory* from an interpretation that led to the neoclassical synthesis. That interpretation, offered in 1937 by Hicks and widely known as the IS-LM framework, incorporates the supply and demand for money into an analysis of income determination that centres on investment and saving. Hicks' (1937) contribution was extended by Alvin Hansen and led eventually to the aggregate supply and demand framework that gave rise to today's large macroeconometric models. Robinson (1962), Keynes's colleague at the University of Cambridge, dismissed Hicks's interpretation as 'bastard' Keynesianism, and much of PKE stems from an effort to offer an alternative that more accurately reflects and extends the central message of Keynes's book.[4]

However, not all PKE can be traced to the aim of rescuing and building on the work of Keynes. PKE also has origins in the work of other economists who were also (at least for a time) associated with the University of Cambridge. Some of those early contributors to PKE pursued work intended to complement Keynes's economics. Others became associated with PKE largely as a consequence of their dissatisfaction with mainstream economic theory and their ties and proximity to the other Post-Keynesians.

Given such origins, it is perhaps not surprising that PKE can be viewed as containing various distinct strands of scholarship. Lavoie (2010) identifies five strands. Each can be associated with at least one major figure in PKE, though all strands involve the work of many people.[5] The five economists are: Keynes, Michael Kalecki, Piero Sraffa, John Kenneth Galbraith, and Nicholas Kaldor.

Keynes

The PKE strand most closely associated with Keynes derives from efforts to build on aspects of *The General Theory* overlooked by conventional economics. Those aspects include Keynes's aim of developing a theory not only appropriate for an economy shaped heavily by expectations (formed, inescapably, in the face of uncertainty) but also relevant to understanding business cycles. An important source of inspiration for much of the work associated with this strand is Keynes's 1937 article, 'The general theory of employment', which offered a response to reviewers of his book and a restatement of its central message.

This strand began to take shape in the 1970s in response to the growing problem of stagflation and to the rise of monetarism in academic and policy circles. Early contributors included Weintraub (1961, 1973), Robinson (1971), Davidson (1972), Minsky (1975), Chick (1983), and Moore (1988). Davidson (2009) continues to be a leading figure in this strand, and his book *The Keynes Solution* shows how Keynes remains relevant to analysing national and international economic activity and to shaping polices that foster prosperity. In particular, Davidson stresses Keynes's emphasis on using government spending to ensure that aggregate demand is sufficient to generate a full-employment level of output.

Kalecki

Kalecki's central interest was explaining business cycles. His writings on output, employment, and cycles anticipated the ideas of Keynes (such as the importance of investment in determining aggregate demand, which, in turn, is a key determinant of output), but had limited initial impact on economics because they were originally published in Polish. Kalecki first visited Cambridge in the fall of 1936 and delivered a presentation, arranged by Joan Robinson, before a seminar group convened by Keynes [Osiatnyski, (1990), pp.503–504]. A year later, Kalecki (1939) moved to Cambridge and wrote *Essays in the Theory of Economic Fluctuations*, one of his most important publications.

Kalecki left Cambridge and moved a number of times after publishing his *Essays*, but his time there influenced Robinson and a subsequent stay in Oxford during the 1940s influenced others, especially Steindl (1952). Lavoie (2010, p.4) offers a list of contemporary Kaleckians, including Malcolm Sawyer, Amitava Dutt, Robert Blecker, and Steve Fazzari. In Kalecki – including his attention to monopoly power, mark-up pricing, class conflict, and the economic significance of profits – such economists find inspiration for analyses of not only macroeconomics in the short-term, but also growth and distribution over the longer-term.[6]

Sraffa

Sraffa was an economics professor in Italy until Keynes invited him to the University of Cambridge in 1927; he called Cambridge home for the rest of his career. Sraffa was invited to England shortly after publication of an article attacking the logical foundation of Alfred Marshall's theory of costs (Sraffa, 1926). After settling in Cambridge, Sraffa compiled and edited the collected works of David Ricardo (which were published between 1951 and 1955, followed by an index in 1973). That project resumed Sraffa's assault on conventional economics: According to Eatwell (1984, p.213),

> His reconstruction of Ricardo's surplus theory, presented in but a few pages of the introduction to his edition of Ricardo's *Principles*, penetrated a hundred years of misunderstanding and distortion to create a vivid rationale for the structure and content of surplus theory, for the analytical role of the labor theory of value, and henceforth, for the foundations of Marx's critical analysis of capitalist production.

Sraffa's assault continued with publication of *Production of Commodities by Means of Commodities: Prelude to a Critique of Economic Theory* (Sraffa, 1960), which used the classical economics of Ricardo to critique the neoclassical theory of value and point to an alternative analysis. Arguments in that book were used by Sraffa and Robinson to question the meaning and role of capital in the economics taught at Harvard, MIT, and most other universities. The book was also an inspiration to others, including Luigi Pasinetti and Pierangelo Garegnani.

Although the Sraffian – also called the Neo-Ricardian – thread is connected to the rest of PKE by a shared dissatisfaction with conventional economics, the matter gets complicated when attention shifts to constructing an alternative framework. As a trio of authors observed nearly 30 years ago, Neo-Ricardian economics is perhaps best understood in the context of Marxist economics, rather than in the context of other strands of PKE: "Neo-Ricardians are firmly fixed to the debates and issues in Marxist theory" [Albelda et al., (1987), p.107]. There is, however, another view. Lee (1998, p.6), for example, credits Sraffa with influencing the Post-Keynesian multi-industry pricing model of Alfred Eichner; and Lavoie (2010, p.3) writes, "Sraffians provide a much needed explanation of prices in an interdependent setting, something that is lacking in the other strands, and they provide a link with multisectoral production systems, which are of particular interest to ecological economists who wish to track the overall impact of production on the use of energy, natural resources, and pollution."

Galbraith

The Galbraithian strand of PKE is a blend of Keynes and institutional economics (a tradition that derives from the work of Thorstein Veblen and John R. Commons).[7] During much of his career, Galbraith, who taught at Harvard, was one of the world's most well-known institutionalists. But Galbraith was also an admirer of the economics of Keynes. In fact, Galbraith first visited the University of Cambridge in 1937 to 1938 with the hope of working with Keynes. However, Keynes was recovering from a heart attack and did not make it to the university that year; instead, Galbraith (1981, p.74) spent his time in the company of Keynes's colleagues – Robinson, Sraffa, and Richard Kahn.

In the 1970s, Galbraith provided substantial support for establishment of the *Journal of Post Keynesian Economics* and contributed his own view of PKE in that journal's first issue. In addition to underscoring that economic life is 'in a process of continuous and organic change', Galbraith's (1978) essay emphasised the market power and influence of large corporations, and stressed that both microeconomics and macroeconomics should reflect that institutional reality. Early contributions to this strand of PKE focused on administered pricing, the role of money in a capitalist economy, the institutional determinants of wages, and the link between market power and stagflation (see, for example, Appelbaum, 1979; Dillard, 1980; Peterson, 1980; Eichner, 1985). More recent work has focused on wage stagnation and income inequality, the rise of money manager capitalism and its part in the global financial crisis, and role of the state (see, for example, Peterson, 1994; Zalewski, 2002; Galbraith, 2008; Whalen, 2010a; Kaboub, 2011).[8]

Kaldor

Kaldor taught at the University of Cambridge after World War II (from 1949 until his retirement in 1975). He contributed widely to economic theory and policy, on subjects ranging from welfare economics and taxation to growth theory. According to Lavoie (2010), the Kaldorian strand is mostly concerned with monetary issues, cumulative causation, productivity growth, and the macroeconomic significance of international finance.

Among the economists associated with the Kaldorian tradition are Wynne Godley, John Cornwall, Mark Setterfield, and Anthony Thirlwall. Godley devoted much attention to implications of the fundamental identity that links private saving, public deficits, and the current account balance (Godley and Lavoie, 2007). Cornwall and his student Setterfield have focused on macroeconomic dynamics, assigning special importance to path dependence and the role of institutions (see, for example, Cornwall, 1977; Setterfield, 1997). Thirlwall's (2013) work centres on economic development and has garnered considerable interest among scholars in Latin America [Lavoie, (2010), p.5].

CORE PRESUPPOSITIONS OF PKE

According to Hein and Lavoie (2015), five presuppositions unite the various strands of PKE and distinguish it from conventional economics. They involve: a conception of the economy; a view of the role of time in economics; a perspective on human behaviour; an approach to economic science; and a standpoint on the role of the state.[9]

The Economy

Post-Keynesians share a 'holistic' conception of the economy, in contrast to the 'atomistic' conception of conventional economists. In PKE, the economic sphere is seen as intertwined with the rest of the social (political, legal, etc.) sphere. As a result, Post-Keynesians "consider individuals as social beings in the context of their environment, given by class, gender, culture, institutions and history" [Hein and Lavoie, (2015), p.2]. In contrast, conventional economists usually start with individual preferences and view the economy and other social institutions as a consequence of those preferences.[10]

Time

Because Post-Keynesians view socio-economic life as constantly changing, they give an important role to time in economics. For example, PKE stresses that production precedes exchange and often gives attention to creation of the resources used in the economic system. In contrast, conventional economics focuses heavily on the allocation of existing resources. Minsky (1975, pp.57–58) captured this distinction by suggesting that PKE is based on a Wall Street paradigm ("the image is that of a banker making deals on Wall Street") while conventional economics is based on a barter paradigm ("the image is that of a yeoman or a craftsman trading in a village market"). In the Wall Street paradigm, profit-seeking economic agents acquire assets and finance investment positions, spurring production of goods and services to be sold at a later date; in the barter paradigm, the time it takes for finance and production falls into the background and the focus is on finding a set of prices that achieves market clearing. Moreover, Minsky's distinction highlights the importance of money in PKE: money and financial commitments link past, present and future.

Human Behaviour

Time also affects the PKE perspective on human behaviour. Since the future is uncertain, Post-Keynesians give attention to the conventions, customs, rules of thumb, and institutions that individuals and organisations use to reduce uncertainty.[11] They also appreciate that people must make decisions despite having imperfect information and limitations on their ability to process the information available. Similarly, PKE highlights the economic significance of changing expectations. In contrast, economic agents in conventional economic models are often assumed to possess so much knowledge and foresight that Lo (2005) describes them as having 'hyper-rational' expectations.

Economic Science

PKE's approach to economic science is described as 'realism'. That is, Post-Keynesians believe that economics should explain the workings of the real-world economy – starting from realistic assumptions such as Kaldor-type 'stylised facts' – and produce research that can contribute to addressing real-world economic problems. In contrast, Hein and Lavoie (2015, p.22) argue that conventional economics adheres to 'instrumentalism', an approach that focuses only on whether economic assumptions "lead to the calculation of equilibrium positions and are conducive to accurate predictions". According to Crotty (2013), instrumentalism contributed to the global financial crisis by making acceptable a wildly unrealistic theory of efficient markets, which justified the international financial deregulation that ultimately added to the severity of the crisis.

The State and Public Policy

PKE stresses the need for continuous state intervention in the economy. In contrast to the conventional economists' view of the state as needing to play a *corrective* role in the economy (that is, correcting market failures), Post-Keynesians see the state as an essential, *creative* entity in economic life. The state is more than an umpire that secures liberties and promotes efficiency: Its legislative, administrative, and judicial decisions give liberty and efficiency their specific meanings, and those meanings evolve over time. To be sure, public policy is not always broadly beneficial and without unintended consequences (and there can certainly be too much government as well as too little government), but state involvement in managing a market economy is unavoidable and one of the roles of PKE is to provide guidance that can lead to judicious policymaking.

Moreover, continuous intervention is more than just a preconception of PKE. It is also a logical consequence of Post-Keynesian analyses. In particular, those analyses often highlight the endogenous nature of money (discussed further in the next section), credit, and business cycles; the inability of wage and price flexibility to achieve and sustain full employment; the importance of aggregate demand in both the short-term and longer-term (including the vital role of government spending when the economy is in a severe recession or depression); and the tendency for oligopoly and monopoly to emerge from competitive markets.

INSIGHT FROM POST-KEYNESIAN RESEARCH

Toward the end of the 1970s, Eichner (1978) edited *A Guide to Post Keynesian Economics*. Just over two decades later, Holt and Pressman (2001) edited *A New Guide to Post Keynesian Economics*. To help provide a clearer picture of PKE, this section highlights some of that volume's enduring observations and findings.

Pricing and Distribution

According to Lavoie [Holt and Pressman, (2001), pp.21–31], PKE offers an approach to the setting of prices by firms that is more realistic than that of mainstream economics. Rather than marginal-cost pricing (setting prices at levels that equate marginal revenues with marginal costs), PKE offers cost-plus pricing. With cost-plus pricing, firms set prices based on what they consider to be normal costs and then add a mark-up, with the aim of achieving a target rate of return (profit). (As Lavoie observes, the PKE approach is incompatible with neoclassical price theory because the latter presumes that overhead costs play no role in determining prices.) That mark-up, in turn, is determined by factors including market power, interest costs, the desire to forestall the entry of new rivals (which points toward a low mark-up), and the need for capital accumulation (which points toward a high mark-up).

PKE also offers an alternative to the marginal productivity theory of distribution. According to James K. Galbraith [Holt and Pressman, (2001), pp.32–41], income distribution depends primarily on the distribution of labour rents, which depends largely on the monopoly power of firms, and on the flow of profit spending (and therefore of investment) that corresponds to the income of the sector producing investment goods (especially technology goods). While the neoclassical view suggests that economic expansions should equalise incomes (by reducing wage dispersion) and recessions should increase inequality (by increasing wage dispersion), Galbraith argues that investment-led booms also increase inequality in advanced economies (while consumption-led booms decrease inequality).

Money and Macrodynamics

Building on the work of Basil Moore, L. Randall Wray [Holt and Pressman, (2001), pp.79–91] outlines the Post-Keynesian 'endogenous' approach to money, which contrasts with the orthodox view that the supply of bank money is determined exogenously by government. According to the endogenous approach, monetary policy operates primarily through the effect of interest rates on the demand and supply of loanable funds; any impact on the quantity of money is indirect. According to Wray, "It is the private demand for loans, plus the willingness of banks to lend, that determines the quantity of loans (and thus deposits) created. The supply of loans is never independent of demand" [Holt and Pressman, (2001), p.85].

Endogeneity also appears in Post-Keynesian macrodynamics. According to Setterfield [Holt and Pressman, (2001), pp.92–101], the conception of endogenous growth in PKE is more expansive than in neoclassical endogenous growth (NEG) models because growth and development processes are determined by their own past history. "Path dependence is, therefore, essential to the Post-Keynesian conception of endogenous growth, something that cannot be said of NEG theory", writes Setterfield [Holt and Pressman, (2001), p.96]. He continues:

> In Post-Keynesian macrodynamics, economic adjustments do more than just select among pre-defined long-run outcomes – they help to determine the very nature of those outcomes. New growth paths arise as economic expansion induces transformative structural changes in consumer preferences, technologies, and social institutions. The economy effectively creates its own future in the course of its growth and development.

Demand factors are also essential in Post-Keynesian macrodynamics. "Increases in supply do not automatically create their own demand, so the supply side cannot be the sole focus of growth analysis", argues Setterfield [Holt and Pressman, (2001), p.94]. In fact, aggregate demand influences not only the use of productive resources at any moment in time, but also the development of productive resources over time. For example, labour force participation rates, the number of hours worked, and the migration of labour are all sensitive to the expansion of demand. Demand also influences the willingness of firms to adopt new technologies. In short, demand influences both the full employment expansion path of the economy and the economy's proximity to that path [Holt and Pressman, (2001), p.95].

PLURALISTIC FEATURES OF PKE

While there is no universally accepted definition of pluralism, this article adopts the perspective of Reardon (2009, p.2), who views the essence of pluralism as "recognition of the legitimate existence of alternative ideologies, frameworks, and references". According to Reardon (2009), pluralism can exist on several dimensions, including epistemology, ontology, theory construction, research methods, and pedagogy. If done right, he argues, pluralism "should instil humility and respectful curiosity about alternative views".[12]

Looking at PKE provides multiple glimpses of pluralism in economics. Pluralistic features can be found in Post-Keynesians' professional engagement as well as in their economic analyses.[13]

Pluralistic Engagement

The pluralistic engagement of Post-Keynesians manifests itself in a couple of ways. One is that most Post-Keynesians reject narrow boundaries on PKE.

They are, in the words of Lavoie, most often 'lumpers', rather than 'splitters' – and are comfortable with a broad tradition that is neither monolithic nor puristic [Lavoie, (2014), pp.42–45]. Another manifestation is that, in addition to allowing broad professional engagement under the 'big tent' of PKE, Post-Keynesians often follow and contribute to the literature of other schools of economic thought, including Marxist, institutionalist, and feminist economics (see, for example, Keen, 1993; Whalen, 2010b; Waller 1999, respectively).[14]

Pluralistic Economic Analysis

Pluralism is also a part of PKE analysis. For example, the Post-Keynesians' holistic view of the economy orients them toward seeing economic relations as embedded in the broader social reality. Thus, socio-cultural factors warrant an integral part of PKE, which is precisely what one would expect from a pluralistic econonomics.[15] In fact, the holism within PKE suggests not just that the socio-economic whole may be greater than the sum of its parts, but also that the functioning of the parts is conditioned by their interrelations [Wilber and Harrison, (1978), p.73; Wilber and Jameson, (1983), pp.154–157].

Another pluralistic feature of PKE is its 'horses for courses' approach to economic theory and analysis. According to Harcourt (1999, p.57), horses for courses means "how and what you do depends on what the purpose is". Thus, Post-Keynesians use different theories, methods, and levels of abstraction in the pursuit of answers to different questions.[16]

Consistent with the horses-for-courses approach, Post-Keynesians have often sought to synthesise various elements from different strands of PKE and even from different schools of economic thought. For example, in his analysis of macroeconomic dynamics, Eichner (1991) incorporated microeconomic elements from institutionalism, pricing elements from Sraffa, and growth and distribution elements from Kalecki. Other Post-Keynesian 'synthesisers' include Philip Arestis, Marc Lavoie, Peter Reynolds, and Zdravka Todorova.[17] A consequence of the horses-for-courses approach is that it can be difficult to assign some individuals to a single strand within PKE.

Another pluralistic feature of PKE is an interest in scholarship beyond economics. For example, Post-Keynesian institutionalist W. Robert Brazelton stresses the value of looking to the fields of psychology and sociology for insight relevant to economics. In particular, he highlights the contributions of psychology to the behavioural finance of Andrew Lo and the microeconomics of Herbert Simon, and he underscores the economic relevance of sociological research on human interaction and cultural change by scholars such as Herbert Blumer and Jeremy Straughn [for further discussion see Whalen (2015)].

PLURALISM AND MINSKY

The publications of Hyman Minsky illustrate how pluralism can fuel a career of innovative Post-Keynesian scholarship. Throughout his professional life, Minsky's research involved efforts to synthesise and build on insight from a diverse group of economists. There are also elements of pluralism in his approach to public policy, which stresses there is no room for 'one size fits all' or 'once and for all' solutions to economic problems.

The Pluralism Driving Minsky's Research

Minsky entered the University of Chicago as an undergraduate in 1937 and was introduced to economics through that university's social-science sequence, which presented all the social sciences as playing integral parts in the study of society.[18] Economists Oscar Lange and Henry Simons had the greatest influence on him. Although Lange was a socialist and Simons is often viewed as having a free-market perspective associated with the 'Chicago School' of economics, Minsky found common ground in their thinking. "As I see it the socialism of Lange had more in common with the capitalism of Simons than with the socialism of Stalin, and the capitalism of Simons had more in common with the socialism of Lange than with the capitalism of Hitler. The important thing is not whether property is private and incomes are derived from owning property, what is important is for society to be democratic and humane", wrote Minsky (1985, p.202).

Minsky's career was motivated by concerns and interests he shared with Simons. Those include: the observed instability of capitalism, the endogenous nature of money, the connection between finance and macroeconomic instability, the relationship between entrepreneurial profit seeking and the development of market power, and the adverse effect of inequality on efficiency and democracy (Minsky, 1985). But Simons did not break with inherited economic theory, so Minsky turned to Keynes who shared his belief that "the inherited theory was incapable of explaining what was happening" [Minsky, (1982), pp.86–87].[19]

Even after turning to Keynes, however, Minsky underscored the common ground shared by Keynes and Simons. For example, according to Minsky (1977, p.305), "Simons was much closer to the views about the monetary-financial process put forward by Keynes than he was to the current Chicago School, which sometimes invokes his authority, or to monetarism". Moreover, Minsky (1982, p.86) stressed that the "fundamental dilemma in economic organization" is the same in Keynes and Simons: how to "preserve the vitality and resilience of decentralized decisions without the instability accompanying decentralized markets".

Building on Keynes – as well as insight from Kalecki and the institutionalists – Minsky developed his financial instability hypothesis, an alternative to the efficient market hypothesis of conventional economics. The financial instability hypothesis maintains that the financial structure of advanced capitalist economies becomes more fragile over a period of prosperity (Minsky, 1975, 1982). The hypothesis includes both an investment theory of business cycles and a longer-term dimension that involves financial-sector evolution over the course of several cycles (Minsky, 1986a).

The financial instability hypothesis provided the foundation for Minsky's work over a number of years, but in the mid-1980s he saw a need for something more. On the occasion of a conference marking the Marx-Keynes-Schumpeter centennial, Minsky (1986b, p.121) wrote: "The task confronting economics today may be characterized as a need to integrate [Joseph] Schumpeter's vision of a resilient intertemporal capitalist process with Keynes's hard insights into the fragility introduced into the capitalist accumulation process by some inescapable properties of capitalist financial structures". The result was Minsky's (1990) theory of capitalist development, which stressed emergence (in the 1980s) of an era he called money manager capitalism.[20]

The pluralism fuelling Minsky's research also inspired him to keep abreast of developments within conventional economics. In an address delivered less than a year before his death, Minsky devoted attention to Thomas Sargent's *Bounded Rationality in Macroeconomics* and stressed that such rationality recognises uncertainty, allowing an appreciation of history, expectations, and learning over time. While acknowledging that 'fundamental differences remain' between Post-Keynesians and new classical economists like Sargent, Minsky (1996, p.362) chose to focus instead on the "room for fruitful discourse".

The Pluralism in Minsky's Policy Views

Elements of pluralism also exist in Minsky's approach to public policy. One of those elements is his belief that there is no 'one size fits all' policy solution. Minsky focused on this most often when discussing the regulation of financial institutions. Because his overarching principles for the financial sector included transparency and compartmentalisation, Minsky (1995a) preferred an industry with specialised institutions, each with different regulatory needs. It was, he often said, a horses-for-courses approach to organising and regulating the financial sector.[21]

Another pluralistic element in Minsky's approach to public policy is his view that there are no 'once and for all' solutions to economic problems. In *Stabilizing an Unstable Economy*, Minsky (1986a) stressed that policy must change over time because economic institutions and relations are always in flux.[22] As a result of that ceaseless economic evolution – driven partly by the efforts of some people to circumvent existing policies – Minsky argued that policy details must constantly evolve and that policy institutions must occasionally receive thoroughgoing reform. Policies that work at one time (at a particular point in the business cycle, within a given institutional framework, or during a certain economic era, for example) may not be effective at another time; and "no institutional structure will be efficient forever" [Minsky, (1995b), p.19].[23]

SUMMARY AND CONCLUSIONS

In response to dissatisfaction with conventional economics after World War II, PKE emerged and produced a body of scholarship united by its own set of presuppositions. That scholarship contains five strands and – although each strand involves the work of many people and some individuals are not easy to place in a single category – each strand can be associated with at least one major Post-Keynesian figure: Keynes, Kalecki, Sraffa, Galbraith, and Kaldor. The presuppositions that give coherence to their economics involve a holistic conception of the economy, an appreciation for the role of time in economic life, an emphasis on economic behaviour in the face of uncertainty, a realist (as opposed to instrumentalist) approach to economic analysis, and a view of the state as a creative entity with an unavoidably continuous role to play in the economy.

In addition to surveying the Post-Keynesian alternative to conventional economics (including some key findings of Post-Keynesian research), this article has highlighted its pluralistic features – by looking first at the tradition as a whole and then at the work of Hyman Minsky. Features identified by looking at the tradition overall include a big-tent approach to PKE, attention to sociocultural factors, a horses-for-courses approach to theory and analysis, and an interest in scholarship beyond economics. Looking at Minsky illustrates how pluralism can fuel a career of innovative research and finds pluralistic elements in his approach to public policy as well as his economic analyses.

PKE does not have all the answers to important economic questions, but it warrants attention from those interested in bringing life back into economics after the global financial crisis of 2007 to 2009 [Reardon, (2009), p.1]. Indeed, Minsky and other Post-Keynesians anticipated and warned of that crisis, while many conventional economists said it could not happen.[24] Perhaps that is because Minsky was introduced to economics at Chicago at a time when pluralism ruled the department (that is, the department treated economics as an integral part of the social sciences and its economists represented, and were open to, a wide spectrum of economic thought) and because so much of PKE can trace its roots to the University of Cambridge, where a similar climate existed.[25]

Attempting to recreate that sort of academic climate in the years ahead seems a worthwhile, joint project of Post-Keynesians and readers of this journal.

NOTES

1. This article uses 'mainstream', 'conventional' and 'orthodox' economics as synonyms. Such economics, which appears in the most widely adopted textbooks, currently includes neoclassical microeconomics as well as new Keynesian, new classical, and 'new consensus' macroeconomic models. For similar characterisations and further discussion, see Niggle (2006), Arestis (2009) and Hein and Lavoie (2015); also see the discussion of the core of contemporary macroeconomics in Caballero (2010).
2. While many other Post-Keynesians could have been highlighted (for example, Eichner, Harcourt, and Robinson immediately come to mind), Minsky was chosen primarily because his ideas have received widespread attention following the onset of the global financial crisis (see, for example, Lahart, 2007; Pollin, 2008; Krugman, 2009).
3. For example, many economists suggest that PKE is rooted in the so-called Cambridge 'capital controversy' of the 1960s, a debate on the nature and role of capital goods in economic theory – between, on one side, economists at the University of Cambridge and, on the other side, economists at Harvard University and the Massachusetts Institute of Technology (MIT) (see for example, Mata, 2004). In contrast, Davidson (2003, p.251) traces the emergence of PKE to publication of Sidney Weintraub's (1958) *An Approach to the Theory of Income Distribution* in 1958. Lavoie (2010, p.2) suggests the roots go back even further, to Keynes's so-called *Circus*, a group of young economists (including Richard Kahn, Joan Robinson, and Piero Sraffa) that met in the early 1930s to discuss his *Treatise on Money*. For an early outline of PKE, see Eichner and Kregel (1975); for a history of PKE, see King (2002).
4. According to Bentolila (2005, pp.116–118), although the IS-LM model is still "the backbone of many introductory macroeconomic textbooks, today's mainstream macroeconomic research is usually conducted using dynamic general equilibrium (DGE) models with microeconomic foundations". However, he adds that "the idea that wage and price rigidities help explain why money affects output and that they can have important effects on business cycle fluctuations, a foundation of the IS-LM model, survives in so-called 'new Keynesian' economics". From the perspective of PKE, the DGE models of new classical macroeconomics (including 'real business cycle' models) are even further removed from the economics of Keynes than new Keynesian models. For further discussion of PKE in relation to conventional macroeconomics, see Niggle (2006).
5. Lavoie (2014, p.43) lists the five strands along with their main research themes and contributors.
6. For further reading on economics from a Kaleckian perspective, see Sadowski and Szeworksi (2004). Also see Asimakopulos (1975, 1983), whose work is often considered a definitive account of Kalecki's theory.
7. Lavoie (2010, p.5) calls economists in this strand 'institutionalist Keynesians'. For an overview of institutional economics (and its connection to pluralism), see

(Adkisson, 2010). For a survey of institutionalist Keynesianism (also called Post-Keynesian institutionalism) after the Great Recession (see Whalen, 2013).

8. Money manager capitalism is what Minsky (1996) called the latest stage of US capitalist development, and is characterised by the influence of institutional investors. In addition to research in the Post-Keynesian institutionalist (Galbrathian) tradition that has already been cited, Todorova (2009) warrants mentioning because her work integrates that tradition and feminist economics to examine the household sector (a part of the economy that has received little attention in PKE); also see Dillard (1948) for an early interpretation of Keynes by an institutionalist.
9. Hein and Lavoie (2015, pp.2–3) do not describe all the presuppositions exactly as I do here, but this section – which parallels Whalen (2013, pp.16–17) – is informed by their essay and makes many of the same points they do. To be sure, the presuppositions mentioned here might also be part of the foundation of other schools of economic thought; what would distinguish other forms of economics from PKE would be adherence to additional presuppositions (involving the centrality of class conflict, a technological/ceremonial dualism, etc.).
10. The holism of PKE helps to highlight the 'paradox of thrift' and other micro-macro paradoxes that often receive little attention in conventional economics; for further discussion of such paradoxes and their connection to holism, see Lavoie (2014, pp.16–22). For further discussion of the role of institutions in PKE, see, for example, King [Holt and Pressman, (2001), pp.65–78].
11. For more on uncertainty in PKE, see Rosser [Holt and Pressman, (2001), pp.52–64], and for more on uncertainty and on methodology in PKE, see Dow [Holt and Pressman, (2001), pp.11–21].
12. For further discussion of pluralism in economics, see Reardon (2009) and Negru (2009).
13. It is beyond the scope of this article to explore the extent to which mainstream economics also exhibits pluralistic features, but Davis (2006) suggests that a number of research programs (involving game theory, experimental economics, complexity theory, behavioural economics, and neuroeconomics) have made economics more pluralistic over the past few decades and may be eroding the dominance of neoclassical theory.
14. In personal correspondence with this author, Lavoie notes that the pluralistic approach of PKE has, in turn, attracted some Marxists (including Gerald Epstein, James Crotty, and Robert Sherman) and Regulation School economists (including Robert Boyer, Dominique Plihon, and Robert Guttmann) to the economics of Keynes, and has helped to infuse their analyses with Post-Keynesian insight.
15. For examples of Post-Keynesian overviews that underscore the importance of socio-cultural factors, see Appelbaum (1979, p.46) and Hamouda and Harcourt (1988, p.25).
16. As Hamouda and Harcourt (1988, p.25) write, seeking to replace the 'complete theory' of mainstream economics with a monolithic alternative "is a misplaced exercise...The important perspective to take away is, we believe, that there is no uniform way of tackling all issues in economics".
17. For a discussion of Arestis, Lavoie, and Reynolds, see King (2002, pp.214–219); also see Todorova (2009).
18. Reflecting on his undergraduate education and on economics education more recently, Minsky (1985, p.194) wrote, "If I had my way the standard course in economics would be eliminated and economics would be introduced in the context of

social sciences and history. The current American way of teaching economics leads to economists who are well trained but poorly educated."

19. According to Minsky (1985, pp.202–203), orthodox economists at Chicago "felt no strong need to revolutionize economic theory" because they anticipated Keynes's main policy conclusion about fiscal policy 'by observing the economy' during the Great Depression.
20. Minsky was Schumpeter's doctoral student at Harvard until Schumpeter's death in 1950. He later completed his degree under the supervision of Wassily Leontief.
21. Minsky (1982, p.14) also maintained that the details of the Federal Reserve's various lender-of-last resort interventions differed, and would continue to differ, because the particulars of each crisis are different.
22. The dynamic nature of economic life is a key reason why Minsky was fond of saying that capitalism comes in as many varieties as Heinz has of pickles (a reference to that company's '57 Varieties' slogan).
23. In *John Maynard Keynes*, Minsky wrote: "It will remain true that we live out our lives in transition; there is no final solution to the problems of organizing economic life" [Minsky, (1975), p.168]. (In light of the earlier discussion of Post-Keynesian ties to the University of Cambridge, it is worth noting that Minsky wrote *John Maynard Keynes* at that university during a sabbatical leave from Washington University.)
24. As early as the mid-1980s, Minsky (1986c) anticipated a global financial crisis triggered by the dangers associated with securitised financial instruments.
25. According to Minsky (1985, p.202), "Between 1937 and 1942, the University of Chicago was a fine place to begin as an economist. The economists at the University covered a wide spectrum of thought; there was no dominant Chicago School. The emphasis upon intellectual rigor and seriousness was combined with a wide definition of the subject".

REFERENCES

Adkisson, R.V. (2010) 'The original institutionalist perspective on economy and its place in a pluralist paradigm', *International Journal of Economics Education and Pluralism*, Vol. 1, No. 4, pp.356–371.

Albelda, R., Gunn, C. and Waller, W. (1987) *Alternatives to Economic Orthodoxy: A Reader in Political Economy*, M.E. Sharpe, Armonk, New York.

Appelbaum, E. (1979) 'Post-Keynesian theory: the labor market', *Challenge*, Vol. 21, No. 6, pp.39–47.

Arestis, P. (2009) *New Consensus Macroeconomics: A Critical Appraisal*, Working Paper No. 564, The Levy Economics Institute of Bard College, Annandale-on-Hudson, NY.

Asimakopulos, A. (1975) 'A Kaleckian theory of income distribution', *Canadian Journal of Economics*, Vol. 8, No. 3, pp.313–333.

Asimakopulos, A. (1983) 'Kalecki and Keynes on finance, investment and saving', *Cambridge Journal of Economics*, Vol. 7, Nos. 3/4, pp.221–233.

Bentolila, S. (2005) 'Hicks-Hansen model', in Segura, J. and Braun, C.R. (Eds.): *An Eponymous Dictionary of Economics*, pp.116–118, Edward Elgar, Cheltenham, UK.

Caballero, R.J. (2010) 'Macroeconomics after the crisis', *Journal of Economic Perspectives*, Vol. 24, No. 4, pp.85–102.

Chick, V. (1983) *Macroeconomics after Keynes*, MIT Press, Cambridge.

Cornwall, J. (1977) *Modern Capitalism: Its Growth and Transformation*, Martin Robertson, London.

Crotty, J. (2013) 'The realism of assumptions does matter: why Keynes-Minsky theory must replace efficient market theory as the guide to financial regulatory policy', in Wolfson, M.A. and Epstein, G.A. (Eds.): *The Handbook of the Political Economy of Financial Crises*, pp.133–158, Oxford University Press, New York.

Davidson, P. (1972) *Money and the Real World*, J. Wiley, New York.

Davidson, P. (2003) 'Setting the record straight on *A History of Post Keynesian Economics*', *Journal of Post Keynesian Economics*, Vol. 26, No. 2, pp.245–272.

Davidson, P. (2009) *The Keynes Solution: The Path to Global Economic Prosperity*, Palgrave Macmillan, New York.

Davis, J.B. (2006) 'The turn in economics: neoclassical dominance to mainstream pluralism?', *Journal of Institutional Economics*, Vol. 2, No. 1, pp.1–20.

Dillard, D. (1948) *The Economics of John Maynard Keynes: The Theory of a Monetary Economy*, Prentice-Hall, New York.

Dillard, D. (1980) 'A monetary theory of production: Keynes and the institutionalists', *Journal of Economic Issues*, Vol. 14, No. 2, pp.255–273.

Eatwell, J. (1984) 'Piero Sraffa: seminal economic theorist', *Science & Society*, Vol. 48, No. 2, pp.211–216.

Eichner, A.S. (1978) *A Guide to Post Keynesian Economics*, M.E. Sharpe, Armonk, NY.

Eichner, A.S. (1985) *Toward a New Economics: Essays in Post-Keynesian and Institutionalist Theory*, M.E. Sharpe, Armonk, NY.

Eichner, A.S. (1991) *The Macrodynamics of Advanced Market Economies*, M.E. Sharpe, Armonk, NY.

Eichner, A.S. and Kregel, J.A. (1975) 'An essay on Post-Keynesian theory: a new paradigm in economics', *Journal of Economic Literature*, Vol. 13, No. 4, pp.1293–1314.

Galbraith, J.K. (1978) 'On post Keynesian economics', *Journal of Post Keynesian Economics*, Vol. 1, No. 1, pp.8–11.

Galbraith, J.K. (1981) *A Life in Our Times: Memoirs*, Houghton Mifflin, Boston.

Galbraith, J.K. (2008) *The Predator State*, Free Press, New York.

Godley, W. and Lavoie, M. (2007) *Monetary Economics: An Integrated Approach to Credit, Money, Income, Production, and Wealth*, Palgrave Macmillan, New York.

Hamouda, O. and Harcourt, G. (1988) 'Post Keynesianism: from criticism to coherence?', *Bulletin of Economic Research*, Vol. 40, No. 1, pp.1–33.

Harcourt, G. (1999) 'Horses for courses: the making of a Post-Keynesian economist', in Heertje, A. (Ed.): *The Makers of Modern Economics*, Vol. 4, pp.32–69.

Hein, E. and Lavoie, M. (2015) 'Post-Keynesian economics', forthcoming in Dimand, R. and Hagemann, H. (Eds.): *The Elgar Companion to John Maynard Keynes*, Edward Elgar, Cheltenham, UK.

Hicks, J.R. (1937) 'Mr. Keynes and the 'classics': a suggested interpretation', *Econometrica*, Vol. 5, No. 2, pp.147–159.

Holt, R.P.F. and Pressman, S. (Eds.) (2001) *A New Guide to Post Keynesian Economics*, Routledge, London.

Kaboub, F. (2011) 'Understanding and preventing financial instability: Post-Keynesian institutionalism and government as employer of last resort', in Whalen, C.J. (Ed.): *Financial Instability and Economic Security after the Great Recession*, pp.77–92, Edward Elgar, Cheltenham, UK.

Kalecki, M. (1939) *Essays in the Theory of Economic Fluctuations*, Allen and Unwin, London.

Keen, S. (1993) 'The misinterpretation of Marx's theory of value', *Journal of the History of Economic Thought*, Vol. 15, No. 2, pp.282–300.

Keynes, J.M. (1936) *The General Theory of Employment, Interest, and Money*, Macmillan, London.

Keynes, J.M. (1937) 'The general theory of employment', *Quarterly Journal of Economics*, Vol. 51, No. 2, pp.209–223.

King, J.E. (2002) *A History of Post Keynesian Economics since 1936*, Edward Elgar, Cheltenham, UK.

Krugman, P. (2009) 'The Night They Reread Minsky', London School of Economics, 10 June [online] http://www.lse.ac.uk/newsAndMedia/videoAndAudio/channels/publicLecturesAndEvents/player.aspx?id=366 (accessed 28 January 2016).

Lahart, J. (2007) 'In time of tumult, obscure economist gains currency', *The Wall Street Journal*, 18 August, p.1.

Lavoie, M. (2010) 'Post-Keynesianism', forthcoming in Faccarello, G. and Kurz, H. (Eds.): *Handbook on the History of Economic Thought*, Vol. 2, Edward Elgar, Cheltenham, UK.

Lavoie, M. (2014) *Post-Keynesian Economics: New Foundations*, Edward Elgar, Cheltenham, UK.

Lee, F. (1998) *Post Keynesian Price Theory*, Cambridge University Press, New York.

Lo, A. (2005) 'Reconciling efficient markets with behavioral finance: the adaptive market hypothesis', *Journal of Investment Consulting*, Vol. 7, No. 2, pp.21–44.

Mata, T. (2004) 'Constructing identity: the Post Keynesians and the capital controversies', *Journal of the History of Economic Thought*, Vol. 26, No. 2, pp.241–259.

Minsky, H.P. (1975) *John Maynard Keynes*, Columbia University Press, New York.

Minsky, H.P. (1977) 'An 'economics of Keynes' perspective on money', in Weintraub, S. (Ed.): *Modern Economic Thought*, pp.295–307, University of Pennsylvania Press, Philadelphia.

Minsky, H.P. (1982) *Can 'It' Happen Again?*, M.E. Sharpe, Armonk, New York.

Minsky, H.P. (1985) 'Beginnings', *Banca Nazionale del Lavoro Quarterly Review*, Vol. 38, No. 154, pp.211–221, reprinted in (2009) in *PSL Quarterly Review* (2009), Vol. 62, Nos. 248–251, pp.191–203.

Minsky, H.P. (1986a) *Stabilizing an Unstable Economy*, Yale University Press, New Haven.

Minsky, H.P. (1986b) 'Money and crisis in Schumpeter and Keynes', in Wagener, H.J. and Drukker, J. (Eds.): *The Economic Law of Motion in Modern Society: A Marx-Keynes-Schumpeter Centennial*, pp.112–122, Cambridge University Press, Cambridge, UK.

Minsky, H.P. (1986c) 'Global consequences of financial deregulation', *Marcus Wallenberg Papers on International Finance*, Vol. 2, No. 1, pp.1–19.

Minsky, H.P. (1990) 'Schumpeter: finance and evolution', in Heertje, A. and Perlman, M. (Eds.): *Evolving Technology and Market Structure: Studies in Schumpeterian Economics*, pp.51–74, University of Michigan Press, Ann Arbor.

Minsky, H.P. (1995a) 'The creation of a capitalist financial system', in Szabo-Pelscoczi, M. (Ed.): *The Global Monetary System after the Fall of the Soviet Empire*, pp.153–170, Avebury, Aldershot, UK.

Minsky, H.P. (1995b) *A Positive Program for Successful Capitalism*, draft paper distributed by Minsky (photocopy).

Minsky, H.P. (1996) 'Uncertainty and the institutional structure of capitalist economies', *Journal of Economic Issues*, Vol. 30, No. 2, pp.357-368.
Moore, B. (1988) *Horizontalists and Verticalists: The Macroeconomics of Credit Money*, Cambridge University Press, Cambridge, UK.
Negru, I. (2009) 'Reflections on pluralism in economics', *International Journal of Pluralism and Economics Education*, Vol. 1, Nos. 1/2, pp.7–21.
Niggle, C. (2006) 'Institutionalist Post-Keynesian economics and the post monetarist consensus', in Setterfield, M. (Ed.): *Complexity, Endogenous Money, and Macroeconomic Theory: Essays in Honor of Basil J. Moore*, pp.368–389, Edward Elgar, Cheltenham, UK.
Osiatnyski, J. (1990) *Collected Works of Michael Kalecki*, Vol. 1, Oxford University Press, New York.
Peterson, W.C. (1980) 'Power and economic performance', *Journal of Economic Issues*, Vol. 14, No. 4, pp.827–869.
Peterson, W.C. (1994) *Silent Depression*, W.W. Norton and Company, New York.
Pollin, R. (2008) 'We're all Minskyites now', *The Nation*, 17 October, pp.5–7.
Reardon, J. (2009) 'Foreword', *International Journal of Pluralism and Economics Education*, Vol. 1, Nos. 1/2, pp.1–6.
Robinson, J. (1962) 'Review of money, trade and economic growth', in Johnson, H.G. (Ed.): *Economic Journal*, Vol. 72, No. 287, pp.690–692.
Robinson, J. (1971) *Economic Heresies: Some Old Fashioned Questions in Economic Theory*, Basic Books, New York.
Sadowski, Z.L. and Szeworksi, A. (2004) *Kalecki's Economics Today*, Routledge, London.
Setterfield, M. (1997) *Rapid Growth and Relative Decline: Modelling Macroeconomic Dynamics with Hysteresis*, Macmillan, London.
Sraffa, P. (1926) 'The laws of returns under competitive conditions', *Economic Journal*, Vol. 36, No. 144, pp.535–550.
Sraffa, P. (1960) *Production of Commodities by Means of Commodities: Prelude to a Critique of Economic Theory*, Cambridge University Press, London.
Steindl, J. (1952) *Maturity and Stagnation in American Capitalism*, Blackwell, Oxford.
Thirlwall, A. (2013) *Economic Growth in an Open Developing Economy*, Edward Elgar, Cheltenham, UK.
Todorova, Z.K. (2009) *Money and Households in a Capitalist Economy: A Gendered Post Keynesian-Institutionalist Analysis*, Edward Elgar, Cheltenham, UK.
Waller, W. (1999) 'Post Keynesian economics', in Peterson, J. and Lewis, M. (Eds.): *The Elgar Companion to Feminist Economics*, pp.622–628, Edward Elgar, Cheltenham, UK.
Weintraub, S. (1958) *An Approach to the Theory of Income Distribution*, Chilton, Philadelphia. Weintraub, S. (1961) *Classical Keynesianism, Monetary Theory and the Price Level*, Chilton, Philadelphia.
Weintraub, S. (1973) *Keynes and the Monetarists*, Rutgers University Press, New Brunswick, New Jersey.
Whalen, C.J. (2010a) 'An institutionalist perspective on the global financial crisis', in Kates, S. (Ed.): *Macroeconomic Theory and Its Failings*, pp.235–259, Edward Elgar, Cheltenham, UK.
Whalen, C.J. (2010b) 'Full employment with liberty: John R. Commons's perspective and its continuing relevance', *Journal of Economic Issues*, Vol. 44, No. 2, pp.559–568.

Whalen, C.J. (2013) 'Post-Keynesian institutionalism after the great recession', *European Journal of Economics and Economic Policies*, Vol. 10, No. 1, pp.12–27.
Whalen, C.J. (2015) 'Pluralism: lifeblood of Post-Keynesian institutionalism', *International Journal of Pluralism and Economics Education*, Vol. 6, No. 1, pp.68–81.
Wilber, C. and Harrison, R. (1978) 'The methodological basis of institutionalism', *Journal of Economic Issues*, Vol. 12, No. 1, pp.61–89.
Wilber, C. and Jameson, K. (1983) *An Inquiry into the Poverty of Economics*, University of Notre Dame Press, Notre Dame, Indiana.
Zalewski, D. (2002) 'Retirement insecurity in the age of money manager capitalism', *Journal of Economic Issues*, Vol. 36, No. 2, pp.349–356.

PART III

Exploring the contemporary relevance of John R. Commons

5. Economic insecurity and the problem-solving approach of John R. Commons

John R. Commons developed and employed a number of theories during his career. But the fundamental motivating force behind Commons's scholarship was an attempt to resolve practical problems (Commons 1950:342). If we are to discuss the contemporary relevance of Commons's ideas, we should first recognize *problem solving* as the foundation of his institutional approach to social inquiry.[1]

While the world has no scarcity of human problems, few within the social sciences are familiar with Commons's insights. A way to bring many of those insights to the fore is to consider the problem of economic insecurity by employing one of Commons's preferred research techniques – the comparative method.[2] This paper reviews Commons's 1921 essay on "Industrial Relations," in which insecurity plays a central role, and compares his remarks to present-day observations on the same subject (Commons 1921a).

COMMONS ON INDUSTRIAL RELATIONS

Although Commons contributed to problem solving in many realms, labor problems constituted his primary area of interest. "Industrial Relations" appears as the first chapter in the 1921 edition of *Trade Unionism and Labor Problems* (Commons 1921a). The essay is derived from a 1919 address, "Bringing about Industrial Peace," presented before the Conference of the National Association of Employment Managers.

Commons's essay allows us to identify four possible means of establishing industrial peace – automatic methods, rough methods, misrepresentation, and investigative methods.[3] One automatic method involves reliance on the forces

Reprinted with permission from P. Voos (ed.), *Industrial Relations Research Association Series: Proceedings of the Fiftieth Annual Meeting* (Industrial Relations Research Association, 1998), 320–327.

of supply and demand via the price system. Another relies on the panacea of socialism. Commons rejects both as ineffective.

There are two dimensions to Commons's critique of the price mechanism as a generator of social harmony. On the macroeconomic front, he points to the disruptions and distress caused by business cycles. On the microeconomic front, he dismisses the suggestion that price theory reflects the reality of individual labor-market bargaining (partly because bargaining power is unequal) and criticizes the competitive process for bringing conditions of employment down to the level offered by the least progressive employer (see also Commons 1919:29, 47).

Socialism, meanwhile, is rejected for its inability to eliminate labor–management conflict without first abolishing the right to strike. Here we see the manifestation of two themes in Commons's writings: the desire to resolve problems in a manner consistent with individual liberty and the belief that conflicts of interest are a normal part of human life. As he wrote in another article a few years later, "[T]his entire idealism of harmony of interests, whether under capitalism or under socialism, falls to the ground once we recognize that social conflict has always been and always will be a fundamental fact in the progress of mankind" (Commons 1925a:692).

"Rough methods" are various devices that force industrial peace. One used by employers is a discharge threat designed to get workers to comply with demands out of fear of unemployment. Commons also identifies union restrictions on workers' entry into employment as a device of this sort, at least with respect to the goal of employment security in the face of slack aggregate demand (see also Commons 1921b:264–66).

Other rough methods include the court injunction, imprisonment of labor leaders, and the impoundment of union funds. Commons is emphatic: the industrial peace achieved through such methods can be neither meaningful nor long lasting. As he writes on government's use of these methods, "[I]f beneath what the leaders are doing there is a real grievance, a real unrest and a mass movement, we cannot permanently suppress it" (Commons 1921a:2). Commons is equally emphatic in rejecting the use of misrepresentation (i.e., distortion or falsification of an opponent's demands or goals) as a strategy for producing labor peace – in fact, he suggests this often serves only to produce greater labor-management unrest.

The key to industrial peace, then, rests in investigative methods. "We must investigate the conditions which cause this industrial unrest" (Commons 1921a:2). But Commons was not content with remedies alone. His preferred investigative method of problem solving was "the method of prevention" – an approach that applied investigative findings "to remove the conditions which cause unrest to awaken" (Commons 1921a:2).

Drawing on his own extensive inquiries into labor problems, Commons maintains that the primary cause of industrial unrest is uncertainty. Since time is an essential element in economic life, uncertainty must be dealt with by everyone (Commons 1921a:3–5; 1934:617–18, 676; 1919:65–6). In Commons's view, however, capitalism in the early 1920s addressed the problem of uncertainty almost exclusively as it related to those engaged in financial transactions. Workers, in contrast, lived in a world filled with economic insecurity.

According to Commons, "confidence in the future" – not labor, management, or physical machinery – is the fundamental source of the vast wealth generated by twentieth century capitalism's large and often highly capital-intensive corporations. Borrowers, lenders, and investors find this confidence in "the expectation of industrial continuity," an expectation secured by the banking system. The key to the capitalistic system, he argues, is that it combines liberty to acquire wealth with "security of expectations" (Commons 1921a:8; see also Commons 1922).

The major weakness of capitalism, however, is "it has not furnished the working people a similar security to that which it has furnished the investors." Like the employer, "the workingman needs to have something to wait for and needs to have confidence in the future." Commons summarizes: "Not until the capitalistic system, not until the great financial interests that control this country, have learned that it is just as important to furnish security for the job as it is to furnish security for the investment will we have a permanent provision for industrial peace" (Commons 1921a:8–10).

Employment insecurity in Commons's day had many dimensions. One was the seasonal or otherwise irregular nature of much work. Another was the fact that workplace dangers threatened continued employment. Still others were the threat of illness and employer practices that produced high turnover. An even more widespread problem was unemployment caused by business cycles (Commons 1921a; 1921b; 1921c; 1922).

Having identified conditions thought to be the source of the problem, Commons then discusses how to remove them. Throughout his career, Commons maintained there was much that business leaders could do to address these conditions.[4] He also stressed that such leaders could serve their own economic interest in the process (see, for example, Commons 1919:65–73; 1921c:5–6; Lewisohn et al. 1925; Commons and Andrews 1936:37–42). Using references to specific firms, Commons argues in "Industrial Relations" that corporations can generate efficiency gains by providing workers with employment security and other reasons to be confident in the future. Discussing one company, he writes:

> I was impressed with the fact that it is not in detailed methods of piece and bonus payments that they try to reach the individual and increase his production, but it is in creating the conviction in every man in that industry that that is *his* industry, that the future of that concern is *his* future. (Commons 1921a:12)

In short, "Get capital to think of the security of the job and it begets efficiency of labor" (Commons 1921a:12).

Despite the potential payoff, Commons recognized that getting capital to think in this manner was seldom easy. He saw two classes of employers: those "who conduct their business in such a superior fashion, who have such personal relations developed with their employees, that labor has no desire to force a collective arrangement upon them" and those "who, either through their own attitude or through the stress of competition, are not free to deal with labor on these higher personal relations" (Commons 1921a:15). By his own estimate, progressive firms accounted for only about 10% to 25% of American employers (Commons 1921b:263). "It appears to me," he writes, "that we cannot get the large capitalistic interests awake to this subject of stabilizing employment unless the government takes hold of it" (Commons 1921a:10).

Accident-compensation law is one part of Commons's policy solution, not merely because it would compensate the injured but more importantly because a properly designed system would give firms an incentive to prevent accidents. Mandatory health insurance was thought to work in a similar manner for the threat of illness – and unemployment insurance was conceived as an initiative with the same effect on irregular work, high turnover, and cyclical employment (Commons 1921a:9–10; 1921b; 1925b). But not all of Commons's policy recommendations involve insurance arrangements. He also calls for a monetary policy that stabilizes the currency – and his later writings expand on the need for both monetary and fiscal components to countercyclical macroeconomic management (Commons 1921a:4–6; Whalen 1993:1165–67).[5]

INSECURITY TODAY

In the quarter century following World War II, America experienced a period of rather tranquil economic growth and widespread prosperity. While this prosperity was not universal, most U.S. citizens thought of themselves as part of an "affluent society." According to John Kenneth Galbraith's book with that title, life's major economic uncertainties "have already been eliminated." Although policy authorities had to remain vigilant in their macro-stabilization efforts, economic insecurity was otherwise considered "finished business" (Galbraith 1958:111–12).

Since the 1970s, however, many have come to believe that the return of economic insecurity has transformed America into an "anxious society." While cyclical fluctuations were the predominant source of insecurity during Commons's time, recent job losses have persisted – and even risen – despite macroeconomic expansion. Unlike the temporary layoffs of the past, unemployment in the present era has increasingly involved permanent job loss due to organizational restructuring (Cappelli et al. 1997; Farber 1997; Davis et al. 1996).[6]

Commons's writings tell us little about the cost of job loss to an individual. Today, though, we know this cost can be substantial. According to a survey by the U.S. Census Bureau, workers losing their jobs between 1990 and 1992 saw their wages drop an average of 23% upon regaining full-time work (Zachary 1995). A U.S. Department of Labor report, meanwhile, finds that only one in three displaced workers is rehired at a full-time position that meets or exceeds the pay of their lost job (U.S. Bureau of Labor Statistics 1996).[7] The duration of unemployment has been on an upward trend since the late 1960s (Cappelli et al. 1997:174–75).

Well-educated employees were once thought to have an especially high degree of employment security. Since the 1980s, however, downsizing "has hit virtually every industry and occupation" (Cappelli et al. 1997:7). Restructuring has increasingly affected managers, professionals, and other salaried employees (Cappelli et al. 1997; Farber 1997).

There are other dimensions to the current trend toward worker insecurity. They include an explosive growth of contingent work, the elimination of intraorganizational job ladders and employer-provided training opportunities, wage stagnation and benefit reductions, and rising income inequality. Today's organizations sometimes give individuals greater autonomy than they had under scientific management; overall, however, "more is expected of employees while less is offered to them" (Cappelli et al. 1997:10). On these dimensions there is much similarity between our time and that of Commons. Indeed, perhaps the major difference here is that the employment-relations system that we seem to be evolving *toward* is very much like the system that America was *moving away from* during his lifetime – one that treats labor as just another "spot market" commodity (Cappelli et al. 1997:5, 7, 11, 16–17).

LESSONS FOR CONTEMPORARY PROBLEM SOLVING

Commons's institutional approach to social research is a problem-solving approach. To apply his perspective to our own era, we must begin by identifying a social problem. We then use investigative methods to identify the problem's underlying causes and propose a remedy (ideally, one that will prevent the problem from recurring).

A commitment to investigative methods compels us to look beyond the temporary expedient of rough methods, such as the threat of unemployment that currently functions much as it did in Commons's time (Cappelli et al. 1997:11). This commitment also requires more than invoking the blind forces that undergird neoclassical economics and Marxism. Solutions generated by investigative methods depend on the choices of individuals and groups, not on the invisible hand of competitive markets.

The institutional approach recognizes the notion of allocative efficiency. But institutionalists understand that other considerations may also be taken into account when evaluating economic performance – ones engendered, for example, by ethical concerns or by an interest in achieving greater efficiency over time. Most economics simply rationalizes existing employment practices in terms of static efficiency. Institutionalism, always searching for ways to locate and reinforce the common ground shared by competing interests, seeks to structure institutions so that security begets *dynamic* efficiency.

Investigation, prevention, and the search for mutual-gains solutions are all important parts of Commons's unapologetically value-infused institutionalism. So is identification and diffusion of best industrial practices – a key element in his attempt to counter the socially harmful effects of both unbridled competition and static economic thinking (Commons 1950:11). Still another valuable component of Commons's institutionalism is the concept of the "advisory committee" or "administrative commission," an investigational body composed of scholars and representatives of diverse economic interests. There is much discussion of "reasonable practices" and "reasonable value" in Commons; these bodies are offered as one effective device for giving shape to what is meant by "reasonable" (Commons 1934:848–49; 1950: 11, 236–37, 257, 374).[8]

While there has been little attention to theory in this paper, many theories are presented in Commons's books and articles – including a general theory of economic transactions, historical theories of labor organization and industrial development, a "transactional" theory of money, and a "profit-margin" theory of business cycles. Numerous aspects of Commons's theories are likely to prove useful as we attempt to resolve the current problem of worker insecurity. But as we begin to dig into his writings for this purpose, we should first recognize that problem solving is the foundation of John R. Commons's institutional approach.

NOTES

1. Commons was critical of those who employed a single theory in problem solving: "Only the foolish, the ignorant, the biased or the arbitrary man ties himself up to a single theory. Every theory has its proper place as an instrument in weighing the facts" (Commons 1919:167). The challenge for an investigator, according to Commons, is to "give due weight" to political economy's many (and often conflicting) theories (Commons 1934:8).
2. The comparative method involves exploring both the similarities and differences to be found when examining activities separated by time or space. It enables

an investigator to identify common (perhaps even universal) events, actions, and relations and to distinguish them from ones unique to a particular phenomenon. According to Commons, comprehensive examinations of similarities and differences should involve inquiry at three levels: facts, purpose, and theory (Commons 1950:120–21). While social researchers are often guided by their own purpose and theory, Commons also saw the need for investigators to understand the purposes and theories that motivated the individuals and groups being studied (Commons 1919).

3. The term "investigative methods" is my own (but see Commons 1950:ix).
4. Commons's investigations revealed that firms occasionally took important steps to promote worker health and safety. The investigations also revealed that some employers sought to prevent unemployment by stabilizing production or redeploying workers within their enterprise as external conditions changed.
5. Commons's fiscal policy measures include public works projects (see Commons 1934:589–90; Commons and Andrews 1936:5, 27–37). His unemployment remedies also call for regulation of private employment agencies, to prevent fraud and other abuses, and for an effective system of public employment offices (Commons 1919:74–82; Commons and Andrews 1936:5–27).
6. Approximately 20% of workers saw their job disappear permanently in the 1980s (Cappelli et al. 1997:68). In the period 1993–1995, nearly 6% of workers lost their jobs to plant closing or restructuring (Farber 1997:Figure 1).
7. The cost of job loss is often particularly great for high-seniority workers, many of whom may never see a return to their previous wage level (Jacobson et al. 1993).
8. Commons's present-day readers will find contemporary relevance not only in his overall approach but also in discussions of specific matters. These range from the need to open lines of job promotion where industry has closed them to the desirability of reorganizing the Federal Reserve's Open Market Committee to include nonbank interests (Commons 1919:140–41; 1950:256–57).

REFERENCES

Cappelli, Peter, Laurie Bassi, Harry Katz, David Knoke, Paul Osterman, and Michael Useem. 1997. *Change at Work*. New York: Oxford University Press.

Commons, John R. 1919. *Industrial Goodwill*. New York: McGraw Hill.

———. 1921a. "Industrial Relations." *Trade Unionism and Labor Problems* 2d. series. Boston: Athenaeum Press, pp. 1–16.

———. 1921b. "The Opportunity of Management." *Industrial Government*. New York: Macmillan, pp. 263–72.

———. 1921c. "Unemployment: Compensation and Prevention." *The Survey*, Vol. 48 (October 1), pp. 5–9.

———. 1922. "Unemployment Prevention." *American Labor Legislation Review*, Vol. 11, no. 1 (March), pp. 15–24.

———. 1925a. "Marx Today: Capitalism and Socialism." *The Atlantic Monthly*, Vol. 136 (November 25), pp. 682–93.

———. 1925b. "The True Scope of Unemployment Insurance." *American Labor Legislation Review*, Vol. 15, no. 1 (March), pp. 33–44.

———. 1934. *Institutional Economics*. New York: Macmillan.

———. 1950. *The Economics of Collective Action*. New York: Macmillan.

Commons, John R., and John B. Andrews. 1936. *Principles of Labor Legislation.* 4th ed. New York: Harper and Brothers.

Davis, Steven J., John C. Haltiwanger, and Scott Schuh. 1996. *Job Creation and Destruction.* Cambridge, MA: MIT Press.

Farber, Henry S. 1997. "The Changing Face of Job Loss in the United States, 1981–1995." ILR-Cornell Institute for Labor Market Policies and Princeton Industrial Relations Section Sixth Annual Policy Conference (Cornell University, May 22–23).

Galbraith, John Kenneth. 1958. *The Affluent Society.* Boston: Houghton Mifflin.

Jacobson, Louis S., Robert J. LaLonde, and Daniel G. Sullivan. 1993. "Long-Term Earnings Losses of High-Seniority Displaced Workers." *Economic Perspectives,* Vol. 17, no. 6 (November/December), pp. 2–20.

Lewisohn, Sam A, Ernest G. Draper, John R. Commons, and Don D. Lescohier, 1925. *Can Business Prevent Unemployment?* New York: Alfred A. Knopf.

U.S. Bureau of Labor Statistics. 1996. *Worker Displacement during the Mid-1990s.* Report USDL 96–446. Washington, DC: U.S. Department of Labor.

Whalen, Charles J. 1993. "Saving Capitalism by Making It Good: The Monetary Economics of John R. Commons." *Journal of Economic Issues,* Vol. 27, no. 4 (December), pp. 1155–79.

Zachary, G. Pascal. 1995. "Census Bureau Confirms Eroding Wages," *Wall Street Journal,* January 25, p. A2.

6. Saving capitalism by making it good: the monetary economics of John R. Commons

> Modern capitalism has been built upon security of investments. It is not labor, or management, or machinery that produces wealth – it is the credit system, and the credit system is nothing but confidence in the future. Without the credit system there might be production of wealth, but it would be the hand-to-mouth production of individuals who dare not trust their products out of their own hands, and society would sink back into feudalism or violence.
>
> John R. Commons, 1921b

While John R. Commons's contributions to social reform and labor studies are widely recognized, his work as a monetary economist is usually ignored – even by students of institutionalist thought. Yet Lafayette Harter [1962, 110] reported in his biography of Commons that Irving Fisher named Commons as one of the world's foremost authorities on money.[1]

This article discusses: (1) the reasons for Commons's interest and involvement in monetary issues; (2) his approach to the institution of money; (3) the role of money and credit in his business-cycle analysis; (4) the policy implications he derived from his analysis; and (5) the fact that Commons's monetary economics played a major role in his effort to "save capitalism by making it good."[2]

LABOR PROBLEMS AND THE MONEY QUESTION

Early in his classic essay on Commons, Kenneth Parsons observed: "Essentially, Commons has been attempting to work out a theory of economics which shall be adequate both for the analysis of economic problems and the guidance of social action in resolving the difficulties."[3]

Reprinted with permission from *Journal of Economic Issues* 27 (4), December 1993, 1155–1179.

According to both Harter [1962, 206] and Edwin Witte [1954], few of Commons's students believed that they fully understood his theoretical formulations, but all recognized that the focus on solving practical problems was unmistakable. In particular, Commons was interested in the difficulties faced by workers. As he told a congressional committee in 1927, "My interest is mainly in labor" [Commons 1927a, 1074]. Thus, as is well known, much of his attention was devoted to what is often referred to today as "labor studies."[4]

The Need to Focus on Macroeconomic Fluctuations

Unemployment was among the labor problems that most troubled Commons.[5] However, both his research and observations – especially between 1919 and 1921 – led him to the conclusion that this problem was primarily due to business cycles. Therefore, he believed it was essential to understand and attack joblessness from a macroeconomic perspective [for example, see Commons 1921a; 1922; 1927a, 1075; 1927b; 1934b, 189–95].

Moreover, Commons's observations during summer 1919 suggested that economic downturns were not the only part of the business cycle to have detrimental effects on workers. Specifically, his studies revealed that the inflationary "boom" phase caused them to "lose all sense of responsibility for their jobs" (and, he might have added, to their fellow employees).[6] As Commons wrote on a number of occasions, the business cycle first demoralizes laborers on the upturn of prices, then pauperizes them on the downturn, then coerces them by lack of jobs during the early stages of recovery [for example, see Commons 1927a, 1075; 1934a, 794, 903].

The Importance of Money and Banking

Commons's attempt to understand and help moderate macroeconomic fluctuations led him – as did most problem-solving efforts – in two directions. One was toward the library to examine cycle theories. The other direction was toward participants in the economic activity of the real world – individuals with insights obtained from practical experience.

From investigations in both directions, Commons concluded that bank credit played an important role in modern capitalist economies. Thus, during the rest of his career he maintained close ties to the banking community and often worked in association with legislators responsible for the nation's monetary policy.[7] While the interest in industrial fluctuations was certainly a major reason why Commons joined with Wesley Mitchell to found the National Bureau of Economic Research, this interest also caused him to become president of the National Monetary Association (the successor to Fisher's Stable Money League) in 1922.[8] In addition, he "spent much time with the Federal Reserve bank in New York and the Federal Reserve Board at Washington." As he wrote in *Myself,* "I saw banker capitalism at work from the inside" [Commons 1934b, 192; Commons 1927a, 1074–75].

While Commons admitted that he "was a late comer in the field of banking," in 1924 (at the annual meeting of the American Economic Association) he became the first person to explain open-market operations and central bank control of the money market to economists.[9] Then in February 1927, he testified in support of a price-level stabilization bill before the House Committee on Banking and Currency. Although the legislation never came to a vote, Representative James G. Strong (of Kansas) was impressed with Commons's testimony and invited him to help draft and promote a new bill in 1928. Commons agreed and worked with Strong for the first five months of that year. In fact, in addition to offering his own testimony, Commons examined other witnesses appearing before the committee. From his perspective, "the money question" had become "the most important of all labor problems."[10]

THE ECONOMIC ROLE AND VALUE OF MONEY

Commons sought to solve the macroeconomic problem of business cycles, and his attempt caused him to first consider the economic role and value of money.[11] His position on these matters stemmed from his view of economic transactions. Commons also recognized the important role of pre-analytic foundations in economics [for example, see Commons 1934a, 612 and Commons et al. 1922].

Method

According to Commons, both the classical and neoclassical economists were concerned with permanent economic tendencies, regardless of perturbations, "frictions," and "accidents," and their method was therefore deductive and quantitative. "They started with certain simple or fundamental causes … and worked these out to their ultimate tendencies" [Commons et al. 1922, 262].

From the work of these orthodox economists came the "equilibrium" view of capitalism. In particular, the argument was that such economies were self-regulating: "There could consequently be no universal overproduction and no universal unemployment in all industries at the same time."[12] Instead, there was (ignoring temporary "frictions") "a full and continuous employment of all factors that cooperate in the great complexity of production" [Commons 1950, 179].

Commons began his "reconstruction of economic theory" by rejecting this fundamental premise of conventional economics. "Modern capitalistic industry has proved," he wrote in 1933, "that there *is* universal overproduction and unemployment." Thus, full employment – indeed "economic order" in general – was no longer seen as arising "from a presupposed harmony of interests, as the older economists believed." Rather, in Commons's view, all order that exists is produced by the purposeful efforts of society's various participants.[13] As Yngve Ramstad [1985, 509] has observed, a "central insight" of Commonsian institutionalism is that institutional adjustment, not the price system, provides the "balancing wheel" of an economy.

In short, instead of adopting the orthodox economists' mechanistic conception of society, Commons saw society as a "going concern" of people who act both individually and collectively. Then, in a move that further distinguished his work from mainstream theorists, Commons incorporated into his analysis a recognition of the fact that all economic activity occurs in actual calendar time. Indeed, he viewed time as "an essential fact of economics" and adopted what today is referred to as a "processual" perspective toward social provisioning [Commons 1934a, 612, 617–21, 119–21, 676; Gruchy 1987, 4].

Transactions

One way that time enters Commons's analysis is through the *activity* of the "transaction," which is his fundamental unit of investigation [Commons 1934a, 117, 619]. While Commons distinguished three types of transactions – bargaining, managerial, and rationing – it is the first that figures most prominently in his analysis of twentieth century capitalism. In part, this is also due to the role of time. In particular, "bargaining" transactions involve voluntary transfers of ownership rights between legal equals, and these must always *precede* both the "managerial" transactions of production and the "rationing" transactions that apportion the benefits and burdens of wealth creation.[14]

Moreover, since bargaining transactions involve action, each "has a beginning and an ending in time." Indeed, such a transaction has three stages – agreement (on intentions), commitment (which imposes future obligations of performance and payment upon the parties), and administration (when parties fulfill their obligations). The transaction ends, or is "closed," at the "date and hour when performance or payment, whichever is last, is completed" [Commons 1934a, 544; 1950, 53].

Commons developed a general theory of transactions in *Institutional Economics (IE)* [Whalen 1989].[15] Specifically, he maintained that a full understanding of such action requires attention to five factors: futurity, efficiency, scarcity, custom, and sovereignty. When the theory is employed to explain a particular bargaining transaction, we see the following: (1) each party has expectations concerning both the future state of the economy and future valuations regarding the particular ownership rights being transferred (futurity); (2)

the parties agree on a particular kind, quality, and quantity of property being transferred (efficiency); (3) they agree on a price (scarcity); (4) they may agree on an interest charge for delayed payment (futurity); (5) they agree on a method of payment (custom); and (6) the state stands ready to enforce performance of the agreement (sovereignty). While it will become necessary to say more about other factors later, we can now begin to explore Commons's monetary analysis by examining the "custom" of money.

Money and the Credit Economy

Commons distinguished four major types of payment systems: barter, precious metals, paper, and credit. He then examined the customs of twentieth century American capitalism and placed our economy in the last category, because he observed that about 90 percent of all bargaining transactions involved payment by means of bank checks against deposits. As a result, he consciously sought to develop a theory that would be consistent with this fact.[16]

According to Commons,

> Money, in its modern meaning, is the social institution of the creation, negotiability, and release of debts arising out of [bargaining] transactions. If payment is made without a lapse of time worth measuring, we name it a purchase or sale [for "cash"], and it differs from the short-time and long-time debts only in that the intervening stage of negotiability of the debt is omitted. Thus money is secondarily a medium of exchange – it is primarily a social means of creating, transferring, and extinguishing debts [Commons 1934a, 513, 415–16, 544, 605].

Moreover, it is the credit economy's negotiability of debts that both gives bankers a prominent role and connects financial and commodity markets [Commons 1934a, 472, 483, 510–12, 559].

In *IE,* this transactional view of money is illustrated by an example involving "a trade acceptance and a single bank dealing with a seller and buyer." In particular, Commons wrote:

> A steel manufacturer sells to an agricultural implement manufacturer 1,000 tons of rolled steel at $40 per ton, payable in 60 days. The debt, "accepted" by the implement manufacturer, is $40,000. The banker buys the debt at six percent discount, or one percent for 60 days, and sets up a deposit on his books to the amount of $39,600 to the credit of the steel manufacturer. At the end of 60 days the implement manufacturer, who has been building up a deposit account at the same bank, pays the debt by a check on his own account payable to the bank for $40,000 and the transaction is closed.

Thus, he concluded:

> Multiply this over-simplified transaction of a supposed single bank by a repetition of billions and even trillions of similar transactions during a year, add all the banks with their clearing houses, and we have, not a *circulation* system of money, but a *forecast* and *repetition* system of money. Each loan or discount transaction creates and extinguishes its own money in expectation of the increase in values which will be added by production and sale.[17]

Another important conclusion produced by this approach is that, over time, the quantity (or, to use Commons's term, "volume") of money varies with expectations about commodity prices and quantities. As Commons noted in *The Economics of Collective Action,* the "total volume outstanding at any period of time depends on whether new debts are being created faster or slower" than they are being canceled [Commons 1950, 240; 1934a, 512, 549].

Money as a Measuring Instrument

So far we have focused on money's role as a means of creating, transferring, and extinguishing debts in a credit economy – Commons's "transactional theory of money" [Commons 1934a, 512]. But money is also a measuring instrument. In fact, according to Commons, money measures both a transaction's scarcity dimension and its entire economic value.

Commons's scarcity dimension – one of his five, interrelated aspects of economic transactions – is measured in monetary terms. This yields the exchange price of an economic quantity. To the neoclassical economist, this price, determined in the present by the interaction of supply and demand, is the "economic value" of the quantity being transferred. For Commons, however, such "value" required attention to more than price.

In Commons's analysis, the magnitude of the whole economic quantity found in a bargaining transaction requires attention to several variables. These are, not surprisingly, reducible to the dimensions of efficiency, scarcity, futurity, sovereignty, and custom.[18] Nonetheless, money still serves as the ultimate, or final, measuring instrument. Thus, he quoted Irving Fisher approvingly: "One of the important functions of money is that it brings uniformity of measurement out of diversity" [Commons 1934a, 514–26].

The Unstable Value of Money

Although Commons accepted money as a measuring instrument, he acknowledged that it is seldom a stable unit. In fact, he observed that money functions more like a barometer – "whose index of atmospheric pressure must be corrected for each change in elevation above the sea level" – than a yardstick or bushel. In particular, determining the value of money was said to require use of a price index to adjust current prices. Thus, such "value" (what today we would call a "real" value) changes inversely with movements in the average level of prices [Commons 1934a, 518–19, 261–62, 478–79].

MONEY, PROFIT MARGINS, AND BUSINESS CYCLES

In Commons's view, macroeconomic fluctuations are a normal part of unregulated capitalism. In particular, he saw them as a by-product of the pursuit of profit [Commons 1934a, 557]. To outline this endogenous theory of cycles, we begin once again by recognizing that economic activity is a process in time.[19]

Credit and Profits

While Commons noted that businesses are organized to seek profit, he stressed the fact that all firms begin as debtors (since production of goods and services must precede their sale). He also noted that firms in a credit economy rely heavily upon banks to provide the funds needed to cover production costs. In other words, enterprises enter into bargaining transactions with banks, and these transactions create the money firms need to pay other debts [Commons 1934a, 527, 538, 560].

Both parties to a loan share the belief that it will be paid (or renewed) when due. Moreover, the borrowing enterprise anticipates (in all but the most unusual situations) that its annual gross earnings will more than cover the year's total costs. Thus, Commons explained that a loan's transfer of purchasing power from the future into the present is based entirely upon an expectation – an expectation of future profitability [Commons 1934a, 527, 538–39, 546, 549, 568–69; 1937].

Expected profits, however, are not always realized. Indeed, Commons observed that profit expectations are not merely matters involving "risk." Rather, they involve "uncertainty" – such expectations concern the unknown, and inherently unknowable, future. As a result, it is quite possible for managers and bankers to find they have made serious forecasting errors when a loan comes due [Commons 1934a, 506–09, 538–39, 601, 608–09; 1937, 687–89].

Moreover, Commons explained that even small errors of estimation can have a profound impact on an enterprise. This is because the corporation's profit margin (the difference between its gross income and total costs) is generally quite narrow, and because a minor change in revenues or costs will have an effect upon such a margin that is many times more powerful than the original change.[20] For example, Commons illustrated this point by using realistic numbers to describe how an unexpected 1 percent decline in the selling price of a firm's output can reduce its margin for profit 33 percent. Small variations in taxes, interest charges, and operating expenses (wages, rents, the price of materials, etc.) can all have similar effects on this margin [Commons 1934a, 580–82].

Macroeconomic Dynamics

Since profit margins are determined by a combination of expectations and an array of cost and revenue determinants, Commons distinguished between "strategic" (or "limiting") and "complementary" (or "routine") factors. In particular, he maintained that while economic outcomes are dependent on thousands of factors, at any time and place there is likely to be one or a small number that take on special significance due to their influence on all others. Thus, it is the strategic factor that deserves special attention as we seek to understand Commons's view of macroeconomic fluctuations [Commons 1934a, 627–29; 1934a, 516, 561, 588, 633, 576; 1950, 194].

Commons indicated that business confidence often plays a strategic role in a stalled economy. If firms and bankers lack confidence (due to unfavorable profit forecasts), the unemployed will not be put to work. On the other hand, favorable profit forecasts can create the new money that, by augmenting purchasing power and allowing firms to acquire labor and materials, engenders a recovery [Commons 1934a, 508–09, 589; 1937, 689; 1950, 255].

Moreover, the prosperity of a recovery breeds optimism. In addition to observing that their own firm is doing well, managers planning economic activity during a recovery often hear encouraging business news and meet optimistic associates, suppliers, and bankers. Thus, corporate executives are likely to both revise profit forecasts upward and feel more confident about their forecasting ability. As a result, enterprises will be more willing to incur debts, and bankers will be more willing to extend credit [Commons 1934a, 508–12, 557–58, 580–81, 608–09; 1937, 689; 1950, 255].

As credit expands, so does investment, employment, output, and aggregate demand. Moreover, the latter causes both profit margins and prices to rise also. Price increases and higher levels of employment could cause firms to estimate that cost increases will reduce or eliminate future profit margins. In the early stages of a boom, however, Commons suggested that it was more likely for the prices of final goods and services to rise faster than factor costs. In fact, he argued that most firms would respond to an increase in the price of their output (regardless of whether it was caused by a change in consumption patterns or by the general price level) by expecting further price and profit increases – expectations that would lead to further borrowing and investing. In short, an upward spiral of expectations and realized profits is set in motion and fueled by the "marvellously elastic" institution of bank credit; it is rather easy for a modest recovery to turn into an inflationary boom [Commons 1934a, 558–60, 581–82; 1925c, 35–36; 1927c, 44].

Yet it is also quite easy for a boom to turn sour. Indeed, as suggested earlier, the potential limiting factors are numerous (and the magnitude of the change that causes one factor to become "limiting" need not be great).[21] All that is required is the reduction of realized and/or expected profits. Once this occurs (and, though years might pass first, Commons saw it as inevitable in a laissez-faire economy), the process that produced a boom is reversed. Finally, the entire business cycle is completed and repeats itself when a recovery, either "automatic" (i.e., due to changing expectations over time) or "managed" (i.e., due to state action) in nature, is once again established [Commons 1934a, 559–61, 577–79, 585–88, 608–12; 1922, 19–20].

POLICY IMPLICATIONS

Commons believed that the private sector could do much to stabilize production and prevent unemployment – even cyclical unemployment [Lewisohn et al. 1925; Commons 1921a; Commons and Andrews 1936, 37–42]. Still, he maintained that "public as well as private efforts are required to reduce unemployment to a minimum" [Lewisohn et al. 1925, 121]. In particular, Commons emphasized the need for two actions that he felt would stabilize the economy by stabilizing credit: a countercyclical macroeconomic policy and unemployment insurance legislation.

Macroeconomic Policy

While Commons saw business cycles as the product of a changing array of limiting and complementary factors, his effort to develop a policy strategy led him to probe further. Looking beyond the kaleidoscope of changing factors and at the cycle as a whole, Commons identified the credit policies of our banking system as a "fundamental cause" of economic fluctuations [Commons 1925c, 43]. He also concluded: "Any improvement that looks to the prevention of unemployment must go back to the period of inflation and prevent the overexpansion that caused the unemployment" [Commons 1922, 20]. Thus, Commons advocated stabilization of the value of money.

In particular, he proposed that macroeconomic policies be used countercyclically in order to stabilize the average level of prices at some point consistent with full (or near full) employment.[22] As Commons [1921c, 4] wrote, "If we could have a system of currency in which the great price movements which have been occuring in these years could be stabilized, we would do more to stabilize industry ... than any other one thing." In short, stable credit and prices were seen as the key to stable production and employment – the key to keeping the economy's various limiting factors under control.[23]

Monetary policy was the most important part of Commons's macroeconomic strategy. Indeed, he gave three monetary instruments special emphasis: the Federal Reserve's discount (or rediscount) rate, open-market operations, and moral suasion (involving both public statements and private conversations).[24] As Commons explained before the Congressional Committee on Banking and Currency, the rediscount rate influences the price of credit, while open-market operations and moral suasion influence its supply and demand, respectively [Commons 1927, 1095].

Commons believed that the Federal Reserve system required no new economic or legal power to stabilize prices; Federal Reserve officials needed only to adopt such a policy. To ensure the adoption of (and adherence to) this policy, however, Commons favored amending the Federal Reserve's legislative mandate to include price stabilization as an explicitly stated objective. While believing that "any proposed standard is better than none," Commons strongly favored a particular stabilization rule – one that would focus on an index of wholesale prices (in which commodities would be weighted according to the levels of employment involved in their production).[25] Moreover, in both congressional testimony (in 1928) and *The Economics of Collective Action,* Commons argued that Federal Reserve actions should be guided by an advisory committee containing representatives of opposing economic interests, instead of an open market committee composed only of bankers [Commons 1929, 67–69, 84; 1950, 256–60].

Three final points are worth mentioning before turning to a discussion of unemployment insurance. Each was discussed by Commons on a number of the occasions during which he addressed macroeconomic stabilization. The first is that Commons did not seek to regulate the price of individual commodities. Indeed, he believed that an important advantage of price-level stabilization was that it allowed individual prices to fluctuate in response to changing economic circumstances [e.g., Commons 1934a, 581; 1937, 695]. Second, Commons recognized that business cycles were an inherent feature of modern capitalism and that some price-level fluctuations were likely to occur even with stabilization as a policy objective. "What is really meant by stabilization of prices," he wrote in 1925, is the avoidance only of "excessive peaks and slumps" [Commons 1925a, 45; 1934a, 557].

Finally, Commons felt the nation could not rely solely on monetary policy for macroeconomic stabilization. In particular, he understood that it is much easier for such policy tools to prevent an inflationary boom than to engender an expansion (and a reduction of unemployment) in the face of low business confidence. Thus, he wrote the following about a period of depression:

> In order to create the consumer demand, on which business depends for sales, the government itself must create the new money and go completely over the head of the entire banking system by paying it out directly to the unemployed, either as relief or for construction of public works, as it does in times of war.[26]

Unemployment Insurance

Commons was clearly interested in the "relief" aspect of unemployment insurance. But he also saw such a policy as much more. In particular, he believed it was "primarily" an unemployment *prevention* measure, one that helped control business cycles by stabilizing credit, production, and employment at the level of the individual firm [e.g., Commons 1934b, 200–201; Lewisohn et al. 1925, 188].

According to Commons's insurance plan, an employer laying off a worker would incur a liability (paid either directly to the employee or to the state). Since this would add a cost to the firm, Commons saw it as a factor that both an employer and a banker would be forced to consider before deciding to allow an enterprise to expand. While expansions that seemed sustainable would not be discouraged, firms would have an incentive to better regulate both the growth and contraction of their operations.

Another feature of Commons's plan was that employers could escape their unemployment liability by securing another job for laid-off workers. As a result, employers would have an interest in the establishment and operation of both public-works programs and public – and private (perhaps even "in-house") – employment offices.[27]

MAKING CAPITALISM "GOOD"

As mentioned at the outset of this essay, the monetary issues addressed by John R. Commons have generally received little attention, even from his closest followers.[28] This is truly unfortunate, for a look at his treatment of money helps us to better understand his overall approach to economics. Moreover, Commons's monetary views had an important impact on his notion of how to "save capitalism by making it good." Indeed, his monetary economics was not separate from his labor studies.

Beyond History

Many have suggested that Commons was not seeking to offer an alternative to orthodox economic theory. Harter [1962, 209], for example, indicated that Commons merely offered a "supplement" to conventional theory in the form of economic history. In fact, however, while the mature Commons was clearly "inclined to minimize the element of novelty in his thinking," a student of Commons's writings on monetary issues cannot avoid the conclusion that Commons intended to offer much more than insight into the historical development of twentieth century economic institutions.[29]

Commons's primary objective was to develop an analysis adequate for investigating and resolving the practical problems of his time. Commons saw unemployment as not only one of our nation's most pressing problems, but also as capitalism's most serious shortcoming and as a condition caused primarily by the business cycle.[30] Furthermore, we now know that Commons's exploration of the cycle led – despite his desire to de-emphasize the heterodox aspects of his views – to the rejection of conventional theory at many levels: at the level of method, Commons felt it necessary to move beyond classical and neoclassical economics and engage in a major "reconstruction of economic theory"; at the level of general economic activity, he chose to replace an analysis based on scarcity with a broader theory of transactions; and at the level of monetary analysis, he saw the need to reject the traditional quantity theory in favor of his "transactional" theory [Commons et al. 1922; 1934a, 510–26, 597–98].

This investigation into Commons's monetary views has also revealed a "profit-margin" theory of endogenous business cycles, a policy program that emphasizes the economic role of credit, and an approach to monetary management that provides an excellent illustration of his "reasonable value" concept.[31] Moreover, while all these individual elements are significant by themselves, they come together as a unified whole only when we give attention to Commons's monetary economics. In short, a look at this aspect of his work elucidates his overall approach to economics, an approach that Commons himself described as an attempt to save capitalism by making it "good."[32]

The Role of Money

Commons's monetary views do not merely serve to unify a number of themes and theories. Rather, the role Commons gave to money and credit in his economics was a central one. Commons did not see money in a credit economy as a mere facilitator of exchange.[33] Instead, he viewed it as essential to the production process of modern capitalism. Without money, which transfers purchasing power from the future into the present, few twentieth century establishments could operate.[34]

From Commons's perspective, then, money is a fundamental element of our economy even before we consider the question of macroeconomic fluctuations. But Commons's analysis of business cycles further underscores the role of money in his approach to economics. In fact, in his view, business cycles are *credit* cycles – a position leading ultimately to both his suggestion that "the credit problem is our biggest labor problem" and his call for credit stabilization.[35]

For Commons, making capitalism "good" required stable credit.[36] Thus, the role of money remained central to his economics even as he moved from positive to normative analysis. Both his countercyclical macroeconomic strategy and his unemployment insurance program were designed to operate by affecting the credit relations of enterprises and their banks. In particular, both policies sought to rely on the profit margin's sensitivity to small changes in costs and expected revenues in an effort to better control bank lending and business expansions [e.g., Commons 1922, 20–21; 1934a, 581, 586–87; 1934c, 364].

The Inseparability of Labor and Money

This article began with the observation that Commons's monetary economics has been ignored even though his contributions to social reform and labor studies are widely recognized. The present investigation into this neglected aspect of Commons's thought leads to two important points regarding that initial statement. One is that attention to the interests that motivated Commons's research on money and credit offers much insight into the relationship between his social reform efforts and his labor studies. Indeed, we find that these endeavors were nearly inseparable.

The second point is that Commons's monetary economics was not separate from his labor studies. Hyman P. Minsky [1982, 280] has written that "monetary economics cannot escape being institutional economics." John R. Commons could have just as easily written that *institutional labor economics cannot escape being (or at least including) monetary economics.*[37]

NOTES

1. Moreover, although Dudley Dillard [1987, 1644] did not examine Commons's ideas in a 1987 article on money as an institution of capitalism, his conclusion included the following statement: "Regretfully, some important institutionalists have been left out, such as John R. Commons … [who] had interesting things to say about money."
2. This quote appears in Commons's [1934b, 143] autobiography. In particular, he wrote: "This nearly thirty years of my own experience … I have written up in my *Institutional Economics.* I was trying to save capitalism by making it good."
3. This essay, "John R. Commons' Point of View," is reprinted in Commons [1950, 342]. At the end of the work is a footnote indicating that Commons [1950, 375] felt Parsons's essay was "a magnificent analysis and summary" of his viewpoint.
4. There appear to be two reasons for Commons's interest in labor. One is a product of his observations and the other is rooted in ethics. The first is suggested by the following quote:

> As I have studied practical problems it has always seemed to me that the life-and-death struggle of making a living and trying to get rich was at the bottom of all other problems. Out of this basic struggle come political parties, constitutional governments, labor unions, corporations, and so on. Always I worked out some administrative task, but the administration grew out of the underlying struggle for making a living [Commons 1950, 118].

The second reason for Commons's interest in labor is found in the following report by Kenneth Parsons:

> [Commons] once remarked to a group of graduate students who had met to discuss what kind of research university professors should do, "As a young man, I decided that I was for whatever helped the common man. What one does with his life depends upon his ethical assumptions and the kind of life he wants to lead. I have had a good time." With that he sat down [Parsons 1985, 757].

For a discussion of the development of Commons's outlook and its connection to his interest in reform, see Harter [1962].

5. In 1925, Commons [in Lewisohn et al. 1925, 152] wrote, "Unemployment is *the* outstanding defect of capitalism." See also Commons [1899; 1905, xiv; 1921a, 5, 9; 1922, 15–16; 1934a, 557, 903; 1950, 285] and Commons and Andrews [1936, 1].
6. Commons [1927a, 1075]. In his testimony before the House Commitee on Banking and Currency, Commons illustrated the demoralizing effect of an inflationary boom by discussing events that occurred during summer 1919. For example, he reported that there was such demand for truck drivers in Cleveland that drivers whose vehicles needed repairs "didn't stop to get any repairs done; they simply deserted their trucks on the street and went and got a job [immediately] with some competing firm" [1927a, 1075]. His testimony also mentions the negative impact of a boom upon the union movement.
7. Early work by Commons suggests he had some familiarity with issues of money, credit, and price fluctuations. See, for example, Commons [1893a; 1893b; 1900a; 1900b]. See also Commons [1934b, 63–67]. Nonetheless, his background in this area was not extensive, and research into labor-management relations consumed most of his time during the first two decades of the twentieth century.
8. Commons served on the National Bureau's Board of Directors from the year it was established (1920) until 1928. See Harter [1962, 75].
9. In *Myself,* Commons notes that the central bank's control of money through open-market operations was something he had not seen in the literature on money and credit:

> This was something new to me. … One of the [American Economic Association] economists, a specialist in banking, said to me, "I have seen it all along and am kicking myself now that I did not understand it." I understood it because Benjamin Strong and his assistants in the [New York Federal Reserve] bank had explained it to me [Commons 1934b, 193].

His discussion of this topic was printed in the *American Economic Review;* see Commons [1925a]. It should be noted that open-market operations were a tool devised by the Federal Reserve system in the face of the financial consequences of World War I – the enormous increase in government debt. The creators of the Federal Reserve had not anticipated the importance of this tool.

10. Commons [1934b, 189–93; 1921c, 4] and Strong [1929, 5]. In 1921, Commons [1921a, 5] began an article on unemployment by stating, "The credit problem is our biggest labor problem." Throughout the rest of his career, the macroeconomic significance of credit was often discussed in his books, articles, and reviews. For example, see Commons [1923b; 1925a; 1927b; 1934a; 1937; 1941; 1950]. For his testimony before (and examination of witnesses for) the Committee on Banking and Currency, see Commons [1927a; 1929].
11. An early product of this effort is Commons et al. [1922]. The need to precede attention to cycles with an examination of money and banking is also illustrated by the structure of the chapter on "futurity" in Commons [1934a, 390–648]. See also Commons [1937].
12. Commons [1934a, 891–2]. Commons added:

    > There might be particular overproduction in one industry or establishment, with a resulting fall in prices and wages for that industry. But this would correct itself by the free movement of capital and labor[.] … The result would be a falling off of production in the overproduced industry and an increase of production in the underproduced industry, so that an automatic tendency towards equilibrium would constantly be going on between different industries, and they would equalize themselves around the comparative costs of production [Commons 1934a, 892].

13. See Commons [1934a, 586, 597, 892, 6, emphasis added; 1921b, 268–72; 1923a, 116–17; 1925b, 690–93; 1937, 681; 1950, 257–58].
14. Commons [1934a, 58, 68, 512; 1950, 53–7]. The ownership transferred in an economic transaction can involve rights to corporeal, incorporeal, or intangible property. See, for example, Commons [1934a, 522–23; 1950, 106–7].
15. This general theory is also described in Commons [1950].
16. See Commons [1934a, 548; 1950, 41–2, 239, 243; 1937, 685–86] and Commons et al. [1922, 245–46].
17. Commons [1934a, 548–49]. Readers familiar with today's Post Keynesian economists will note that Commons's transactional perspective anticipates the Post Keynesian endogenous-money approach. For a Post Keynesian discussion of endogenous money, see Wray [1990].
18. While classical economists (including Marx) saw value as determined in the past, and neoclassical economists find it in the present, the dimension of "futurity" led Commons [1950, 103, 145–53] to conclude that value is instead shaped by current expectations of the future.
19. Like most cycle analysts, Commons believed that "business cycles" were recurrent but not necessarily periodic.
20. Commons used data from 1919–1929 to estimate the average profit margin as 3 percent of sales for American manufacturing firms during normal times. See Commons [1934a, 561–62, 570].
21. For example, the source of the problem might be a sudden lack of business confidence; an over-committed firm that starts a cascade of business and bank failures (and/or engenders a wave of financial pessimism); competitive pressure from new enterprises (with less debt and more efficient production techniques); or rising costs (i.e., operating expenses, taxes, or interest charges).
22. The level of employment Commons had in mind is called the "full employment level of unemployment" [i.e., no cyclical unemployment] in today's economics

texts. Subsequent references to "full" employment in this work are to be viewed as referring to this level.

23. See, for example, Commons [1921c; 1929; 1937; 1982; 1934a] and Commons and Andrews [1936].
24. For Commons's discussion of these and other instruments (including international concerted action), see Commons [1925a; 1927a; 1927b; 1927c; 1929; 1934a, 596, 605–06; 1934c; 1937, 683; 1950, 246–60].
25. Commons [1929, 431]. See also Commons [1927a, 1113–21, 1120; 1927b; 1929, 100–101; 1950, 258]. In addition to believing in the need for price stabilization, Commons was concerned that the Federal Reserve system gave a few individuals great power and almost no guidance. As he said in a 1927 congressional hearing, the Federal Reserve "is the only administrative body in our system which Congress has created and to which it has given no standards or rule of policy." On this, see Commons [1927, 1120; 1925a, 44].
26. Commons [1934a, 589–90]. See also Commons [1925a, 47–9; 1934a, 609–11; 1934c, 365], Commons and Andrews [1936, 5, 27–37], and Lewisohn et al. [1925, 121–51].
27. On Commons's view toward unemployment insurance, see Commons [1921a; 1922; 1923c; 1925c; 1934a, 586–7, 840–73], Commons and Andrews [1936, 306], and Lewisohn et al. [1925, 152–210].
28. An important exception is Harlan L. McCracken, a macroeconomist who studied with Commons at the University of Wisconsin.
29. Mitchell [1937, 340]. It should be noted that Commons *did* offer a theory of capitalist development (and this theory gave some attention to the role of money and credit). But he *also* offered much more, as will soon be discussed. For more on this theory and on Commons's overall approach as described in the first chapter of *IE,* see Whalen [1989].
30. On the matter of unemployment as one of capitalism's most serious shortcomings, see note number five above.
31. Commons's theory of "reasonable value" emphasized the use of advisory, or administrative, commissions (through which competing economic interests would jointly shape public policy) and the need for experimentation, investigation, and adoption of "best" existing practices. His call for an advisory committee to the Federal Reserve incorporated both of these elements. For more on Commons's "reasonable value," see Ramstad [1991a; 1991b].
32. It should be noted that Commons was one of a number of early twentieth century economists – such as Wesley Mitchell, Irving Fisher, Henry Simons, Gustav Cassel, Knut Wicksell, Ralph Hawtrey, and John Maynard Keynes – seeking to save capitalism through work similar to that described above. In fact, one of Commons's essays on monetary theory and policy caused Keynes to write the following to him in a 1927 letter:

    > Many thanks for sending me your article in the "An[n]alist." I am entirely in sympathy with it. Indeed, a good deal of your analysis runs on very closely similar lines to some material which I already have in my manuscript for a forthcoming book [i.e., the *Treatise on Money*]. … [Moreover,] I quite agree with your practical proposals … I should very much like to have some conversations with you on this and other matters. Judging from limited evidence and at great distance, there seems to be no other economist with whose general way of thinking I feel myself in such genuine accord [Keynes 1927].

In light of these remarks, we should not be surprised by the compatibility of contemporary institutionalism and Post Keynesianism.

33. Commons rejected the conventional belief that real and monetary sectors can be analyzed independently. For example, see Commons et al. [1922, 259–60]. Note also that in 1923, Commons [1923b, 646] wrote: "Money … is the center of economic theory, instead of an afterthought."
34. Note that this view of money is strikingly similar to that of Keynes. Indeed, in one of the few italicized sentences in *The General Theory,* Keynes [1964, 293] wrote: *"[T]he importance of money essentially flows from its being a link between the present and the future."*
35. Commons [1921a, 5]. The suggestion that business cycles are credit cycles is perhaps most clearly indicated in Commons [1921a, 5–6; 1922, 20; 1925c, 43].
36. Commons rejected both the socialist/communist and fascist alternatives to capitalism. While the latter was seen as inherently flawed, so were both alternatives. In particular, he believed that only capitalism could foster innovation and protect personal liberty. This is why Commons [1934b, 118] chose to "regulate but not destroy the [capitalist] sytem." For more on this matter, see Commons [1925b; 1934a, 557, 902–03; 1935].
37. Further evidence in support of this last point is Commons's [1934a, 888] suggestion in *IE* that both labor legislation and trade unionism can play an important role in economic stabilization.

REFERENCES

Commons, John R. "Economic Reform." *The Voice* (1893a). Reproduced in John R. Commons Papers (microfilm edition, 1982), State Historical Society of Wisconsin.

———. "Sound Currency." *The Voice* (1893b). Reproduced in John R. Commons Papers (microfilm edition, 1982), State Historical Society of Wisconsin.

———. "The Right to Work." *The Arena* 21 (February 1899). Reproduced in John R. Commons Papers (microfilm edition, 1982), State Historical Society of Wisconsin.

———. "Index Numbers of Prices, Freight Rates, Etc." *Quarterly Bulletin of the Bureau of Economic Research* 1 (July 1900a): 1–34.

———. "Wholesale Prices 1896 to 1900." *Quarterly Bulletin of the Bureau of Economic Research* 2 (October 1900b): 35–54.

———. *Trade Unionism and Labor Problems.* Boston: Ginn, 1905.

———. "Unemployment: Compensation and Prevention." *The Survey* 48 (October 1, 1921a): 5–9.

———. *Industrial Government.* New York: Macmillan, 1921b.

———. *Trade Unionism and Labor Problems,* Second Series. Boston: Ginn, 1921c.

———. "Unemployment Prevention." *American Labor Legislation Review* 12 (March 1922): 15–24.

———. 'Wage Theories and Wage Policies." *American Economic Review Supplement* 13 (March 1923a): 110–17.

———. "Robson's 'Economics of Unemployment'." *American Economic Review* 13 (December 1923b): 638–47.

———. "Unemployment: Prevention and Insurance." In *The Stabilization of Business,* edited by Lionel D. Edie, 164–205. New York: Macmillan, 1923c.

———. "The Stabilization of Prices and Business." *American Economic Review* 15 (March 1925a): 43–52.

———. "Marx Today: Capitalism and Socialism." *Atlantic Monthly* 136 (November 25, 1925b): 682–93.

———. "The True Scope of Unemployment Insurance." *American Labor Legislation Review* 15 (March 1925c): 33–44.

———. "Statement Before the Committee on Banking and Currency." In *Stabilization*, 1074–121. Washington, D.C.: United States Government Printing Office, 1927a.

———. "Price Stabilization and the Federal Reserve System." *The Annalist* 29 (April 1, 1927b): 459–62.

———. "Reserve Bank Control of the General Price Level: A Rejoinder." *The Annalist* 30 (July 8, 1927c): 43–4.

———. "Statements and Remarks Before the Committee on Banking and Currency." In *Stabilization*. Washington, D.C.: United States Government Printing Office, 1929.

———. *Institutional Economics: Its Place in Political Economy*. New York: Macmillan, 1934a.

———. *Myself*. New York: Macmillan, 1934b.

———. "Price Stabilization." In *Encyclopaedia of Social Sciences*, vol. 12, edited by Edwin R. A Seligman, 362–66. New York: Macmillan, 1934c.

———. Review of *Capitalism and Its Culture*, by Jerome C. Davis. *American Economic Review* 25 (September 1935): 491–92.

———. "Capacity to Produce, Capacity to Consume, Capacity to Pay Debts." *American Economic Review* 27 (December 1937): 681–97.

———. Reviews of *The Triumph of American Capitalism* and *The Dynamics of War and Revolution*, by Louis M. Hacker and Lawrence Dennis, respectively. *American Economic Review* 31 (March 1941): 122–24.

———. *The Economics of Collective Action*, edited by Kenneth Parsons. New York: Macmillan, 1950.

———. "Control of the Price Level Through Changes in the Rate of Discount and Rediscount." Reproduced in John R. Commons Papers (microfilm edition, 1982), State Historical Society of Wisconsin, undated manuscript.

Commons, John R., and John B. Andrews. *Principles of Labor Legislation*, 4th ed. New York: Harper and Brothers, 1936.

Commons, John R., H. L. McCracken, and W. E. Zeuch. "Secular Trends and Business Cycles: A Classification of Theories." *Review of Economic Statistics* 4 (October 1922): 244–63.

Dillard, Dudley. "Money as an Institution of Capitalism." *Journal of Economic Issues* 21 (December 1987): 1623–47.

Gruchy, Allan G. *The Reconstruction of Economics*. Westport, Conn.: Greenwood, 1987.

Harter, Lafayette G. *John R. Commons: His Assault on Laissez Faire*. Corvallis: Oregon State University Press, 1962.

Keynes, John Maynard. Letter to John R. Commons, 26 April 1927. Reproduced in John R. Commons Papers (microfilm edition, 1982), State Historical Society of Wisconsin.

———. *The General Theory of Employment, Interest, and Money*. 1936. Reprint. New York: Harcourt Brace Jovanovich, 1964.

Lewisohn, Sam A, Ernest G. Draper, John R. Commons, and Don D. Lescohier. *Can Business Prevent Unemployment?* New York: Alfred A Knopf, 1925.

Minsky, Hyman P. *Can "It" Happen Again?* Armonk, N.Y.: M. E. Sharpe, 1982.

Mitchell, Wesley Clair. *The Backward Art of Spending Money and Other Essays.* New York: McGraw Hill, 1936.

Parsons, Kenneth H. "John R. Commons: His Relevance to Contemporary Economics." *Journal of Economic Issues* 19 (September 1985): 755–78.

Ramstad, Yngve. "Comments on Adams and Brock Paper." *Journal of Economic Issues* 19 (June 1985): 507–12.

———. "From Desideratum to Historical Achievement: John R. Commons's Reasonable Value and the 'Negotiated Economy' of Denmark." *Journal of Economic Issues* 25 (June 1991a): 431–39.

———. "Towards an Economics of the Just Price: John R. Commons and Reasonable Value." Paper presented to the Association For Institutional Thought, April 25, 1991b, Reno, Nevada.

Strong, James G. "Statement to the Committee on Banking and Currency." In *Stabilization,* 3–11. Washington, D.C.: United States Government Printing Office, 1929.

Whalen, Charles J. "John R. Commons's *Institutional Economics:* A Re-Examination." *Journal of Economic Issues* 23 (June 1989): 443–54.

Witte, Edwin E. "Institutional Economics as Seen by an Institutional Economist." *Southern Economic Journal* 21 (October 1954): 131–40.

Wray, L. Randall. *Money and Credit in Capitalist Economies: The Endogenous Money Approach.* Aldershot, England: Edward Elgar, 1990.

7. Social security: a view from beyond the beltway

Since late 2004, President George W. Bush has aggressively paved the way for his plan to partially privatize social security. Part of his strategy has involved trotting out privatization supporters as "regular folks" and apolitical "experts." A little digging by journalists, however, has revealed that these "fellow citizens," as the president calls them, are often career political operatives.

That's no surprise to me. After examining the subject of retirement for over two years with a diverse group of citizens in upstate New York, I know there is no mandate for the Bush plan. In fact, social security privatization is just the latest retirement-related policy promoted by national policymakers but opposed by ordinary Americans. The citizens with whom I worked believe President Bush has squandered an excellent chance to initiate a meaningful discussion on retirement security in the new century.

CIVIC ENGAGEMENT

In 2002, shortly after the president's Commission to Strengthen Social Security (CSSS) issued its final report, I recruited and convened fourteen panelists for a civic engagement project on the future of retirement in the United States.[1] The Retirement Security Project panel was sponsored by the nonpartisan, nonprofit Interactivity Foundation, and met monthly in Rochester, New York, for a year and a half.

The panel discussion process operated as follows. As project facilitator, I posed a series of questions for the panel to explore in succession (with an opportunity to revisit topics at any time), including: What is retirement? Why do people retire? How do people view retirees? What are Americans' concerns and anxieties about retirement? What are the dimensions of retirement security? What realities must public retirement policies consider? In what alternative ways might private institutions and public policies be structured to address

Reprinted with permission from *Challenge* 48 (4), July–August 2005, 5–10.

retirement security? What might be the consequences of pursuing each of the policy possibilities identified?[2]

Panelists were not asked to reach consensus on any of these questions. Rather, their task was to craft a report that could stimulate public discussion by offering a broad range of viewpoints and options. Still, a number of points of unanimous agreement emerged during the project and were at least hinted at in the final report.[3] They suggest a wide gulf between the dominant political direction in Washington, DC, and the wishes of those "beyond the beltway." The agreement was particularly remarkable because panel members maintained that their individual philosophical orientations placed them at different places across a wide political spectrum.[4]

SOCIAL SECURITY

In the course of examining a number of possible approaches to social security and to saving for retirement, panelists examined the CSSS proposals. At the heart of those proposals are personal retirement accounts created by funds diverted from payroll taxes, and the president has subsequently made such accounts the centerpiece of his approach to social security reform. Prior to the project's start, most panelists were at least somewhat familiar with the CSSS work. The project gave all panelists an opportunity to review the CSSS report and related documents written by commission members.

The Retirement Security Project's discussion revealed that panelists had two main objections to the president's privatization plan: they saw it as harmful to both the social security system and retirement security. Panelists immediately recognized that creating private accounts out of existing payroll taxes requires a huge transition cost that only exacerbates the system's funding problem. The most financially sound proposal presented by the CSSS requires about a trillion dollars of new taxes or government borrowing by 2029 to pay for the transition, according to economist and CSSS member Olivia S. Mitchell.[5] Other analysts say it requires even more borrowing. In contrast, social security trustees report that the existing program can pay full benefits through 2042, and 70 percent of currently promised benefits will be available thereafter.[6]

Panelists were deeply concerned that the personal accounts common to all CSSS proposals would undermine retirement security by exposing a sizable portion of "social security" contributions to the swings and uncertainties of financial markets.[7] Moreover, this concern was not based on idle panel speculation. A member of the panel who was a retired benefits manager for a large company was attracted to our retirement project because his nest egg lost more than one-third of its value in the year prior to the project's start. Another panel member, a union leader, represented workers and retirees affected by a corporate stock meltdown that wiped out the assets of many dedicated employees.

The Rochester panelists are not opposed to policies that encourage workers to save more for retirement. They are generally supportive of tax breaks for individual retirement accounts and of finding new ways to promote saving and foster personal responsibility for retirement planning. But the consensus was that personal accounts should be a supplement to – not carved out of – social security.

PENSIONS AND HEALTH CARE

Looking beyond social security, project panelists lamented the general trend away from defined-benefit pension plans. Recognizing the many existing opportunities for workers to save for their own retirement (via various forms of individual retirement accounts, for example), panelists thought policymakers should work to stem the private-sector movement toward defined-contribution retirement programs as a replacement for traditional pensions. Panel members argued that employer plans should spread investment risk and administrative costs across large numbers of people, not concentrate the risk and costs upon individuals.[8]

The gap between the thinking of policymakers and of ordinary citizens also appears in the health-care area, which is a major source of retirement insecurity. Medicare reform legislation passed in 2003 prohibits using the purchasing power of the federal government to contain drug costs. That is precisely the opposite of what the Retirement Security Project participants believe is necessary.

In fact, the policy possibility that the overwhelming majority of retirement project panelists favored most strongly was adoption of a universal health-care system that serves all Americans. A single-payer system, they argued, would remove a huge administrative burden from employers (thus helping them to compete more effectively in the global economy). It would also cut costs by removing the complexity, redundancy, and expense associated with a huge medical-insurance industry. Panelists stressed that such a system would avoid "socialized medicine" while providing basic care for everyone, because a private market for health-care services would still be permitted.[9]

NEEDED: A THOUGHTFUL NATIONAL DISCUSSION

To be sure, the Rochester panelists recognized that a thoughtful national discussion is needed before revamping health care, pensions, or social security. By deeming social security to be broken and then requiring that all "solutions" include diverting funds to personal accounts, however, the Bush administration has distracted the nation from an opportunity to take a fresh look at retirement and its many financial, medical, and social aspects and implications. The Retirement Security Project panelists believed that Americans must discuss more fully the nature of the retirement they want. Only then can the nation decide what policies are appropriate. Clearly, when participants were forced to analyze the options fully and were able to look beyond the political rhetoric, they became highly skeptical of privatization plans.[10]

Recent opinion polls suggest that participants in the Retirement Security Project are not alone in their opposition to a major overhaul of social security. Now it is time for Congress to listen, and maybe even foster the kind of dialogue that their "fellow citizens" in Rochester and across the nation truly deserve.

NOTES

1. The project panel, drawing equally on people with professional experience in an area related to retirement and on those without such experience, included residents from a three-county area surrounding Rochester, New York. The panel reflected the region's urban, suburban, and rural mix and included participants whose age ranged from the mid-twenties through the mid-seventies. Most were not lifelong residents of the region (one panelist spent her youth in the Caribbean).
2. In the course of answering these questions, panelists decided what material they wanted to read and what to share with each other (usually current news stories about retirement dimensions or dilemmas). The facilitator tracked down information for the panel (trends in health expenditures, the fraction of elderly in nursing homes, eligibility requirements for existing programs, a widely acclaimed textbook that surveys retirement policies around the globe, etc.) only when asked.
3. In mid-2004, the Retirement Security Project produced a report that comports with the nonadvocacy mission of the Interactivity Foundation (based in Parkersburg, West Virginia). The project's final report, *The Future of Retirement Security in the United States: Policy Possibilities for Public Discussion*, was a collaborative effort by the panel. The present article is based on interacting with the panelists for more than two years.
4. Agreement among the diverse panelists was also remarkable because the nature of the project guarded against discussions designed to persuade participants to favor any particular policy direction. Efforts by a panelist (or the facilitator) to steer the panel toward a particular way of thinking would have been glaringly incompatible with the project's objectives.
5. Olivia S. Mitchell, *Testimony Before the Senate Finance Committee Hearing on the Final Report of the President's Commission to Strengthen Social Security*, October 3, 2002; available at www.commtostrengthensocsec.gov.
6. Social Security and Medicare Boards of Trustees, *Status of the Social Security and Medicare Programs: A Summary of the 2004 Annual Reports*, March 23, 2004; available at www.ssa.gov/OACT/TRSUM/trsummary.html. See also Greg Anrig Jr. and Bernard Wasow, *Twelve Reasons Why Privatizing Social Security Is a Bad*

Idea, December 14, 2004, Century Foundation, New York; available at www.soc-sec.org/publications.asp?pubid=503/.

7. Under the plan favored by the president and the CSSS, personal accounts would be accompanied by a reduction in guaranteed benefits.
8. The traditional defined-benefit pension promises to pay a specified monthly benefit upon retirement (usually based on factors such as age, years of service, and compensation level). In a defined-contribution plan, employers contribute a specified amount regularly to a worker's individual retirement account. In the case of the former, employers, not workers, bear the risk of unfavorable investments; in the case of the latter, employees bear the investment risk. Individual accounts permit workers to move easily from one employer to another. Although many defined-benefit pension programs have been created as single employer plans, they can be designed as multiemployer plans and can be structured to allow portability (the transfer of funds from one employer's plan to another).
9. Panelists saw the link between employment and health-care provision as a product of historical events, and said the link was not all that attractive from the perspective of employers or workers (who might need care most when not employed). Not only did panelists see the insurance industry as adding to the cost of care, but they also noted that coverage gaps often leave insured families in financial trouble. (A recent study supports the panelists' view that most families are "just one serious illness away from bankruptcy." See David U. Himmelstein, Elizabeth Warren, Deborah Thorne, and Steffie Woolhandler, "MarketWatch: Illness and Injury as Contributors to Bankruptcy," *Health Affairs*, February 2, 2004; available at www.healthaffairs.org.) It was striking to watch a fiscally conservative panelist, who "never voted for a Democrat," speak about the possibility of a tax-financed system of universal coverage with as much enthusiasm as another panelist long active in progressive causes.
10. It is impossible to say just how much of the agreement observed in this project was the result of panelists' devoting time to thinking about this issue and how much was a product of their interaction with other panelists (who often had very different life experiences and political views). However, participants were unanimous in their view that the interactive process – which often generated ideas that were in no individual panelist's mind at the outset – enriched their own thinking about retirement issues and policies. In fact, consensus on some points may have emerged precisely because panelists were asked to consider a wide terrain of policy possibilities and spend time examining them from a variety of angles *without* needing to reach any agreement (a need that might have led to strong advocacy rather than open exploration). In any event, at the end of the project, the panelists expressed a strong belief that the most appropriate way forward on retirement for the nation is by means of a national dialogue that looks broadly at this topic and at a wide range of alternative policy possibilities.

8. Sending jobs offshore from the United States: what are the consequences?

In the United States, the Fourth of July is usually a day of celebration. But the date has a darker meaning for families of more than a thousand workers in central New York. That is because Independence Day, 2004, was when Carrier Corporation halted its Syracuse-area production of cooling equipment, and 1,200 hourly and salaried employees watched their jobs move to Asia (Fay 2005). Carrier workers are not alone. In July 2005, U.S. manufacturing employment totaled 14.3 million, down three million since July 2000. That is a loss of about 20 percent of America's manufacturing jobs in just a few years.

Of course, not all of these jobs moved outside the U.S. But competition from lower-paid foreign workers is a major cause of the decline, according to the Congressional Budget Office (2004). Josh Bivens, an economist at the Economic Policy Institute in Washington, DC, estimates that as many as two-thirds of the domestic manufacturing jobs lost since the mid-1990s can be blamed on the substitution of imports for goods that had been produced in the U.S. (Bivens 2004).

In short, U.S. consumers are substituting goods produced by foreign labor for goods produced by their fellow citizens. And often this occurs because U.S.-based multinationals close U.S. operations and either relocate their production facilities overseas or contract with foreign-based producers. This sounds like "offshoring", and it certainly is. But it has been happening since the 1960s; in fact, U.S. manufacturing employment has been falling since 1979. Offshoring, however, has appeared more recently in the lexicon of economists, policymakers, and journalists. This article explains the term's more recent appearance and often very limited meaning. It also explores the magnitude of the phenomenon, identifies the jobs affected or "at risk", describes the impact on enterprises, workers, and communities, and recommends some steps that could help policymakers achieve a more prosperous economy in the face of this trend.

Reprinted with permission from *European Journal of Economics and Economic Policies: Intervention* 2 (2), November 2005, 33–40.

THIS IS PROGRESS?

A brief historical sketch will set the stage for a closer look at the current wave of offshoring. By most accounts, manufacturing jobs represented the Old Economy, and could not or should not be saved. These jobs were heavily blue-collar and unionized, did not require more than a high-school diploma, got your hands dirty, and, according to the conventional wisdom, paid workers "too much". When the jobs disappeared, workers were told to pull themselves up by their bootstraps and join the New Economy: learn to use – or even program – computers, and jump on the service-economy bandwagon. More than anything else, this transition was considered a sign of economic progress.

I recall that in the early 1990s, Buffalo, New York, landed a call center employing a few hundred people. Local leaders touted that center's customer-service phone jobs as a sign that western New York was part of the high-tech economy.

But enthusiasm over the New Economy never really made it into the new millennium. The technology-driven investment boom went bust, as did the dot-com frenzy – and the stock market. Call-center workers were just a fraction of the many service-sector employees suddenly finding themselves out of work or at risk of unemployment as jobs were relocated to places such as the Caribbean and China.

It was not so easy to call this "progress" any longer, and the term "offshoring" began appearing in news accounts and academic papers. Moreover, although offshoring can be applied to both blue-collar and white-collar jobs, it has become most closely associated with the substitution of foreign labor in white-collar, service jobs. In short, offshoring (also called international outsourcing) is used most often to describe the loss of positions previously considered insulated from foreign competition.

"AT RISK" JOBS RUN THE GAMUT

Who is being affected by services offshoring? The federal government does not collect reliable statistics. Some private sector researchers estimate that services offshoring has cost the U.S. a half-million jobs over the past three years; others suggest that close to a half-million jobs were lost in 2004 alone. The consulting firm Forrester Research predicts that 830,000 U.S. service jobs will be lost to offshoring this year – and it projects that a total of 3.4 million will be lost from this sector by 2015 (Associated Press 2004).

Assuming the Forester projection for 2005 proves accurate, that is still less than six percent of the workers who involuntarily lose their jobs each year. Moreover, the U.S. economy ended 2004 with a total of 1.7 million jobs more than existed at the end of 2003; the economy has not lost its ability to create jobs.

Nevertheless, job loss can be traumatic, and the creation of new jobs does not always benefit those who see their positions go offshore. So, who in the service sector is at risk to lose their job to offshoring? A recent study by economists at the University of California at Berkeley concludes that 14 million Americans are in jobs that are at risk, which means the job of one out of every ten non-agricultural workers is threatened. Their estimate is based on a combination of historical data, announced business plans, and job attributes (Bardhan/Kroll 2003[1]).

Among the most "at-risk" occupations mentioned by the Berkeley economists are the following:

- office and administrative support jobs, which include about two-dozen occupations such as computer operator, switchboard operator, data enterer, and a range of office clerks;
- many business and financial occupations, including financial analyst, credit card and insurance-claim processor, tax preparer, accountant, and payroll record keeper;
- paralegals, legal assistants, and medical workers, including x-ray readers and medical transcriptionists;
- graphic designers, technical writers, and computer and math professionals (such as programmers, software engineers, statisticians and actuaries).

These economists also offer another glimpse at what jobs are at risk. They report a saying among companies providing outsourcing services to businesses: "Any job that involves mostly sitting at a desk, talking on the phone, and working on a computer is under potential threat." (Bardhan/Kroll 2003: 4)

That statement lends support to a point buried in a 2003 study by the McKinsey Global Institute (MGI), the research arm of the McKinsey & Company consulting group. The McKinsey study suggests that up to 30 percent of the economy's jobs can be offshored (MGI 2003: 9). The study also makes it clear that work currently offshored runs the gamut (MGI 2003: 6):

- back-office processing of documents and data;
- customer contact jobs, such as customer service and telemarketing;
- corporate services, such as finance, accounting, human resources and information-technology support;
- knowledge services and decision analysis, such as research services, portfolio analysis, risk management and credit underwriting;

- and even path-breaking research and development, such as engineering, design, and testing of new products.

SIXTY-FOUR CENTS AN HOUR

The prime motivation behind offshoring is the desire to reduce labor costs. There is a huge difference between the U.S. and developing countries when it comes to compensation of workers with equivalent skills. For example, a U.S.-based software developer who costs a company $60 an hour can be replaced by an Indian developer with the same skills for $6 an hour (MGI 2003: 6). A programmer in the Philippines who is paid $1.50 an hour can replace a U.S.-based computer programmer who costs $10 an hour (Outsource Philippines 2005). And if we include manufacturing in our definition of offshoring, then a U.S.-based factory worker hired for $21 an hour can be replaced by a Chinese factory worker who is paid 64 cents an hour. In addition to the wage difference, employers believe that workers are motivated to be dependable and highly productive in nations to which jobs are offshored (Coy 2004).

The main reason offshoring is happening now is because it can. Innovations in information technology have given us personal computers, the ability to computerize and digitize most business services, and the opportunity to cheaply connect operations around the globe by means of international telecommunications. Toss into the mix sagging profits from the tech bust, and a fear that competitors are already doing it, and there is no surprise companies have been rushing to relocate jobs.

According to McKinsey, the top destinations for services offshoring have been Ireland, India, Israel, and Canada. Other destinations include China, Eastern Europe, the Philippines, Australia, South Africa, Russia, and Thailand. A major factor is access to English-speaking workers; 70 percent of worldwide services offshoring is done by U.S.-based businesses (MGI 2003).

WINNERS AND LOSERS

What are the consequences of offshoring? According to mainstream U.S. economists, offshoring is just another form of international trade, which means they see it as benefiting America and its trading partners. Dislocations are acknowledged, but conventional economists stress that "the economy overall benefits" (Mankiw 2004a, 2004b). American heterodox economists and labor unions, meanwhile, draw attention to the dislocations, and emphasize that negative effects (job loss, a lower standard of living, etc.) may be felt by many more than those who watch their jobs disappear overseas. Indeed, such economists argue a "crisis of demand" could be triggered, which might result in a deep recession and a prolonged period of weak economic performance. Even worse, offshoring can mean the loss of jobs and production capabilities vital to national defense (Public Citizen 2005, Connell 2005, Parks 2004, Sleigh et al. 2004).

Offshoring certainly produces winners and losers. Big winners are stockholders and consumers. For every dollar of services offshored, McKinsey estimates that a company's shareholders and/or consumers gain 62 cents in the form of higher profits and/or lower prices. Some of the gain in profits might even lead to further job creation in the U.S., and there is evidence that many U.S.-based companies continue to create jobs here even while they offshore others (Slaughter 2004).

For enterprises, offshoring means substantially lower production costs. When companies offshore jobs, the huge gap between U.S. and overseas wages is offset somewhat by higher telecommunications costs and the expenses associated with coordinating global operations. Still, researchers estimate that even when these offsetting costs are considered, companies save at least 50 percent over U.S. production. In fact, the savings are often increased to 70 percent by means of a reorganization of the work process (MGI 2003: 2).

Here is a specific offshoring example: BellSouth Corporation plans to send the jobs of about 650 computer programmers and software maintenance technicians to India by 2007, for an estimated five-year savings of $275 million. No wonder India's National Association of Software Companies reports that the number of Indian workers producing software for export to the U.S. increased by over 100,000 between 2000 and 2004. Over the same period, U.S. software employment fell by almost 200,000 jobs (Economic Policy Institute 2005).

The clearest gain from offshoring is found in corporate profits. Two years into the current recovery, which began in late 2001, the profit share of national income grew 33 percent (on a pretax basis), compared with only a three percent gain in the recovery of 1992–1993. Worker compensation, however, was *down* four percent – which, according to economists at the Brookings Institution, represents a steeper decline than in any previous recovery of the last 40 years (Brainard/Litan 2005: 11). The gain in corporate profits relative to wages translates into a substantial redistribution of income. That is because half of the households in America hold no stock in any form, including mutual funds and 401(k)-style pension plans. In fact, half of the workers with 401(k) plans have less than $10,000 in their accounts (Gleckman 2005). At the same time, the top 20 percent of the nation's stockholders own almost 95 percent of all stocks (Mishel et al. 2005: 277).

BIG LOSERS

Workers who watch their job offshored are the big losers. After losing their job, sixty percent of service workers reported taking a pay cut when becoming reemployed, according to U.S. Department of Labor surveys conducted between 1979 and 1999. One out of every five of those re-employed reported taking a pay cut of 30 percent or more. Even worse, 30 percent of service workers losing their job to offshoring were unemployed for an extended period, often a year or more. Losses from offshoring are even more substantial among manufacturing workers (Kletzer 2001: 31).

Long periods of unemployment and large declines in income are likely to persist among those affected by offshoring. Of the dozen occupations projected by the U.S. Department of Labor to produce the most jobs in the nation by 2008, half of them pay poverty wages. These high-growth jobs include janitors, cashiers, and home health aides.

Of course, workers who do not lose their jobs might gain from slower growth in product prices (it is possible that offshoring might restrain inflation by a couple tenths of one percent), but there are also negative effects on these workers. For example, offshoring means a larger portion of payroll taxes has to be paid out in the form of unemployment benefits; that leaves less tax dollars for other public initiatives. Further, since most workers losing jobs to offshoring take a pay cut when rehired, everyone is affected by the reduction in consumer purchasing power. The continuously employed also lose because the threat of having their own jobs outsourced means they settle for lower wage increases – and may even accept a pay cut or benefit concessions.

Offshoring of goods and services has other negative consequences. At the national level, for example, offshoring adds to the U.S. trade deficit, which was a record $620 billion last year. The largest imbalance was with China, from which America imported $162 billion in goods and services more than it exported. At the community level, offshoring has ripple effects. For example, Robeson County, in southeastern North Carolina, lost 8,700 manufacturing jobs to international trade between 1993 and 2003. As those employment losses rippled through the community, another 10,000 jobs were lost according to a recent study (Hossfeld/Legerton 2004). Another example is Galesburg, Illinois, a small city in the western part of that state. Last September, it lost its largest employer, as Maytag Corporation moved a refrigerator plant and its 1,600 jobs to Mexico. A Western Illinois University study estimates the total job losses in the area will be 4,200 (Rural Economic Technical Assistance Center 2003). These ripple effects run through two main channels. First, when jobs are offshored, suppliers often reduce their workforces too. Second, households affected by job loss tend to spend less on local goods and services – so all establishments feel the pinch, including restaurants, the local post office, the hardware store, the neighborhood bank, and so on. Even local charities are affected. At the family level, meanwhile, job loss has long been shown to have economic, social, medical, and psychological costs. For example, unemployment is associated with increased rates of suicide, homicide, mental hospital admission rates, and alcohol abuse.

ACHIEVING A MORE PROSPEROUS ECONOMY

There are at least three constructive steps U.S. policymakers can take in the face of offshoring. First, they can ease the dislocation faced by workers who lose their jobs. Today, there are training, healthcare, and income benefits for manufacturing workers who lose jobs to foreign trade. Service workers, however, are not eligible for such benefits. Trade Adjustment Assistance needs to be extended to service workers.

Second, policymakers can keep the overall economy running hot so the unemployment rate is as low as possible. In the year 2000, for example, the unemployment rate was four percent. Last year, it was 5.5 percent, and it was even higher in 2002 and 2003. More budget discipline would help by allowing the Federal Reserve to keep interest rates low. (Recent tax cuts, tilted toward the wealthy, have produced much red ink without adding much consumer demand.) Low overall unemployment means higher national output, greater demand by households, and a smoother transition to re-employment for job seekers (Bernstein/Baker 2003).

Finally, companies in the United States should be encouraged to compete by treating their domestic workers as a source of innovation, high productivity, and product quality, rather than to compete by viewing employees as a cost to be minimized. There are two routes to competitiveness. When firms compete by focusing on innovation, productivity and quality, they take the "high road" – and there are benefits for workers, shareholders and consumers; when firms search the globe for low wages and compete by using cheap labor to undercut each other, they set out on a "low road" that sets up a "race to the bottom". At first, it is just displaced workers who suffer from the "low road" approach, but eventually communities and corporate profits can be hurt too, as purchasing power stalls. Policymakers could encourage more companies to take the high road by making more effective existing programs such as the Manufacturing Extension Partnership (based loosely on the national agricultural extension concept) and by expanding tax incentives for employers who support workers' continuing education and training.

Of course, it won't be easy to achieve a high-employment economy in which companies choose the competitive high road over the low road, and in which displaced workers are given a helping hand. But achieving such an economy would certainly give Americans more reason to celebrate on Independence Day.

NOTE

1. With data updated in 2005.

REFERENCES

Associated Press (2004): Study: Offshoring of U.S. Jobs Accelerating, www.MSNBC.com (18.05.2004)
Bardhan, Ashok D./Kroll, Cynthia (2003): The New Wave of Outsourcing, University of California, Berkeley, Fisher Center Research Reports No. 1103, updated data on "at risk" occupations provided to the author in March 2005
Bernstein, Jared/Baker, Dean (2003): The Benefits of Full Employment, Washington, DC: Economic Policy Institute
Bivens, Josh (2004): Shifting Blame for Manufacturing Job Loss, Economic Policy Institute Briefing Paper, No. 149
Brainard, Lael/Litan, Robert (2005): Services Offshoring, American Jobs and the Global Economy, in: Perspectives on Work, Vol. 8, No. 2, pp. 9–12
Congressional Budget Office (2004): What Accounts for the Decline in Manufacturing Employment?, CBO Economic and Budget Issue Brief, February 18, 2004
Connell, Tula (2005): America Needs Good Jobs, in: America at Work, Vol. 10, No. 1, p. 12 to p. 14
Coy, Peter (2004): Just How Cheap is Chinese Labor, in: BusinessWeek Online, December 13, 2004, www.businessweek.com
Economic Policy Institute (2005): EPI Issue Guide: Offshoring, www.eipnet.org
Fay, Timothy A. (2005): The Carrier Move from Syracuse, in: Perspectives on Work, Vol. 8, No. 2, pp. 4–6
Gleckman, Howard (2005): Social Security: Three New Ideas, in: BusinessWeek Online, February 21, 2005, www.businessweek.com
Hossfeld, Leslie/Legerton, Mac (2004): The Economic and Social Impact of Job Loss in Robeson County, North Carolina, 1993–2003, in: Sociation Today, Vol. 2, No. 2, www. ncsociology.org/sociationtoday
Kletzer, Lori G. (2001): Job Loss from Imports: Measuring the Costs, Washington, DC: Institute for International Economics
Mankiw, N. Gregory (2004a): Press Briefing on the 2004 Economic Report of the President, The White House, Washington, DC, February 9, 2004
Mankiw, N. Gregory (2004b): Ask the White House, www.whitehouse.gov/ask/jan04.html (22.01.2004)
McKinsey Global Institute (2003): Offshoring: Is It a Win-Win Game?, San Francisco, CA: McKinsey & Company
Mishel, Lawrence/Bernstein, Jared/Allegretto, Sylvia (2005): The State of Working America 2004/2005, Washington, DC: Economic Policy Institute
Outsource Philippines (2005): Why the Philippines: Quality of Knowledge Workers and Comparison of Labor Costs, www.outsourcephilippines.org

Parks, James (2004): The Future of Manufacturing and America's Middle Class, in: America at Work, Vol. 9, No. 3, pp. 10–13

Public Citizen (2005): The Politics of Offshoring, www.citizen.org/trade/offshoring/views

Rural Economic Technical Assistance Center (2003): Maytag Plant Closure: IMPLAN Economic Impact Analysis, Macomb, IL: Illinois Institute for Rural Affairs

Slaughter, Matthew J. (2004): Globalization and Employment by U.S. Multinationals: A Framework and Facts, in: Daily Tax Report, March 26, 2004

Sleigh, Steve/Almeida, Paul/Khan, Faraz (2004): Losing Altitude: Employment in the Aerospace Sector, in: Perspectives on Work, Vol. 7, No. 2, pp. 10–12

9. Social unionism in western New York: the case of the Economic Development Group

In June 2009, United Auto Workers (UAW) vice president Bob King looked back on the past half century, noting, "Unions probably did too much through collective bargaining and not enough socially." He concluded that unions must represent the interests of all workers, not simply members (King 2009). Labor-community engagement, often called *social unionism*, has a long history, but both it and academic attention to it have been growing since 1980. This article examines one manifestation in western New York: the labor-led Economic Development Group.

The Economic Development Group (EDG) emerged in the late 1990s to enable western New York union leaders to jointly engage in regional economic development activities. During the past decade, the EDG has operated a variety of initiatives to foster shared regional prosperity. While the organization has had only a modest impact on its area's economic well-being, a number of EDG projects appear to be on the leading edge of innovation with respect to regional development. Thus, the EDG warrants attention from academics and practitioners, including national policy makers interested in the retention and expansion of family-supporting jobs.

This article is based on close observation of the western New York (WNY) labor movement for more than two decades, including interaction with area workers, union representatives, employers, and community leaders. In addition to serving as a participant observer in the region for a number of years, the author conducted a series of formal and informal interviews with members of the WNY community over an extended period.

LABOR-COMMUNITY ENGAGEMENT

The U.S. labor movement's involvement in metropolitan-level community issues can be traced to at least 1827, when members of Philadelphia's craft

Reprinted with permission from *Labor Studies Journal* 35 (4), December 2010, 540–565.

unions formed the Mechanics' Union of Trade Associations. Its purpose was to raise the condition of the city's skilled workers, but also to promote the "happiness, prosperity and welfare of the whole community" (Commons et al. 1918, 190). The Mechanics' Union pursued its aims – including free public education – through political action, leading to establishment of a Working Men's Party in various cities.

In less than a decade, the union and party disbanded, but similar groups took their place. By 1836, at least thirteen "trades' unions" operated, most in northeastern communities. Some lobbied against competition from prison labor. Others galvanized grassroots support for a ten-hour workday and for strikes designed to achieve that end. The trades' unions met with some success, but were wiped out by the financial panic of 1837 (Commons et al. 1918, 190–395).

The Knights of Labor, whose prominence peaked in the mid 1880s, sought widespread unity aimed at a broad reform of society. They wanted to foster solidarity among all producers of wealth (not merely among members of a particular craft or even all workers) and to replace the wage system with worker-owned cooperatives by means of education and peaceful politics. In addition to traditional trade assemblies, the local structure of the Knights included mixed assemblies. "The mixed assemblies included all kinds of workers, employers, and members of community social-action groups such as eight-hour-day leagues, women's suffragettes, and temperance societies," writes Hoyt Wheeler (2004, 84–85).

Labor-community engagement has also been part of the AFL, CIO, and combined AFL-CIO. This has often involved lobbying and political education, but also organizing strategies linking the workplace and community as well as engagement through local councils and community-service programs (Zieger 1995). The federation has frequently been a leading voice for working families, regardless of union membership, on matters including social security, health-care policy, and the minimum wage (Robinson 1981). There has also been involvement by individual unions, such as the UAW, which campaigned for national health insurance and supported Americans for Democratic Action and other policy-oriented groups (Jacobs 1987).

David Jacobs's 1987 article on the UAW connects that union's social engagement to "social unionism," which he defines as "union concern for social issues beyond the immediate workplace" (Jacobs 1987, 119). Jacobs argues the term becomes operational when union leaders respond as follows to a problem of concern to members: "by choosing from among a variety of possible responses the one strategy that unites (1) the interests of members as workers and citizens, (2) the interests of all trade unionists, and (3) the interests of the poor and unorganized." Jacobs also explains that social unionism is expressed "through political institutions parallel to the institutions of collective bargaining" (Jacobs 1987, 134–35).

According to Wheeler (2004, 85), social unionism includes any of at least three strategic endeavors: emphasizing political action and coordination with other community groups; establishing and supporting worker-rights organizations; and using workers' capital as an instrument of power. The literature on labor-community coordination at the metropolitan level has seen explosive growth in the past few decades, giving attention to issues including the fight against plant closings (Haines and Klein 1982; Lynd 1983; Craypo and Nissen 1993), revitalization of union organizing (Wial 1992–1993; Bronfenbrenner et al. 1998; Turner, Katz, and Hurd 2001; Clawson 2003; Ness 2005), living-wage campaigns (Nissen 2000; Reynolds and Kern 2001–2002; Luce 2004), and the prospect of regional power building (Craft 1990; Reynolds and Ness 2004; Reynolds 2009). There is also emerging literature on worker-rights organizations and worker centers (Karson 2004; Fine 2006; Heckscher and Carre 2006) and robust literature on community renewal through worker ownership (Whyte et al. 1983; Mackin 2001; Gates 2001; Fung, Hebb, and Rogers 2001; Croft 2004).[1]

Other dimensions of social unionism include labor-management involvement in city and regional revitalization and the revival of city central labor councils. The literature on labor-management participation at the city and regional level was strongest in the 1980s, but has never disappeared and may indeed be resurgent (Leone et al. 1982; Woodworth, Meek, and Whyte 1985, 97–178; Whalen 1987; Miller and Zeller 1991; Bernhardt, Dresser, and Rogers 2001–2002). Meanwhile, the literature on central labor councils, which often intersects with research on previously mentioned aspects of social unionism, has expanded over the past dozen or so years (Eimer 1999; Ness and Eimer 2001; Colburn 2004; Byrd and Rhee 2004; Schurman 2008–2009).[2]

Economic development is a common concern of city and regional labor-management partnerships and central labor councils. Since the mid 1990s, Pittsburgh, Milwaukee, and San Jose have been among the metropolitan areas best known for union involvement in economic development. In Pittsburgh, the Steel Valley Authority (SVA) has operated as an inter-municipal economic development agency since 1986. Catalysts for the SVA were local steelworkers, religious leaders, and area public officials seeking to address the region's loss of manufacturing jobs. The SVA focuses on saving jobs through its Strategic Early Warning Network, creating jobs and rebuilding neighborhoods through community projects and strategic research, and promoting industrial innovation through pension-financed venture capital funds (Croft 2004).

Vehicles for such union involvement in Milwaukee have included the Wisconsin Regional Training Partnership (WRTP) and Campaign for Sustainable Milwaukee (CSM). Business, labor, and government officials in Milwaukee formed the WRTP in 1992. It develops and administers workforce development initiatives (Parker 2004; WRTP 2009). Representatives of organized labor and community activists created the CSM in 1993 to craft and promote a community-generated plan for Milwaukee economic development. The organization folded in 2001, but not before spearheading successful local and county living-wage campaigns and partnering with the business community to establish an eight-year (1997–2004) Milwaukee Jobs Initiative that trained and assisted job seekers (Rogers 1994; Abelson 2001; Dresser 2009).

In San Jose, unions channel most of their economic development activities through Working Partnerships USA (WPUSA). Established in 1995 as a coalition of labor, faith organizations, and other community groups, WPUSA combines research, advocacy, and policy development with attention to the needs of working people. Through a series of research reports, WPUSA documented widening economic inequality in Santa Clara County, provided support for San Jose living-wage advocates, and promoted the notion of "accountable development," whereby public development funds are aimed at creating affordable housing and other community benefits. Drawing on WPUSA's work, the South Bay AFL-CIO Labor Council has influenced two San Jose development projects and continues to press for a citywide accountable development policy (Brownstein 2000; Rhee 2004; Rhee and Sadler 2007; WPUSA 2008).

Western New York (WNY) has also been the site of labor involvement in economic development. In the 1980s, that involvement caught the attention of labor scholars and practitioners (see, for example, Woodworth, Meek, and Whyte [1985] and Whalen [1987]). After a period during which union energy was redirected to plant-level matters (see, for example, Klingel and Martin [1988, 51–70]), labor's focus shifted back to the community in the late 1990s. One sign of this was revitalization of the area's Coalition for Economic Justice, which mounted a successful living-wage campaign in Buffalo. Another was establishment of the EDG.

Ian Greer, Barbara Byrd, and Lou Jean Fleron co-authored a 2007 chapter on Buffalo and Seattle. It offers a wide-ranging survey of labor's engagement in those communities' economic development – broadly defined to include trade policy protests, strike support, and living-wage initiatives, as well as more conventional development topics. The EDG is discussed, but the chapter focuses on the parallels of social infrastructure building in the two cities (Greer, Byrd, and Fleron 2007).

The essay by Greer, Byrd and Fleron draws on two earlier articles about Buffalo. Using the same broad conception of economic development as in 2007, Greer and Fleron (2005) describe the contours of labor's social infrastructure in Buffalo, emphasizing the role of researchers and educators and addressing how development politics present challenges similar to those found in Europe. Fleron and Applegate (2004) focus on the EDG and describe it as pursuing a development strategy that includes independent action akin to the work of U.S. community development corporations. As explained below, this article yields a different perspective.

EDG ORIGINS AND EARLY DEVELOPMENT

In the early decades following World War II, the WNY economy boomed; during the 1970s, however, the region was seen as an archetypal "Rust Belt" community. A rash of huge, permanent layoffs and plant closings diminished local economic prospects and fueled urban decay. The region has been struggling to recover ever since.

National, State, and Local Influences

By the mid 1980s, there was widespread concern about the entire nation's ability to prosper in an increasingly competitive, global economy (President's Commission 1985). Two paths to economic revitalization emerged – the "high road" versus the "low road." The low road involves competing on the basis of low wages; the alternative involves competing on the basis of productivity, skills, innovation, and product quality. Many argued that America had taken the low road in the 1970s and 1980s, and that the high road was needed to achieve broadly shared prosperity and to enable a steadily improving quality of life (Harrison and Bluestone 1990).

The AFL-CIO's Human Resources Development Institute (HRDI) promoted pursuit of a high-road strategy at the city and regional levels in a book called *Economic Development: A Union Guide to the High Road* (HRDI 1998). The common feature of the organizations it described, including the SVA and WRTP, was that each forged business, labor, and community partnerships. Labor leaders in Buffalo were intrigued by its strategy for retaining and creating family-supporting jobs.

Thanks in large part to Cornell University School of Industrial and Labor Relations (Cornell ILR), the notion of creating labor-management partnerships resonated with WNY union leaders. Since 1946, Cornell ILR has helped to establish and maintain joint labor-management initiatives across the state of New York. The school's Buffalo office has encouraged union participation in area economic development since the mid 1960s, when it inaugurated a series of labor-management forums on the region's economy (Merrill 1997; *Courier Express* 1964; *Buffalo News* 1983).

A regional summit organized by Cornell ILR in 1975 – attended by over five hundred representatives of area workers and employers – supported creation of the Buffalo-Erie County Labor Management Council (BELMC). The BELMC's small staff of professionals brought area union leaders and managers together to address common economic concerns (Whalen 1987).

The BELMC focused on achieving positive labor relations across the county. At the heart of that work was an ongoing effort to form and sustain plant-level labor-management committees. In the late 1980s, when the BELMC was most active, it worked with about ninety committees operating in over forty WNY workplaces and in various industries. More than thirty thousand hourly and salaried workers were involved, meeting regularly to address workplace concerns ranging from staffing levels and occupational safety to productivity and product quality. The record shows that these committees improved employee morale, labor relations, and customer service (Woods et al. 1991, 10–13). A sharp reduction in the region's record of work stoppages since the mid 1970s can also be attributed at least in part to the committees.[3]

The BELMC began to fade when its executive director left the region in 1993. Nevertheless, for a generation of local leaders the BELMC served as a proving ground for collaborative approaches to union-management relations. In the late 1990s, as a result of the efforts of the BELMC and the Cornell ILR work that fostered and complemented it, most of the region's union members were as comfortable engaging with employers in cooperative endeavors as in hard-nosed negotiations. This laid a foundation for establishment of the EDG.[4]

Organizing for Action

At first glance, it might seem strange that WNY labor leaders organized to participate in regional development during the boom of the late 1990s. Although the local manufacturing sector had struggled for decades, the economies of WNY and the nation were expanding as the new millennium approached. Unemployment rates locally and nationally were lower than they had been in years, and union-management relations were generally harmonious. In fact, a number of WNY labor-relations partnerships won national awards in this period.

The leaders' decision to organize for action is partly explained by the fact that WNY residents felt they were not sharing adequately in the nation's prosperity. In early 1999, economists at Buffalo's Canisius College reported that, for the decade, personal income in the area was growing only about half as fast as in the nation as a whole (Palumbo and Zaporowski 1999). Statistics of that sort struck a nerve in the region. As a participant observer in WNY during that period, this author often heard residents say the investment boom was bypassing the area and that action was needed to partake in the country's robust expansion.

There was also a critical incident prompting the labor leaders to act. In the spring of 1999, the Buffalo area's Chamber of Commerce (Buffalo Niagara Partnership) and eight WNY county industrial development agencies established a nonprofit, business development and regional marketing organization. Members of the group, called the Buffalo Niagara Enterprise (BNE), pooled resources and set ambitious goals for attracting capital investment and jobs to the Buffalo-Niagara region (see Figure 1).

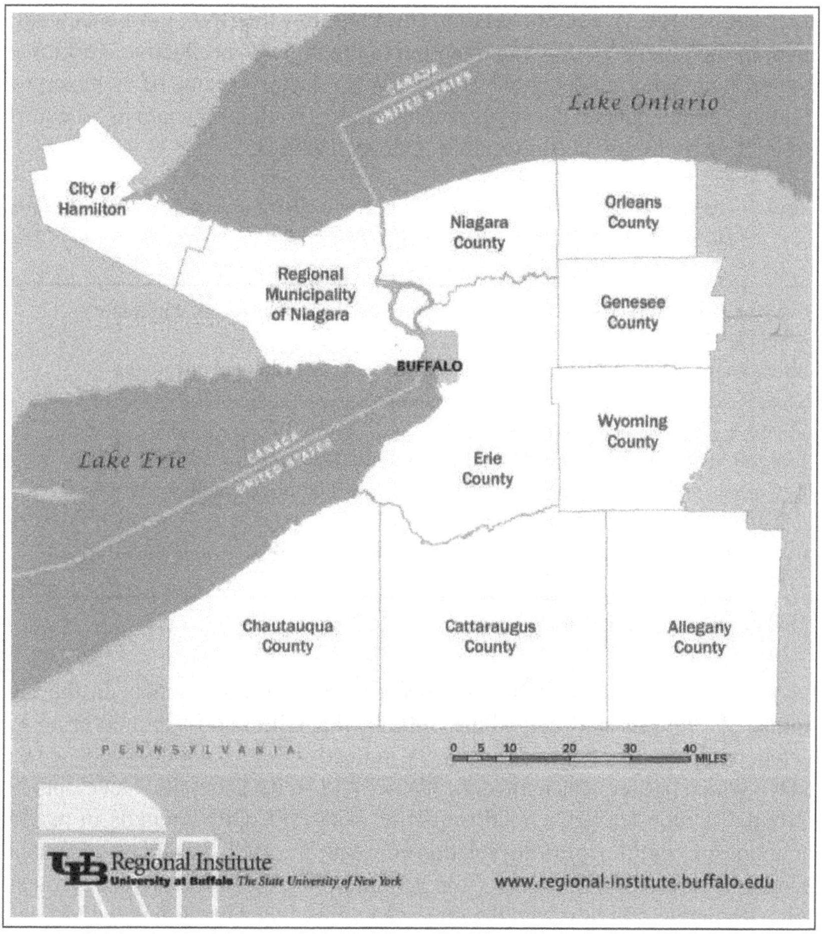

Source: University at Buffalo Regional Institute, Regional Knowledge Network. Used with permission.

Figure 1 Buffalo-Niagara region (eight counties in WNY)

Union leaders believed they could play a valuable role in the regional marketing effort. Buffalo's image as a "union town" was embedded in the national psyche, and for good reason: the area had the highest unionization rate in the country in the 1980s and 1990s. The leaders wanted to spread the word about the region's many successes traceable to worker-management cooperation, thereby undermining unfounded stereotypes. Development Counsellors

International (DCI), a public relations firm hired by the BNE, gave encouragement to the unions by drawing attention to the region's productive workforce. Noting that General Motors described a WNY factory as one of its most productive engine plants, DCI suggested promoting Buffalo-Niagara as "the most productive region in North America" (Meyer 1999, B7).

Table 1 Objectives of the WNY AFL-CIO Economic Development Group (as declared on June 25, 1999 and presented to the region's public leaders on July 22, 1999)

Create a strong, diversified economy with living-wage jobs for all and quality standards of living in WNY
Strengthen a highly skilled workforce as a competitive regional advantage
Secure a voice for organized labor in economic development in the region
Mobilize organized labor to seize and expand opportunities for partnership with regional job creation efforts, building on mutual interests
Actively promote progressive, constructive labor relations throughout WNY, and publicize the successes as a regional advantage
Coordinate and build labor cohesion in regional economic development efforts, learning from one another

Source: Buffalo AFL-CIO Council (1999).

As in the past, Cornell ILR stepped forward with assistance. In the late spring of 1999, its staff helped the Buffalo AFL-CIO Labor Council bring together union leaders from various WNY industries. The dialogues produced the EDG, which participants named the "WNY AFL-CIO Economic Development Group."[5] Union leaders agreed to partner with AFL-CIO councils in nearby counties and build a working relationship with the BNE in pursuit of mutual economic development interests. On July 22, 1999, the EDG convened a meeting with public officials from the region and introduced the group and its goals (see Table 1).

By late 1999, the EDG was ready for action. AFL-CIO labor councils in seven WNY counties backed its structure and mission.[6] Services of a day-to-day coordinator had been secured – through an in-kind gift from Niagara Mohawk Power Corporation in conjunction with the International Brotherhood of Electrical Workers (IBEW) – and specific project areas were identified. Progress was also being made on chartering the group as a nonprofit corporation and securing funding for its operations through local foundations (both goals were achieved by 2002, when annual funding via local grants totaled just under $33,000).

LABOR RELATIONS

At the outset, a primary EDG goal was to promote cooperative labor-management relations at the enterprise and community levels within WNY. Such cooperation was viewed as essential not only to retaining and improving existing jobs, but also to creating new ones via local business expansion, new enterprise startups, and the attraction of corporations from outside the region.

The "Champions at Work" Study

In late 1999, the EDG partnered with the BNE to commission a study of WNY employment relations and workplace practices. The New York State legislature funded the study and Cornell ILR faculty members supervised the research. It was published in 2000 as *Champions at Work: Employment, Workplace Practices and Labor-Management Relations in Western New York* (Fleron, Stanger, and Patton 2000).

Champions at Work was the organization's first accomplishment. The final report, based on employer and union survey responses, regional economic data, and case studies, demonstrated that WNY "is a world-class region" in terms of workforce quality, workplace practices, and labor relations. It also confirmed the results of earlier academic studies that show "unions contribute to the success of high-performance workplaces" (Fleron, Stanger, and Patton 2000, 7).

The *Champions* report garnered media attention in the region and in the nation's business press; it was also well received by local leaders. The *Wall Street Journal* mentioned the findings on its front page (Tejada 2000). EDG chairman Kevin Donovan said that while he thought WNY labor relations were very good, "this study exceeded my expectations." BNE president Thomas Kucharski felt the study could help dispel some misconceptions about the region. When asked whether the report would make corporate site-selection professionals change their views of WNY, Lance Yoder, managing editor of *Expansion Management,* said he expected it would cause them to "take a second look" at the area (Williams 2000).

The EDG study does seem to have made an impact on site-selection consultants and business decision makers. In 2005, the BNE (co-sponsor of the *Champions* study) was named by *Site Selection Magazine* as one of the Top 20 local economic development groups in North America (Starner 2005). In early 2006, meanwhile, *Expansion Management* named Buffalo to its list of "America's 50 Hottest Cities" for business expansion or relocation (Kirzner 2006).

The Champions Network

The goal of promoting labor-management cooperation also resulted in establishment, in 2000, of a business-labor practitioners' Champions Network. That group was intended to extend the EDG-BNE relationship and help spread the use of cooperative labor relations in the region. It was also created to assist in attracting companies – union or nonunion – to WNY by fielding business relocation inquiries and by participating in ongoing public-private regional marketing initiatives. Moreover, the network was conceived as a mechanism to alert unions and the community to possible job loss in the region, thus allowing sufficient time for intervention and collaborative problem solving by area stakeholders.

However, the Champions Network was never able to get off the ground as intended. Its roster included more than fifty labor and business leaders in 2000, but the organization exhibited few signs of life for about three years.

In 2003, Cornell ILR revived the Champions Network. There were three network task forces by 2004. One was convened to examine the coordination of economic development functions in the region. Another worked to encourage civic involvement, voter registration, and election-day turnout. A third was established to address the image of the region as seen by outsiders; its main work has been to support a grassroots campaign called "Believe in Buffalo Niagara," designed to collect one hundred thousand signatures to a letter, promoting the region's vitality and promise, which would then be sent to hundreds of corporate leaders (Cornell ILR 2003; Believe in Buffalo Niagara n.d.; Cornell ILR n.d.).[7]

Members of the Champions Network task forces deserve praise for their volunteer efforts to make WNY a better region in which to live and work, but there is no solid evidence that the network has achieved its original aims of improving enterprise-level labor relations and employment prospects in WNY. Since 2004, Cornell ILR has continued to draw attention to the link between constructive labor relations, organizational performance, and worker gains by creating a "Champions@Work Award" and bestowing it annually – initially on behalf of the EDG, but later on its own – upon WNY union-management partnerships (see, for example, Cornell ILR [2008]). There is surely merit to highlighting joint labor-management endeavors, but since the network has so far relied only on raising community awareness – rather than, for instance, fostering workplace labor-management committees – its impact on WNY employment relations remains indirect, difficult to measure, and probably quite small.

While Cornell ILR keeps the Champions Network alive and some EDG board members participate in the network, the EDG no longer considers it an EDG project. Like the earlier BELMC, the EDG chose from the outset to avoid both partisan politics and feel-good boosterism. In part, then, one senses that the EDG leadership feels the Champions Network has moved too much in the directions of political action and cheerleading, but the BNE may also be partly responsible for the EDG's decision regarding the network. If the BNE had taken steps to better integrate the Champions Network into its regional development and marketing efforts – and recognized the Network's establishment as an opportunity to begin working more closely with the EDG – then perhaps the network would still be an EDG project.

Despite its experience with the Champions Network, the EDG has not given up on partnering with the business community on economic development issues. In 2007, for example, the EDG joined with the National Electrical Contractors Association to convene a regional business exposition showcasing WNY and its constructive employment-relations climate. The event attracted fifty-five potential employers from as far away as Japan and China, all interested in exploring the benefits of doing business in WNY.

REGIONAL POWER

Reliable and affordable supplies of electricity and heat are essential to WNY, where winters are long and as many as half of the jobs depended on manufacturing at the start of the new millennium (Maguire 2002). As a result, the EDG has pursued two projects designed to retain and expand low-cost energy in the region.

The Niagara Power Project

Shortly after the EDG was established, it took the lead in working to renew the federal license governing the region's hydropower plant on the Niagara River, the Niagara Power Project (NPP), which needed renewal by August 2007. The relicensing of a power plant involves a multitude of issues, including allocation of power and the plant's environmental impact. The EDG members were particularly interested in retaining the plant's low-cost electric power, upon which many area residents and employers had come to depend. For example, when U.S. industrial users were paying an average of five cents per kilowatt-hour in early 2004, many WNY employers were paying 1.5 to 2.5 cents for Niagara power (Pataki 2004).

The EDG became involved in the NPP license renewal at the urging of Phil Wilcox, an EDG founder and member of the IBEW. At a meeting with labor, business, and government representatives in the fall of 1999, he explained that the NPP's plant supplied inexpensive power to about 110 companies, responsible for fifty thousand jobs. Wilcox also stressed that rapid relicensing could favorably affect regional development: uncertainty over NPP power allocation had already led one area employer to shelve a $40 million expansion, he reported (Williams 1999).

The traditional approach to relicensing does not involve community stakeholders until a plant operator submits its license renewal application with the Federal Energy Regulatory Commission. As a result, renewal usually gets bogged down in an adversarial process involving lengthy legal challenges. Wilcox was aware a community-involvement alternative was available and advocated that the EDG initiate it.

The consensus building, community-involvement approach to license renewal had never been initiated by a labor organization, but EDG members found the project attractive. Beyond the impact of relicensing on economic development, the EDG was attracted by the project's focus on a process of negotiations (familiar union territory); the opportunity for organized labor to take the initiative on a regional issue; and the chance to show the community that the EDG could serve as an honest broker. By July 2000, the EDG shepherded into existence the WNY Relicensing Consensus Committee. Co-chaired by the EDG's Donovan and a local government official, it brought interested stakeholders together to shape the relicensing effort.

In August 2005 – two years prior to license expiration – the NPP's operator filed its application for a fifty-year license renewal. The application eventually received federal approval and the plant has been operating under the new license since September 1, 2007. The settlement agreements (determining power allocation and the community impact of plant operations) and the EDG's leadership in the process received praise from all corners of the community. The inclusive approach provided stakeholders with "an integral say in the project's future," said Assemblywoman Francine DelMonte (quoted in Saltzman [2005]; [2007]).

The project gave labor "a place at the table" and ensured that the renewal process was used "for purposes of improving the WNY economy," adds Richard Lipsitz (2006), a Teamsters leader who helped found the EDG. "Without the EDG, environmentalists and developers would have had a voice, but not area workers." The initiative also demonstrated labor's ability to galvanize the entire community in a project requiring cooperation and compromise.

Buffalo District Energy

When the EDG was established, a number of its members were interested in sustainable development and the generation of environmentally friendly sources of low-cost energy. EDG members then learned the city of Buffalo has a gas-fired, heating plant that delivers thermal energy to downtown, city-owned structures. This prompted discussions with the city about using WNY farm crops as fuel and expanding the heating loop to include noncity buildings.

When it became clear there were legal restrictions preventing the city from expanding the loop, the EDG offered to lead the expansion initiative, and city leaders supported the idea.

To pursue this project, the EDG teamed with Siemens Building Technologies, Inc. The near-term plan was to convert the downtown plant into a biomass-fueled facility and expand it to heat workplaces and residences. From the start, however, the long-term goal of the EDG's Buffalo energy project has been establishment of a cogeneration plant that provides customers with heating and cooling and that sells "green" (clean and renewable) electricity to the power grid. The EDG has also envisioned establishing a similar facility in Niagara Falls and elsewhere; despite the NPP, much of WNY still relies heavily on expensive, imported energy resources.

Providing reliable, low-cost energy to private sector employers is seen as a way to help retain and expand job opportunities in the city, but the EDG also has other goals for its Buffalo energy initiative. Fueling the plant with willow shrubs and other "energy" crops grown in WNY would keep energy dollars in the local economy, support the region's farmers, and reduce pollution. Moreover, construction associated with the plant's expansion would provide jobs for skilled workers and training opportunities for area youth. Indeed, the EDG considers "training the underrepresented to take advantage of new opportunities" to be a cornerstone of the project (Economic Development Group 2004, 17; Buffalo District Energy 2006).

The EDG has been working on this energy project since 2001. To get the ball rolling, it created the nonprofit Buffalo District Energy Corporation (BDEC). It then had to address an Internal Revenue Service challenge to its nonprofit status. BDEC also needed engineering expertise, so the project became a joint venture with Siemens. By the end of 2005, the BDEC had a clear plan: it would issue bonds, take over operation of the existing heating loop, install biomass boilers, and begin to expand the distribution system. The addition of a cooling system would come at a later phase.

The Buffalo energy project is modeled after a system that heats over 75 percent of downtown St. Paul, Minnesota. That facility – which provides, heat, hot water, chilled water, and electricity – can be fired by coal, natural gas, or wood waste. In fact, the nonprofit "District Energy St. Paul" recently constructed a heat and power plant fuelled with wood waste – the largest wood-fired district energy system in the United States (District Energy St. Paul 2008).

Reducing energy costs is an essential part of the Buffalo project. In 2004, BDEC estimated the city would reduce thermal energy costs by 30 percent in the project's first year – and save more than $21 million over thirty years. Expanding the system to county buildings was projected to generate a savings of nearly $30 million for the county over the same three decades (Economic Development Group 2004, 13). Expanding the system further would make cost savings available to additional consumers, including low-income Buffalo residents.

The project stalled in 2006, however, due in part to election of a new city mayor and approval of new real estate developments near the plant. Those developments would require relocation of the biomass plant, and BDEC is reexamining the feasibility of the project (Donovan 2009). Nevertheless, the EDG's work on district energy has subsequently caught the attention of groups elsewhere in the region and in other parts of the Northeast, and, as will be discussed below, the timing of its pursuit of green energy may ultimately prove fortuitous.

WORKFORCE DEVELOPMENT AND NEIGHBORHOOD REVITALIZATION

The EDG has been engaged in workforce development initiatives since 2000, when it created the Buffalo Niagara Jobs Initiative (BNJI). EDG jobs projects seek to meet local needs by preparing low- and moderate-income Buffalo residents for skilled employment. "It's not a high-road economy unless the whole community can benefit," says Lipsitz (2006). "We need to enable participation by those who have been excluded from paths to prosperity in the past."

The Buffalo Niagara Jobs Initiative

In 2000, the EDG convened representatives from the business, labor, government, and education communities to consider how area workforce development resources might be coordinated and better utilized. The BNJI evolved out of those discussions. The core idea of the jobs initiative was to link training and other employment support services to a ten-year project to renovate Buffalo's public schools, a venture that included a project labor agreement requiring construction unions to meet certain targets for employment of women and minorities.

A sixteen-member community advisory board, co-chaired by the president of a local construction company and the EDG's Donovan, leads the BNJI. To get the program started, the board met regularly with members of the EDG staff and about a dozen additional community participants. The BNJI board held its meetings at an inner-city Baptist church, a sign of its ability to bring together labor, industry, government, community organizations, and local religious leaders. It later worked with a host of local organizations to identify interested job seekers and to provide education and support services.

The BNJI completed its first year of providing educational services in mid 2006. In that year, 127 participants were registered (106 men and twenty-one women) and sixty-nine completed its life-skills and construction-skills classroom programs (fifty-nine men and ten women). Of the sixty-nine, nine were subsequently employed in union apprenticeships, and twenty-five found related employment or work as a private contractor. Another twenty-one found jobs unrelated to construction, and fourteen were unemployed. Many of those not completing the program were hired directly into a union apprenticeship, found another job, or elected to stay in school to earn a degree. The vast majority of the BNJI enrollees were African American and their median age was thirty-three (BNJI 2006).

By the end of 2008, the BNJI had graduated three cohorts of approximately one hundred students in total (Lipsitz 2008). The second and third cohorts were smaller than the first because the EDG decided to move away from engaging its staff in the direct operation of training programs. In June 2009, however, the EDG began a dialogue with the AFL-CIO to explore ways the two organizations could work together to revitalize the BNJI (Donovan 2009).

According to the EDG's executive director, Janice Barrett, its strength in the education and training realm involves serving as a catalyst and facilitator. The EDG can forge teams of local leaders and help such teams find the financial resources they need to address specific workforce development needs. The EDG is also willing to "stay in the trenches" and work with the parties until new projects get off the ground. Operating and managing such programs on a long-term basis, however, is best assigned to others outside the EDG, says Barrett (2008).

A new initiative provides an example of the role the EDG wishes to play. Working with area hospitals, nursing homes, healthcare unions, community organizations, and educational institutions, the EDG created a workforce development advisory board to focus on allied health professions. It then secured public and private grants to pursue establishment of a charter high school – the Health Sciences Charter School (which opened in August 2010) – that will prepare students for work and further study in healthcare fields (Donovan 2009). The overall goal of the healthcare partnership is to train new and incumbent workers in a way that meets industry needs. The group "won't train for training's sake," Barrett says, emphasizing a workforce development principle that has governed the EDG from its inception (Barrett 2006; 2008).

Housing Rehabilitation

EDG leaders have long envisioned linking workforce development and housing rehabilitation, especially in neighborhoods targeted for school renovations. "It was one of our original ideas," says Lipsitz. "If school reconstruction can be accompanied by improving the housing stock, whole neighborhoods can be improved" (Lipsitz 2006). In late 2003, schools were being fixed, but many neighborhoods remained blighted by abandoned and deteriorating homes (Moses and Koch 2005), so the EDG created its Joint Neighborhood Stabilization

Initiative. An outgrowth of the BNJI, the neighborhood stabilization initiative is a construction-skills program designed to provide BNJI enrollees paid employment for hands-on training at worksites where area houses are being rehabilitated. To support this effort, the EDG hired a crew of skilled craft workers to teach BNJI enrollees by involving them in housing reconstruction.

In the first six months of 2006, three homes in one of the city's most neglected neighborhoods were renovated. A few more homes were refurbished later, but the entire housing rehabilitation project has been on hold since the start of 2007. The notion of such an initiative (including the opportunity to enable local residents to benefit from both skills training and home ownership) remains attractive to the EDG, but the group has not yet found a viable way to cover the costs involved and does not want the initiative to displace area residents.[8]

CURRENT CHALLENGES, NEW OPPORTUNITIES

The lack of a dedicated funding source constitutes one of the biggest current challenges for the EDG, according to Barrett and other board members. The EDG's limited funding and dependence on soft-money (project-oriented, fixed-term grants) has restricted staffing levels and constrained its ability to plan and begin new initiatives. Projects such as Buffalo district energy and the jobs initiatives take years of preparation, and that advance work is made more difficult when operational resources and "capacity-building" grants are scarce (Barrett 2008).[9]

A 2007 report by the nonpartisan, Albany-based Fiscal Policy Institute (FPI) indicates that the region served by the EDG is also facing persistent economic challenges. Between 2000 and 2006, a time when total U.S. employment rose 1.7 percent and overall New York state employment fell by just 0.6 percent, employment in each of the two western-most regions of the state (as categorized by the FPI) fell by more than 2 percent – and job losses were especially significant in manufacturing. During the same period, a group of counties the FPI calls Western and Northern New York experienced an average annual decline in real wages (0.2 percent), while the other parts of the state saw wages rise (by at least 0.7 percent) (FPI 2007, 15, 48).[10]

The FPI report, the latest to provide a detailed examination of the state's demographic and economic trends by region, also shows a population decline of 2.7 percent in Western New York for the period 2000–2006. In contrast, during the same period, New York City experienced a population increase of 2.6 percent, and Eastern New York (the Capital region, Hudson Valley, and Long Island) experienced an average population expansion of 2.8 percent. Some parts of the state saw small population declines (Central New York and the Mohawk Valley, for instance), but none were nearly as large as WNY (FPI 2007, 53).[11]

Today, in the midst of a state fiscal crisis, deep national financial trouble, and a disquieting recession, the EDG leadership remains cautiously optimistic. The region has been hit hard by the recent downturn, but President Barack Obama's effort to revitalize the U.S. economy by means of a major public-investment initiative provides a reason for hope. Indeed, the EDG is well positioned to work in partnership with key domestic-policy branches of the Obama administration, which has from the outset expressed an interest in modernizing schools, improving the nation's infrastructure, boosting job training, and promoting "green collar" jobs that address the nation's energy and transportation needs in an environmentally friendly manner (Kuhnhenn 2008). According to the EDG's leaders, the key is to forge ahead in a way that treats the group's experience and the region's characteristics (including its skilled workforce and tradition of manufacturing) as "a bundle of assets" (Lipsitz 2008; Barrett 2008).

While the EDG's experience over the past decade has produced an asset bundle with three core competencies (labor relations, energy production, and workforce development), its experience also provides lessons applicable to any future EDG initiative. One is the value of not merely taking advantage of opportunities, but also creating them. For example, when the business-led BNE was formed, the unionists in WNY did not complain about being excluded or simply ask to be involved in a BNE project; instead, they organized, fashioned an agenda, and invited the BNE to partner with them to examine and then promote the productive character of the workforce as a regional asset. Similarly, when the unionists learned that power plant relicensing was an important economic development topic and that a consensus-building relicensing process existed, they did not ask an area legislator to form a group that could initiate such a process; instead, the EDG took the lead and created a chance to demonstrate its interest in finding common ground with other area stakeholders. Time and again, the EDG sought to create opportunities as a way to pursue its agenda, and those efforts have paid off.

Another lesson of the EDG experience is the importance of combining self-reliance with openness toward forging regional partnerships. Other observers have described the EDG as building a "two-lane high road" to regional economic development: one lane involving collaboration with willing members of the business community and another involving independent action reminiscent of the work of community development corporations (Fleron and Applegate 2004, 11). While that interpretation has some merit, it also obscures a deeper point: every time the EDG has taken the initiative it has also sought to find a partner, establish a dialogue with other stakeholders, build on shared interests, and fashion opportunities for mutual gains. If the EDG involves a "two-lane" road, then one of its strengths is that EDG initiatives aim to straddle the lane dividers.

Still another lesson that comes from the EDG experience is the need to remain undaunted in the face of broader economic and political currents. "There's a lot we can't control, and we recognize our accomplishments can be overshadowed by forces beyond our influence," says Lipsitz. What he and other EDG leaders describe is a marathon, not a sprint, and the EDG seeks to remain active for the long haul. From their perspective, there are plenty of constraints and no quick fixes, but there is also no excuse for giving up. As Lipsitz explained to this author in 2006:

> Judging us by looking at aggregate statistics misses the whole point. We are making a difference in people's lives, and we hope to make more of a difference over time. We don't try to be overly optimistic about the EDG's potential – which is a reason we don't seek to draw attention to ourselves – we just try to make a difference as we can. Meanwhile, if the community comes to realize that union people aren't the enemy, then that's all the better. (Lipsitz 2006)

Looking ahead, the EDG is especially hopeful about opportunities involving renewable energy. EDG members are convinced that environmentally friendly energy systems and technologies have a boundless future as engines of job growth. In fact, the EDG's Donovan retired from the UAW at the end of 2008 to pursue such projects on a full-time (unpaid) basis via a new nonprofit EDG spin-off and partner called Northeast District Energy Corporation (NDEC).

In Buffalo, the EDG's downtown energy loop may have stalled, but the idea has attracted interest in other WNY communities and across the northeastern United States, including Vermont and New Hampshire. Northeast District Energy entered 2009 with a $250,000 Vermont Clean Energy grant to conduct technical and feasibility studies on construction of a biomass plant that would serve two Brattleboro schools, and with optimism about possible New York State Energy Research grants for projects in WNY (Barrett 2008; Pierce 2008). Today (mid 2010), the NDEC has three district-heating projects in Vermont and a new project at Paul Smith's College in the Adirondacks. The EDG is also exploring the possibility of using the district energy concept to heat and cool its new health-professions charter school and other nearby structures (Donovan 2009; Barrett 2010).

SUMMARY AND CONCLUSIONS

The ten-year experience of the EDG represents part of the latest chapter in a long history of labor-community engagement in the United States. With a survey of that labor history as a backdrop, this article has examined the EDG's origins, development, and major initiatives. Current challenges and opportunities have also been identified, in the process drawing attention to lessons that shed light on the EDG's past and that are likely to guide its future.

Although the EDG has had limited impact on WNY overall – in part due to a lack of resources, but also because of the overwhelming impact of national and international economic trends – a number of its projects appear to be on the leading edge of innovation with respect to regional development. The EDG successfully charted a new path for power plant relicensing. Its efforts to pursue renewable energy and associated "green-collar" jobs are now recognized as prescient.[12] Its workforce development initiatives involve nonprofit metropolitan labor-market intermediaries and sectoral strategies linked to regional economic needs, which are precisely the institutions and approaches that researchers see as the future of regional development and national labor-market policies (Benner, Leete, and Pastor 2007; Glover and King 2010).[13] Moreover, the high-performance workplace practices highlighted and promoted by the EDG continue to be recognized as vital to future U.S. industrial competitiveness (Lynch 2009).

As a case study in social unionism, the EDG experience offers more than insights for practitioners seeking retention and expansion of family supporting jobs. It also provides a starting point for further research on unions. For example, by comparing this with other cases of union engagement in regional development, scholars can test and further develop frameworks that help understand how and when labor-community coalitions are forged (see, for example, Tattersall [2008a] and [2008b]; and Turner and Cornfield [2007, 1–19]). Further research can also draw on the EDG experience to deepen our understanding of the dimensions and challenges of regional power building (following the work of Reynolds [2009] and Reynolds in Turner and Cornfield [2007, 79–94]). It can also increase our knowledge of the overall effectiveness and limits of labor-community engagement (see Craft 1990; Nissen 2004; and Shantz 2009).

The UAW's Bob King may be right when he says unions probably did too much through collective bargaining in the past half-century and not enough through broader forms of social engagement. Early in the twentieth century, however, labor economist Robert F. Hoxie argued that unionism "has its finger in practically every social pie that is baking" (Hoxie 1917, 4). Today, with the spread of social unionism in forms such as the EDG, Hoxie's statement may be more accurate than it has been in decades.

NOTES

1. Wheeler uses "social unionism" interchangeably with the terms social movement unionism, reformist unionism, and uplift unionism, but others draw distinctions, including Turner and Cornfield (2007, 15) and Hyman (1996, 69–72).

Social unionism also overlaps with "community unionism;" see, for example, Fine (2001), Lipsig-Mumme (2003), and Tattersall (2008a; 2008b).

2. In addition to the literature on specific aspects of social unionism, there are also compilation volumes on a variety of labor-community coalitions. See, for example, Breecher and Costello (1990), Reynolds (2004), and Turner and Cornfield (2007). See also the survey volume by Reynolds (2002) and the extensive literature review in Nissen (2004), including attention to matters not mentioned in the present article, such as labor-environmental alliances, religion-labor partnerships, unions and the global justice movement, and coalitions supporting union contract campaigns. Along with Shantz (2009), works by Nissen (2004) and Turner and Cornfield (2007) are also part of the literature assessing social unionism's prospects, challenges and limitations.
3. Work stoppages were at record-low levels across the nation in the 1990s, but WNY rates of lost work time had by then fallen to just a fraction of the national level (Fleron, Stanger, and Patton 2000, 33).
4. The BELMC closed its doors in 2002, but Cornell ILR still operates in WNY. Other regional institutions contributing to the WNY labor-relations climate of the 1990s included the WNY Employee Involvement Council (1985–1999) and the WNY chapter of the Industrial Relations Research Association, established in 1965.
5. In 2003, the EDG severed official ties to the Buffalo AFL-CIO Labor Council and its name was shortened to the Economic Development Group, Inc. Nevertheless, the organization still functions much as envisioned at the outset. At present (mid 2010), a full-time executive director and a part-time office assistant manage the organization's daily operations. (Additional part-time staffers and volunteers have been assigned to specific initiatives, and that number has fluctuated with project needs and the availability of funds.) The executive director is in regular contact with the EDG's officers, and convenes EDG board meetings eight times per year. Each of the thirteen board members must belong to a union, and the board continues to contain members from a diverse set of occupations and industries. (Unions include, for example, the UAW, Teamsters, CWA [representing nurses as well as telecommunication workers], AFSCME, NYSUT (teachers), SEIU, and IBEW.) The organization strives for consensus, though the board can operate by majority rule when necessary. The group has no official ties to the state labor council or national labor federations. In short, it is a group of WNY union leaders who meet to identify and pursue local economic development initiatives (in partnership with other local groups and constituencies whenever and wherever possible).
6. The EDG represents union members in the following WNY counties: Allegany, Cattaraugus, Chautauqua, Erie, Genesee, Niagara, and Orleans. The business community's BNE includes an additional county, Wyoming, a largely rural area with few union members. The total population of these eight counties was just under 1.6 million in 2000 (Institute for Local Governance and Regional Growth 2006).
7. The "Believe in Buffalo Niagara" campaign appears to have subsequently folded without accomplishing its objective.
8. While the EDG shuns involvement in public policy battles in addition to political campaigns, housing rehabilitation might be one area where the EDG could benefit from reconsidering its detachment from policy matters. Recalling the real estate development projects that have become an obstacle to the EDG biomass initiative, one could envision a city policy that requires a certain amount of neighborhood renovation in exchange for development rights.

9. A review of the EDG's financial statements through 2008 shows its annual grants revenue was highest in 2006, at just under $150,000. (It was also able to generate income by co-sponsoring the WNY business exposition in 2007.) In addition, the EDG has generated revenue – from public and private sources – to support its workforce development and neighborhood revitalization initiatives, but that revenue has merely covered associated program expenses.
10. The BNE, meanwhile, fell far short of its initial five-year employment and investment goals. Instead of achieving its target of creating fifty thousand new jobs, for example, it created or retained 14,500 (Fink 2004). In its sixth year (2004–2005 fiscal year), the BNE's most successful to date in terms of employment, it helped create or retain 4,730 jobs and attract $229 million in capital investment (Buffalo Niagara Enterprise 2005, 9). (The group's record year for attracting investment was 2005–2006, when it attracted $258 million [Buffalo Niagara Enterprise 2006, 7].)
11. Buffalo, meanwhile, can accommodate about six hundred thousand residents, but now has fewer than half that number.
12. For recent research on the economic benefits of investing in clean energy, see Pollin, Heintz, and Garrett-Peltier (2009) and Pollin, Wicks-Lim, and Garrett-Peltier (2009).
13. Speaking to a reporter a few days before the Health Sciences Charter School opened, principal Hank Stopinski explained that the industry and labor partnership gives the school a vital knowledge base and that it is already receiving attention as a model for other schools. "We are getting calls from all over the nation right now [and] we haven't had our first students through the door yet" (quoted in Habuda 2010).

REFERENCES

Abelson, Richard. 2001. Hard lessons in political deceit and real friends. AFSCME District Council 48 *Direct talk* (the executive director's web-based news and opinion column). http://www.afscme48.org/directtalk1.html (accessed June 26, 2009).

Barrett, Janice P. 2006. Interview with the author. June 19.

Barrett, Janice P. 2008. Interview with the author. December 29.

Barrett, Janice P. 2010. E-mail correspondence with the author. August 19.

Believe in Buffalo Niagara. N.d. We believe in Buffalo Niagara (a letter writing campaign that began October 4, 2004). http://www.believeinbuffaloniagara.org/, last (accessed October 21, 2006; website no longer active).

Benner, Chris, Laura Leete, and Manuel Pastor. 2007. *Staircases or treadmills? Labor market intermediaries and economic opportunity in a changing economy*. New York: Russell Sage Foundation.

Bernhardt, Annette, Laura Dresser, and Joel Rogers. 2001–2002. Taking the high road in Milwaukee: The Wisconsin Regional Training Partnership. *WorkingUSA* 5 (3): 109–30.

Breecher, Jeremy, and Tim Costello, eds. 1990. *Building bridges: The emerging grassroots coalition of labor and community*. New York: Monthly Review Press.

Bronfenbrenner, Kate, Sheldon Friedman, Richard W. Hurd, Rudolph A. Oswald, and Ronald L. Seeber, eds. 1998. *Organizing to win: New research on union strategies*. Ithaca, New York: ILR Press.

Brownstein, Bob. 2000. Working partnerships: A new political strategy for creating living-wage jobs. *WorkingUSA* 4 (1): 35–48.
Buffalo AFL-CIO Council. 1999. News release: Buffalo AFL-CIO announces formation of Western New York AFL-CIO Economic Development Group. June 25. Buffalo, New York: Buffalo AFL-CIO Council.
Buffalo District Energy. 2006. Project overview. Buffalo, NY: Economic Development Group, Inc.
Buffalo News. Public forums will focus on WNY recovery. 1983. April 13.
Buffalo Niagara Enterprise. 2005. *Buffalo Niagara Enterprise annual report 2004–2005*. Buffalo, NY: Buffalo Niagara Enterprise.
Buffalo Niagara Enterprise. 2006. *Buffalo Niagara Enterprise annual report 2005–2006*. Buffalo, NY: Buffalo Niagara Enterprise.
Buffalo Niagara Jobs Initiative. 2006. Participant statistics: June 2005-June 2006. June 19. Buffalo, NY: Economic Development Group, Inc.
Byrd, Barbara, and Nari Rhee. 2004. Building power in the new economy: The South Bay Labor Council. *WorkingUSA* 8 (2): 131–53.
Clawson, Dan. 2003. *The next upsurge: labor and the new social movements*. Ithaca, NY: ILR Press.
Colburn, Bruce. 2004. Taking back America for working people: Community by community. *WorkingUSA* 8 (2): 229–31.
Commons, John R., David J. Saposs, Helen L. Sumner, E. B. Mittleman, H. E. Hoagland, John B. Andrews, and Selig Perlman. 1918. *History of labour in the United States*, vol. 1. New York: Macmillan.
Cornell ILR. 2003. Seeing 2020: From shared vision to focused action. Champions at Work meeting agenda and printed copy of PowerPoint presentation containing results of labor and management focus groups. September 23. Buffalo, NY.
Cornell ILR. 2008. Cameron Compression Systems & International Association of Machinists receive Cornell ILR champions@work award. August 27. http://www.ilr.cornell.edu/wied/news/2008-Champions-Award.html (accessed June 26, 2009).
Cornell ILR. N.d. Research highlight: Champions@work network. http://www.ilr.cornell.edu/profiles/championsAtwork.html/ (accessed June 26, 2009).
Courier Express. 1964. City's economic issues discussed. March 11.
Craft, James A. 1990. The community as a source of union power. *Journal of Labor Research* 11 (2): 145–60.
Craypo, Charles, and Bruce Nissen, editors. 1993. *Grand designs: The impact of corporate strategies on workers, unions, and communities*. Ithaca, NY: ILR Press.
Croft, Thomas. 2004. Saving jobs and investing in labor's future: The Steel Valley Authority. *Perspectives on Work* 8 (1): 4–6.
District Energy St. Paul. 2008. Our story. http://www.districtenergy.com/about/story.html (accessed June 26, 2009).
Donovan, Kevin. 2009. Interview with the author. July 1.
Dresser, Laura. 2009. Milwaukee Jobs Initiative project details. Center on Wisconsin Strategy. http://www.cows.org/collab_projects_detail.asp?id=2 (accessed June 26, 2009).
Economic Development Group. 2004. Reinventing Buffalo: Buffalo District Energy Project. Printed copy of PowerPoint presentation. April 22. Buffalo, NY: Economic Development Group, Inc.
Eimer, Stuart. 1999. From "business unionism" to "social movement unionism": The case of the AFL-CIO Milwaukee County Labor Council. *Labor Studies Journal* 24 (2): 63–81.

Fine, Janice. 2001. Community unionism in Baltimore and Stamford: Beyond the politics of particularlism. *WorkingUSA*. 4 (3): 59–85.

Fine, Janice. 2006. *Worker centers: Organizing communities at the edge of the dream*. Ithaca, NY: Cornell University Press.

Fink, James. 2004. BNE releases 5-Year Report, *Buffalo business first*. August 24. http://buffalo.bizjournals.com/buffalo/stories/2004/08/23/daily21.html (accessed June 26, 2009).

Fiscal Policy Institute. 2007. *The state of working New York, 2007*. Albany, NY: Fiscal Policy Institute.

Fleron, Lou Jean, and Ron Applegate. 2004. Building a two-lane high road: Unions and economic development in Western New York. *Perspectives on Work* 8 (1): 10–12.

Fleron, Lou Jean, Howard Stanger, and Eileen Patton, 2000. *Champions at work: Employment, workplace practices and labor-relations in Western New York*. Buffalo, NY: Cornell University School of Industrial and Labor Relations.

Fung, Archon, Tessa Hebb, and Joel Rogers, eds. 2001. *Working capital: The power of labor's pensions*. Ithaca, NY: ILR Press.

Gates, Jeff. 2001. Labor must reckon with ownership. *Perspectives on Work* 5 (2): 10–13.

Glover, Robert, and Christopher King. 2010. Sectoral approaches to workforce development: Toward an effective U.S. labor market policy. In *Human resource economics and public policy: Essays in honor of Vernon M. Briggs Jr.*, ed. Charles J. Whalen, 215–52. Kalamazoo, MI: W. E. Upjohn Institute for Employment Research.

Greer, Ian, Barbara Byrd, and Lou Jean Fleron. 2007. Two paths to the high road: The dynamics of coalition building in Seattle and Buffalo. In *Labor in the new urban battlegrounds: Local solidarity in a global economy*, ed. Lowell Turner and Daniel B. Cornfield, 111–28. Ithaca, NY: Cornell University Press.

Greer, Ian, and Lou Jean Fleron. 2005. Labor and regional development in the USA: Building a high road Infrastructure in Buffalo, New York. *International Journal of Action Research* 1 (2): 219–42.

Habunda, Janice L. 2010. Charter school prepares students for jobs in health care field. *Buffalo News*. August 9.

Haines, Pamela, and Gary Klein. 1982. Citizens and unions respond. In *Community and capital in conflict: Plant closings and job loss*, ed. John C. Raines, Lenora E. Berson, and David McI. Gracie, 234–54. Philadelphia: Temple University Press.

Harrison, Bennett, and Barry Bluestone. 1990. *The great u-turn: Corporate restructuring and the polarizing of America*. New York: Basic Books.

Heckscher, Charles, and Francoise Carre. 2006. Strength in networks: Employment rights organizations and the problem of coordination. *British Journal of Industrial Relations* 44 (4): 605–28.

Hoxie, Robert F. 1917. *Trade unionism in the United States*. New York: D. Appleton and Company.

Human Resources Development Institute. 1998. *Economic development: A union guide to the high road*. Washington, DC: AFL-CIO.

Hyman, Richard. 1996. Changing union identities in Europe. In *The challenges to trade unions in Europe: Innovation or adaptation?* Ed. Peter Leisink, Jim Van Leemput, and Jaques Vilrokx, 53–73. Cheltenham, UK: Edward Elgar.

Institute for Local Governance and Regional Growth. 2006. State of the region: Regional overview. http://regional-institute.buffalo.edu/sotr/regi_over_popu.cfm (accessed June 25, 2009).

Jacobs, David C. 1987. The UAW and the Committee for National Health Insurance: The contours of social unionism. *Advances in Industrial and Labor Relations* 4: 119–40.
Karson, Tom. 2004. Confronting Houston's demographic shift: The Harris County AFL-CIO. *WorkingUSA* 8 (2): 207–27.
King, Bob. 2009. Remarks at the Labor and Employment Relations Association National Policy Forum, June 11, 2009. Notes transcribed by the author.
Kirzner, Ken. 2006. Expansion management magazine publishes its 8th annual "America's 50 hottest cities" ranking. *Expansion management* press release. January 25. http://www.expansionmanagement.com/cmd/articledetail/articleid/16977/default.asp (accessed June 26, 2009).
Klingel, Sally, and Ann Martin, eds. 1988. *A fighting chance: New strategies to save jobs and reduce costs*. Ithaca, NY: ILR Press.
Kuhnhenn, Jim. 2008. Obama stimulus package could top $800B. *NorthJersey.com*. December 18. http://www.northjersey.com/news/nation/36362679.html (accessed June 26, 2009).
Leone, Richard, Michael F. Eely, David W. Watkins, and Joel E. Gershenfeld. 1982. *The operation of area labor-management committees*. Washington, DC: U.S. Department of Labor, Labor-Management Services Administration.
Lipsig-Mumme, Carla. 2003. Forms of solidarity: Trade unions and community unionism. Published online by the Australian Council of Trade Unions. May 9. http://www.actu.asn.au/ecc/news/1053579943_13456.html (accessed June 26, 2009).
Lipsitz, Richard. 2006. Interview with the author. June 22.
Lipsitz, Richard. 2008. Interview with the author. December 20.
Luce, Stephanie. 2004. What happens after laws pass? Implementing and monitoring living wage ordinances. *Perspectives on Work* 8 (1): 37–39.
Lynch, Lisa. 2009. Labor market policy reform during economic crisis. PowerPoint slides prepared for presentation before the Labor and Employment Relations Association National Policy Forum. June 12.
Lynd, Staughton. 1983. *The fight against shutdowns: Youngstown's steel mill closings*. San Pedro, CA: Singlejack Books.
Mackin, Christopher. 2001. Employee ownership: A primer for industrial relations. *Perspectives on Work* 5 (2): 5–9.
Maguire, Matthew. 2002. Study: Manufacturing still matters to New York economy, especially upstate, and new state policies can help it thrive. News release of The Business Council of New York State, Inc. September 17. http://www.bcnys.org/whatsnew/2002/0916mfg2.htm (accessed June 26, 2009).
Merrill, Theresa. 1997. *Reflections on progress at work*. Buffalo, NY: Cornell University School of Industrial and Labor Relations.
Meyer, Brian. 1999. WNY needs a "killer" slogan, marketers tell BNE. *Buffalo News*. July 17.
Miller, Robert W., and Frederick A. Zeller. 1991. Critical factors in the successful development of an area labor-management committee. *Employer Responsibilities and Rights Journal* 4 (3): 215–30.
Moses, Jamie, and Peter Koch. 2005. Buffalo schools, part II: Kids out in the cold. *Artvoice* 4 (49). December 8. http://artvoice.com/issues/v4n49/buffalo_schools (accessed June 26, 2009).
Ness, Immanuel. 2005. Community labor alliances: Organizing greengrocery workers in New York City. In *The new urban migrant workforce: Innovative models for*

labor organizing, ed. Sarumathi Jayaraman and Immanuel Ness, 57–70. Armonk, NY: M. E. Sharpe.

Ness, Immanuel, and Stuart Eimer, eds. 2001. *Central labor councils and the revival of American unionism*. Armonk, NY: M. E. Sharpe.

Nissen, Bruce. 2000. Living wage campaigns from a "social movement" perspective: The Miami case. *Labor Studies Journal* 25 (3): 29–50.

Nissen, Bruce. 2004. The effectiveness and limits of labor-community coalitions: Evidence from South Florida. *Labor Studies Journal* 29 (1): 67–89.

Palumbo, George P., and Mark P. Zaporowski. 1999. The economic outlook for the Buffalo region. *Western New York Economic News* 2 (2). http://www.canisius.edu/images/userImages/creans/Page_8187/wnyen2.doc (accessed June 26, 2009).

Parker, Eric. 2004. Workforce development and family-supporting jobs: The Wisconsin Regional Training Partnership. *Perspectives on Work* 8 (1): 7–9.

Pataki, George. 2004. Low-cost hydropower to help create 245 new WNY jobs. Governor's press release. January 27. http://www.ny.gov/governor/press/04/jan27_04.htm (accessed October 21, 2006; no longer available – author has printed copy).

Pierce, Morris A. 2008. Opportunity for Vermont clean energy development fund grant. Economic Development Group, Inc. Draft report. September 15.

Pollin, Robert, James Heintz, and Heidi Garrett-Peltier. 2009. The economic benefits of investing in clean energy: How the economic stimulus program and new legislation can boost U.S. economic growth and employment. Political Economy Research Institute, University of Massachusetts, Amherst. http://www.peri.umass.edu/236/hash/cb09819d9c/ publication/350/ (accessed June 29, 2009).

Pollin, Robert, Jeannette Wicks-Lim, and Heidi Garrett-Peltier. 2009. Green prosperity: How clean-energy policies can fight poverty and raise living standards in the United States. Political Economy Research Institute, University of Massachusetts, Amherst. http://www.peri.umass.edu/236/hash/f6ce6c3f78/publication/349/ (accessed June 29, 2009).

President's Commission on Industrial Competitiveness. 1985. *Global competition: The new reality*, vol. 1. Washington, DC: U.S. Government Printing Office.

Reynolds, David B. 2002. *Taking the high road: Communities organize for economic change*. Armonk, NY: M. E. Sharpe.

Reynolds, David B., ed. 2004. *Partnering for change: Unions and community groups build coalitions for economic justice*. Armonk, NY: M.E. Sharpe.

Reynolds, David B. 2009. Challenges in the spread of regional power building. *WorkingUSA* 12 (1): 1–6.

Reynolds, David B., and Jen Kern. 2001–2002. Labor and the living wage movement. *WorkingUSA* 5 (3): 17–45.

Reynolds, David B., and Immanuel Ness. 2004. Labor builds regional power. *WorkingUSA* 8 (2): 123–29.

Rhee, Nari. 2004. Living wage jobs and quality of life: The community benefits initiative in San Jose. *Perspectives on Work Online* 1 (Fall). http://www.lera.uiuc.edu/Pubs/Perspectives/onlinecompanion/fall04-rhee.html (accessed June 26, 2009).

Rhee, Nari, and Julie A. Sadler. 2007. Building an inclusive city: Labor-community coalitions and the struggle for urban power in San Jose. In *Labor in the new urban battlegrounds: Local solidarity in a global economy*, ed. Lowell Turner and Daniel B. Cornfield, 178–90. Ithaca, NY: Cornell University Press.

Robinson, Archie. 1981. *George Meany and his times*. New York: Simon & Schuster.

Rogers, Joel. 1994. Sustainable Milwaukee: A community strategy for high-wage, low-waste, democratic economic development. Paper submitted to the

Rockefeller Foundation on behalf of the Center on Wisconsin Strategy, University of Wisconsin-Madison.
Saltzman, Michael. 2005. NYPA files application for a new license for the Niagara Project reflecting participation of area communities. New York State Power Authority news release. August 18. http://www.nypa.gov/press/2005/050818a.htm (accessed June 26, 2009).
Saltzman, Michael. 2007. New 50-year license for Niagara Power Project, now effective, signifies substantial new benefits for region. New York State Power Authority news release. September 6. http://www.nypa.gov/press/2007/070906a.htm (accessed June 26, 2009).
Shantz, Jeff. 2009. The limits of social unionism in Canada. *WorkingUSA* 12 (1): 113–29.
Schurman, Susan J. 2008–2009. Creating organizational change through leadership education: The AFL-CIO State and Local Labor Federations Leadership Institute. *Perspectives on Work* 12 (1–2): 9–11.
Starner, Ron. 2005. Southern comfort. *Site Selection Magazine*. May. http://www.siteselection.com/issues/2005/may/p250/ (accessed June 26, 2009).
Tejada, Carlos. 2000. Work week. *Wall Street Journal*. September 26.
Tattersall, Amada. 2008a. Common themes in community unionism in industrialized countries: Lessons from long-term coalitions in Australia and Canada. *Illawarra Unity, Journal of the Illawarra Branch of the Australian Society for the Study of Labour History* 8 (1): 43–68.
Tattersall, Amada. 2008b. A little help from our friends: Exploring and understanding when labor-community coalitions are likely to form. *Labor Studies Journal*. December 30. OnlineFirst.
Turner, Lowell, and Daniel B. Cornfield, eds. 2007. *Labor in the new urban battlegrounds: Local solidarity in a global economy*. Ithaca, NY: Cornell University Press.
Turner, Lowell, Harry C. Katz, and Richard W. Hurd, eds. 2001. *Rekindling the movement: Labor's quest for relevance in the twenty-first century*. Ithaca, NY: ILR Press.
Whalen, Charles J. 1987. Consensus mechanisms and community development: The Buffalo experience. *Journal of Economic Issues* 21 (2): 763–74.
Wheeler, Hoyt. 2004. Producers of the world unite! A return of reformist unionism? *Labor Studies Journal* 29 (3): 81–100.
Whyte, William Foote, Tove Helland Hammer, Christopher B. Meek, Reed Nelson, and Robert N. Stern. 1983. *Worker participation and ownership*. Ithaca, NY: ILR Press.
Wial, Howard. 1992–1993. The emerging organizational structure of unionism in low-wage services. *Rutgers Law Review* 45: 631–738.
Williams, Fred O. 1999. Labor group urges state lawmakers to preserve cheap power for local firms. *Buffalo News*. September 17.
Williams, Fred O. 2000. A bright side to unions. *Buffalo News*. October 1.
Wisconsin Regional Training Partnership. 2009. About us; history – WRTP timeline. http://www.wrtp.org (accessed June 26, 2009).
Woods, Susan, Bill Ganley, Chuck Smith, and Susan Davis. 1991. *Case studies in cooperative labor-management relations: Examples in Western New York*. Buffalo, NY: Cornell University School of Industrial and Labor Relations.
Woodworth, Warner, Christopher Meek, and William Foote Whyte, eds. 1985. *Industrial democracy: Strategies for community revitalization*. Beverly Hills, CA: Sage Publications.

Working Partnership USA. 2008. Current projects: Accountable development. http://www.wpusa.org/Focus-Areas/govCurrentProjects.htm (accessed June 26, 2009).

Zieger, Robert H. 1995. *The CIO, 1935–1955*. Chapel Hill: The University of North Carolina Press.

10. Full employment with liberty: John R. Commons's perspective and its continuing relevance

On June 10, 2009, Paul Krugman delivered a lecture at the London School of Economics. Most of it focused on John Maynard Keynes's contribution to understanding the Great Depression (Krugman 2009). According to Krugman, *The General Theory of Employment, Interest and Money* helped economists understand and solve the most pressing problem of the early 1930s — mass unemployment.

Krugman suggests Keynes broke three barriers preventing the economics profession from addressing widespread joblessness. One was its belief that "supply creates its own demand," which suggests a Great Depression could not be possible. Another was business cycle analysis, which obscured the study of depressions in the early 1930s on both sides of the Atlantic. "Economists obsessed with the ups and downs of investment, but skipped the step of explaining why the point at which people realize they overextended themselves leads to mass unemployment." The third was the apparent inability of institutional economics to provide a clear strategy for economic recovery despite being the most influential school of U.S. economic thought at the onset of the Great Depression. Keynes moved economics forward by disengaging the analysis of depressions from the broader cycle, demonstrating that the level of spending in an economy could fall short of that needed to make full use of productive capacity, and instructing policymakers to "turn this dial — increase G [government spending]" (Krugman 2009).

Most institutionalists would probably agree with Krugman that Keynes's contributions were helpful in the 1930s and remain useful today as economies around the globe seek to address what journalists have dubbed the Great Recession. There is also no denying that John R. Commons's 900-page, *Institutional Economics* — which addresses a range of topics including business cycles and mass unemployment — may be an excellent example of the pre-*General Theory* literature that Krugman (2009) described as "impenetrable" and of which

Reprinted with permission from *Journal of Economic Issues* 44 (2), June 2010, 559–568.

he said, "[i]t makes you want to bang your head on the table." Nevertheless, Commons's contribution on the subject of high unemployment is worth deciphering, and that is the purpose of this article. It also underscores the continuing relevance of Commons's perspective, which extends beyond "increase G" in important ways. While a severe page constraint adds to the formidability of the task, it also provides an opportunity to show institutionalism can address unemployment with clarity and concision.

Still, why dig through the writings of Commons, especially a book that begins by acknowledging "perhaps nobody" (Commons 1934a, 1) will grasp the author's message? And why should others take interest in this effort? One reason is that, as Krugman (2009) acknowledges and Keynes recognized, economists must eventually return to business cycle analysis — and, given the severity and consequences of the most recent global financial crisis, the sooner the better. Another reason is we know Commons had important insights. Indeed, Kates (2009) suggests Commons contributed key ideas used by Keynes when overturning Say's Law. The article is also motivated by recognition that even Keynes needed interpreters: As Krugman (2009) observes in his lecture, "[m]y generation mostly encountered Keynes refracted through John Hicks."

THE CASE FOR SAVING CAPITALISM

Commons saw unemployment as the "outstanding defect of capitalism" (Lewisohn et al. 1925, 52). He also considered the business cycle the most important cause of unemployment (Commons 1922). Nevertheless, he was unwilling to reject capitalism because he saw it as the only alternative that retains a meaningful degree of individual liberty and the hope of high living standards. In *Institutional Economics*, published in 1934, Commons stresses that "capitalism is not a single or static concept," and in his autobiography, published that same year, he writes that the central aim of his research for nearly thirty years was to "save capitalism by making it good" (Commons 1934a, 766; 1934b, 143).

Commons divides world economic history into three stages: scarcity, abundance, and stabilization. The era of abundance begins with the industrial revolution in the eighteenth century. But the period also ushers in business cycles, destructive ("cut-throat") competition, labor strife, and large-scale unemployment. Although classical economics had no place for widespread overproduction and joblessness, the problems had become undeniable and resulted in emergence of the era of stabilization in the late nineteenth century (Commons 1925a, 95–120; 1934a, 773–789, 892).

In the era of stabilization, business and government developed various approaches designed to achieve and sustain a recovery in economic production.

Efforts to promote a "managed" recovery replaced reliance on the "automatic" method of price-system adjustment. At first, the private sector led the way through cartels, investment banks and holding companies. By the mid-1930s, however, the public sector had taken the lead in major nations across the globe (Commons 1934a, 611–612; 1925b).

Communism and fascism were very real alternatives to capitalism in the 1930s. They also promised — indeed, demonstrated — an ability to cure joblessness. But Commons rejected both.

What troubled Commons most about communism and fascism was they required citizens to sacrifice key political, civil-rights and economic dimensions of individual liberty to achieve employment security. In the political realm, restrictions were imposed to severely constrain — and often prohibit — popular elections, involvement in political parties, and representative government. In fact, in such societies, legislatures were abolished and judges were appointed and removed by dictators, replacing the rule of law with that of the iron fist. In the realm of civil rights, freedom of speech, the press and association — including the right to join labor unions and farmers' cooperatives — were all curtailed; "compulsory membership in regulated associations" replaced participation in voluntary associations. And in the realm of economic freedom, individuals were prohibited from withholding property and labor from the market in search of a satisfactory bargain. Transactions were instead coerced, and although citizens were employed they were most often also poor, a condition which itself "deprives people of economic liberty," argued Commons (1934a, 898–903).

Meanwhile, a number of factors contributed to economic liberty in the United States in the early twentieth century. One was the opportunity for many wage earners to "take up free land or return to their families on the farms when capitalistic industry collapsed."[1] Another was the opportunity for promotion within the ranks of American industry on the basis of demonstrated ability and ambition. ("Europe has not yet learned this trick of promotion. Class feeling keeps the manual worker in his inferior class, and the higher executives come in from the families of privileged and educated classes," Commons wrote.) A third factor was that the nation's various freedoms provided a thriving climate for individual originality and genius — in the arts, sciences, engineering, journalism, and all fields within the academy. Indeed, while Commons was critical of aspects of the "banker capitalism" that he observed in the United States in the 1930s, opportunities for worker advancement and free investigation help explain why he wrote, "[i]t is probable that huge corporations do not grow so much by Marx's technological efficiency as by the booms and depressions of banker capitalism" (Commons 1934a, 886–891).

The American system's ability to generate abundance is a key element in Commons's analysis. "The fundamental contrast between the European and American systems is the contrast of poverty with abundance, of low standards of living with high standards of living," he wrote in *Institutional Economics* (1934a, 886). Commons credits America's high living standards with providing an important reason why the bulk of U.S. citizens remained wedded to the preservation of capitalism in the early 1930s despite the nation's history of macroeconomic instability. The U.S. economy's capacity to produce the output that permitted those high standards — that is, its capacity to deliver a key aspect of economic liberty — also helps explain his preference for saving capitalism rather than replacing it (Commons 1934a, 886–887).

Commons's strategy for saving capitalism — for achieving and sustaining full employment with liberty — can be treated as having three dimensions: financial, human and political. Each is discussed below. A fourth component could also be identified, a conceptual dimension devoted to economic theory. But Commons never developed theory in a vacuum; he incorporated it into the examination and resolution of real-world problems. This article follows his lead.[2]

MONEY

Saving capitalism must begin with the financial system argued Commons, who viewed the ability to finance large corporations and new inventions as capitalism's main strength. "The banks float the securities of the corporations and arrange commercial credits," Commons wrote, but there is still more to the story; they must also gain the confidence of millions of investors (Commons 1934a, 890). In fact, when searching for the ultimate source of wealth in capitalist society, Commons did not settle upon labor, management or machinery, but on "confidence in the future" (Commons 1921, 268). Thus, financial-market protections — laws regulating the issue and sale of financial instruments to protect investors from corrupt practices and foster confidence in financial markets — are considered essential to a sustained recovery from Commons's perspective (Commons 1934a, 887–891).

Commons supported expansionary monetary policy during an economic downturn, but also argued that preventing future unemployment involves requiring the Federal Reserve to pursue a policy of stabilizing the rate of inflation once the economy recovers (Commons 1934a, 804–805). In Krugman's brand of Keynesian economics, government spending can be used to restore full employment and then economists and policymakers can return to the issues and tools of conventional microeconomics (Krugman 2009). From Commons's business-cycle perspective, however, preventive measures are needed to control the overall extension of credit and the rise in prices during prosperous times; if not, credit will be overextended and another crisis will eventually emerge. Commons (1934a, 611) added: "It is more difficult, by concerted action, to start a recovery from a long period of depression than it is, by similar action, to stop an inflation that causes the succeeding deflation." He maintained that pursuit of such price stabilization would cause the Federal Reserve to influence the supply, demand and price of credit in at least four ways: through the discount rate, open-market operations, moral suasion, and international concerted action (Commons 1934a, 789–805; 1922, 19–21; 1925c).

A broad diffusion of stock ownership — and of personal investment instruments, such as savings accounts and insurance policies — is also part of Commons's strategy for saving capitalism. A nation with millions of shareholders would, of course, be less attracted to alternative economic systems, but there are also economic benefits. For example, the diffusion helps stabilize stock-market values and augment business capital, suggested Commons (1934a, 887–890).

The continuing relevance of the financial dimension of Commons's recovery and reform agenda is unmistakable. His call for strict financial-market regulation, for example, appears as fresh as today's headlines.

Today, Tymoigne (2009, 17) proposes a "proactive regulatory framework" in response to the recent global financial crisis. He offers the following principles as a guide to financial-system regulatory reform: 1) manage innovations ("not all innovations are good"); 2) modify views of creditworthiness to accommodate a cash-flow view (default probability asks, "Will you pay?" but a cash-flow view asks, "*How* will you pay?"); 3) realign the financial sector with the broader needs of the economy (reward long-term performance, for example); and 4) devote more attention to systemic risk (via national cash-flow accounting and detection of Ponzi-type activity). These principles have the same aim as Commons's call for regulation of investment instruments; they seek to channel the profit motive in a direction that fosters investor confidence and a more sustainable financial system (see also Commons 1935). A proposal by the U.S. Treasury Department (2009) also reflects this spirit and is even more comprehensive.[3]

Although price increases are not currently a major U.S. economic concern, Commons's version of inflation targeting, which would take effect only after restoration of full employment, also remains relevant. Rather than seek price-level control in a rigid manner and for its own sake, Commons sought only broad stabilization of the "general credit situation" and the aim was to avoid price-level fluctuations that would eventually disrupt investment and employment (Commons 1925c, 45; 1937). This amounts to a proactive monetary-policy framework that dovetails with the just-mentioned regulatory framework. Moreover, with Commons's ends as a guide, there is little doubt that a modern version of his approach to monetary policy would include stabilization of asset price inflation — to prevent run-ups in, for instance, the market for stocks or real estate.

Commons devoted little attention to broadly extending an investment stake in the economy, but even the mention of it puts him ahead of many contemporary economists. President George W. Bush often spoke of fostering an "ownership society," but Jacob S. Hacker (2006, 6) demonstrates that this was largely the gloss on a "great risk shift" that transferred financial burdens from corporations and government to "the fragile balance sheets of American families." Nevertheless, broader ownership has been investigated by a number of serious scholars and practitioners (see for example, Ashford and Shakespeare (1999), Ackerman and Alstott (1999), and Gates (1998)). The potential civic and economic benefits — including those mentioned by Commons — indicate it deserves greater consideration from today's institutionalists.

PEOPLE

Turning from the financial to the human aspects of Commons's effort to make capitalism "good," one finds that he calls for the following policy initiatives: direct government spending to tackle joblessness, a public unemployment insurance program financed in part by a tax on employers that would increase with the tendency to discharge workers (called "experience rating"), and legislation protecting workers (via minimum wages and maximum hours, for instance) and trade unionism (Commons 1934a). Each of his recommendations was incorporated into the New Deal, not just to assist workers directly, but also to aid recovery by boosting and stabilizing aggregate demand. It is particularly notable that Commons looked to fiscal policy in the way Keynes would later make famous:

> To create the consumer demand, on which business depends for sales, the government itself must create the new money and go completely over the head of the entire banking system by paying it out directly to the unemployed, either as relief or for construction of public works. (Commons 1934a, 589–590)

In the current Great Recession, Commons's recommendations continue to provide assistance. The American Recovery and Reinvestment Act of 2009 rests on the Commons-Keynes view of the need for fiscal stimulus. The value of unemployment insurance (UI) with an experience rating has been demonstrated by Anderson and Meyer (2000), who analyze past state policy variations and show that the rating system reduces UI claims; this suggests unemployment today would be even more severe without the policy Commons promoted. The minimum wage and collective bargaining also help contain the severity of the downturn.

Commons's perspective also leads us to additional insights. For example, it underscores the potential macroeconomic benefit of labor-law reform that reduces some of the current obstacles to worker organizing and collective bargaining. It also draws attention to the value of the following: proposals that would call on the government to serve as employer of last resort (Kaboub 2007); the comprehensive human-resource development strategies inspired by Vernon Briggs (Whalen 2010); and the initiatives of the Obama administration's Middle Class Task Force, which aims to protect the incomes of America's working families and retirees.

POLITICS

Finally, there is what Commons considered the biggest challenge to capitalism, freedom, and democracy: the difficulty of restraining the power of the "high-salaried executives and political machines" of the banking establishment. Near the end of *Institutional Economics*, Commons writes that American banker capitalism "is an economic government of bankers more powerful than the political government. Its sanctions are not the physical force of the state — they are the more powerful sanctions of credit, profit and loss" (Commons 1934, 895–903). It is remarkable how his concerns resonate in our time.

Skepticism over the appropriateness and implementation of the $700 billion Troubled Asset Relief Program is just the tip of the iceberg. In the 1990s, Minsky (1996) warned of the arrival of "money-manager capitalism." Others have used different terms, including "plutocracy" (Phillips 2002), "plutonomy" (Frank 2007), and oligarchic "corporatism" (Brooks 2008). Thomas Palley (2007) and Krugman (2009) call it "financialization," a process whereby the markets, institutions, and elites of the financial sector acquire tremendous influence over public policy and economic outcomes. Regardless of its name, however, all agree the trend is accompanied by widening U.S. inequality and an erosion of the living standards of many working families. The high living standards of a democratic capitalism are threatened in our time as in that of Commons.

Commons saw only one solution: processes that give voice to representatives of diverse economic interests must shape the nation's policies. For example, he long maintained that an advisory committee containing elected representatives of all economic stakeholders should guide the Federal Reserve. Could it work in the 1930s? On the one hand, Commons looked at the Italian experience with proportional representation of economic interests and saw failure. On the other hand, he looked to countless American administrative commissions and observed that the most effective operate with the help of a diverse, stakeholder advisory committee (Commons 1934a, 900–901).

Can it be done today? Not without much effort, especially since U.S. workers are largely unorganized. The challenges are exacerbated by the global scope of labor, product and financial markets. Nevertheless, Commons's vision of full employment with liberty offers the hope of greater macroeconomic stability and unrivaled abundance. Even the establishment should find that attractive.

NOTES

1. In the mid 1930s, Commons (1934a, 886) recognized "farms are less and less a refuge for the unemployed," which underscored the need to foster full employment via managed recovery.
2. Two notes on Commons's theories are warranted. First, Commons develops and applies a variety of theories in his books and essays, including a general theory of economic transactions, a theory of reasonable value, theories of world history and capitalist development, a theory of labor movements, a transactional theory (rather than a quantity theory) of money, and a profit-margin theory of business cycles; see, for example, Atkinson (2004) and Whalen (1989; 1993). Second, institutionalists like Commons saw no need for a formal theory to explain why a loss of business confidence leads to large-scale unemployment because they operated from the vantage point of what Dudley Dillard (1987), drawing on Keynes, calls a monetary theory of production. It recognizes not only that production precedes exchange, but also that finance precedes production. Finance is based on a mere expectation of returns, and when expectations are disappointed anywhere in the economy a loss of confidence can sweep through the system, cutting off credit. Without financing, production eventually (often quickly) grinds to a halt, workers are discharged, and fewer goods and services are available for purchase.
3. *Financial Regulatory Reform: A New Foundation* is organized around the following goals: 1) Promote robust supervision and regulation of financial firms; 2) establish comprehensive supervision of financial markets [including enhanced regulation of securitization markets and comprehensive regulation of over-the-counter derivatives]; 3) protect consumers and investors from financial abuse; 4) provide the government with the tools to manage financial crises; and 5) raise international regulatory standards and improve international cooperation (U.S. Treasury 2009, 3–4).

REFERENCES

Ackerman, Bruce and Anne Alstott. *The Stakeholder Society*. New Haven: Yale University Press, 1999.

Anderson, Patricia and Bruce Meyer. "The Effects of the Unemployment Insurance Payroll Tax on Wages, Employment, Claims and Denials." *Journal of Public Economics* 78, 1–2 (2000): 81–106.

Ashford, Robert and Rodney Shakespeare. *Binary Economics*. Lanham, MD: University Press of America, 1999.

Atkinson, Glen. "Labor and the Menace of Competition." In *The Institutionalist Tradition in Labor Economics*, edited by Dell P. Champlin and Janet T. Knoedler, pp. 39–49. Armonk, NY: M.E. Sharpe, 2004.

Brooks, David. "The Establishment Lives!" *The New York Times*, September 23, 2008. http://www.nytimes.com/2008/09/23/opinion/23brooks.html. Accessed December 5, 2009.

Commons, John R. *Industrial Government*. New York: Macmillan, 1921.

———. "Unemployment Prevention." *American Labor Legislation Review* 12, 1 (1922): 15–24.

———. *Reasonable Value*. Ann Arbor: Edwards Brothers, 1925a. Contains the typeset notation: To Be Revised.

———. "Marx Today: Capitalism and Socialism." *The Atlantic Monthly* 136, November (1925b): 682–693.

———. "The Stabilization of Prices and Business." *American Economic Review* 15, 1 (1925c): 43–52.

———. *Institutional Economics: Its Place in Political Economy*. New York: Macmillan, 1934a.

———. *Myself*. New York: Macmillan, 1934b.

———. Review of *Capitalism and Its Culture*, by Jerome C. Davis. *American Economic Review* 25, 3 (1935): 491–492.

———. "Capacity to Produce, Capacity to Consume, Capacity to Pay Debts." *American Economic Review* 27, 4 (1937): 680–697.

Dillard, Dudley. "Money as an Institution of Capitalism." *Journal of Economic Issues* 21, 4 (1987): 1623–1647.

Frank, Robert. "Plutonomics." *The Wall Street Journal*, WSJ Blogs, The Wealth Report, January 8, 2007. http://blogs.wsj.com/wealth/2007/01/08/plutonomics/. Accessed December 5, 2009.

Gates, Jeff. *The Ownership Solution*. Reading, MA: Addison-Wesley, 1998.

Hacker, Jacob S. *The Great Risk Shift*. New York: Oxford University Press, 2006.

Kaboub, Fadhel. "Institutional Adjustment Planning for Full Employment." *Journal of Economic Issues* 41, 2 (2007): 495–502.

Kates, Steven. "Subverting Say's Law: Keynes, Commons and Harlan McCracken." Twenty-Second Conference of the History of Economic Thought Society of Australia, July 10, 2009. http://hetsa2009.com/abstracts_index.html. Accessed December 4, 2009.

Krugman, Paul. "The Return of Depression Economics: The Night They Reread Minsky." Lionel Robbins Lecture, London School of Economics, June 10, 2009. http://cep.lse.ac.uk/_new/interviews/ default.asp. Accessed December 4, 2009.

Lewisohn, Sam A., Ernest G. Draper, John R. Commons and Don D. Lescohier. *Can Business Prevent Unemployment?* New York: Alfred A. Knopf, 1925.

Minsky, Hyman P. "Uncertainty and the Institutional Structure of Capitalist Economies." *Journal of Economic Issues* 30, 2 (1996): 357–368.

Palley, Thomas. "Financialization: What It Is and Why It Matters." Working Paper No. 525. Annandale-on-Hudson, NY: The Levy Economics Institute of Bard College, 2007.

Phillips, Kevin. *Wealth and Democracy*. New York: Broadway, 2002.

Tymoigne, Eric. "Securitization, Deregulation, Economic Stability, and Financial Crisis." PowerPoint slides. Allied Social Science Associations Annual Meeting, San Francisco, CA. January 4, 2009.

U.S. Treasury Department. *Financial Regulatory Reform: A New Foundation.* Washington, DC: Department of the Treasury, 2009.

Whalen, Charles J. "John R. Commons's Institutional Economics: A Re-examination." *Journal of Economic Issues* 23, 2 (1989): 443–454.

———. "Saving Capitalism by Making It Good: The Monetary Economics of John R. Commons." *Journal of Economic Issues* 27, 4 (1993): 1155–1179.

——— (ed.). *Human Resource Economics and Public Policy: Essays in Honor of Vernon M. Briggs Jr.* Kalamazoo, MI: W.E. Upjohn Institute for Employment Research, 2010.

11. Human resources: the key to institutional economics after the Great Recession

INTRODUCTION

In the wake of the recent global financial crisis, many economists have asked what went wrong, how can economists do a better job of anticipating or preventing financial trouble in the future, and how can economic theory better incorporate financial institutions into macroeconomics? Addressing those questions is appropriate, and this author has even led one inquiry of that sort (Whalen, 2011).

But learning from the global financial crisis and what has become widely known in the USA as the Great Recession must involve more than recognizing what can go wrong. It must also involve learning as the crisis winds down and as the economy moves into the recovery phase and then into the next expansion. If, as is almost certain, the jobs that will be required in that expansion will be different and often even in different places from where they were before, then unless we take these issues into account we will not have properly or fully addressed the recession problem. This chapter leaves a retrospective analysis of the downturn to others and instead takes an institutional economist's perspective on what we can learn from how the crisis was brought to a close.

From an institutionalist perspective, resolving the Great Recession required a two-pronged strategy: recovery and reform. The recovery agenda included monetary stimulus and expansionary fiscal policy to stabilize aggregate demand, Federal Reserve (Fed) 'lender-of-last-resort' action to stabilize financial markets, and temporary financial market policies to address dimensions of the Great Recession that required more extensive intervention. The reform agenda included financial regulatory reform, a national commitment to the challenges facing USA's working families, and US participation in efforts that promote

Reprinted with permission from S. Kates (ed.), *The Global Financial Crisis: What Have We Learnt?* (Edward Elgar, 2011), 204–217.

international economic stability and job creation (Whalen, 2010a). Most of this was addressed by US policy-makers in response to the recent crisis, but a key part was given short shrift in both the recovery and reform agendas: the part focusing on working families.

Writing in *Macroeconomic Theory and Its Failings* (*MTIF*), the precursor to the current volume, this author stressed that 'the overarching policy objective should be greater macroeconomic stability and *broadly shared prosperity* in the USA and abroad' (Whalen, 2010a: 250, emphasis added). This is consistent with the view he expressed in an essay co-written in the mid-1990s with the late Hyman Minsky. They wrote:

> In the current era, economic success requires more than economic growth, low unemployment and minimal inflation. It requires that every citizen has the opportunity to develop and utilize his or her talents and capacities, and it requires an economy that rewards workers with rising standards of living and the prospect of an even better life for their children. (Minsky and Whalen, 1996: 161)

In the institutionalist reform agenda presented in *MTIF*, attention to issues affecting American workers and their families was impossible to miss, but the recovery agenda was also supposed to help millions of American families by reducing unemployment and resolving the mortgage crisis.

As the Great Recession wound down in late 2009, however, unemployment rose to 10 per cent (nearly hitting its post-war peak) and stayed above 9 per cent into mid-2010 as this chapter was written. Meanwhile, the federal effort to address the mortgage problem remained inadequate – indeed, an independent bank analyst called it a 'dud' (Puzzanghera, 2010). Thus, what resolution of the global financial crisis and Great Recession reveals is that the recovery and expansion ahead are shaping up to look like the previous expansion, which left most middle-class and working families behind (Weller, 2006).

How should institutionalism respond? In the wake of the Great Recession, among the most promising ways forward for institutional economists involves focusing on what American institutionalist Vernon M. Briggs calls *human resource economics* (HRE). HRE is a policy-oriented field that views human resources as the key to economic progress and personal development and is one that is frequently ignored and neglected. It also puts the attention of economics squarely on workers, their capacities and contributions, and their well-being.

This chapter explores the emergence, evolution and contemporary relevance of HRE. Following the lead of Briggs, a pioneer in HRE, the discussion of contemporary relevance has five dimensions: labor supply and demand, workforce quality, employment opportunities, personal development, and international well-being. HRE offers insights for dealing with future downturns, but is also relevant to preparing adequately for future expansions.[1]

A DISTINCT FIELD

Economists and politicians have long pointed to human resources as the source of national strength and prosperity. Adam Smith ([1776] 1935: 734) put worker 'skill, dexterity and judgment' at the heart of his explanation for the wealth of nations, and other economists followed his lead. As a result, the labor theory of value was a cornerstone of classical economics.

Despite that long history, HRE emerged as a distinct field within economics only in the wake of World War II. The breakthrough came when post-war economists conducted research to explain economic progress in industrialized nations. Their research demonstrated that the human resources side of the resource base has 'enormous implications for national and international well-being' (Briggs, 1987).

Yet the story of HRE does not begin entirely after World War II. That is because institutional economist John R. Commons (1862–1945) provides HRE with vital intellectual grounding. Commons responded to the economic booms and depressions of the early twentieth century by forging a 'third way' between laissez-faire and a planned economy (Whalen, 2008a: 45). HRE takes that path as its starting point.

The centerpiece of this 'third way' is pragmatic reform. Commons believed that economic and human adjustment problems are an inevitable part of the advance of industrialization. Thus, he concluded that social institutions and public policy have to evolve to deal with the changing circumstances. There is no utopia beyond a dynamic, 'reasonable' and harmonious society. In short, Commons put the aim of practical problem-solving at the heart of institutional economics, and this is where HRE gets its reformist bent.

GROWTH AND STABILIZATION

HRE emerged from the post-war work of labor economists influenced by institutional economics. It originated with research on the relationship between human resources and economic growth. But these labor economists soon realized that human resource development could also play a constructive role in addressing other difficult economic issues, including stabilization of employment, output and prices.[2]

A starting point for HRE is *Education, Manpower, and Economic Growth*, by Frederick H. Harbison and Charles A. Myers (1964).[3] It examined 75 countries on the basis of a composite human-resource development index and compared those findings with national indicators of economic development and growth. Its main conclusion was that nations could make the greatest strides in growth and development by crafting and implementing a coherent strategy for human resource development. According to Harbison and Myers, that strategy would set clear priorities for an economic agenda that recognizes and reflects broad social goals, not merely narrow economic objectives.

The link between human resources and aggregate economic growth has remained a focal point for HRE. For example, Briggs demonstrated in 1987 that although much post-war economic research assumed physical capital was the main source of productivity increases and long-term growth, human resource development was actually the major contributor. 'It is a fact of economic life that deserves prominence in policy formulation', concluded Briggs (1987: 1213–14). This emphasis continues to influence the work of US human resource economists such as Robert Glover and Christopher King (2010), and on a global scale it drives the human development research agenda of the United Nations, which has kept attention on the matter for over two decades in its reports on human development (United Nations Development Program, 2010).

HRE also emerged as economists began to grapple with structural unemployment in the 1960s. Careful observers of the early post-World War II economy noted that the average US unemployment rate was rising with each successive period of cyclical prosperity. This 'creeping prosperity unemployment' triggered a debate among economists over whether structural economic change posed a growing problem (Marshall and Briggs, 1989: 590).

The two economists at the center of this debate were Walter Heller, President John Kennedy's chief economic adviser, and Charles Killingsworth, a professor at Michigan State University. Heller argued that expansionary fiscal policy, in the form of a tax cut proposed by Kennedy, would be sufficient to reduce unemployment. Killingsworth countered that an increasing proportion of unemployment was structural and would not respond to tax cuts. He argued that automation, the emergence of computers, and other technological changes were affecting more and more workplaces, reducing demand for unskilled workers and increasing demand for engineers, programmers, repairmen and other skilled workers.[4]

In the wake of Kennedy's assassination, policy-makers passed both the tax cut supported by Heller and experimental programs consistent with Killingsworth's position. The latter included worker-training and labor-market assistance for the jobless, initiatives initially called 'manpower' policies and later renamed employment and training policies. Other programs with structural components would follow, especially under the Comprehensive Employment and Training Act of 1973 (CETA), but also the Job Training Partnership Act of 1982 and the Workforce Investment Act of 1998.

Another aspect of HRE emerged in the 1970s: use of employment and training policies to counteract recession. In the 1960s, US policies aimed at the labor market were applied 'without any countercyclical intent' (Levitan et al., 1972: 359). But that changed with the Emergency Employment Act of 1971 and then CETA, which sought to address business-cycle fluctuations by offering workers temporary positions in periods of high unemployment. Such work is often called public-service employment, and the same strategy was part of the American Recovery and Reinvestment Act of 2009 (ARRA). In February 2010, the US Congressional Budget Office estimated that ARRA boosted real US gross domestic product by as much as 2 per cent in 2009 and 4 per cent in 2010 and that it lowered the unemployment rate by as much as 0.5 percentage points in 2009 and 1.8 percentage points in 2010 (US Congressional Budget Office, 2010: 9).

Under CETA, local governments (and later also non-profits) hired the unemployed to serve in any of a range of positions, including teacher's assistant, home-health aide, and police dispatcher. Program participants also worked on community conservation and weatherization projects. ARRA was designed to provide similar employment. Assessments of CETA found that it boosted aggregate spending and employment more quickly than tax cuts. The assessments also found little evidence that federal spending merely substituted for local spending (Marshall and Briggs, 1989, 598–601).

In the late 1970s, employment and training policies were also implemented to help stabilize prices in the face of stagflation. Since economists and policymakers feared that merely stimulating aggregate demand further would worsen inflation, Ray Marshall, President Jimmy Carter's Labor Secretary, and other human resource economists proposed attacking joblessness through targeted employment and training programs. The aim was to eliminate labor bottlenecks in the economy, and thus ease inflation pressures, while simultaneously reducing unemployment. The same goal was, and remains, a key driver of active labor market policies in Western Europe.

CIVIL RIGHTS AND EQUITY

The civil rights movement was another major development that contributed to emergence of HRE and national human-resource policy in the United States. Human resource economists such as Marshall and Briggs viewed civil rights as a matter of human rights and social equity, but also as a matter of enhancing economic efficiency. For these economists, ensuring equal opportunity meant tackling not only overt discrimination but also institutional forms of discrimination, which range from procedural matters that affect hiring decisions to 'the preparation of people for jobs' (Marshall and Briggs, 1989: 593). Moreover, this group of economists was not interested in equity and opportunity for racial and ethnic minorities alone; they also supported equal opportunity for women – indeed, equal opportunity for all.[5]

In the 1970s, new structuralist research demonstrated that minorities, women, and youth were entering the labor force in larger numbers and often faced employment challenges. Marshall and Briggs (1989: 592) responded by emphasizing that this structuralist research dovetailed with Killingsworth's earlier findings. They argued that both research streams point to 'the necessity of human-resource policies as the most equitable and efficient way to reduce aggregate unemployment rates'.

CONTEMPORARY RELEVANCE

Drawing on a 1987 essay by Briggs titled 'Human resource development and the formulation of national economic policy', one can identify five policy dimensions of HRE. They are: labor supply and demand, workforce quality, labor-market opportunities, personal development, and international well-being. An examination of these dimensions reveals the contemporary relevance of HRE.

Labor Supply and Demand

One way to look at the labor supply or quantitative dimension of human resources is to begin with the number of employed people in the United States. In August 2010, the official number was just under 139.3 million. Following the international standard set by the template produced by the International Labour Organization (ILO), to be counted among the employed by the US Bureau of Labor Statistics (BLS), as in all other economies following the ILO standard, a person must first be viewed as part of the civilian labor force. To be included in the labor force, one must be sixteen or older, reside in one of the fifty states or the District of Columbia, and not be confined to an institution (home for the aged, prison, or mental-health facility). In August 2010, the US labor force totaled 154.1 million (US BLS, 2010).

Of course, not everyone in the labor force is counted as employed, a category that requires paid employment within a certain BLS reference period, which again follows the ILO standard. A member of the labor force can also be 'unemployed', which requires one to be available and either searching for work or waiting to be recalled by an employer. As of August 2010, the unemployed comprised 14.9 million, 9.6 per cent of the US labor force (US BLS, 2010).

The 9.6 per cent unemployment rate in August 2010 is one measure of unutilized labor, but there are also potential workers who are part of the US population and not currently part of the labor force. Many of those potential workers fall within a BLS category of people considered 'marginally attached' to the labor force. They are

> persons not in the labor force who want and are available for work, and who have looked for a job sometime in the prior twelve months (or since the end of their last job if they held one within the past twelve months), but were not counted as unemployed because they had not searched for work in the four weeks preceding the [most recent BLS employment] survey. (US BLS, 2008)

Marginally attached workers in August 2010 numbered 2.4 million, including 1.1 million 'discouraged workers', who were no longer looking because they believed no jobs were available to them (US BLS, 2010).[6]

There is also underutilized labor. For example, in August 2010 the BLS identified 8.9 million of the employed labor force as involuntary part-time workers. These people would like to work full-time, but had their hours cut back or were unable to find full-time jobs (US BLS, 2010). Another category of underutilized labor is underemployment, which involves people in positions that require less skill and education than they possess.

Surveying this terrain, human resource economists such as Briggs and Marshall have often called for a comprehensive, national human resource strategy that would include a commitment to full employment. They envision a strategy that would address not just the unemployment rate, but also the challenges surrounding marginal attachment and underutilization. That strategy would have a macroeconomic component, involving fiscal and monetary policies, but also a battery of labor-market and education policies that recognize the need for remedies tailored to fit different circumstances.[7]

Workforce Quality

In addition to a quantitative dimension, HRE has a qualitative dimension. A nation interested in the qualitative dimension of human resources would address the needs of its most economically disadvantaged residents, but would also engage in preventive maintenance and embrace the notion of long-run educational development.

For those who cannot find employment on a regular and self-supporting basis, or who must rely on the underground economy, Briggs (1987: 1225) envisions a *lifeline of opportunity.* This would include job training and other employment preparation, which he sees as both just and economically pragmatic. Writing in the late 1980s, he described the case for an opportunity lifeline by focusing on three US economic problems: the declining labor-force participation of black males, the poverty challenge facing female-headed households, and increasing adult illiteracy. These problems still exist.

In fact, the problems remain serious and economic conditions since the global financial crisis have only made them worse. A 2006 volume edited by Ronald B. Mincy (2006) found that the labor force participation rate of black men continued to decline even during the economic boom of the 1990s. A 2004 report by Andrew Sum and his colleagues at Northeastern University found an ongoing decline in the employment-to-population ratio of black men that began in the mid-1950s. It also found a high and rising rate of year-round joblessness among black men (one out of every four were idle all year in 2002) (Sum et al., 2004). Both studies conclude by recommending the sort of targeted education and workforce-development strategies that Briggs has been promoting for decades.

Poverty among female-headed households and the illiteracy problem are also worrisome. In 1985, one out of every three families headed by a woman was living in poverty (Briggs, 1987: 1225–6). In 2005, the poverty rate for such families was 29 per cent, ten times the rate found in two-parent families (Gosling, 2008: 175–6). A 2002 report on an adult literacy survey, sponsored by the US Department of Education, concluded that about 44 million of the 191 million adults in the United States – nearly one out of four (23 per cent) – have skills that place them in the lowest of five possible proficiency levels for reading, comprehension of documents, and quantitative reasoning. The skills of many respondents were so limited that 'they were unable to respond to much of the survey' (Kirsch et al., 2002: 18). The following year, another literacy study estimated that 50 million Americans cannot read or comprehend above the eighth-grade level and that nearly 75 per cent of the unemployed were illiterate (Morry, 2003). (Note that the study was conducted prior to the Great Recession.) Viewing the labor force in this light puts a wholly different dimension on our labor force problems.

Along with a lifeline for the unemployed and working poor, Briggs envisions a *preventive maintenance* component that offers assistance to anyone who becomes vulnerable to unemployment, regardless of salary history. This is warranted, he argues, by the increasingly dynamic nature of the workplace and the economy's increasing skill and educational requirements. Believing it is impractical to expect the entire workforce to adjust to these changing employment patterns on its own, Briggs suggests a network of initiatives to assist individuals with the labor-market adjustment process. They would include providing reliable information on labor-market trends and job requirements, and offering workers opportunities for educational upgrading, job retraining, employment counseling, and even relocation when appropriate (Briggs, 1987: 1227–30).

Since education is at the heart of Briggs's understanding of what is needed to achieve national success in a dynamic, global economy, he also envisioned *long-run educational development* as contributing to the qualitative dimension of human resources. He offered five educational objectives: preventing students from dropping out of school; boosting the average literacy and educational proficiency level across American society; ensuring that education is contingent on ability to learn, not ability to pay; making educational opportunities accessible to adults throughout their working lives; and linking education reform to a national industrial policy.[8] Briggs recognized this would require extensive changes within US educational institutions (affecting administrative practices, teacher certification and compensation, school decision-making, student assessment methods, and more), but he insisted such changes would enable education to 'contribute to the answer and not worsen the problem' of contemporary labor-force adjustment (Briggs, 1987: 1230–31).

Equal Employment Opportunity

A workforce-opportunity dimension to human resources exists alongside the quantitative and qualitative dimensions. Conventional economics argues that discrimination is irrational and thus should not persist. On the basis of extensive research, Briggs responded that experience 'has demonstrated that it cannot be realistically assumed that labor markets function solely on the basis of merit and productivity'. He added: 'The roots of discrimination run deep into the institutional practices that prepare workers to compete in the labor market' (Briggs, 1987: 1231).

In Briggs's view, equal employment opportunity should be supported by anti-discrimination mechanisms that monitor hiring patterns and offer redress in the event of discriminatory actions. In some cases it is enough to insist that hiring requirements are job-related and that employment practices are fair. Other times, however, biases and discrimination go much deeper, and help explain why certain groups within the labor force might not appear in the applicant pool of a fair-minded employer.[9] Thus, Briggs stresses that active outreach, training, apprenticeship, and placement programs contribute to pursuit of equal employment opportunity (Briggs, 1987: 1231–4; Curington, 2007).

Personal Development and International Well-being

The two remaining dimensions of human resources look beyond the national economy and focus on personal development and international well-being. Some individual benefits of human resource development come from being adequately prepared for employment. Indeed, this is where HRE touches on worker incomes, retirement security, and quality of working life, all of which deserve attention from human resource economists.[10] However, there are also other benefits associated with education and the development of individual talents and abilities, some accruing to the individual and some to society.

Economists have long recognized there are social as well as individual benefits of an investment in human resources. In fact, education offers the classic case of a good that generates a positive externality. Yet Briggs (1987: 1235) suggests that the need for an educated citizenry has become increasingly great, owing to the awesome ability of science and technology to create, destroy and 'reshape the relationship of human beings to their natural environment'. He writes that 'it is imperative that the uses of these forces be the result of the decisions made by an informed citizenry and not by an opinionated or indifferent society'.

That last point connects the personal to the political, but it also connects the individual to the rest of global humanity. Most HRE has focused on well-being at the national level, suggesting that a prosperous and humane US economy, for example, provides Americans with the best position from which to address problems on an international scale. Over the years, however, these institutionalists have given increasing attention to international issues, especially international coordination, global standards and worldwide codes of conduct. Not surprisingly, their message centers on leveling the global economic playing field to bring up those at the bottom and prevent a global race to the bottom.

THE WEALTH OF NATIONS

In response to the Great Recession, economists and policy-makers devoted much attention to shoring up the financial sector of the economy and introducing reforms that might help anticipate or even prevent future financial crises. That was appropriate.[11]

After the Great Recession, however, it seems useful for economists to turn their attention to human resources, the ultimate source of the wealth of nations. HRE, rooted in institutional economics, offers one way forward. It is pragmatic, aimed at practical problems, and attuned to the multiple dimensions of human resources. There are certainly plenty of human resource issues to explore, and devoting attention to them now will pay off at all stages of the business cycle.[12]

NOTES

1. For an excellent discussion of HRE, see Briggs (1987). For more on HRE, see Whalen (2010b). Some other economists in the HRE tradition include Eileen Appelbaum, Barry Bluestone, Christopher King, Robert Glover, Garth Mangum, Ray Marshall, Paul Osterman, Michael Piore, Richard Santos and Andrew Sum, though these individuals often disagree on policy specifics. The late Eli Ginzberg and Sar Levitan can also be considered part of this tradition.
2. HRE was not the economics profession's only post-World War II tradition to focus on the importance of human skills and knowledge. The other tradition, called human-capital theory, emerged from neo-classical economics and is associated with the work of Theodore Schultz and Gary Becker. For critical assessments of

human-capital theory from the perspective of HRE, see Briggs (1987) and Piore (1974).
3. See also Ginzberg (1958) and Harbison (1973).
4. On structural unemployment, see Killingsworth (1965a; 1965b; 1979). On the Heller-Killingsworth debate and its continuing relevance, see Bluestone (1996).
5. HRE is concerned not merely with the *level* of employment, but also with the *composition* of employment (Marshall and Briggs, 1989: 594). Reflecting on the civil rights era from the vantage point of the mid-1980s, Briggs wrote: 'There had to be changes in the racial and gender composition of employment patterns, as opposed to an exclusive policy focus merely on the level of employment. As a black leader once expressed it, "After all, we had full employment back on the plantations"'. At the same time, Briggs recognized that any successful equal-employment opportunity strategy would need to be accompanied by a full-employment strategy, or the former would only heighten job-security concerns among groups that previously benefited from exclusionary employment practices (Briggs, 1987: 1233–4).
6. Other marginally attached workers indicate they have not recently looked for work due to reasons such as family responsibilities and school attendance (US BLS, 2010).
7. Immigration is also an important part of the quantitative dimension of human resources. For more on this, see Whalen (2010b).
8. On linking education and training with industrial policy, Briggs writes: 'There can be little purposeful long-term educational preparation of the labor force for employment if there is little direction provided as to where the economy is thought to be going' (Briggs 1987: 1231).
9. For example, recruitment and job-posting practices can be structured (even inadvertently) in a way that favors some groups over others. In addition, inequality and discrimination can shape the institutions that educate, train and prepare people for employment. Past patterns of discrimination can cause even those with educational or training opportunities to temper their occupational aspirations and forgo some opportunities out of discouragement.
10. For a related discussion of income and retirement insecurity in recent decades, see Whalen (2008b).
11. But, as suggested earlier in this chapter (and in Whalen, 2010a), the mortgage crisis deserved greater attention than it received, as did unemployment.
12. This chapter was prepared in the spring of 2010 (and updated in the summer), when there was widespread agreement among economists that the US economy was in a recovery, although the unemployment rate, at over 9 percent, remained close to its post-World War II peak.

REFERENCES

Bluestone, Barry (1996), 'Economic inequality and the macrostructuralist debate', in Charles J. Whalen (ed.), *Political Economy for the Twenty-First Century: Contemporary Views on the Trend of Economics*, Armonk, NY: M.E. Sharpe, pp. 171–94.

Briggs, Vernon M. (1 987), 'Human resource development and the formulation of national economic policy', *Journal of Economic Issues*, **21**(3), 1207–40.

Curington, William P. (2007), Interview with Vernon M. Briggs Jr., conducted via telephone, May, deposited in the Martin P. Catherwood Library, Cornell University, Kheel Center for Labor Management Documentation and Archives.

Ginzberg, Eli (1958), *Human Resources: The Wealth of a Nation*, New York: Simon & Schuster.

Glover, Robert W. and Christopher T. King (2010), 'Sectoral approaches to workforce development: toward an effective US labor-market policy', in Charles J. Whalen (ed.), *Human Resource Economics and Public Policy: Essays in Honor of Vernon M. Briggs Jr.*, Kalamazoo, MI: W.E. Upjohn Institute for Employment Research.

Gosling, James J. (2008), *Economics, Politics; and American Public Policy*, Armonk, NY: M.E. Sharpe.

Harbison, Frederick H. (1973), *Human Resources as the Wealth of Nations*, New York: Oxford University Press.

Harbison, Frederick H. and Charles A. Myers (1964), *Education, Manpower, and Economic Growth: Strategies of Human Resource Development*, New York: McGraw-Hill.

Killingsworth, Charles. C. (1965a), 'Automation, jobs, and manpower: the case for structural unemployment', in Garth L. Mangum (ed.), *The Manpower Revolution: Its Policy Consequences*, Garden City, NY: Anchor Books, pp. 97–117.

Killingsworth, Charles C. (1965b), 'Unemployment after the tax cut', in William G. Bowen and Frederick H. Harbison (ed.), *Unemployment in a Prosperous Economy*, Princeton, NJ: Industrial Relations Section, Princeton University, pp. 82–97.

Killingsworth, Charles C. (1979), 'The fall and rise of structural unemployment', in Barbara D. Dennis (ed.), *Proceedings of the Thirty-First Annual Meeting*, Madison, WI: Industrial Relations Research Association, pp. 1–13.

Kirsch, Irwin S., Ann Jungeblut, Lynn Jenkins and Andrew Kolstad (2002), *Adult Literacy in America: A First Look at the Findings of the National Adult Literacy Survey*, 3rd edn NCES 1993–275, Washington, DC: National Center for Education Statistics, Office of Educational Research and Improvement, US Department of Education.

Levitan, Sar A., Garth L. Mangum and Ray Marshall (1972), *Human Resources and Labor Markets: Labor and Manpower in the American Economy*, New York: Harper and Row.

Marshall, Ray and Vernon M. Briggs (1989), *Labor Economics: Theory, Institutions, and Public Policy*, 6th edn, Homewood, IL: Irwin.

Mincy, Ronald B. (ed.) (2006), *Black Males Left Behind*, Washington, DC: Urban Institute Press.

Minsky, Hyman P. and Charles J. Whalen (1996), 'Economic insecurity and the institutional prerequisites of successful capitalism', *Journal of Post Keynesian Economics*, **19**(2), 155–70.

Morry, Chris (2003), 'Illiteracy in the United States', Communication Initiative Network (Summary of Findings of the Words are Your Wheels Literacy Program), available at http://www.comminit.com/en/node/17040, accessed 13 February 2009.

Piore, Michael J. (1974), 'The importance of human capital theory to labor economics: a dissenting view', in Barbara D. Dennis (ed.), *Proceedings of the Twenty-Sixth Annual Winter Meeting*, Madison, WI: Industrial Relations Research Association, pp. 251–8.

Puzzanghera, Jim (2010), 'Foreclosure prevention program is struggling', *Los Angeles Times*, 21 August, available at http://articles.latimes.com/2010/aug/21/business/la-fi-obama-foreclosures-20100821, accessed 24 August 2010.

Smith, Adam ([1776] 1935), *An Inquiry into the Nature and Causes of the Wealth of Nations*, New York: Modern Library.

Sum, Andrew, Iswar Khatiwada, Frimpomaa Ampaw, Paulo Tobar and Sheila Palma (2004), *Trends in Black Male Joblessness and Year-Round Idleness: An Employment Crisis Ignored*, Chicago, IL: Alternative Schools Network, available at http://www.nlc.org, accessed 13 February 2009.

United Nations Development Program (2010), 'Summary – the real wealth of nations: pathways to human development', available at http://hdr.undp.org/en/reports/global/hdr2010/summary/, accessed 31 May 2010.

US Bureau of Labor Statistics (BLS) (2008), 'Marginally attached workers (Current Population Survey)', in 'BLS Information Glossary', available at http://www.bls.gov/bls/glossary.htm, accessed 13 February 2009.

US Bureau of Labor Statistics (2010), 'The employment situation: August 2010', Washington, DC: US Department of Labor, available at http://www.bls.gov/news.release/empsit.nr0.htm, accessed 4 September 2010.

US Congressional Budget Office (2010), *Estimated Impact of the American Recovery and Reinvestment Act on Employment and Economic Output From October 2009 Through December 2009*, February, Washington, DC: Congressional Budget Office.

Weller, Christian E. (2006), 'America needs a more balanced economy', *Perspectives on Work*, **10**(1), 14–16.

Whalen, Charles J. (2008a), 'Post-Keynesian institutionalism and the creative state', *Forum for Social Economics*, **37**(1), 43–60.

Whalen, Charles J. (2008b), 'Post-Keynesian institutionalism and the anxious society', in Sandra S. Batie and Nicholas Mercuro (eds), *Alternative Institutional Structures: Evolution and Impact*, New York: Routledge, pp, 273–99.

Whalen, Charles J. (2010a), 'An institutionalist perspective on the global financial crisis', in Steven Kates (ed.), *Macroeconomic Theory and Its Failings: Alternative Perspectives on the Global Financial Crisis*, Cheltenham, UK and Northampton, MA, USA: Edward Elgar Publishing, pp. 235–59.

Whalen, Charles J. (ed.) (2010b), *Human Resource Economics and Public Policy: Essays in Honor of Vernon M. Briggs Jr.*, Kalamazoo, MI: W.E. Upjohn Institute for Employment Research.

Whalen, Charles J. (ed.) (2011), *Financial Instability and Economic Security after the Great Recession*, Cheltenham, UK and Northampton, MA, USA: Edward Elgar Publishing.

12. John R. Commons and government as employer of last resort: three paths to a progressive right to work

> Unemployment is the outstanding defect of capitalism.
>
> Lewisohn, Draper, Commons, and Lescohier (1925)

Today in the United States, a number of congressional Democrats endorse proposals that would establish a job guarantee for all Americans seeking work. Within academia, much recent research providing an intellectual foundation for such proposals comes from economists writing about the need for government to serve as an "employer of last resort," a notion often traced to the work of Hyman Minsky (1986).[1] However, arguments for such a policy can be traced back much further: John R. Commons, a pioneer in institutional economics, wrote in favor of government jobs for the unemployed as early as the 1890s.

This article demonstrates that there are actually three arguments in Commons's writings that provide a case for government as employer of last resort. The first, which can be called the *legal* path to the right to work, was offered by Commons at the beginning of his career. The second, the *financial* path, is rooted in work on money and business cycles that Commons undertook in the 1920s. The third, the *historical* path, can be pieced together by drawing on his *Institutional Economics* (Commons 1934a), published as Commons embarked on retirement and President Franklin Roosevelt grappled with the Great Depression. Each path is considered in turn, and a brief conclusion underscores the continuing relevance of Commons's contributions.

Reprinted with permission from *Journal of Economic Issues* 54 (2), June 2020, 428–435.

SECURING LIFE AND LIBERTY: LEGAL PATH TO THE RIGHT TO WORK

In the United States, the "right to work" is associated most often with state laws that allow workers to refuse to join a labor organization or even pay fees to cover the cost of union representation. However, the term originally referred to a progressive call for the right to employment. In three early works, Commons (1893, 1899, 1900) presented the right to work as a logical extension of the right to life and liberty, which must be secured by government.

A Bundle of Rights

In those publications, Commons described the right to liberty as "a bundle of rights." That bundle grants us freedom to do many things, including contract with others, leave one employer and work for another, and establish a new enterprise. The bundle evolves over time—evolving as society recognizes that conditions have changed.

According to Commons, changes to the American economy in the second half of the nineteenth century threatened the right to life and liberty because wage labor had for many people become the only route to providing for one's self and family, which left them in a weak bargaining position relative to employers and extraordinarily vulnerable during periods of joblessness. Thus, Commons argued that society's bundle of rights must be updated to contain the right to work. That right would be defined and enforced by a web of laws aimed at unemployment prevention, unemployment compensation, and public employment—and the latter would include giving the unemployed the right "to have work furnished by the government" (Commons 1893, 81).[2]

The Next Great Human Right

The thrust of Commons's public employment recommendation was aimed at the loss of employment caused by business-cycle downturns. But he also suggested that public employment would be needed to help some displaced workers at all stages of the cycle. In addition, Commons saw public employment as a wage policy as well as an employment policy. Commons (1899, 141) wrote: "The right to employment would give laborers steady work throughout the year, and … abolish involuntary poverty among the able-bodied."

To summarize: the new bundle of rights Commons envisioned would expand the liberty of working people—by reducing coercion and capricious use of power in employment relations, by increasing employment security and economic security, by providing new economic opportunities, and by bolstering incomes. Taken as a whole, Commons (1893, 80–81) saw a web of laws establishing the right to work—"the next great human right." Securing the right to life and liberty in this way is Commons's *legal* path to the right to work.

TAMING BUSINESS CYCLES: FINANCIAL PATH TO THE RIGHT TO WORK

Between World War I and the start of the Great Depression, the American economy experienced several inflationary booms and deflationary busts with high unemployment.[3] That decade is when Commons (1921, 1922, 1925a) came to see business cycles as the most important of all labor problems. His investigations produced a profit-margin theory of cycles and policy recommendations aimed at dampening and coping with such cycles. Those investigations are where we find his second argument in favor of government as employer of last resort—a *financial* path to the right to work.

Commons on Business Cycles

Commons's cycle theory focuses on expectations, bank credit, and profit margins (Commons 1922, 19–20; 1934a, 508–589; 1937, 689; 1950, 255). He argued that the key to igniting a stalled economy is business confidence. If firms and bankers lack confidence, due to unfavorable profit forecasts, then the unemployed will not be put to work. In contrast, favorable profit forecasts encourage the banking system to create the new money that sparks a recovery by augmenting purchasing power and allowing firms to acquire labor, machinery, and materials. And since a recovery boosts confidence, expansions often evolve into booms. Unfortunately, profit expectations are fragile, Commons emphasized, so it's easy for a boom to turn sour, causing the economy to stall.[4]

Commons preferred to prevent cyclical downturns rather than cope with them. Since he identified the credit policies of the banking system as a "fundamental cause" of business cycles, Commons sought to stabilize credit—that is, safeguard "the general credit situation" (Commons 1925a, 43; 1925b, 43). "Any improvement that looks to the prevention of unemployment must go back to the period of inflation and prevent the over-expansion that caused the unemployment," wrote Commons (1922, 20).

Commons believed unemployment insurance and monetary policy had important roles to play in preventing economic downturns. His unemployment insurance proposal was designed so employers would incur a financial liability for laying off workers (Commons 1922, 1934b, 198–199; Lewisohn et al. 1925, 188). Commons saw the liability as a factor that both employers and bankers would need to consider before allowing enterprises to expand. Thus, he believed firms would have an incentive to better regulate their growth and contraction. Meanwhile, Commons (1925b, 1927a, 1927b, 1929, 1982) wanted the Federal Reserve to use open-market operations, the discount rate, and moral suasion, to stabilize the average price level. That, he believed, was the most effective way to stabilize the general credit situation.

However, Commons recognized that cycles could at best be tamed, not eliminated. "What is really meant by stabilization of prices," he wrote, is the avoidance of "excessive peaks and slumps" (Commons 1925b, 45; 1934a, 557). Thus, the financial path to the right to work runs through Commons's analysis of business cycles and the policy tools designed to dampen them and brings us to the need to cope with a downturn once it hits. Because Commons understood that it's much easier for monetary policy to prevent an inflationary boom than to ignite a recovery and reduce joblessness in the face of low business confidence, he wrote that a more direct form of public action is needed during a recession or depression:

> In order to create the consumer demand, on which business depends for sales, the government itself must create the new money and go completely over the head of the entire banking system by paying it out directly to the unemployed, either as relief or for construction of public works, as it does in times of war. (Commons 1934a, 589–590)

Commons on Public Works

Writing in the mid 1920s, Commons argued that public employment—in particular, public works—has a key role to play during an economic downturn. In 1925, for example, he joined a colleague and two business leaders to coauthor *Can Business Prevent Unemployment?* In their chapter on "Public Policies to Relieve Unemployment," Commons and his collaborators argued: "There are large possibilities in the wise use of public works to alleviate unemployment" (Lewisohn et al. 1925, 150).

The chapter demonstrates that cities and states accelerated public works in periods of depression at least since 1914—and that a bill was introduced before Congress in 1919 to create an Emergency Public Works Board, so that federal, state, and local agencies could cooperate in using public works to address unemployment after World War I. The chapter also approvingly cites the work of William Clark, a Canadian economist who drew on international research to stress the importance of countercyclical government spending for public works and advance planning to ensure such projects would be ready for use in downturns (Lewisohn et al. 1925, 121–125).

The rest of the chapter by Commons and his colleagues (Lewisohn et al. 1925, 126–151) reviews various public-works initiatives in America and abroad, highlighting lessons and challenges. For example, they maintain that public works must legitimately provide a public good or service (rather than charity in the form of a "make-work" job) and should avoid displacing employed workers by taking work from private employers: Public-works jobs should "permanently increase the wealth of the community, and be performed by labor employed in the ordinary way, i.e., on an efficiency basis and at current rates of wages." For maximum program effectiveness, they also stress the importance of anticipating a downturn by giving preemptive attention to details of program administration: "Work must be planned in advance, places approved, contracts drawn, and everything ready."[5]

SAVING CAPITALISM: HISTORICAL PATH TO THE RIGHT TO WORK

Commons's third argument for having government serve as an employer of last resort, the *historical* path to the right to work, can be pieced together from his analysis of stages of economic history. To be sure, Commons left this path a bit incomplete, but the elements are there to fashion a historically grounded argument in addition to the legal and financial arguments outlined above. Commons's discussion of stages of history is most fully developed in *Institutional Economics*, so that will be our focus.

Scarcity, Abundance, and Stabilization

In *Institutional Economics*, Commons (1934a, 773–788) divides economic history into three epochs: eras of scarcity, abundance, and stabilization.[6] The era of scarcity, characterized by shortages of the material means of life and minimal individual liberty, extended from the earliest days of human civilization until the late eighteenth century. The era of abundance, a product of the industrial revolution and characterized by the rise of individualism and laissez-faire capitalism, lasted until the late nineteenth century. The era of stabilization followed, continuing to the present.

In the era of stabilization, individual liberty is constrained (but may also be secured and enhanced) through collective action initiated by either the public or private sector. Such constraints emerged as a way to control economic booms and busts at the national level as well as to address labor-management disputes and other conflicts at the enterprise and industry levels. In the 1930s, stabilization took various forms across the globe: communism in Russia; fascism in Italy and Germany; and managed capitalism in the United States and England, owing to business combinations, industry-wide collective bargaining, and government regulation.

In capitalist democracies, the shift to an era of stabilization was far from a settled matter—a point John Maynard Keynes recognized and stressed in a 1925 lecture based on material by Commons that was later included in *Institutional Economics* (see Whalen 2008). Keynes warned: "The transition from economic anarchy to a regime which deliberately aims at controlling and directing economic forces in the interests of social justice and social stability, will present enormous difficulties both technical and political." The way forward was not clear: "We have to invent new wisdom for a new age," wrote Keynes (1972, 305–306).

Communism, Fascism, and Capitalism

By the time Commons published *Institutional Economics*, the challenge of inventing new wisdom for the era of stabilization had become even more difficult—and the stakes were greater than ever. The Great Depression gripped the world economy, and communism and fascism were emerging as serious threats to capitalist nations. Commons (1934b, 143)—who believed in liberty and democracy and saw fascism and communism as incompatible with both—wanted to "save capitalism by making it good." In 1934, however, Commons (1934a, 902–903) wasn't convinced that his desired real-world outcome was a sure thing.

The form of managed capitalism that existed at the start of the Great Depression is what Commons called "banker capitalism." According to Commons (1934a, 773), investment bankers "arose out of their former intermittent activity in special flotations of securities of corporations and nations, into a dominant position in the consolidation of industries, the sale of foreign and domestic securities to the public, and the control of boards of directors." But a huge problem remained: banker capitalism proved itself incapable of preventing an economic collapse. "In fact it appears that fluctuations of overproduction and unemployment are more extreme with large corporations than with little employers," wrote Commons (1934, 896).

The Great Depression also created a new problem for Commons and others interested in liberty and democracy. That's because the crisis put even more power in the hands of bankers—namely, those in charge of the government's Reconstruction Finance Corporation and, of course, central bankers. In the end, observed Commons (1934a, 773), the economic crisis meant that "bankers rise to new importance, and banker capitalism comes into control of industries and nations."

As a result of observing the expanding power of bankers as well as growing support for a national planning council to rationalize industry and stabilize output, Commons expressed concern that America might be on the road to fascism. It left him troubled. While Commons was deeply committed to liberty and democracy, he believed that large numbers of workers would not miss liberty and democracy as long as fascism or communism gave them the employment security that capitalism failed to deliver (Commons 1934a, 902–903).

Employer of Last Resort as the New Wisdom

Commons did not complete the argument for government as employer of last resort when discussing economic history in *Institutional Economics*. While a chapter does call for public works to put people to work during depressions, chapters dealing with economic history focus instead on the need for economic and political institutions to involve voluntary associations and give voice to a wide range of economic stakeholders (Commons 1934a, 876–903; see also Commons 1935). But Commons did provide a prominent discussion of the need for government job creation "in bad years and slack seasons" when updating *Principles of Labor Legislation* in 1936 (Commons and Andrews 1936, 27).[7] Moreover, history completed the argument for him. It turns out that government as employer of last resort has, in practice, become an important part of the "new wisdom" of the stabilization era.

In the years following publication of *Institutional Economics*, the United States (and other industrial democracies) avoided fascism and communism by finding another way forward. In the face of economic downturns, countercyclical macroeconomic policies have been used to moderate recessions. And when downturns have been particularly severe, the federal government has indeed furnished work for at least some of the unemployed.[8] The approach that has emerged is not nearly as thoroughgoing as what Commons envisioned in his writings on public works and government job creation, nor is it as ambitious as what Commons advocated when he called for workers to have the legal right to such employment, but it does represent a step in that direction.

CONCLUSION: RECLAIMING THE RIGHT TO WORK

This article has identified three arguments in Commons that provide a case for government to serve as employer of last resort. The legal path navigates through the right to life and liberty. The financial path makes its way via a profit-margin theory of cycles. And the historical path traverses a series of economic stages and threads the needle between fascism and communism.

But these are not just paths. Each provides insight with contemporary relevance. The legal discussion highlights the often overlooked problem of economic coercion. The financial discussion leads to a still pertinent analysis of how public-works employment can be made most effective. And the historical discussion reminds us of the fragile nature of democratic capitalism. Since joblessness—the threat of it as well as the reality—remains among the most serious of all labor problems, the survival of liberty and democratic capitalism may continue to depend on our ability to provide public employment to those willing but unable to find work.[9]

It's been more than a century since Commons outlined the right to work as a bundle of liberties that should include the right of the unemployed to have work furnished by the government. Yet unemployment remains an outstanding defect of capitalism, and important lessons from Commons's scholarship remain to be learned and used as a foundation for public policy. The work of saving capitalism "by making it good" continues. It's time to rediscover Commons's arguments and build on them to reclaim the right to work as a progressive cause.

NOTES

1. For an example of that literature, see Tcherneva (2011).
2. For more on Common's discussion of unemployment prevention, unemployment compensation, and public employment in his early essays, as well as a more detailed discussion of his legal path to the right to work, see Whalen (2019, 322–324).
3. The National Bureau of Economic Research (2019) identifies four contractions in that period, one of which—between January 1920 and July 1921—is widely referred to as a depression.
4. For a further discussion of Commons's cycle theory, see Whalen (1993).
5. Writing with his former student, John B. Andrews, Commons returned to the subject of public works in the opening chapter (on unemployment) of the 1936 edition of *Principles of Labor Legislation* (Commons and Andrews 1936). In a section on emergency public works, they conclude that although results of such work projects "have not always been gratifying, … the opinion has been growing that the flaws are not inherent, … [and] may be largely overcome by proper administration. Against the added cost [owing to inefficiencies], which may be a serious problem, must be placed the value of the work accomplished and also the human resources which are conserved and even improved" (Commons and Andrews 1936, 27–31). Another section of the chapter stresses the importance of labor-market information (such as current data on hirings and layoffs), which "would make possible intelligent action for the prevention and relief of unemployment through the systematic distribution of public work and the pushing of necessary projects when private industry's demand for labor is low." They conclude: "Public work would then act as a sponge, absorbing the reserves of labor in bad years and slack seasons, and setting them free again when the demand for them increases in private business" (Commons and Andrews 1936, 27).
6. For an earlier, but less detailed, discussion of stages of history, see Commons (1925c). See also Commons (1934a, 876–903).
7. For some discussion of Commons and Andrews (1936), see note 5 above.
8. For a discussion of countercyclical job creation in the United States, see Levine (2003); Congressional Research Service (2010); and Whalen (2019, 324–326).

9. For more on the continued significance of addressing unemployment and job insecurity, see Whalen (2019). It is also worth observing that University of Chicago economist Raghuram Rajan recently warned that capitalism "is under serious threat" because it currently fails to provide opportunity for most people (BBC News 2019).

REFERENCES

BBC News. 2019. "Raghuram Rajan says Capitalism is 'Under Serious Threat.'" BBC News, March 12, 2019. https://www.bbc.com/news/business-47532522. Accessed December 12, 2019.

Commons, John R. 1893. *The Distribution of Wealth*. New York: Macmillan and Company.

———. 1899. "The Right to Work." *The Arena* 21 (2): 131–142.

———. 1900. "A Sociological View of Sovereignty, Part VI." *American Journal of Sociology* 5 (6): 814–825.

———. 1921. "Unemployment: Compensation and Prevention." *The Survey* 48 (October 1): 5–9.

———. 1922. "Unemployment Prevention." *American Labor Legislation Review* 12 (March 1922): 15–24.

———. 1925a. "The True Scope of Unemployment Insurance." *American Labor Legislation Review* 15 (March): 33–44.

———. 1925b. "The Stabilization of Prices and Business." *American Economic Review* 15 (1): 43–52.

———. 1925c. "Marx Today: Capitalism and Socialism." *Atlantic Monthly* 136 (November 25): 682–93.

———. 1927a. "Price Stabilization and the Federal Reserve System." *The Annalist* 29 (April 1): 459–62.

———. 1927b. "Statement Before the Committee on Banking and Currency." In *Stabilization*, 1074–1121. Washington, DC: United States Government Printing Office.

———. 1929. "Statements and Remarks Before the Committee on Banking and Currency." In *Stabilization*. Washington, DC: United States Government Printing Office.

———. 1934a. *Institutional Economics*. New York: Macmillan.

———. 1934b. *Myself*. New York: Macmillan.

———. 1935. "Communism and Collective Democracy." *American Economic Review* 25 (June): 212–223.

———. 1937. "Capacity to Produce, Capacity to Consume, Capacity to Pay Debts." *American Economic Review* 27 (4): 681–97.

———. 1950. *The Economics of Collective Action*. New York: Macmillan.

———. 1982. "Control of the Price Level Through Changes in the Rate of Discount and Rediscount." Reproduced in John R Commons Papers (microfilm edition, 1982), State Historical Society of Wisconsin, undated manuscript.

Commons, John R., and John B. Andrews. 1936. *Principles of Labor Legislation*, 4th ed. New York: Harper and Brothers.

Congressional Research Service. 2010. *Countercyclical Job Creation Programs*. Washington, DC: Congressional Research Service.

Keynes, John M. 1972. "Am I a Liberal?" In *The Collected Writings of John Maynard Keynes, Volume 9, Essays in Persuasion*, edited by Donald Moggridge, 295–311.

London: Macmillan. (Address delivered in Cambridge, United Kingdom, August 1925.)

Levine, Linda. 2003. *Countercyclical Job Creation Programs of the Post-World War II Era*. Washington, DC: Congressional Research Service.

Lewisohn, Sam A., Ernest G. Draper, John R. Commons, and Don D. Lescohier. 1925. *Can Business Prevent Unemployment?* New York: Alfred A Knopf.

Minsky, Hyman P. 1986. *Stabilizing an Unstable Economy*. New Haven: Yale University Press.

National Bureau of Economic Research. 2019. U.S. "Business Cycle Expansions and Contractions." https://www.nber.org/cycles.html. Accessed February 23, 2019.

Tcherneva, Pavlina. 2011. "The Case for Labor Demand Targeting." *Journal of Economic Issues* 42 (2): 401–410.

Whalen, Charles J. 1993. Saving Capitalism by Making It Good: The Monetary Economics of John R. Commons." *Journal of Economic Issues*, 27 (4): 1155–1179.

———. 2008. "John R. Commons and John Maynard Keynes on Economic History and Policy: The 1920s and Today." *Journal of Economic Issues* 42 (1): 225–242.

———. 2019. "Institutional Economics and Chock-Full Employment." *Journal of Economic Issues* 53 (2): 321–340.

13. The "middle way" of John R. Commons: pursuing reasonable value in the age of unreason

John R. Commons (1862–1945) and his University of Wisconsin students influenced economic reform in the United States from the Progressive Era through the Great Society. For much of his career, however, capitalism and democracy in the United States faced internal and external threats from fascism and communism.[1] Commons responded by seeking to "save capitalism by making it good," settling on a solution that was more an approach to policymaking than a concrete policy agenda. At bottom, that solution was a society oriented toward pursuit of *"reasonable value"* (Commons 1934a, 143 and 1950, 138, 164).

Commons's goal of achieving and sustaining a humane form of capitalism can be called a "middle way" between socio-political extremes, and looks similar to the social democratic systems found in Nordic countries. In fact, the economy described in a book called *Sweden: The Middle Way,* written in the 1930s by American journalist Marquis Childs (1936), sounds very much like it was constructed using Commons's reasonable value as a blueprint. In particular, Childs presented Sweden as a nation in which the public is committed to democratic institutions; "capital and labor realize that violence means death for both;" and "wisdom … lies above all in … willingness to adjust, to compromise, … [and to ensure] the workability of the social order" (Childs, quoted in Unstad 1936, 305). More recently, Yngve Ramstad (1991) offered the "negotiated economy" of Denmark as the best real-world illustration of Commons's vision of a nation focused on reasonable value.

Recent work by Kota Kitagawa (2017 and 2020) highlights the two paths to reasonable value in Commons's writings: judicial sovereignty and collective democracy. Judicial sovereignty centers on representative democracy and the right to due process, combined with the Supreme Court's role in the United States as final arbiter of reasonableness from a legal standpoint (which, of course, has consequences for all socioeconomic activity). Collective democracy centers on the reasonableness embodied not only in collective bargaining

Reprinted with permission from *Journal of Economic Issues* 54 (4), December 2020, 1161–1173.

between business and labor, but also in any joint investigation, bargaining, and administration of disputes by stakeholder representatives. This policy note considers—with help from flashbacks to Commons's era—a number of present-day obstacles to pursuit of both sorts of reasonable value. Some possible ways forward are also suggested.

JUDICIAL SOVEREIGNTY

It would certainly be comforting to look at judges, especially those on the Supreme Court, as impartial and eminently reasonable individuals, willing to give due weight to all the facts and to keep personal philosophies and biases out of the process of deliberation. But, of course, it would also be a mistake. Judges (like all of us) always come to a dispute with a perspective, and courts reflect society's political realities, no matter what code of ethics jurists have sought to cultivate and pass down over time. The main political reality of recent decades in the United States has, unfortunately, been the tendency toward an increasingly polarized system of politics and governance.

It Can Happen Here

At the end of 2017, with President Donald Trump nearing the end of his first year in office, *The New Republic* published an article with the title "How a Democracy Dies." According to the essay's authors, political scientists Steven Levitsky and Daniel Ziblatt (2017) of Harvard University, history shows that constitutional rules aren't sufficient to safeguard democracy: "Even well designed constitutions can fail." Instead, the key safeguard is "the development of strong democratic norms." In particular, two norms are vital: "mutual toleration, or accepting one's partisan rivals as legitimate (not treating them as dangerous enemies or traitors); and forbearance, or deploying one's institutional prerogatives with restraint—in other words, not using the letter of the Constitution to undermine its spirit."

Levitsky and Ziblatt maintain that for most of U.S. history those norms "served as crucial bulwarks against authoritarian tendencies," such as when illegal activities were traced to the Oval Office in the early 1970s and bipartisan pressure forced the resignation of President Richard Nixon. But the authors also identify a turning point when democratic norms began to erode: the election of Newt Gingrich to Congress in the late 1970s. What Gingrich brought to Washington was "a blunter, more cutthroat vision of politics" than either party had practiced previously:

> Backed by a small but growing group of loyalists, Gingrich launched an insurgency aimed at instilling a more "combative" approach in the party … He described Democrats in Congress as corrupt and sick. He questioned his Democratic rivals' patriotism. He even compared them to Mussolini and accused them of trying to destroy the country. (Levitsky and Ziblatt 2017)

Sensing and stoking growing public discontent toward the federal government, Gingrich rode that wave to become Speaker of the House, "and his leadership helped to establish 'politics as warfare' as the GOP's dominant strategy" (Levitsky and Ziblatt 2017). Tracing the Gingrich team's trek on the road to their impeachment of President Bill Clinton, Levitsky and Ziblatt write:

> After the Republicans' landslide 1994 election, the GOP began to seek victory by 'any means necessary.' House Republicans refused to compromise, for example, in budget negotiations, leading to a five-day government shutdown in November 1995 and a 21-day shutdown a month later. This was a dangerous turn. As norms of forbearance weakened, checks and balances began to devolve into deadlock and dysfunction. (Levitsky and Ziblatt 2017)

Gingrich eventually left Congress, but his strategy has remained, leading to the present era in which candidates threaten to lock up their rivals and parties use legislative majorities "to steal Supreme Court seats" (Levitsky and Ziblatt 2017).

As a consequence of politics as warfare, American society is deeply divided. As Levitsky and Ziblatt (2017) write toward the end of their essay: "Democrats and Republicans have become much more than just two competing parties, sorted into liberal and conservative camps. Their voters are now deeply divided by race, religious belief, culture, and geography." Even worse, political dysfunction may be the least of our worries; it could very well be leading us to authoritarianism: "the mounting assault on the norms that sustain [our political order and its institutions] should strike fear in anyone who hopes to see the United States secure a democratic future" (Levitsky and Ziblatt 2017).

Others agree about the danger of American democracy devolving into authoritarianism. In fact, historian and journalist Anne Applebaum warned of this in her own 2017 essay, highlighting ominous parallels between, on the one hand, contemporary right-wing leaders in the United States and elsewhere, and, on the other hand, leaders of the Russian revolution a century earlier (Applebaum 2017). For example, she observes that, "to an extraordinary degree," today's right-wing has "adopted Lenin's refusal to compromise, his anti-democratic elevation of some social groups over others, and his hateful attacks on his 'illegitimate' opponents."[2]

In a more recent essay, Applebaum (2020) explores the various arguments Republicans use to defend not speaking out against "a president whose operative value system—built around corruption, nascent authoritarianism, self-regard, and his family's business interests—runs counter to everything that most of them claim to believe in." Their arguments remind her of "the strategies, tactics, and self-justifications that the inhabitants of occupied countries have used in the past." Applebaum's article, which outlines the damage done by the current administration and warns clearly about the authoritarian danger of having President Trump serve a second term, bears a title with a blunt message to those who have not spoken out: "History Will Judge the Complicit."

As this policy note is being wrapped up for production and publication, the U.S. presidential election of 2020 is a month away. No matter how that election turns out, the threat of America's continued slide toward authoritarianism remains real. If President Trump is reelected, the danger will certainly be immediate. But even if Trump is not reelected, it's hard to see how the nation moves forward appreciably, given that, in recent years, there has been so much talk of "fake news;" so much labeling of opposing politicians, journalists, and others as "enemies of the people;" and so much reliance on "alternative facts" by public officials, political commentators, and news outlets that shape and amplify partisan talking points. Regardless of the election outcome in 2020, if we assume the sharp divides and dysfunction continue, then it's quite possible that a cunning observer could mount a successful assault on our democratic institutions in perhaps four, eight, or a dozen years. Moreover, even without Trump the Republican Party has for decades been moving (at the state and federal levels) in the direction of "a private governing elite of corporate power … wholly released from public accountability" (Parramore 2018).[3] As Sinclair Lewis warned in 1935, it *can* happen here (Lewis 1935).

It Could Have Happened Here

Looking back at Commons's writings, it's clear that he thought authoritarianism certainly *could* happen here. In the 1930s and 1940s, he pointed to a number of troubling signs that America was heading in the direction of fascism. He saw evidence of this at the state and local level: "We know that universal suffrage has broken down in the Southern states and our biggest cities. These are the places from which the business and professional classes look with longing to a businessman's government, which is our fascism" (Commons 1934b, 899). He also saw evidence at the federal level, in steps toward national economic planning as well as in concentration and control of economic power—with Washington's blessing—by the financial sector.[4] And he saw it in the suppression (for both political and economic reasons) of left-wing ideas and labor unions (Commons 1934b, 889–903 and 1950, 262–266, 290).[5]

In fact, Commons saw very little standing in the way of full-blown authoritarianism. In 1934, he wrote that it would only take legislatures to be discredited (Commons 1934b, 902), which wouldn't be extraordinarily difficult in the midst of a prolonged depression and in the face of (manufactured or real) military threats from abroad (Commons 1934b, 884).[6] Moreover, Commons feared that large numbers of workers would not miss liberty and democracy as long as fascism or communism gave them the employment security that capitalism failed to deliver (Commons 1934b, 903).

Saving Judicial Sovereignty

Can judicial sovereignty be saved as a path to reasonable value? Can we end politics as warfare, political deadlock, and dysfunctional government—without sacrificing representative government, democratic norms, and civil liberties? There is no silver bullet to our challenge, no single answer. There is also no guarantee of success; but here are five complementary suggestions that are worth pursuing as part of a multifaceted initiative.

First, we need a genuinely progressive *economic nationalism* that shores up the middle class, attacks economic inequality and discrimination, reduces economic insecurity, recommits the public sector to service rather than predation, rebuilds America's global alliances, and tackles climate change (see, for example, Robert Kuttner 2018).[7] This sort of policy agenda certainly makes sense as a way to ensure that citizens view democracy, and a judiciary aimed at reasonableness, as worth saving. But how does such an agenda make its way through our confrontational and divided political and cultural climate (including polarized news and information sources)? It requires large-scale social mobilization, won't be easy, and many of us have been in this fight for decades, but it's definitely a worthwhile goal.

Second, institutionalist William Waller (2015, 327) argues that policies not based on reason must be met with a determined effort—by "educators, policy analysts, researchers, and decent human beings"—to identify and challenge decisions based instead on myths, misrepresentation, and outright lies. Waller writes: "Reason cannot overcome fantasy if the ideology and myths contained in the conventional wisdom are not challenged and discredited." He also stresses the need to remember history, which teaches us both how democratic crises have unfolded (thereby offering warning signs) and how such crises have been addressed in the past (thereby providing lessons of what worked, what didn't work, and why) (see also Levitsky and Ziblatt 2018; Applebaum 2017 and 2020).

Third, democratic norms—especially mutual toleration for political opponents—must be restored. In fact, in a book that followed their essay for *The New Republic*, Levitsky and Ziblatt (2018, 231) argue that democratic norms must not merely be restored: they must be *extended* into every corner of society. To be sure, democratic norms must be taught, but if such norms are to become widely held as an internalized ethic, then democratic principles and methods of engagement must be practiced regularly and in a wide range of organizational settings, including schools and the workplace.

Commons defended the democratic norm as the only way to retain individual liberties, and others in both our time and his have put forth corresponding arguments. Levitsky and Ziblatt (2018, 231) stress that previous generations made great sacrifices to craft and preserve the democratic system we inherited, and that we must now renew and fortify that system—to "prevent it from dying from within." Theologian Reinhold Niebuhr ([1944] 2011, xxxii) offered his case for democracy in 1944: "Man's capacity for justice makes democracy possible; but man's inclination to injustice makes democracy necessary." Niebuhr's reasoning was based in pragmatism, not morality: "Liberal democracy is worth defending not because it fulfills a moral ideal or because modern civilized types deserve nothing less, but because it is the best way to restrain human egotism and will-to-power" (Dorrien, in Niebuhr [1944] 2011, xx). Commons would have certainly agreed.

Fourth, it is worth exploring a suggestion that Commons offered at various times in his career: proportional representation. Instead of deciding legislative elections in a winner-take-all manner, relying on proportional representation—which gives voice to majority and minority parties in proportion to their votes—would be more representative of diverse economic and political interests (Commons 1934b, 898).[8] Winner-take-all elections are designed with the aim of "assuring majoritarian control over the government." Systems with proportional representation have a different aim: "[They] are based fundamentally on the idea that all significant points of view in society should be represented directly in the councils of decision making [in proportion to their incidence in the electorate]" (Gardner 2020, 12, 15, 26).

Those divergent aims lead to two very different conceptions of the common good. In the winner-take-all system, majority opinion decides the common good; in proportional representation, it is determined through "pluralistic bargaining among interest groups" (Gardner 2020, 22). In fact, representatives in winner-take-all systems "need not answer to or even consider the views of [political] minorities—in some cases, quite substantial minorities."

From the preceding comparison, one can see why Commons was attracted to proportional representation. It is consistent with his pragmatic conception of truth; it forces all perspectives to receive a hearing and thus be given "due weight" in decision making; and it enables legislatures to reflect diverse economic interests.[9] In addition, Commons knew the system worked in some U.S. cities and had worked for over a decade in Prussia (before being abolished by the military dictatorship of Germany). However, he also observed that it created only more political deadlocks and dysfunction in Italy, where "it furnished Mussolini with his most persuasive argument for the suppression of the legislature." In the end, Commons included a call for proportional representation in *Institutional Economics*, but he admitted, and was concerned, that the outcome in the United States could be the same as in Italy (Commons 1934b, 898–900).[10]

The fifth suggestion aimed at making democracy more effective, thereby helping to save judicial sovereignty as a path to reasonable value, also comes from Commons: it is a call for the widest possible use of government-established administrative commissions, in conjunction with stakeholder advisory committees, as a way to resolve public disputes and make rules and government regulations. The commission method of investigation and negotiation—which Commons championed in Wisconsin to address a variety of public issues including regulation of utilities and workplace safety—was offered in *Institutional Economics* not just as a sensible way to solve problems, but also as a method of preventing authoritarianism by "improving and retaining" federal, state, and local legislatures.[11] According to Commons (1934b, 900–901), such commissions can relieve legislatures of many "overwhelming details," enabling lawmakers to focus on activities at which they can be most effective: the fashioning of "general laws and general standards of administration." The expanded use of such commissions is also consistent with the recommendation (discussed above) by Levitsky and Ziblatt to bolster democratic norms through the extension of democratic practices across society.[12]

COLLECTIVE DEMOCRACY

Collective democracy can be seen as a broad term encompassing both the work of administrative commissions and the collective bargaining that takes place between parties such as labor unions and businesses.[13] But each of these lanes on the road to reasonable value is fraught with obstacles, including some that are common to both. Since Commons's conception began with labor-management relations and then expanded from there, this discussion also begins in the realm of industrial relations.

Industrial Relations

Collective bargaining in the field of labor-management relations—which Commons (1934a, 72) called "constitutional government in industry"—has a few prerequisites. For example, employees must be organized and have representatives that can negotiate with management on workers' behalf. In 2019, however, only 10.3 percent of wage and salary workers in the United States were members of unions—about half of the 20.1 percent unionization rate of 1983, and far below the peak of 34.8 percent in 1954 (Bureau of Labor Statistics 2020; Mayer 2004, 12). That decline in U.S. unionization contrasts sharply with survey data on worker preferences: in 2017, nearly half of those in the non-unionized, non-managerial workforce reported that they would join a union if they could, up from about one-third of workers surveyed forty years earlier (Kochan et al. 2019, 19–20).

Those findings on unionization and worker preferences—and the fact that many workers in today's "gig economy" are classified as self-employed contractors, rather than employees, and are therefore ineligible for union membership—are consistent with a sizable literature on the need for pragmatic labor law reform.[14] Such reform would make meaningful the existing right of workers to organize and bargain collectively, and extend that and other labor rights and benefits to gig workers and others currently excluded from protective labor legislation. For example, reform could also benefit many workers hired by subcontractors, which large companies often use to avoid responsibility for wages and working conditions (see McIntyre and Ramstad 2004; Weil 2014).

To be sure, there's good reason to have low expectations from efforts to achieve labor law reform. Supporters of workers' union rights have been unsuccessfully trying to reform labor law since 1947 (when Congress weakened union rights with the Taft-Harley Act), and recent Supreme Court decisions have not been favorable to organized labor.[15] But such reform could be enacted in 2021 if the Democratic Party has a major electoral victory on November 3, 2020. And, even without such reform, there are still a variety of innovative paths (including formation of citywide unions, community-labor partnerships, worker centers, and international coordination) available to those seeking to advance workers' interests on the collective bargaining front (see, for example, Fine et al. 2018). It must also be kept in mind that unions did not have the legal right to organize and bargain collectively in the United States until after Commons retired from the University of Wisconsin (in the early 1930s); that workers' efforts to organize and bargain collectively were, until the New Deal, often met with deadly force; and that for all but a few years at the end of Commons's life, unions covered a smaller fraction of the U.S. workforce than they do today (Mayer 2004, 11). In short, low expectations may be warranted, but giving up on worker organizing is not.[16]

Another prerequisite for meaningful collective bargaining is that both parties must bargain in good faith. For collective bargaining to succeed, both parties must recognize some shared interests and mutual dependence—otherwise, instead of constructive bargaining we could see (alas, as we have seen all too often in the United States) labor leaders fired for their union work (which is illegal, but still happens frequently), corporate facilities damaged, strikes that are long and violent, and jobs shipped offshore. Unfortunately, there are a myriad of reasons for parties to resist good faith negotiations—including lack of trust, a belief in retaining management prerogatives at all cost, and fear of "the uncertainties of experimentation" (Commons 1934b, 875 and 1934a, 73).

Yet there is also a large and decades-long literature, with real-world examples, on how collective bargaining can turn mutual dependence into substantial mutual gains.[17] That literature demonstrates how "investigative methods" and persuasion are often more advantageous to both sides than using "rough methods" (such as threats or illegal acts) and power.[18] It also shows that there is usually an ebb and flow to good faith and mutual-gains bargaining. Commons devoted much of his career to contributing to that literature, and this continues to be a useful way for institutionalists to help advance collective democracy.[19]

Commissions and Related Forums

Commons's commissions have frequently faced resistance for many of the same reasons that business and labor often resist good-faith bargaining. In fact, on the basis of his work with labor and management in the commission setting, Commons (1934b, 742–743) writes: "Malthusian passions and stupidity [often] put up a desperate front against even a social ideal that can be demonstrated to be practical." At the same time, Commons explains that his belief in pursuit of "what can be shown to be the best practicable" comes from seeing too many practitioners pursue *untried* solutions to problems and then become "disillusioned and turned into pessimists and reactionaries."

An innovation similar to Commons's commissions was envisioned for rulemaking within the federal government in the 1970s. Drawing inspiration and encouragement from labor economist John Dunlop (who served as President Gerald Ford's first Secretary of Labor), law professor Philip Harter and others worked in the 1970s and 1980s to bring negotiated rulemaking (also called "regulatory negotiation" or "collaborative governance") to agencies within the federal government (Harter 1982). As Harter (2009, 436) describes it, the aim of this "process innovation" was straightforward: "an open-minded collaboration with the shared quest of reaching an agreement that will be implemented."

In the rulemaking setting, bad-faith behavior by the participating stakeholders is not the only potential obstacle to success. For example, agencies "may be reluctant to lose control over the process;" and facilitators must take care to ensure that the voices of less organized interests are not excluded (Harter 2009, 414, 440; Freeman 1997, 97). Nevertheless, regulatory negotiation did achieve considerable initial successes, especially in the areas of health-and-safety and environmental regulation, including negotiated rules for off-road diesel emissions as well as for equipment leaks at chemical plants (Harter 2009; Freeman 1997). When this system of collaboration ultimately broke down in the late 1990s, it was in large part because many companies decided to exert political influence on agencies rather than engage in negotiations.[20]

Can agency-level collaborative governance be revived? Harter (2020) continues to think so. After all, Harter (2009, 431) asks, how else can the *public interest* be determined except "through careful analysis and the clash of ideas and interests, precisely the stuff of deliberative collaboration?" Looking back on the U.S. experience with negotiated rulemaking, he concludes: "Considerable benefits can result if the agency actually shares the decision-making by engaging representatives of those who will be substantially affected by the policy in its development" (Harter 2009, 418). Commons would concur; and would probably add, as he did in his autobiography, that we should not be discouraged by setbacks for collective democracy, since humans tend to exhaust all the alternatives before finally pursuing a path that works (Commons 1934a, 174).[21]

Another type of forum similar to Commons's commissions provides collective democracy at the community level: the area labor-management committee. These regional labor-management partnerships emerged after World War II and existed in over forty U.S. communities in the 1980s, providing an opportunity for representatives of workers and area businesses to improve labor relations and collaboratively address regional economic issues (Cutcher-Gershenfeld 1985). As industrial-relations scholar Joel Cutcher-Gershenfeld (1985, 101) observed at the time: such organizations "have been and remain somewhat fragile," but they have also "proved an important source of [community and labor-management] innovation."

In the 1980s, I conducted research on an area labor-management committee in Western New York. Then I returned to the region about a decade later as a participant observer. Perhaps the most significant difference I observed was that organized labor in the 1990s found the business community had become, at best, a reluctant partner. The area's unions felt strongly that Western New York had been left behind by the U.S. economic expansion of the 1990s and they wanted to join with the area's Chamber of Commerce and other community organizations to promote the region, its highly skilled workers, and its history of cooperative labor relations. The business community, however, wasn't interested (see Whalen 2011).

The local Chamber office (the Buffalo Niagara Partnership) had its own approach to promoting the region, its own activities, and its own agenda. It saw no need to engage with the local Buffalo Labor Council and other union groups. As a result, the labor movement created a nonprofit corporation, the Western New York Economic Development Group, and reached out to local public officials, educators, churches, and other community groups in pursuit of its own initiatives (including projects involving education, energy issues, and neighborhood revitalization). The business situation was the same across the country; and in 2006, when I met with executive directors of area labor-management committees who were trying to rebuild an association of such groups, there were only about ten remaining in the nation. Unions were in decline; business power was on the rise; and, to a large extent, the corporate sector in communities across the nation decided it just didn't need to engage with unions.

Commons actually understood this problem. In *The Economics of Collective Action*, he wrote that there is one dispute that can't be settled by an administrative commission: "the issue of economic power." According to Commons (1950, 266), matters involving economic power can be settled only though legislation, which, of course, is ultimately subject to judicial review. For the country as a whole, only the federal government has the clout to encourage, demand, or establish commissions, collective bargaining, and even a national network of regional labor-management partnerships. And if that doesn't succeed in achieving stakeholder negotiations "on something like an organized equilibrium of equality" (Commons 1934a, 73), only the federal government can go further and alter the ground rules: only it can insist upon "collective agreements between opposing organizations of power" in place of the exercise of sheer economic power (which Commons called "class war"). Thus, in the end, judicial sovereignty and collective democracy function as mutually reinforcing complements (Commons 1950, 266–270).

In fact, the federal government *did* create a network of area labor-management committees—just as it legislated the groundwork for (union-management) collective bargaining, administrative dispute resolution, and negotiated rulemaking.[22] The number of such committees grew rapidly in the 1970s and early 1980s, with some support from the Commerce Department and the Labor Department, but mostly as a result of a grants program managed by the Federal Mediation and Conciliation Service. That program was created by the National Labor-Management Cooperation Act of 1978, expressly for the purpose of fostering the establishment of community and enterprise-level labor-management partnerships (Cutcher-Gershenfeld 1985, 112). When the federal government signaled this was a national priority, such collective democracy flourished; when government support diminished toward the end of the 1980s, collective democracy began to wither. The lesson, and the route forward for all who seek to pursue reasonable value via collective democracy, is obvious.

CONCLUSION: PURSUING THE "MIDDLE WAY" WITH EYES WIDE OPEN

Some might think that an economist who focused so much on achieving "reasonable value" must have been a naive idealist. Commons was certainly not. In fact, Commons (1934b, 846) wrote: "Capitalism, like dictatorship and party politics, thrives on the stupidity of mankind. Is it not better, therefore, for peace of mind, to recognize in advance the foundations of capitalism than to turn out eventually disillusioned, hopeless, reactionary, revolutionary, or contented with 'natural law' instead of a better organized collective action?" Moreover, pragmatism and realism account not only for Commons's emphasis on solutions that have demonstrated their practicality, but also for his attention to two paths, rather than a single path, to reasonable value. To be sure, the two paths—judicial sovereignty and collective democracy—are there because they are complementary and mutually reinforcing, but given Commons's concern about authoritarianism, two paths also exist to provide reasonable value with a second chance in the event that one path becomes impassable for a time.

Commons also had exceptional foresight. He understood that, when left unchecked, a society's clash of economic classes would not resolve itself into a harmony of interests. Instead, it would lead to an endless succession of vicious conflicts, as one "top dog" seeks to replace the other. Thus, he tried to find a way to temper such conflicts by allowing for "the slow infiltration of reason" (Commons 1934b, 846). As he wrote in an article on capitalism and socialism:

> This entire idealism of harmony of interests, whether under capitalism or under socialism, falls to the ground once we recognize that social conflict has always been and always will be a fundamental fact in the progress of mankind ... There has not been and never will be an *automatic* harmony of interests ... If a harmony of interests is actually attained, it can be accomplished only as we go along, from day to day, dealing with each conflict as it arises, and settling it the best we know how. This is what is meant by the concepts of reasonable value and reasonable practice. (Commons 1925, 692, emphasis added)

Commons's pursuit of a "middle way" based on reasonable value remains a worthy goal. Indeed, as he wrote in his autobiography, it might be "the only way to save us" from greater social conflict, less freedom and opportunity, and more economic distress in the years to come (Commons 1934a, 73). Reasonable value could be just the antidote we need in an age of unreason.

NOTES

1. Commons, widely regarded as a founder of institutional economics and a pioneer in the study of labor, began his career in 1890; although he "retired" from the University of Wisconsin in 1932, Commons continued to teach for a number of years, and wrote about economics and the economy until his death in 1945. For an excellent recent biography of Commons, see John Dennis Chasse (2017).
2. In the mid-1990s, newspaper columnist and political analyst James Pinkerton (1994) made a similar observation when writing about Newt Gingrich: "Gingrich [whose staff freely describes him as a Leninist] is no Bolshevik, but he plots and prepares like one."

3. For a similar view on the Republican Party, see Jacob Hacker and Paul Pierson (2020).
4. That concentration and control of power by the financial sector is what Commons called "banker capitalism." To a large degree, the seat of such power was (and still is) the city of New York, not Washington, DC. But the Federal Reserve coordinated banker capitalism with authority granted by Congress, so the system was (and still is) a New York-Washington nexus, which Commons (1934b, 895) called "an economic government of bankers more powerful than the political government." Moreover, Commons observed that the "alliance of banking and industry is complete" because "great industrial corporations are represented on the boards of directors of the twelve reserve bank boards" (Commons 1934b, 890–891).
5. For additional discussions of authoritarian elements in the American experience, ranging from presidential wartime authority to suppression of investigative research, see Commons (1934b, 883–884 and 1934a, 165–181).
6. Writing in 1934, Commons (1934b, 897–902) suggested that the credibility of democratic legislatures was already on shaky ground in many countries; that many intellectuals were losing faith in democracy; that liberals across the world were being "gradually or violently squeezed out;" and that even supporters of democracy like him were not entirely sure that representative government was competent to manage a modern economy.
7. On the problem of public-sector predation, a situation in which government officials do not recognize the public interest and instead manage the public sector to serve private interests, see James Galbraith (2008). Also, one could add campaign finance reform to the broad agenda outlined above, including a constitutional amendment to overturn the Supreme Court's Citizens United ruling, which prohibits restrictions on corporate spending for political campaigns. Although Commons usually focused on judicial sovereignty, constitutional amendment is, of course, always available as a way to keep the Court in check.
8. In *Institutional Economics*, Commons (1934b, 900) writes: "Only when legislatures can be made representative of economic interests through their own freely elected leaders, can it be expected that they will have the experience and ability to hold in check the high-salaried executives and political machines of American banker capitalism."
9. On the matter of truth, Commons was influenced by the pragmatic philosophy of Charles S. Peirce, who wrote: "The opinion which is fated to be ultimately agreed to by all who investigate is what we mean by truth" (quoted in Commons 1934b, 152).
10. For evidence of growing interest in proportional representation, discussion of what it might look like in practice, and suggestions on how to prevent the deep conflicts that concerned Commons, see Greenblatt (2017); Drutman (2017); and Amy (n.d.).
11. For a discussion of the Wisconsin commission that Commons fashioned to address workplace safety, see Commons (1913, 395–424).
12. Since this policy note is being completed after the death of Supreme Court Justice Ruth Bader Ginsburg but before the 2020 presidential election, it seems a discussion of saving judicial sovereignty is incomplete without some comment on whether Joe Biden and the Democratic Party should increase the number of judges on the Court in the event that they have the opportunity in 2021. My view is that adding a seat (or two, if retaining an odd number of judges is deemed essential) would be appropriate in light of the Senate's unprecedented and indefensible refusal to grant Judge Merrick Garland a hearing in 2016, which has skewed the Court and thus

warrants a remedy. Nevertheless, the political fallout would likely only deepen the partisan divide and intensify the combativeness of U.S. politics. The nation's respect for judicial sovereignty stands to be harmed either way.

13. Commons's (1950, 256–257) vision of collective democracy extended even to the Federal Reserve, which he thought should be guided by "a powerful advisory committee" with a wide range of economic stakeholders.
14. For some practical reform proposals, see Kochan (2020); Marvit (2019); and Harris and Krueger (2015). Also see Rosenberg (2020), which discusses California's move in this direction by means of a "gig economy" law that took effect at the start of 2020.
15. An example of such a Supreme Court decision is *Janus v. AFSCME* (decided in 2018), which prohibits state and local government unions from collecting representation fees from non-union members of a bargaining unit, despite each union's legal obligation to represent all workers in the unit.
16. Employee representation in the form of government-mandated works councils, which are found in some parts of Europe, could also be established by federal law.
17. See, for example, Cohen-Rosenthal and Burton (1993); Fleron, Stanger, and Patton (2000); Preuss and Frost (2003); Barrett and O'Dowd (2005); Cutcher-Gershenfeld, Sleigh, and Pil (2006); Dabney (2015); and Beck (2018).
18. For Commons's discussion of "rough methods" (and misrepresentation) and the alternative of "investigative methods" (and prevention of problems), see Commons (1921).
19. Unions also bolster judicial sovereignty by strengthening representative democracy, see Chasse (2018).
20. According to Harter (2020), "Instead of trying to persuade agencies, companies decided to buy their bosses." He also argues that collaborative governance found itself out of step with the tone that Newt Gingrich set as Speaker of the House.
21. Of course, Commons (1913, 404–407) also stressed that collaborative governance requires a highly professional and nonpartisan staff that can conduct independent research. Lindsey and Teles (2017, 159–164) make the same argument and offer some recommendations to that end.
22. Such legislation includes the National Labor Relations Act of 1935, the Administrative Dispute Resolution Act of 1990, and the Negotiated Rulemaking Act of 1990. The first is discussed in Cutcher-Gershenfeld, Sleigh, and Pil (2006); the others are discussed in Harter (2009).

REFERENCES

Amy, Douglas J. n.d. "What is 'Proportional Representation' and Why Do We Need This Reform?" FairVote blog post. https://tinyurl.com/y4ar7zxe.

Applebaum, Anne. 2017. "100 Years Later, Bolshevism is Back. And We Should Be Worried." *The Washington Post.* November 6. https://tinyurl.com/yco4wees.

———. 2020. "History Will Judge the Complicit." *The Atlantic.* June 1, 2020. https://tinyurl.com/ya4w4zry.

Barrett, Jerome, and John O'Dowd. 2005. *Interest-Based Bargaining: A User's Guide.* Victoria, BC: Trafford.

Beck, Allison. 2018. "The Case for Dialogue and Dispute Resolution in the Future@Work." *Perspectives on Work* 22 (1): 14–19.

Bureau of Labor Statistics, United States Department of Labor. 2020. "Union Members Summary." *Economic News Release*, January 22. https://www.bls.gov/news.release/union2.nr0.htm.

Chasse, John Dennis. 2017. *A Worker's Economist: John R. Commons and His Legacy from Progressivism to the War on Poverty*. New York: Transaction Publishers.

———. 2018. "How Necessary are Unions? Insights from John R. Commons." *Journal of Economic Issues* 52 (2): 413–421.

Childs, Marquis. 1936. *Sweden: The Middle Way*. New Haven: Yale University Press.

Cohen-Rosenthal, Edward, and Cynthia E. Burton. 1993. *Mutual Gains: A Guide to Union-Management Cooperation*, second edition. Ithaca, NY: ILR Press.

Commons, John R. 1913. *Labor and Administration*. New York: Macmillan.

———. 1921. "Industrial Relations." In *Trade Unionism and Labor Problems*, second series. Edited by J. R. Commons, 1–16. Boston: Ginn and Company.

———. 1925. "Marx Today: Capitalism and Socialism." *Atlantic Monthly* 136 (11): 682–693.

———. 1934a. *Myself*. New York: Macmillan.

———. 1934b. *Institutional Economics: Its Place in Political Economy*. New York: Macmillan.

———. 1950. *The Economics of Collective Action*, edited by K. H. Parsons. New York: Macmillan.

Cutcher-Gershenfeld, Joel. 1985. "The Emergence of Community Labor-Management Cooperation." In *Industrial Democracy: Strategies for Community Revitalization*. Edited by Warner Woodworth, Christopher Meek, and Warner F. Whyte, 99–120. Beverly Hills, CA: Sage.

Cutcher-Gershenfeld, Joel, Steven R. Sleigh, and Fritz K. Pil. 2006. "Collective Bargaining: Keeping Score on a Great American Institution." In *Contemporary Issues in Employment Relations*. Edited by David Lewin, 39–68. Champaign, IL: Labor and Employment Relations Association.

Dabney, Dennis. 2015. "The Case for Partnership." *Perspectives on Work* 19 (1): 6–9.

Drutman, Lee. 2017. "This Voting Reform Solves Two of America's Biggest Political Problems." *Vox*. July 26. https://tinyurl.com/ycnrr96n.

Fine, Janice, Linda Burnham, Kati Griffith, Minsun Ji, Victor Narro, and Steven Pitts, eds. 2018. *No One Size Fits All: Worker Organization, Policy, and Movement in a New Economic Age*. Champaign, IL: Labor and Employment Relations Association.

Fleron, Lou Jean, Howard Stanger, and Eileen Patton. 2000. *Champions @ Work: Employment, Workplace Practices and Labor-Management Relations in Western New York: A Study*. Buffalo, NY: Western Region, ILR School, Cornell University. https://digitalcommons.ilr.cornell.edu/reports/11/.

Freeman, Jody. 1997. "Collaborative Governance in the Administrative State." *UCLA Law Review* 45 (1): 1–98.

Galbraith, James K. 2008. *The Predator State*. New York: Free Press.

Gardner, James A. 2020. "Conceptions of Politics in Comparative Perspective." In *Comparative Election Law*. Edited by James A. Gardner. Cheltenham (UK): Edward Elgar. Chapter posted online, June 7, 2020. https://tinyurl.com/yde2bhsb.

Greenblatt, Alan. 2017. "What's 'Proportional Voting,' and Why Is It Making a Comeback?" *Governing: The Future of States and Localities*. September. https://tinyurl.com/y9jh43eu.

Hacker, Jacob S., and Paul Pierson. 2020. *Let them Eat Tweets*. New York: W.W. Norton.

Harris, Seth D., and Alan B. Krueger. 2015. "A Proposal for Modernizing Labor Laws for Twenty-First-Century Work: The 'Independent Worker'." Discussion Paper 2015–10. The Hamilton Project, Washington, DC. https://tinyurl.com/yyu2uasb.

Harter, Philip J. 1982. "Negotiating Regulations: A Cure for Malaise." *Georgetown Law Journal* 71 (1): 1–118.

———. 2009. Collaboration: The Future of Governance. *Journal of Dispute Resolution* 2009: 411–488.

———. 2020. Personal correspondence with the author. June 8.

Kitagawa, Kota. 2017. "Two Methods of Institutional Reform in the *Institutional Economics* of John R. Commons." In *Contemporary Meanings of John R. Commons's Institutional Economics: An Analysis Using a Newly Discovered Manuscript*. Edited by Hiroyuki Uni, 73–98. Singapore: Springer.

———. 2020. "From Judicial Sovereignty to Collective Democracy: The Development of J.R. Commons' Perspective on Progressive Institutional Change." *Journal of Economic Issues* 54 (2): 316–321.

Kochan, Thomas A. 2020. "Worker Voice, Representation, and Implications for Public Policies." Research Brief, MIT Task Force on Work of the Future. July 2020. https://tinyurl.com/yyrzhne4.

Kochan, Thomas A., Duanyi Yang, William Kimball, and Erin L. Kelly. 2019. "Worker Voice in America: Is there a Gap between What Workers Expect and What They Experience?" *ILR Review*, 72 (4): 3–38.

Kuttner, Robert. 2018. *Can Democracy Survive Global Capitalism?* New York: Norton.

Levitsky, Steven, and Daniel Ziblatt. 2017. "How a Democracy Dies." *The New Republic*. December 7. https://tinyurl.com/y7e7zo9h.

Levitsky, Steven, and Daniel Ziblatt. 2018. *How Democracies Die*. New York: Crown.

Lewis, Sinclair. 1935. *It Can't Happen Here*. Garden City, New York: Doubleday, Doran. and Company.

Lindsey, Brink, and Steven M. Teles. 2017. *The Captured Economy*. New York: Oxford University Press.

Marvit, Moshe. 2019. "The PRO Act Is the Labor Reform that Workers Need and Deserve." Online Commentary, The Century Foundation. https://tinyurl.com/y8l84pka.

Mayer, Gerald. 2004. *Union Membership Trends in the United States*. Washington, DC: Congressional Research Service.

McIntyre, Richard, and Yngve Ramstad. 2004. "Not Only Nike's Doing It: 'Sweating' and the Contemporary Labor Market." In *The Institutionalist Tradition in Labor Economics*. Edited by Dell P. Champlin and Janet T. Knoedler, 297–314. Armonk, NY: M.E. Sharpe.

Niebuhr, Reinhold. (1944) 2011. *The Children of Light and the Children of Darkness: A Vindication of Democracy and a Critique of Its Traditional Defense*. With an introduction by Gary Dorrien. Chicago: University of Chicago Press.

Parramore, Lynn. 2018. "Meet the Economist Behind the One Percent's Stealth Takeover of America." Institute for New Economic Thinking. May 30. https://tinyurl.com/y5kdjnlk.

Pinkerton, James P. 1994. Gingrich's Window of Opportunity. *Los Angeles Times*. November 8. https://tinyurl.com/yaudm83a.

Preuss, Gil A., and Ann C. Frost. 2003. "The Rise and Decline of Labor-Management Cooperation: Lessons from Health Care in the Twin Cities." *California Management Review* 45 (2): 85–106.

Ramstad, Yngve. 1991. "From Desideratum to Historical Achievement: John R. Commons's Reasonable Value and the "Negotiated Economy" of Denmark." *Journal of Economic Issues* 25: 431–439.

Rosenberg, Eli. 2020. Can California Rein in Tech's Gig Platforms? *Washington Post* January 14. https://tinyurl. com/y8vw7fjg

Unstad, Lyder L. 1936. Review of *Sweden: The Middle Way. American Economic Review* 26 (2): 304–305.

Waller, William. 2015. "Policy in an Era of Unreason: Remarks Upon Receiving the Veblen-Commons Award." *Journal of Economic Issues* 49 (2): 321–327.

Weil, David. 2014. *The Fissured Workplace.* Cambridge: Harvard University Press.

Whalen, Charles J. 2011. "Union Engagement in Western New York Economic Development." In *Advances in Industrial and Labor Relations*, Volume 18. Edited by David Lewin, Bruce E. Kaufman, and Paul J. Gollan, 177–214. Bingley (UK): Emerald.

PART IV

Standing on the shoulders of Hyman Minsky

14. Stabilizing the unstable economy: Minsky and Simons on business cycle theory and policy

In the first issue of the *Journal of Post Keynesian Economics*, John Kenneth Galbraith argued that market mechanisms are losing their authority as a regulatory force in America. Thus, he suggested that economists "are faced with a three-way choice." One possible response is "to deny that anything much has happened to the market." Another is "to accept that the market has declined but to believe that it can be retrieved." The third is "to accept the decline of the market" and "address oneself to considering how the resulting economic performance can be made socially acceptable to as many people as possible" [Galbraith 1978, pp. 8–11].

According to Galbraith, the last of these approaches "is central to post-Keynesian economics" [Galbraith 1978, p. 11]. This is, of course, consistent with the fact that incomes policies and consensus-building mechanisms are often advocated by individuals in the "post-Keynesian" movement. Indeed, a willingness to "accept the decline of the market" is an important element that binds many post-Keynesians and institutionalists [Brazelton 1981, p. 541].

Hyman P. Minsky's *Stabilizing an Unstable Economy (SUE),* however, offers an agenda for economic reform that is not consistent with Galbraith's position. An industrial policy promoting competitive markets is a major element in the Minsky program. In fact, in his first chapter, Minsky notes that Henry C. Simons's "A Positive Program for Laissez-Faire" contains "a model of political economy" that is (despite the passage of over fifty years) "still worth considering" [Minsky 1986a, p. 9, n. 7].[1] Since Minsky is a major figure in the post-Keynesian movement, the connection between his policy recommendations and those of an individual associated with the so-called "Chicago School" of economics is one that deserves attention.

The present work addresses this matter by outlining Minsky's economic-policy program. In the process, recommendations that also appear in the writings of Henry Simons—one of Minsky's university professors—will be

Reprinted with permission from *Journal of Economic Issues* 25 (3), September 1991, 739–763.

identified and discussed. The article then considers how its findings affect our view of not only Simons and Minsky, but also Galbraith's remarks on post-Keynesianism and the decline of the market. The work closes by suggesting that attention to the Minsky-Simons connection might serve as a starting point for the revival of non-neoclassical business-cycle research.

While this essay relies heavily upon *SUE,* ideas from other works by Minsky are integrated into the analysis. We begin, however, by reviewing the pre-analytic and analytic elements shared by Minsky and Simons. The connection between their policy prescriptions can be fully appreciated only after recognizing that both hold a similar interpretation of how our economy functions.

MINSKY, SIMONS AND BUSINESS-CYCLE THEORY

Hyman Minsky is best known for the development of an investment theory of business cycles known as the "financial-instability hypothesis." Although the relationship between this theory and the ideas of John Maynard Keynes often receives attention, Minsky has indicated that the fundamentals of his hypothesis can be derived from the writings of three individuals: Keynes, Irving Fisher, and Henry Simons. In a recent essay in this journal, the present author outlined this connection between Minsky and Simons. Most of the economic policies recommended by Simons and Minsky were produced in response to their business-cycle analyses [Minsky 1986a, pp. 172–73; Whalen 1988a].

Theory

The cycle theories of Minsky and Simons rest upon some common pre-analytic elements. Specifically, both economists: (a) maintain that the U.S. economy is prone to endogenously generated booms and recessions; (b) reject a general-equilibrium point of view; and (c) seek to understand (and suggest ways to resolve) what they perceive as actual economic problems. Thus, their foundation contrasts sharply with the one adopted by neoclassical economists such as Robert E. Lucas.[2]

Turning to the succession of system states, one finds that Simons and Minsky also share a similar approach to economic dynamics. In particular, both maintain that our system's financial structure plays a central role in the production of industrial fluctuations. Specifically, both view business earnings as affecting future earnings (and prices and employment) through a process involving expectations, loan credit, and private investment. In a recovery, for example, a rise in business earnings engenders increased profit expectations, credit extensions, greater private investment, and increases in both industrial production and prices.[3]

Another similarity is that both analysts can explain an initial fall in business earnings as the product of endogenous economic-system forces. In particular, they maintain that cash-payment commitments will rise relative to cash receipts during the ordinary course of economic expansion. This is because production expenses are believed to rise late in the boom and eventually reduce the margin between sales prices and production costs.[4]

A final similarity involves the movement from recession back to recovery. Specifically, Minsky and Simons both offer two explanations of the return to an earnings level that is rising instead of falling. One requires government intervention (that is, expansionary monetary or fiscal policy) while the other requires a psychological change that increases investment (and aggregate demand) by raising earnings expectations.

The Need for Comprehensive Reform

In 1936, Simons wrote that "no real stability of production and employment is possible" without the drastic public- and private-sector reforms of a "genuine economic reconstruction" [Simons 1948, pp. 166, 170]. Today, Minsky's message is the same. As he noted in both *SUE* and *Can "It" Happen Again,* while "thoroughgoing reform" might engender "a closer approximation to a tranquil expanding economy," economic fluctuations are both "an observed characteristic of our economy" and a "natural" consequence of "noninterventionist capitalism" [Minsky 1982a, pp. xii–xxiv; 1986a, pp. 9–10, 292].

Thus, according to Minsky, the financial-instability hypothesis suggests the need for an entire "system of changes, not for isolated changes" [Minsky 1986a, pp. 332, 314]. As he wrote in *SUE,* "policy must range over the entire economic landscape and fit the pieces together in a consistent, workable way" [Minsky 1986a, p. 290]. Indeed, Minsky warns that "standing by themselves, unaccompanied by the requisite companion measures, the individual parts of an integrated reform program might be futile" [Minsky 1986a, p. 293].[5]

In *SUE,* Minsky's "agenda for an integrated program of reform" is presented as comprising four elements (Big Government, an employment strategy, financial reform, and a structure-of-industry policy). Instead, the present work divides his recommendations into two categories: those that address the symptoms of economic instability and those that address its causes. The following two sections examine these categories respectively.

ADDRESSING THE SYMPTOMS OF INSTABILITY

Although Minsky's agenda includes efforts to attack the causes of capitalist instability, he maintains that no capitalist economy can ever be entirely stable.[6]

Thus, the best course of action, he argues, is one that develops institutions and policies to attenuate and contain the thrust to instability. As he writes in the closing chapter of *SUE*, "even though all capitalisms are flawed, we can develop a capitalism in which the flaws are less evident than they have been since [the mid-1960s]" [Minsky 1986a, pp. 295, 10, 284, 288; 1982a, p. xxiii].

To contain industrial fluctuations, Minsky recommends stabilizing both employment and prices through the use of countercyclical macroeconomic policies. In particular, he calls for the federal government to produce a budget that would be balanced at some "readily attainable level of performance" (such as an unemployment rate of five percent). If economic activity fell below this level, a deficit capable of sustaining aggregate profits would be produced. Moreover, if inflation appeared, indicating a drift toward financial fragility, a budget surplus would be triggered and profits would be constrained [Minsky 1988, p. 27; 1986a, pp. 295–99, 302–4, 332].[7]

Although Minsky views fiscal policy as the primary tool of macroeconomic stabilization, he recognizes that monetary policy must also play a countercyclical role. For example, monetary authorities must intervene when faced with the threat of a serious debt deflation. Such a lender-of-last-resort intervention "allows particular units and branches of industry to fail even as it assures that the total available financing does not collapse" [Minsky 1986a, pp. 322, 324, 327].

In *John Maynard Keynes*, Minsky notes that an important theme in post-Keynesian economics involves the future's fundamental uncertainty [Minsky 1975b]. Moreover, in *SUE* he explains that he is seeking to reduce "the overall cyclical uncertainty" of capitalism by addressing the symptoms of instability with monetary and fiscal policies [Minsky 1986a, pp. 293, 327]. Yet while *JMK* maintains that Minsky's views are compatible with those found in Keynes's *The General Theory of Employment, Interest and Money*, readers familiar with the writings of Henry Simons will observe that Minsky's stabilization ideas are also quite similar to those expressed by Simons.

Simons

Throughout most of this century, free-market advocates have been characterized as proponents of a "do-nothing" policy. Simons disagreed:

> The representation of laissez faire as a merely do-nothing policy is unfortunate and misleading. It is an obvious responsibility of the state under this policy to maintain the kind of legal and institutional framework within which competition can function effectively as an agency of control. … Laissez faire, to repeat, implies a division of tasks between competitive and political controls; and the failure of the system, if it [fails or] has failed, is properly to be regarded as a result of failure of the state … to do its part [Simons 1948, pp. 42, 55].

According to Simons, "the [capitalist] state is charged ... with heavy responsibilities and large 'control' functions" [Simons 1948, p. 42]. Moreover, in his view, among the state's most important responsibilities is macroeconomic stabilization.

Although Keynes's *General Theory* introduced many American economists to the idea of countercyclical economic policies, Simons (and some of his colleagues at the University of Chicago) was writing in favor of such policies even before the *General Theory* was published. Specifically, Simons called for deliberate and combined monetary and fiscal actions to both achieve some level of "relatively full employment" and then stabilize aggregate profits, prices, incomes and employment [Simons 1933, pp. 5, 12; 1948, pp. 38–39, 74, 81, 108–20, 173, 175–77, 180–83, 332–35; 1938, pp. 221–24].[8]

One statement of this position can be found in Simons's famous "Rules versus Authorities" article of February 1936. To address the symptoms of capitalist instability, "we must," he wrote, "rely on government action." In particular, Simons suggested a reliance "on such injections of fiscal [and monetary] stimulants as may be necessary to prevent recurrence of wholesale liquidation; and, above all, on the prompt and drastic measures for debt retirement which may soon become imperatively necessary to prevent a disastrous inflationary boom" [Simons 1948, pp. 173].[9]

In short, the stabilization policies advocated by Minsky and Simons are indeed quite similar. Moreover, both recommend such policies for the same reason. In particular, both seek profit stability to—as Simons described it—"minimize the economic uncertainties" inherent in a system prone to industrial fluctuations [Simons 1938, p. 222; 1948, p. 183].

But if instability is an "inherent and inescapable" flaw of capitalist economies, it seems fair to ask why Minsky and Simons have not recommended the elimination of capitalism [Minsky 1986a, p. 120]. Indeed, Abba P. Lerner's conclusion upon studying Minsky's cycle analysis was as follows: "The only hope is to transform the system into a considerably more socialistic society with a more centrally planned economy" [Lerner 1976, p. 70].

Capitalism versus Socialism

To understand Minsky's reason for retaining a capitalist form of economic organization, one must first recognize that he views both capitalism and socialism as being inherently flawed. In particular, in addition to business cycles, capitalism is believed to engender an unreasonable distribution of income and enterprises with market power. Socialism, meanwhile, is said to have an "inherent totalitarian bias." It must also be recognized that Minsky's policy positions are inspired by what he refers to as "democratic ideals" and a commitment to "individual liberty." Thus, he is not interested in replacing capitalism with socialism [Minsky 1986a, pp. 8–9, 296, 332; 1975b, pp. 156–57, 169].

Finally, there are two other reasons why Minsky seeks to retain a capitalist system. One is that he agrees with Keynes, who wrote:

> [A decentralized market mechanism,] if it can be purged of its defects and its abuses, is the best safeguard of personal liberty in the sense that, compared with any other system, it greatly widens the field for the exercise of personal choice. It is also the best safeguard of the variety of life, which emerges precisely from this extended field of personal choice, and the loss of which is the greatest of all the losses of the homogeneous or totalitarian state. For this variety preserves the traditions which embody the most secure and successful choices of former generations; it colours the present with the diversification of its fancy; and, being the handmaid of experiment as well as of tradition and of fancy, it is the most powerful instrument to better the future [quoted in Minsky 1975b, p. 148].[10]

Perhaps even more important, however, is the fact that Minsky believes there are indeed policies that will permit capitalism to improve its "approximation to a tranquil expanding economy." Any need for "thoroughgoing socialism" is therefore eliminated by strategic intervention into "an economy that remains basically capitalist" [Minsky 1982a, p. xxiii; 1975b, pp. 149, 156, 168–69].

Like Minsky, Simons believed that both capitalism and socialism contain inherent flaws. In fact, Simons saw the same weaknesses as Minsky. Indeed, Simons's most well-known essay, "A Positive Program for Laissez Faire," is structured by a concern over instability, inequality and the development of market power. Moreover, Simons deeply believed that the alternative of socialism produced a "totalitarian, collectivist state" [Simons 1948, pp. 109, 30, 40–77, 165; 1933, pp. Al, A5; Minsky 1985a, p. 219].

Simons also matched Minsky's commitment to democracy and liberty [Simons 1948, pp. 1–11, 40–43, 56, 78, 89, 105, 181]. Further, both agree that personal liberty requires decentralized, competitive markets. As Simons wrote in 1934, "It seems clear ... that there is an intimate connection between freedom of enterprise and freedom of discussion and that political liberty can survive only within an effectively competitive economic system" [Simon 1948, p. 43].

Finally, as suggested earlier, Simons and Minsky both believe there is some economic reform program that, "if it could be realized politically, would suffice to permit tolerable functioning of a free-enterprise system and to prevent (or postpone) revolutionary change in our whole institutional framework." In short, each writer has indicated that "making capitalism a better system" is both desirable and possible [Simons 1948, pp. 56, 109, 111–12, 119–20].

ADDRESSING THE CAUSES OF INSTABILITY

In Minsky's view, a variety of elements engender instability in today's United States economy. To directly attack some of these elements, he believes that macroeconomic policies must be supplemented with the following: (a) federal fiscal policies that decrease the economy's dependence on private investment, and (b) a structure-of-industry policy that promotes competitive markets and reforms financial institutions in a comprehensive manner. Each of these supplements is considered here in turn.

Minsky on Fiscal Policy and Private Investment

Minsky's reason for seeking to decrease our economy's dependence on private investment is one that flows directly from his macroeconomic analysis. In particular, this analysis indicates that investment is the portion of aggregate demand that is most volatile. Indeed, it is for this reason that the financial-instability hypothesis can be considered an "investment theory of the business cycle" [Minsky 1988, p. 23]. Thus, the effort to decrease the significance of investment is an attempt to shift the weight of the economy toward its more stable spending components [Minsky 1986a, pp. 291–93, 300, 306, 308, 311–12, 314; 1978, p. 44; 1982a, p. 113; 1975a, p. 13; 1975b, pp. 93–94, 162–69].

This preference for fiscal policies that decrease the economy's dependence on private investment leads Minsky to recommend both spending and tax changes. For example, since military expenditures are a powerful investment stimulant, he has suggested a reduction of spending in this area.[11] Instead, he recommends expenditures that both enhance other public resources and reduce cyclical unemployment through the direct employment of labor. In fact, he advocates an employment strategy that would make public employment (at some modest income level) available for all who are without work [Minsky 1986a, pp. 270–71, 289, 291, 300–301, 308–12; 1982a, pp. xxiv, 1975b, pp. 154–69; 1975a, p. 13].[12]

Of course, it might be somewhat difficult for the federal government to provide the spending that Minsky suggests and simultaneously maintain the system of public transfers that exists today. But, argues Minsky, the government would not need to do both. For example, it is suggested that his system would greatly reduce unemployment insurance expenditures. In fact, he believes that the system could "allow us to dispense with almost all aid to families with dependent children" if introduced along with a universal children's allowance and other efforts to remove employment barriers [Minsky 1986a, pp. 300, 309–10, 312; 1982a, p. 201; 1981–82, p. 53].

On the tax side, Minsky recommends a more progressive personal income-tax structure (more brackets, higher rates, especially for those with very high incomes, and an increased personal exemption). In addition to generating more revenue and equality than the present income-tax system, it is believed that a more progressive structure would enhance economic stability [Minsky 1988, p. 27; 1986a, pp. 296, 305, 308, 1975b, pp. 158–60, 166–69]. Minsky also seems to favor steeper taxes on inherited wealth [Minsky 1975b, pp. 150–51, 159–60, 167]. As discussed in *John Maynard Keynes*, a more egalitarian society would contribute to the aim of "decreasing the dependence of the system upon private investment" [Minsky 1975b, p. 167].[13]

Another tax change that would contribute to this aim would replace employer contributions to Social Security with what Minsky calls a "universal" value-added tax (VAT). As he writes in *SUE*,

> [Since] employer contributions to Social Security are a VAT on labor's contribution to value added, tax avoidance leads business to substitute capital for labor in choosing production techniques. Inasmuch as capital-intensive techniques and the debt-financing by business to which it leads are destabilizing, the employer's contribution to Social Security is a doubly pernicious tax, reducing employment and fostering instability. A universal VAT is superior to our partial VAT [Minsky 1986a, p. 306].

In particular, Minsky suggests that "a comprehensive VAT to yield 3.0 percent or so of GNP seems a very modest revenue target" [Minsky 1986a, p. 307; 1988, p. 27; 1982a, p. 201].[14]

Simons on Fiscal Policy and Private Investment

While Simons's writings are unlike Minsky's in that they do not contain an explicit call for the decreased macroeconomic significance of private investment, the former's monetary reforms contain an element that amounts to nearly the same thing. In particular, although Simons seeks to avoid government control over the *direction* of private investment, his "quantitative control of credit" (achieved through banking and other financial reforms) would regulate the aggregate *size* of such investment [Simons 1948, p. 332]. At least in prosperous times, then, this credit control would constrain the growth of private investment and shift the weight of the economic system toward its more stable components.

Moving from the level of policy strategy to specific fiscal components, we find even more agreement. For example, both Minsky and Simons propose a greater emphasis on public-goods creation. As Simons wrote in 1934, if his economic reforms were implemented, we could

> look forward confidently to continued augmenting of the "free income" of the masses, in the form of commodities and services made available by government,

> either without charge or with considerable modification of prevailing price controls. There are remarkable opportunities for extending the range of socialized consumption (medical services, recreation, education, music, drama, etc.) and, especially, for extending the range of social welfare activities [Simons 1948, pp. 68, 318].

Simons's works also suggest that he shared Minsky's belief in the need for government to serve as employer of last resort. As J. Ronnie Davis has noted,

> There is no question but that Simons and his [Chicago] colleagues argued throughout the early 1930s for large and continuous deficit budgets as the key to checking and reversing the massive unemployment and deflation, played an important role in the development of the notion of compensatory public spending, and attempted to persuade Washington to adopt large budgetary deficits [Davis 1969, pp. 388–89].

Indeed, in 1944 Simons stated his position succinctly: "If expansion of private output and investment does not provide adequate employment, governmental enterprise and investment must fill the gap" [Simons 1948, p. 117].

On the matter of taxation, meanwhile, one finds still more harmony in the views of Minsky and Simons. In particular, both favor a fiscal system with progressive taxation of personal income "as its centerpiece" [Minsky 1986a, p. 305].[15] Moreover, it appears that Simons and Minsky also agree on the need for a more aggressive approach to inheritance taxation [Simons 1948, pp. 65–69, 76, 148].[16]

Minsky on Competitive Markets and Financial Reform

The recommendations outlined so far seek to retain (indeed, strengthen) the stabilizing power of macroeconomic policy while modifying fiscal policies in a way that reduces the likelihood of industrial fluctuations. Minsky's structure-of-industry policy, meanwhile, is designed to promote competitive markets and reform financial institutions—defined so as to include even ordinary firms—in a comprehensive manner. This "industrial policy" is consciously based upon the writings of Simons. Indeed, according to Minsky the coupling of such a policy with those described above is not merely "appropriate" but rather "a natural union" [Minsky 1987a, p. 31; 1986b, pp. 63–64; 1982a, p. 201; 1986a, p. 329].

Although decentralized, competitive markets cannot put an end to business cycles (which is why the aforementioned policies are needed as well), Minsky maintains that they can constrain or eliminate some sources of instability. For example, such markets allow us to avoid the "moral hazard" problem associated with giant enterprises. Further, competition reduces both the inflationary pressures engendered by market power and the instability caused by income inequality [Minsky 1985b, pp. 17–18; 1986a, pp. 8–9, 199, 296, 318, 332; 1982a, p. 201].

Moreover, decentralized markets are "fine social devices for taking care of [most of] the particular outputs and prices of an economy" (especially in light of the fact that "there are limitations to what can be administered competently" by any public body) [Minsky 1986a, pp. 295–96, 291, 293]. They also permit a release of "the undoubtedly strong entrepreneurial drives that exist in our nation" [Minsky 1986b, p. 64].[17] Thus, "once we achieve an institutional structure in which upward explosions from full employment are constrained even as profits are stabilized, then [most of] the details of the economy can be left to market processes" [Minsky 1986a, pp. 295–96].

Of course, this industrial policy requires a variety of positive, public-sector interventions to constrain market power and promote competition. A first step would be the federal chartering of corporations. This is because such action would offer a way to "revise and make uniform the rules of corporate governance" [Minsky 1987a, pp. 30–31]. Moreover, since money plays a critical role in Minsky's cycle analysis, the primary focus of his proposed interventions is a reform of financial relationships [Minsky 1986a, p. 314].

The reforms establishing and enforcing Minsky's "good financial society" would produce smaller firms and a greater emphasis on direct ("to-the-asset") financing than we have at present [Minsky 1982a, pp. 69, 201; 1986a, pp. 315, 318, 321–22]. In particular, he believes that there should be limits (varying, perhaps, by industry) on the size of assets or employees that any private organization can deploy.[18] He also calls for a uniform, bank capital-asset ratio ("a 5 percent asset-equity ratio seems reasonable" [Minsky 1986a, p. 320]) and an increased payout ratio for bank earnings. As Minsky stated in a recent interview, "The [economic] system would be more stable if the banking system were decentralized, with many small and independent banks serving an industrial and commercial structure of small and medium-size firms" [Minsky 1988, p. 28; 1986a, pp. 318–22, 330–31; 1982a, p. 201; 1985b, pp. 17–18].[19]

Minsky's industrial policy would also require changes in the practices of our central bank. For example, as he wrote in *SUE*,

> a *major* necessary reform is for the Federal Reserve to shift from the open-market technique to discounting. The discount window method for creating the reserve base induces favorable terms for the hedge financing of short-term positions and blunts the tendency toward fragile financing structures [Minsky 1986a, p. 325].[20]

Relying on the discount window is important because it enables the Federal Reserve to "look over the shoulder and comment on the adequacy of a bank's practices." In short, bank examination would be "a natural outgrowth of the banking relation between banks and the Federal Reserve" and in this way the latter could "continuously 'lean against' the use of speculative and Ponzi finance" [Minsky 1986a, pp. 326, 328].[21]

Still another element in the Minsky corporate-reform program is elimination of the corporate income tax. There are many reasons given for this. For example, the tax is said to induce debt-financing (since it "allows interest to be deducted prior to the determination of taxable income"), increase prices (since it tends to "show up in product prices just as a sales tax"), and encourage both market power and nonproductive, executive expenses (since "advertising, marketing, and the pleasures of the executive suites can be charged against revenues in determining taxable income"). Moreover, to handle the problem of tax avoidance, Minsky would treat corporations as if they were proprietorships or partnerships. In particular, this "would require a full imputation of per-share income to the stockholders regardless of whether or not dividends were paid" [Minsky 1986a, pp. 305–6].[22]

While Minsky views decentralized markets as useful social instruments, he also believes that some industries—because of externalities and/or capital intensity—require additional forms of public regulation and intervention. He is especially concerned that financing the most capital-intensive processes and expensive capital assets requires market power. Thus, he suggests it may be appropriate (and stabilizing to the macroeconomy) to provide government financing—and perhaps even public ownership—in industries requiring such processes and assets [Minsky 1982a, pp. 86, 201, 329–31; 1986a, p. 295; 1985c, p. 64; 1988, p. 31].

There are enterprises in two industries, moreover, to which Minsky gives particular attention—railroads and electric utilities (especially nuclear power facilities). This is because they both "combine capital intensity with enormous externalities" [Minsky 1986a, p. 331]. Here he calls for public ownership and operation (perhaps through a government agency like the Tennessee Valley Authority). Although he recognizes the political difficulties that such a suggestion raises, he views this approach as the most straightforward and effective way of managing these two industries [Minsky 1986a, pp. 331–32; 1982a, p. 201].

Finally, while Minsky believes it is possible to improve economic performance relative to the past, he stresses that "there is no economic organization, no magic formula which, once achieved and set in motion, solves the problem of economic policy for all times" [Minsky 1982a, p. 113]. Indeed, he notes that while the whole of any economic system is constantly in a state of evolution, the financial structure is particularly dynamic in a capitalist society. Thus, he concludes *SUE* in the following manner: "There is no possibility that we can ever set things right once and for all; instability, put to rest by one set of reforms will, after time, emerge in a new guise" [Minsky 1986a, pp. 333, 7, 243–44, 287, 314, 328, 323; 1977, pp. 306–7; 1982a, pp. 113–14; 1975b, p. 168; 1988, p. 28; 1982b, p. 380].

Simons on Competitive Markets and Financial Reform

As mentioned above, Minsky's call for government intervention to promote and sustain competitive markets is based consciously on the ideas of Simons. It is not surprising, therefore, that these economists offer strikingly similar recommendations in the area of industrial policy. We begin this subsection by comparing their reasons for seeking to remove monopoly elements from most industries.

Of course, both Minsky and Simons believe that corporate market power has often been a source of much economic instability.[23] But they also agree that competitive markets are useful devises for guiding the allocation of most resources.[24] As Simons noted in 1934,

> The existence (and preservation) of a competitive situation in private industry makes possible a minimizing of the responsibilities of the sovereign state. It frees the state from the obligation of adjudicating endless, bitter disputes among persons as participants in different industries and among owners of different kinds of productive services [Simons 1948, p. 42].

Moreover, Minsky and Simons share a critical view of the modern corporation's efficiency and capacity for innovation. Thus, they expect their anti-monopoly reforms to promote, not retard, economic progress.[25] As Simons wrote in *Economic Policy for a Free Society*,

> The profligate dispensation of privileges under incorporation laws may have accelerated the industrialization of America. Existing corporation laws may have been somewhat appropriate to an agricultural nation bent on rapid change. They may, by their extravagances, have accelerated progress. But they are surely ill designed to sustain progress or tolerable operation of the economy they promoted. Turned loose with inordinate powers, corporations have vastly over organized most industries. Having perhaps benefited briefly by corporate organization, America might now be better off if the corporate form had never been invented or never made available to private enterprise [Simons 1948, p. 34].[26]

But how would the "urgent task of deorganizing industry and deconcentrating industrial control" proceed? Simons and Minsky would both begin with a "thoroughgoing reform in corporation law"—reform that would vest the right to charter private corporations exclusively in the federal government [Simons 1948, pp. 34–35, 57–60, 81–83, 101]. Further, both men view their corporate reforms as part of a comprehensive reconstruction—establishing what Simons called "the financial good society"—of our nation's financial structure [Simons 1948, pp. 171–72, 191, 239, 331].

Both the overall goals and details of the financial reforms proposed by Minsky and Simons are also similar. These men see "our financial system [as] simply too elaborate and too complex" and agree that a restructured financial system should "promote smaller and simpler organizations weighted more toward direct financing than they are now" [Simons 1948, pp. 38, 171, 229–30; Minsky 1982a, p. 201]. Moreover, they each support size limitations on firms and rules prohibiting operating corporations from owning the securities of other companies.[27]

Simons's banking reforms are more drastic than those proposed by Minsky. For example, Simons recommended the following changes: (a) "complete separation, between different classes of corporations, of the deposit and lending functions of existing deposit banks;" (b) "legislation requiring that all institutions which maintain deposit liabilities and/or provide checking facilities (or any substitute therefor) shall maintain reserves of 100 per cent in cash and deposits with the Federal Reserve banks;" and (c) "displacement by notes and deposits of the Reserve banks of [private-bank credit and] all other forms of currency in circulation, thus giving us a completely homogeneous national circulating medium" [Simons 1948, pp. 62–63]. Nonetheless, the banking recommendations of these men are linked by an important similarity—both desire a "radical decentralization" that would facilitate "new [bank and non-bank] enterprise" and the multiplication of "small and moderate-size firms" [Simons 1948, pp. 34, 117–20, 236–38; 1933, p. 2].

Turning to the matter of corporate income taxes, we find still more agreement between Simons and Minsky. In particular, there are three important commonalities. First, both mention "the unhappy influence of interest deductions in the corporation tax" [Simons 1948]. Second, both propose the repeal of this income tax [Director 1946, pp. 16, 18]. Finally, both are not only concerned about "evasion of the personal income tax by stockholders with respect to undistributed earnings of corporations" but also recommend the same strategy to prevent such action. As Simons noted in "A Positive Program for Laissez Faire," effective provision against this type of evasion involves "taxing shareholders in corporations in exactly the same manner as members of partnerships" [Simons 1948, pp. 59, 66–67].

As suggested above, a discussion of the corporate income tax leads Minsky to express a negative view of advertising and marketing. Indeed, it appears that he hopes such practices will receive much less attention after the corporate tax is repealed and the size of enterprises is constrained. While this hope is shared by Simons, the latter goes further and writes: "The strongest case can be made for heavy taxation of advertising, provided rates can be made much higher than revenue considerations would dictate" [Simons 1948, p. 73].

Yet there is another similarity on the subject of merchandising in addition to the common desire to see the curtailment of such activities. It is that Minsky and Simons are critical of these efforts for the same reasons. In particular, both criticize advertising and marketing for the following reasons: (1) they breed market power and erect a barrier to competition in industry; (2) they waste economic resources on nonproductive activities; (3) they impose inflationary pressure on the economic system; and (4) they often result in what Minsky has called the "artificial stimulation" of consumption [Simons 1948, pp. 57, 71–73, 85, 95; Minsky 1986a, pp. 260, 306; 1975b, pp. 153–54, 165].

While Simons and Minsky agree on the need to rely heavily upon decentralized markets, they also agree that "competition cannot be made to function effectively as an agent of control" in every industry. Further, both maintain that it may be most appropriate to depend on "direct government ownership and operation" in industries unable to sustain competitive arrangements [Simons 1948, p. 57]. Moreover, both note that the public sector "should plan definitely on socialization of the railroads and utilities" [Simons 1948, pp. 57–58, 61–62, 83, 86, 102].

Additional Similarities

Our look at the policy perspectives of Minsky and Simons concludes by noting three final similarities. First, though suggested earlier, it is worth underscoring the fact that both Simons and Minsky believe "instability is an inherent and inescapable flaw of capitalism" [Minsky 1986a, p. 120]. While each proposes "thoroughgoing reform" to minimize the causes and effects of industrial fluctuations, neither believes that business cycles can be eliminated completely. As Simons wrote in "Rules versus Authorities in Monetary Policy," one should expect some "occasional [macroeconomic] disturbances" from even the best form of capitalism [Simons 1948, pp. 165, 172].

Second, both Minsky and Simons maintain that minimizing capitalist instability requires a comprehensive, "system of changes." Both men treat economic policy as a unified whole and offer specific reforms as parts of the "total arrangements" necessary to achieve a more stable, democratic and humane society. Moreover, at the heart of each of their comprehensive sets of arrangements is a common belief in the need for "a genuine 'division of labor' between competitive and political controls" [Simons 1948, pp. vi, 40–43, 56–57, 78–79, 160, 170].

Finally, neither Minsky nor Simons have a static conception of the "good society." For example, both recognize that not even the adoption of a comprehensive set of reforms will permit our society to experience tranquil economic progress for all time. As Simons noted in "Rules versus Authorities,"

> [In time, many reforms] may prove ineffective and disappointing because of the reappearance of prohibited practices in new and unprohibited forms. It seems

> impossible to predict what forms the evasion[s] might take or to see how particular prohibitions might be designed in order that they might be more than nominally effective [Simons 1948, p. 172].

Further, both recognize that the "good society" can only be maintained if society progresses "not only in terms of prevailing criteria but also in [its conception of] the criteria themselves" [Simons 1948, p. 2; Minsky 1986a, p. 7; 1975b, p. 168].

IMPLICATIONS AND CONCLUSIONS

The preceding discussion demonstrates that the economic-policy strategies of Hyman Minsky and Henry Simons have a great deal in common. This work concludes by considering some implications of what we have found. In particular, what has been shown above affects how we view not only Simons and Minsky, but also Galbraith's remarks on post-Keynesian economics and "the decline of the market."

Simons

Many economists from across the spectrum of economic thought view Simons as an originator of monetarism, a member of the camp that believes markets are self regulating, and an opponent of both government intervention and the economics of Keynes.[28] Indeed, Robert Lucas has even maintained that much of his business-cycle research "is simply an attempt to understand and make more explicit the implicit model underlying the policy proposals of Henry Simons ... and other critics of activist aggregative policy" [Lucas 1981, p. 260]. It is clear from our discussion, however, that such views are not correct.

Lucas's approach to macroeconomic fluctuations is an attempt to find a general-equilibrium explanation. Moreover, as he noted in 1976, "By seeking an equilibrium account of business cycles, one accepts *in advance* rather severe limitations on the scope of governmental countercyclical policy which might be rationalized by the theory." Simons, meanwhile, rejected both the equilibrium starting point and the severe limitations on government policy. While Lucas explicitly acknowledges that his account of business cycles is nothing more than an "elegant rationalization" of a monetarist approach to economic stabilization, there is no doubt that Simons would have opposed both the purpose and conclusions of Lucas's work [Lucas 1981, pp. 2, 234–35, italics in original].

Indeed, it seems that Simons would find the macroeconomics of Lucas and other modern neoclassical theorists far more objectionable than the economics of Keynes. As even Milton Friedman [1967] has acknowledged, Simons and

Keynes shared both a similar interpretation of industrial fluctuations (both in general and with respect to the Great Depression in particular) and many parallels in the realm of policy advice. The similarities in the views of Keynes and Simons have also been mentioned by J. Ronnie Davis. As Davis noted in a 1969 article entitled "Henry Simons, the Radical," Simons's review of the *General Theory* indicates not only that he accepted Keynes's argument regarding the source of deflationary pressures, but also that he was "not inclined to be more generous toward monetary orthodoxy than is Mr. Keynes." In fact, Simons concluded by welcoming the "opportunity to defend Mr. Keynes against all advocates of reactionary monetary policies" [quoted in Davis 1969, p. 394].

Minsky

While this work has demonstrated that the policy recommendations of Minsky and Simons have much in common, it has also suggested that Minsky is conscious of the similarities between his views and those of his former University of Chicago professor. The acknowledged connection is especially strong with respect to Minsky's industrial policy; but this is not the only area where one finds such ties.[29] Moreover, as mentioned in the introduction to the present essay, Minsky's *SUE* indicates in its first chapter that he finds a valuable and still relevant "model of political economy" in Simons's writings.[30]

Minsky has often noted that Simons was one of three teachers who had a great impact on his thinking.[31] In fact, during a recent professional gathering Minsky remarked that he may have learned as much economics through his many informal conversations with Simons as he did in the classrooms of Chicago and Harvard [Minsky 1987b].[32] Nonetheless, the Minsky-Simons connection is absent from almost every examination of Minsky's writings. Instead, nearly all economists focus exclusively on Minsky's intellectual ties to Keynes.[33]

The fact that this thread in the history of economic thought is overlooked is truly unfortunate. A major implication of the present work is that one cannot fully understand and appreciate Minsky's views on theory and policy unless his ties to Simons are recognized. While Minsky has been a student of the writings of John Maynard Keynes for a long time, it must be recalled that he was first a student of the ideas of Henry Calvert Simons.[34]

Post-Keynesianism and the "Decline" of the Market

Finally, we return to the remarks of John Kenneth Galbraith and the suggestion that accepting the decline of the market is "central" to post-Keynesian economics. It is clear from our analysis that Galbraith's position is unacceptable.

It is a position that simply cannot accommodate Minsky—one of the towering figures in American post-Keynesianism.

While Galbraith's attempt to characterize a school of economic thought by a policy stance is not uncommon, it involves a method that is almost always unsuccessful. Moreover, it often leads to factionalism and disputes among individuals sharing a common view of how our economic system (or some other economy that is the subject of analysis) functions.[35] Thus, it seems best to identify post-Keynesians and those of the other so-called "schools" (such as institutionalists, Marxists, and neoclassicals) by the theories they employ, or perhaps even by the set of methodological preconceptions to which they adhere.[36] In short, focusing on how economists approach their professional task of understanding and predicting economic-system behavior seems a much more appropriate way to identify (and distinguish among) various traditions in our science.

But the suggestion that post-Keynesians should be identified by their preconceptions and/or theories raises an intriguing question. Would such definitions lead one to view Simons as a member of the post-Keynesian camp? Exposing the various preconceptions of Simons's work and comparing them with the views of Minsky and other post-Keynesians are tasks that cannot be accomplished in the present work. Nonetheless, it is clear from Simons's description of laissez-faire (discussed above) that he adopts a more holistic and less deterministic view of economic systems than many conventional economists. It is also clear that Simons has accepted one fundamental starting point of post-Keynesian and institutional economics: that institutional adjustment, not the price system, provides the "balancing wheel" of an economy.[37]

Meanwhile, despite the somewhat inappropriateness of the label, Minsky's "post-Keynesian" theory of business cycles is in many ways a refined version of Simons's analysis. While Simons did not share the Keynesian view that wage and price flexibility might have a negative effect on profit flows and expectations, it is clear that Simons's theory of cycles is closer to Keynes—and institutionalists such as Thorstein B. Veblen and John R. Commons—than it is to either the "classicals" of Keynes's time or the neoclassicals of our own. If the theories of so-called classicals and neoclassicals are used to define the "orthodox" school, then Simons's cycle analysis belongs instead in the "heterodox" (yet non-Marxian) camp with Keynes, Minsky, Veblen, Commons and others.[38]

In closing, then, although Minsky and Simons are not willing to accept the decline of the market, both would accept Galbraith's suggestion that market mechanisms have been losing authority as a regulatory force throughout twentieth-century America.[39] This is a significant similarity and should not be overlooked. Keynes and Simons can be interpreted as founders of opposing camps only if we suppress a common, central insight of each author—that the structure of advanced capitalist economies engenders industrial fluctuations and involuntary unemployment. By studying the Minsky-Simons connection and the writings of other early twentieth-century business-cycle theorists, it becomes clear that modern neoclassical economics, not post-Keynesianism and institutionalism, represents an aberration from the historical mainstream in macroeconomics.

NOTES

1. While Minsky has written more about the similarity between his views and those of Simons in recent years, he has hinted at this for some time. In a 1969 work, for example, he wrote: "For the entire issue of the good financial society various writings of Henry Simons are still relevant" [Minsky 1982a, p. 191, n. 5].
2. For a more detailed discussion of the cycle theories of Simons and Minsky—and a comparison with the macroeconomics of Lucas—see Whalen [1988a].
3. A decline in business earnings will, of course, reverse this process.
4. The firm experiencing such a cash shortage can seldom acquire new loans. As Thorstein Veblen—whose approach to business cycles has much in common with the analyses of both Simons and Minsky (see Whalen [1989a])—writes, this firm cannot obtain a new loan because "its obligations have already been augmented to the extent which its recent earnings-capacity would warrant" [Veblen 1904, pp. 202–3].
5. In *SUE*, for example, Minsky notes that lender-of-last-resort action by the central bank "virtually assures that there will be another crisis in the near future" unless legislated and/or administered policy changes prohibit (or at least discourage) "fragility inducing financial practices" [Minsky 1986a, p. 327].
6. In Minsky's analysis, capitalism is defined by the existence of certain institutions and elements that engender financial instability and industrial fluctuations [Minsky 1975b, p. 57; 1982a, pp. 71–72]. As he wrote in 1982, "No matter how industry and government finances are structured, as long as the economy remains capitalist ... there will be business cycles ... The basic shortcomings of a capitalist economy that lead to [such] cycles are related to the ownership, creation and financing of capital assets" [Minsky 1982a, pp. xxiii–xxiv].
7. From Minsky's (and Simons's) perspective, the stabilization of aggregate profits is, of course, central to macroeconomic stabilization. If profit fluctuations are contained, then the likelihood of changes in output and employment levels is significantly reduced.
8. Although Simons often wrote about the need for a price-level stabilization rule, it is clear that his ultimate objective was more than just stable prices. In fact, in his 1936 "Rules versus Authorities" article, Simons explicitly mentioned that this rule was designed to achieve "the end of profit [and thus production and employment] stability" [Simons 1948, p. 169]. For discussions of the advantage that a price-level rule has over the fixed quantity of money rule, see Simons [1948, pp. 164, 331].
9. Simons's link between fiscal and monetary policy is the financing of public budgets. As he wrote in "Rules versus Authorities,"

> The powers of the monetary authority should have to do primarily or exclusively with fiscal arrangements—with the issue and retirement of paper money (open-market operations in government securities) and perhaps with the relation between government revenues and expenditures; in other words,

> the monetary rules should be implemented entirely by, and in turn should largely determine, fiscal policy [Simons 1948, pp. 182, 175, 320–31].

Indeed, in another work Simons wrote:

> [F]iscal policy cannot be separated from monetary (or banking) policy, however convenient the separation might be for academic specialists. We must talk about budgetary problems as monetary problems (and vice versa) or talk irrelevant nonsense about them both [Simons 1938, p. 222].

Because of this connection, both the monetary and fiscal policies of Simons would operate in a countercyclical manner.

10. See also Minsky [1986a, pp. 291, 295–96, 329].
11. A government that relies heavily upon military expenditures is also criticized by Minsky because it augments the demand for consumer goods and services without producing a corresponding increase in their supply. Government transfers receive the same criticism. For example, see Minsky [1986a, pp. 260, 270].
12. While it is impossible to discuss all aspects of Minsky's fiscal-policy strategy, four points deserve to be mentioned. First, Minsky identified what we might call an "added benefit" of public-resource creation in a 1982 essay. In particular, this "benefit" is that such assets "increase the efficiency of privately owned capital." In other words, "A government which is big because it engages in resource creation and development will encourage a greater expansion of output from private investment than is the case for a government which is big [for other reasons]" [Minsky 1982a, p. xxiv].

    Second, training and human-resource development are important elements in Minsky's employment strategy [Minsky 1986a, pp. 308–12]. Third, much of his public employment seems directed toward work that is labor-intensive. Although the issue is never discussed directly, it appears (from Minsky [1982a, p. 113], for example) that at least part of Minsky's intention here is to minimize the stimulative impact of federal spending on private investment. Finally, Minsky makes it clear that one reason for his emphasis on employment programs is his belief that "dignity and independence are best served" by a system in which an adult "earns his or her way through the exchange of income for work" [Minsky 1986a, p. 9].
13. Minsky suggests that a more progressive income tax would enhance economic stability in a number of ways. Contributing to the aim of decreasing the system's dependence on investment is only one of these ways. For discussions of others, see Minsky [1986a, pp. 296, 305].
14. Another change suggested by Minsky would raise gasoline and oil taxes. Although this is recommended "to promote conservation and divert imports to non-oil-producing nations," such a change also appears consistent with his desire to reduce the attractiveness of private investments in capital assets [Minsky 1986a, p. 307; 1988, p. 27].
15. In light of the fact that Minsky supports increasing the tax on gasoline (see note 14 above), it is interesting to observe that Simons calls for the abolition of all excise taxes with the exception of the one on this product. The latter's justification, however, is quite different from that used by Minsky. In particular, Simons explains that gas taxes are "eminently defensible as charges for special services of government to a class (or to a form of consumption) which does not merit subsidy" [Simons 1948, pp. 68, 83; 1938, pp. 38–39, 220].

16. Simons summarized his preferred approach to taxation in "A Positive Program for Laissez Faire" as follows: "Such a policy requires the establishment of the [progressive] personal income tax as the predominant element in our whole fiscal system and the rescue of inheritance taxation from its miserable failure" [Simons 1948, p. 66]. Moreover, as in the Minsky tax plan, a desire to reduce inequalities of wealth and income is evident in the Simons recommendations (and explicitly mentioned in the accompanying discussions) [Simons 1948, pp. 57, 65, 83].
17. While some might argue that large firms are essential to economic growth and innovation, Minsky believes that "enterprises on the scale of the American giant firms tend to become stagnant and inefficient" [Minsky 1975b, p. 167]. Indeed, in 1985, he wrote that "the corporate form has degenerated to the point where it no longer is a reliable engine of progress" [Minsky 1985c, p. 62]. See also Minsky [1986a, pp. 8–9; 1986c, p. 64; 1988, p. 31].
18. In addition, Minsky [1985c, pp. 61–62] has written: "One possible path of [corporate] reform is to forbid operating corporations from owning the stock or the bonded debts of other corporations." For more on his view of corporate financial reform, see Minsky [1982a, pp. 57, 71–72, 86, 113; 1975b, pp. 167–68; 1988, p. 28; 1986a, p. 332; 1975a, p. 13].
19. Minsky also indicates that ease of entry into markets, including those in the field of banking, should be a policy objective. He also suggests that small banks should be allowed to function as investment and merchant bankers as well as commercial bankers; "they should be allowed to underwrite and place equity and bond issues of smaller businesses" [Minsky 1986a, pp. 319–21, 329–30].
20. On the same page, Minsky [1986a, p. 325] adds: "Each bank should have a line of credit at the discount window and be able to borrow up to its line at a preferred rate; borrowings above the line of credit [would] be at a penal rate."
21. For more on central bank action and suggested changes, see Minsky [1986a, pp. 252–53, 314, 318, 321–28; 1982a, p. 190]. In addition, note Minsky's [1986a, pp. 326–27] acknowledgment that "after a financial trauma, the Federal Reserve needs to facilitate deficit-financing by making bank reserves available outside the normal discounting channel [that is, by purchasing Treasury bills from the open market]."
22. As an alternative, Minsky notes that the real estate investment trust provision could be generalized to all corporations. This would keep the corporate income tax "on the books" but exempt firms "that pay out 85 percent or 90 percent of profits in dividends" [Minsky 1986a, p. 306]. For some additional remarks on the corporate income tax, see Minsky [1982a, p. 201; 1988, p. 27].
23. While citations regarding Minsky's view on this matter have been offered above, see Simons [1948, pp. 42–43, 45–46, 53–55, 114–19, 170; 1933, pp. Sl, Al–2] for supporting evidence concerning the position of the latter. Further, it is worth noting that in addition to the unequal market power of firms, Minsky and Simons are concerned about inequalities of individual income and opportunity. Both men have suggested that the establishment and maintenance of competitive markets would reduce these latter forms of inequality (and complement, not contravene, stabilization efforts in the process) [Simons 1948, pp. 6–7, 51–53, 65–69; 1938, pp. 221–24; Minsky 1986a, pp. 9, 296; 1975b, pp. 150–69].
24. See Simons [1948, pp. 42–43, 46–49] for supporting evidence.
25. Further, both Simons and Minsky indicate that even if large firms promote economic growth, it would be best to sacrifice this growth in the interest of freedom, equality, and social justice [Simons 1948, pp. 6, 52; Minsky 1986a, p. 8].
26. See also Simons [1948, pp. 34–35, 59–60, 101, 117–18].

27. Two notes seem warranted at this point. First, in addition to a general size limitation for all firms, both Simons and Minsky suggest that special limitations might be needed on an industry-by-industry basis (in accordance with the desire to preserve competition wherever possible) [Simons 1948, pp. 58–60, 81–83; Minsky 1986a, p. 330]. Second, while both Minsky (see note 18 above) and Simons write about prohibiting "operating" corporations from owning the securities of other firms, only Simons comes close to defining an "operating" corporation. Such a firm is distinguished from an "investment trust" and appears to be defined as follows: a "corporation which engages in the manufacture or merchandising of commodities or services" [Simons 1948, pp. 58–61, 82].
28. For example, see Liebhafsky [1971, pp. 567–69]; Weintraub [1978, p. 84, n. 2]; and Lucas [1981, p. 260].
29. For example, see Minsky [1982a, pp. 71, 73, 97, 178, 191, 289; 1977, pp. 305, 307; 1986a, pp. 172, 329; 1975b, p. 5]. In these works, he acknowledges that he and Simons share common views on the following matters: financial reform, central bank abilities, the countercyclical usefulness of expansionary fiscal and monetary policy, the endogenous nature and macroeconomic significance of money, and the inability of policymakers to solve economic problems once and for all.
30. Although the economic views and recommendations of Simons and Minsky are often very similar, it is important to keep in mind that their perspectives are not identical. Perhaps the most significant element found in Simons's reconstruction proposal but absent from Minsky's program is the abolition of fractional-reserve banking. In addition, it is significant that Simons is hostile to labor unions (he views them as a major obstacle to establishment and maintenance of competitive-market arrangements and would like to see them disappear) while Minsky does not consider them to be a significant source of instability [Simons 1948, pp. 35–36, 48–49, 60–61; Minsky 1986a, pp. 261, 279–83]. (Nonetheless, Minsky does write that "those devices in agriculture, labor, manufacturing, and trade that constrain downward price flexibility [would not be] relevant to a properly organized Big Government capitalism, because they tend to exacerbate inflationary pressures" [Minsky 1986a, p. 331].)
31. For example, see Minsky [1986a, p. xiv; 1982a, p. viii; 1985a]. The other two influential professors were Oscar Lange and Josef Schumpeter.
32. For a brief discussion of Minsky's many conversations with Simons at a tavern near the University of Chicago, see Minsky [1985a, p. 220].
33. For more on this, see Whalen [1988b, p. 161].
34. Indeed, works containing early versions of Minsky's financial-instability hypothesis make no reference to Keynes. (See, for example, "Central Banking and Money Market Changes," "Can 'It' Happen Again?" and "Longer Waves in Financial Relations." These essays—found in Minsky [1982; 1964]—were published in 1957, 1963, and 1964, respectively.) In the earliest of these articles, meanwhile, one finds a footnote—at the end of the final paragraph—in which Minsky notes that his perspective "is not unlike that of" Henry Simons and Lloyd W. Mints (also of the University of Chicago) [Minsky 1982, p. 178, n. 23]. Keynes does not appear as a reference, and the links to Keynes are not mentioned, until the late 1960s.
35. For an example of an unsuccessful attempt to characterize a school of economics by a particular policy stance, see Gruchy [1978].
36. For one approach that relies on the preconceptions of economic analysis in its attempt to compare schools of thought, see Whalen [1990].
37. On the regulatory role of institutional adjustment, see Ramstad [1985, p. 509].

38. On the cycle analyses of Veblen and Commons and the extent to which they are similar to the views of Keynes, Simons and Minsky, see Whalen [1989a; 1989b] and Lawlor [1987].
39. According to Simons, our public officials "have never really tried to maintain effectively competitive conditions in industry" [Simons 1948, p. 42].

REFERENCES

Brazelton, Robert. 1981. "Post Keynesian Economics: An Institutional Compatibility?" *Journal of Economic Issues* 15 (June): 531–42.
Davis, J. Ronnie. 1969. "Henry Simons, the Radical: Some Documentary Evidence." *History of Political Economy* 1 (Fall): 388–94.
Director, Aaron. 1946. "Simons on Taxation." *The University of Chicago Law Review* 14 (December): 15–19.
Friedman, Milton. 1969. "The Monetary Theory and Policy of Henry Simons." *The Journal of Law and Economics* 10 (October): 1–13.
Galbraith, John Kenneth. 1978. "On Post Keynesian Economics." *Journal of Post Keynesian Economics* 1 (Fall): 8–11.
Gruchy, Allan G. 1978. "Institutional Economics: Its Influence and Prospects." *American Journal of Economics and Sociology* 37 (July): 271–81.
Lawlor, Michael S. 1987. "Minsky and Keynes on Speculation and Finance," Presented at the Association For Evolutionary Economics Annual Meeting, Chicago, Illinois.
Lerner, Abba P. 1976. Review of *John Maynard Keynes,* by Hyman P. Minsky. *Challenge* 19 (May–June): 69–70.
Liebhafsky, H.H. 1971. *American Government and Business.* New York: John Wiley and Sons.
Lucas, Robert E. 1981. *Studies in Business-Cycle Theory.* Cambridge, Mass.: The MIT Press.
Minsky, Hyman P. 1988. "Back from the Brink." *Challenge* 31 (January–February): 22–28.
———. 1987a. "Bashing Bigness ... But with Blinders." *Challenge* 30 (July–August): 29–31.
———. 1987b. "Discussion." Association For Evolutionary Economics Meeting, Chicago, Illinois (session entitled "The Economic Ideas of Hyman P. Minsky").
———. 1986a. *Stabilizing an Unstable Economy.* New Haven: Yale University Press.
———. 1986b. Review of *The Zero-Sum Solution*, by Lester C. Thurow. *Challenge* 29 (July–August): 60–64.
———. 1985a. "Beginnings." *Banca Nazionale Del Lavoro Quarterly Review* 38 (September): 211–21.
———. 1985b. "Money and the Lender of Last Resort." *Challenge* 28 (March–April): 12–18.
———. 1985c. Review of *The Second Industrial Divide*, by Michael J. Piore and Charles F. Sabel. *Challenge* 28 (July–August): 60–64.
———. 1982a. *Can "It" Happen Again?* Armonk, N.Y.: M.E. Sharpe.
———. 1982b. "Debt Deflation Processes in Today's Institutional Environment." *Banca Nazionale Del Lavoro Quarterly Review* 35 (December): 375–93.
———. 1981–82. "The Breakdown of the 1960s Policy Synthesis." *Telos* No. 50 (Winter): 49–58.

———. 1978. "The Carter Economics." *Journal of Post Keynesian Economics* 1 (Fall): 42–45.
———. 1977. "An 'Economics of Keynes' Perspective on Money." In *Modern Economic Thought.* Ed. Sidney Weintraub, pp. 295–307. Philadelphia: University of Pennsylvania Press.
———. 1975a. "Financial Resources in a Fragile Financial Environment." *Challenge* 18 (July–August): 6–13.
———. 1975b. *John Maynard Keynes.* New York: Columbia University Press.
———. 1964. "Longer Waves in Financial Relations: Financial Factors in the More Severe Depressions." *American Economic Review* 54 (May): 324–35.
Simons, Henry C. 1948. *Economic Policy for a Free Society.* Chicago: University of Chicago Press.
———. 1938. *Personal Income Taxation.* Chicago: University of Chicago Press.
———. 1933. "Banking and Currency Reform (with Supplement and Appendix)." Department of Economics, University of Chicago.
Veblen, Thorstein. 1904. *The Theory of Business Enterprise.* New York: Charles Scribner's Sons.
Weintraub, Sidney. 1978. *Capitalism's Inflation and Unemployment Crisis.* Reading, Mass.: Addison-Wesley.
Whalen, Charles J. 1990. "Schools of Thought and Theories of the State: Reflections of An Institutional Economist." Presented at the Hobart & William Smith Colleges Conference on Institutionalist Theories of the State, Geneva, New York.
———. 1989a. "The Minsky-Simons-Veblen Connection: Reply." *Journal of Economic Issues* 23 (September): 891–95.
———. 1989b. "The Monetary Economics of John R. Commons." Presented at the Association For Evolutionary Economics Annual Meeting, Atlanta, Georgia.
———. 1988a. "The Minsky-Simons Connection: A Neglected Thread in the History of Economic Thought." *Journal of Economic Issues* 22 (June): 533–44.
———. 1988b. *Beyond Neoclassical Thought: Economics from the Perspective of Institutionalists and Post Keynesians.* Ph.D. Dissertation, The University of Texas at Austin.

15. Budget amendment offers toxin, not tonic

Washington seems unable to let a bad idea die. The balanced budget amendment, which failed to pass Congress in 1994, is back as the first major legislative issue of the new year. And once again, it failed (but only barely) to gain the support it needed for passage. Economists, political scientists, and other concerned individuals again united to oppose this legislation. They believed this amendment would be a political and economic toxin, not a tonic.

POLITICAL DANGERS

By defeating the amendment, we have avoided several political pitfalls. Among them are:

- The balanced budget amendment would distract us from the real task at hand—setting national priorities and making difficult policy choices. Resources required for its ratification would be used better, if they were directed toward substantive issues rather than to symbolism.
- The amendment is merely a statement of intention. Its objective cannot be achieved without political will. Moreover, judicial enforcement is neither likely or viable.
- The amendment invites increased use of federal mandates (on corporations and state and local governments) and other types of evasion. In addition, it sets the stage for partisan disputes over the appropriateness of particular evasions. This is the lesson we have learned both from state-level experience and the federal Gramm-Rudman experiment.

Reprinted with permission from *Challenge* 38 (3), May–June 1995, 50.

ECONOMIC DANGERS

There are also dangers of an economic nature. Some of those are:

- The amendment would mandate an objective that almost no private economic actor could or should meet. Contrary to the stated position of many amendment supporters, the proposal does not require Congress "to live under the same budget restraints as families and businesses." Balancing the federal annual budget is *not* the same as balancing a checkbook.
- The amendment would preclude development of federal "capital-budgeting" procedures. Such procedures have been used effectively by states, localities, and even some of our international competitors. They would help us bring a stronger investment orientation to federal expenditures.
- The amendment would severely hinder the public sector's ability to compensate for cyclical fluctuations. A mandatory balanced budget would eliminate one of the few mechanisms that can prevent mild downturns from developing into severe recessions.

The frustration Americans feel about our federal budget is understandable. Passing a balanced budget amendment might fill us with a sense of accomplishment for a short while. In the end, however, it will produce a more fragile economy, greater citizen frustration, and a further loss of confidence in our political institutions.

16. Destabilizing an unstable economy: the erosion of automatic stabilizers

Co-authored by Jeffrey Wenger

In his 1986 book, *Stabilizing an Unstable Economy*, Hyman Minsky argued that the major flaw of modern capitalism is that it is unstable. But Minsky also insisted that business cycles could be moderated—and that another depression could be prevented—through the use of sensible economic policies. "We can, so to speak, stabilize instability," he wrote (Minsky 1986, 10).

U.S. economic instability has indeed been contained during the last half century. The economy has weathered nine contractions and an even larger number of domestic or international financial crises since 1950. Yet a repeat of the 1929–33 macroeconomic collapse has been avoided. The reason, according to Minsky: sound fiscal and monetary policies. In particular, public spending has offset reductions in private spending. Government debt has helped to steady financial markets. And the central bank has stepped in with monetary accommodation and lender-of-last-resort interventions (Minsky 1986; Fazzari and Minsky 1984).

Minsky's brand of fiscal policy—which he called "Big Government"—has a critical role to play during upswings and downturns. The Federal Reserve cannot do the job alone:

> Monetary policy to constrain undue expansion and inflation operates by way of disrupting financing markets and asset values. Monetary policy to induce expansion operates by interest rates and the availability of credit, which do not yield increased investment if current and anticipated profits are low. (Minsky 1986, 304)

Big Government depends heavily on automatic stabilizers. Fiscal policy may have a discretionary component, such as the introduction of new taxes in a boom or new spending in a downturn. But Minsky understood that discretionary action usually comes with a long lag, when it comes at all: His goal was

Reprinted with permission from *Challenge* 45 (6), November–December 2002, 70–92.

to present a *structure* of capitalism that would be more prosperous and stable. Minsky stressed that "the budget structure of Big Government must have the built-in capacity" to produce sizable deficits when the economy plunges, and to run surpluses during inflationary booms (Minsky 1986, 292).

But here is the rub: Instead of reinforcing the economy's automatic stabilizers, U.S. policymakers have allowed them to erode throughout the last few decades. Important progressive elements of the tax structure are gone. Unemployment insurance is in dismal shape, due to declining eligibility and shrinking real benefits. Welfare is now a block-grant program with strict time limits. The minimum wage is no longer enough to keep a family of three out of poverty.

This article discusses the importance of built-in stabilizers and the risks their erosion poses for the American economy. It reviews the erosion in each of the four areas listed in the last paragraph, and describes what corrective action can be taken. It also explores why the economy has, to date, avoided a more serious downturn despite the gradual weakening of its stabilizers.

THE IMPORTANCE OF AUTOMATIC STABILIZERS

Capitalism requires built-in fiscal-policy stabilizers because business cycles are an inherent feature of capitalist economies. Conventional economic theory misses this fact because it cannot shed light on economic performance through time, a problem that has been thoroughly examined by numerous scholars, including Joan Robinson and Nobel laureate Douglass North. Fortunately, an analysis of capitalist dynamics is at the heart of Minsky's perspective, which he called "financial Keynesianism" or "post-Keynesian economics."

Endogenous Cycles

Minsky's post-Keynesian theory stresses that macroeconomic conditions are transitory. Booms are generated endogenously during recoveries. Conditions that lead to a contraction are an unavoidable by-product of robust expansions.

The precise path taken by the economy over time is not predetermined, however. As John Maynard Keynes stressed in 1937, the economic future is uncertain. We cannot even place firm probabilities on the matter: "We simply do not know" (Keynes 1937, 213–14). Business cycles have no natural periodicity. Rather, their path depends heavily on the nature and evolution of expectations and economic institutions.

To understand expectations, institutions, and the possibility of government stabilization, Minsky rejected the conventional notion that the economy can be thought of as a village bazaar. Instead, he started with the real world, where production must come before exchange—and where financing precedes production. Minsky's economy is one held together by financial relations, "a world of commitments to pay cash today and in the future" (Minsky 1982, 63).

That starting point explains why the institutions of money and credit are so important to Minsky's economics. Financial commitments are a crucial link between past, present, and future. They are shaped by expectations formed in the past because that is when existing contracts were negotiated. They are influenced by existing cash flows because those flows affect the ability to meet such commitments. And they look to the future because expectations are what determine decisions about new lending and borrowing (including refinancing).

The financial relations of businesses are crucial to the analysis of business cycles. Household demand is primarily dependent on current and expected near-term income. Investment demand by firms, however, is based heavily on the state of long-term expectations. The two are interrelated, to be sure. Still, the latter is more prone to fluctuate widely and suddenly. As Keynes wrote of the factors determining aggregate demand, "It is those which determine the rate of investment which are most unreliable, since it is they which are influenced by our views about the future about which we know so little" (Keynes 1937, 221). Moreover, business relations can have more enduring repercussions: Spending decisions by firms often involve a longer-term financial commitment than decisions by consumers.

The focus on investment means that profits are at the heart of cycle analysis. "Business profits are the key element in determining how well a capitalist economy works" (Minsky 1986, 303). In a recovery, for example, robust earnings raise expectations about future earnings, which causes loans to rise and investment to increase. That investment growth lifts aggregate demand and helps push expectations higher. The result is an increase in output, employment, and stock prices, all of which increase expectations even further.

Since an expanding economy rewards risk-taking enterprises, corporate debt rises as an expansion picks up steam. No corporate leader wants to be left behind due to underinvestment. That is why, over time, more and more firms move away from conservative financing and toward increasingly fragile cash flows—from what Minsky called "hedge" financing to what he called "speculative" and "Ponzi" financing. And it is not just business executives that give the boom its momentum: Rising profits ease financiers' worries that new loans might go unpaid, which adds further fuel to the fire.

The recent U.S. experience demonstrates that booms can last a long time, but not forever. A new reality eventually introduces chaos to the environment of increasingly risky investment and financing practices. The market for labor—and often for other inputs and for credit—starts to tighten, constraining expansion and pushing up business expenses. Overexpansion begins to reveal itself in selected sectors. Disappointing earnings in portions of the economy cause a quick and widespread reassessment of debt structures, lending terms, and investment decisions.

Stabilization Policy

To stabilize the economy, policy "needs a handle by which it can affect profits" (Minsky 1986, 303). Monetary policy is one crucial tool. In a downturn, for example, the central bank can lower interest rates across the entire economy by cutting the federal funds rate. It can even step in to arrange refinancing for specific banks and other large institutions that are in trouble. Both actions help stabilize overall profits by shoring up cash flows, thus preventing financial trauma from spreading.

But monetary policy is not sufficient. Central bank action affects profits after a six- to eighteen-month lag, and only sizable interest-rate cuts have a meaningful effect on earnings in a contraction. The Fed has even less impact on long-term profit expectations, which are central to investment decisions. Using monetary policy to contain a boom has its own shortcoming: Financial-market disruptions caused by interest-rate hikes often trigger a downturn.

In addition to sensible monetary policy, sound economic management requires the "automatic income and financial stabilizing effects of Big Government" (Minsky 1986, 38). Government expenditures provide the quickest and most effective way to stabilize the economy in the face of a fall in business investment. Big Government means a federal budget structure that injects spending into a stalling economy and generates a sizable public deficit in the process. Big Government must also help counteract the tendency toward an inflationary boom by reducing public spending, increasing revenues, and generating budget surpluses during periods of widespread prosperity.

The expenditures of Big Government help stabilize a contracting economy regardless of whether they purchase goods and services or provide income to households. While government purchases will instantly raise aggregate demand, which means they stimulate income and employment, most transfers are also spent quickly. That is why a program like unemployment insurance can be a powerful stimulant. As Minsky noted, "Unemployment insurance, which was at a $5.3 billion annual rate in the second quarter of 1974, rose to a $19.4 billion annual rate during the second quarter of 1975. Such a dramatic rise in unemployment insurance payments helps to explain why the sharp downturn [of 1974–75] was reversed so quickly" (Minsky 1986, 26).

The income effects of government spending are important to individual households and enterprises, but the secret to the macroeconomic success of Big Government is its size. Government budgets must be large enough to generate deficits that can offset falling private-sector debt during a contraction. "The full import of government as ... sustainer of economic activity cannot be appreciated without recognizing the significance of the proposition that the sum of the surpluses and deficits over all sectors must equal zero," wrote Minsky (1986, 30). That means Big Government needs to prop up business profits by running a sizable deficit at a time when the private sector is pulling back. (Fiscal policy at the federal, state, and local levels together determines the overall budget effect of Big Government. The federal government is especially important, though, because of its relative size and because it can run deficits more easily than states and localities.)

In particular, rising public expenditures need to make up for declining private investment. According to Minsky, government can easily be structured to provide that spending if outlays and revenues are both "of the same order of magnitude" as private investment when the economy is at full employment. In prosperous times, this translates into government budgets that are balanced (and are tending toward surplus as the economy continues to expand) and that account for about 17 percent of gross domestic product (Minsky 1986, 297–99).

In addition to its income and budget (deficit spending) effects, Big Government has an important portfolio effect. Government bonds—used to finance the federal deficit—provide households, businesses, and financial institutions with an asset that is both marketable and free of default risk. During a downturn, this asset improves the liquidity of portfolios, which helps contain the private sector's credit contraction (Minsky 1986, 36).

The 1974–75 period again provides a perfect example. Minsky wrote:

> [B]ecause of Big Government and the large increase in government debt, the default risk of business and bank portfolios decreased. As businesses liquidated inventories, they decreased their indebtedness to banks and acquired government debt. Banks and other financial institutions acquired liquidity by buying government debt rather than by decreasing their assets and liabilities. The public, both households and business, not only acquired safe assets in the form of bank deposits and savings deposits but were also able to decrease their indebtedness relative to income. The existence of a large and increasing government debt thus acted as a significant stabilizer of portfolios during the threatening period. (Minsky 1986, 37)

Successful Capitalism

In *Stabilizing an Unstable Economy* (*SUE*), Minsky stressed that undoing Big Government threatens economic stability. "Government is frequently disparaged as an inefficient bureaucratic maze serving the interests of officeholders and time-servers rather than of the public," he wrote. But Minsky insisted "political and intellectual resources must be invested in the creation and maintenance of an effective government apparatus because Big Government is here to stay if we are to avoid great depressions." Similarly, he noted: "The Reagan effort to reduce government ... would ... make our economy more susceptible to downside instability. The Big Government impact was clearly evident in the recession of 1982–83 and the recovery of 1983–84 [the episodes most immediately preceding release of *SUE*]. The power of Big Government and enormous deficits to contain downside instability was demonstrated" (Minsky 1986, 22, 300).

Minsky insisted that the existence of automatic fiscal stabilizers meant the difference between failed and successful capitalism. His was a historical perspective: At the end of the first third of the twentieth century, capitalism was "a failed economic order," Minsky often wrote. In the decades that followed, Big Government capitalism turned out to be much more successful (Minsky 1996, xii). One writer summarized Minsky's views on the matter as follows: "The success of capitalism rests on the government's ability to sustain profits when the normal profit-sustaining mechanisms of investment break down. In 1929 government debt could not offset the effect on profits of the collapse of investment. In contrast, in 1990 the government deficit contained the [contraction]" (Spring 1994, 14).

EROSION OF THE STABILIZERS

In the United States, key Big Government stabilizers have included progressive taxation, unemployment insurance, and welfare expenditures (Aid to Families with Dependent Children [AFDC] and, more recently, Temporary Assistance to Needy Families [TANF]). The minimum wage has also provided a stabilizing force by providing a floor for wages during downturns. At least since the mid-1970s, however, the corrective power of these elements has eroded.

Taxes

Progressive income taxation gives the revenue structure automatic stabilizing power. An expanding economy pushes more and more families into higher brackets. A contracting economy does the reverse.

But the stabilizing elements of the federal tax system are now much weaker than in the1970s. The federal income-tax rate structure had twenty-five brackets in 1977—ranging from 0 percent for taxable income up to $3,200 (for a married couple filing jointly) to 70 percent for income at $203,200 and above. The highest rates applied only to capital income: Labor income above $47,200 was taxed at a maximum rate of 50 percent. Today, the top rates are much lower, there are far fewer brackets, and brackets are adjusted for inflation.

The current income tax structure is still a graduated system, but not as it was a few decades ago. A series of rate changes, which began in 1981, have left a system with only five brackets and marginal tax rates ranging from 15 percent to 39.1 percent. Capital gains (on assets held for eighteen months or more) are now treated preferentially: Their rate is capped at 28 percent.

Adjusting brackets for inflation, required since 1981, also erases a stabilizing element of the tax system. Before these adjustments were made, revenues automatically rose with the inflation that pushed families into a higher bracket. As a result, the growth of aggregate demand was somewhat constrained in booms. That stabilizer is now gone.

Unemployment Insurance

Minsky considered unemployment insurance (UI) one of the U.S. economy's most important stabilizers. Recent empirical evidence supports that contention. Looking at the combined impact of discretionary and automatic UI spending in recessions since the late 1960s, Lawrence Chimerine, Theodore S. Black, and Lester Coffey find that losses in gross domestic product would have been 15 percent deeper, on average, in the absence of UI (Chimerine et al. 1999, 67).

But changes in UI since the late 1970s have limited the program's effectiveness as an automatic stabilizer. For example, Congress began taxing UI benefits as income in 1979. All UI income became taxable by 1987. This reduces the stabilizing effect of these benefits by taking money out of the hands of the unemployed.

In 1981, meanwhile, lawmakers eliminated the trigger that extended UI benefits across the nation during slowdowns, and raised the trigger for state extended-benefits programs. (An extension of UI benefits is triggered in each state by its insured unemployment rate, the ratio of those receiving benefits to those in covered employment. The rate that activates extended benefits, which are jointly funded by states and the federal government, was raised from 4 percent to 5 percent.) These changes "virtually disabled" the part of UI that engaged in a recession without congressional action, according to program experts Stephen Woodbury and Murray Rubin (1997, 257). A weaker system of extended benefits can spell trouble for the unemployed, who often exhaust their benefits before finding new work during downturns, and it means that UI provides less automatic stimulus to a faltering economy.

Congressional pressure on states has also reduced the fraction of workers eligible for UI. Federal legislation, passed in 1981, was designed to shore up state-level UI financing. The states responded by taking steps that resulted in tighter restrictions on eligibility (Vroman 1990, 25).

Figure 1 shows the erosion of UI since the 1970s. It displays the trend in the insured unemployment rate divided by the total unemployment rate, a fraction that approximates the percentage of the unemployed receiving UI benefits. The decline in that fraction over the past few decades is startling—and the proportion receiving benefits has been lower in each successive recession. (Shaded areas in the figures indicate recessions.)

Further evidence of the erosion of this stabilizer comes from data on UI spending as a percentage of gross domestic product (GDP). UI payments represented 0.75 percent of GDP in 1975 and only 0.66 percent of GDP in 1982. Yet the 1981–82 recession was more severe than that of 1974–75: Unemployment reached a post-World War II high of 10.8 percent in November and December 1982, but peaked at only 9 percent in May 1975.

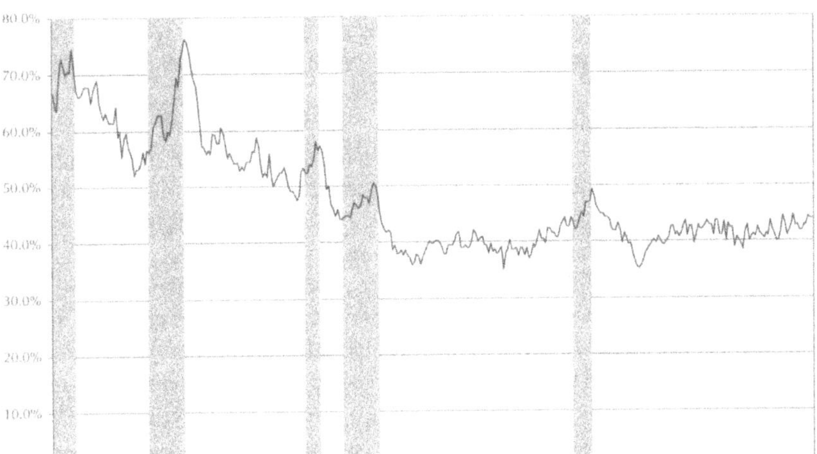

Figure 1 Insured unemployment rate/total unemployment rate, 1970–1999, seasonally adjusted

Welfare

Welfare as we knew it (AFDC) was an entitlement program that showed a distinct pattern over the business cycle. Since eligibility was based in part on financial need, AFDC injected money into the economy in a countercyclical manner. Periods of job loss and slow growth brought about increases in poverty. Welfare caseloads and expenditures, therefore, increased during recessions and declined during economic expansions. AFDC's funding formula matched federal expenditures to state expenditures at a fixed rate.

Welfare reform ended AFDC in 1996. The entitlement feature and the funding formula were both eliminated. These changes stripped welfare of much of its countercyclical effect (Blank 2001).

The new federal program (TANF) is fundamentally different from AFDC. TANF provides welfare money to states in the form of federal block grants that are fixed in size. Attached to those funds is a strict time limit: No adult may receive assistance for more than five years over their lifetime, regardless of the state of the economy when that eligibility period runs out. (This article discusses elements in TANF as authorized through September 30, 2002. Before this article is published, Congress could change the program during reauthorization.)

The size of the block grants is not determined by caseloads, and there is no provision in the law to adjust the grants for inflation. This means that no additional federal funds will be forthcoming as caseloads increase in a recession. The block grant amount is fixed at $16.5 billion per year, which means its overall impact shrinks over time: The real size of the TANF grant fell 12 percent between 1996 and 2002 (Weaver 2002).

What happens if states need more money for welfare during a contraction? That is a problem for each state to solve on its own. TANF allows unspent portions of state grants to be set aside for use in more difficult times. It also permits states to borrow from the federal government. But both paths lead to serious practical concerns for states. According to Janice Peterson of the U.S. General Accounting Office, the future of carryover—or "rainy day"—funds "has been very uncertain," and some states have not built them up "for fear that they could lose them" if Congress decides to reallocate unspent TANF dollars. Borrowing from the U.S. government to make welfare expenditures, meanwhile, involves market-rate interest charges and requires repayment within three years (Peterson 2002, 437).

As Figure 2 indicates, AFDC and TANF expenditures as a percentage of GDP have declined sharply and rather steadily since the 1970s, from a high of 0.65 percent of GDP in 1975 to 0.24 percent of GDP in 1998. Thus, even

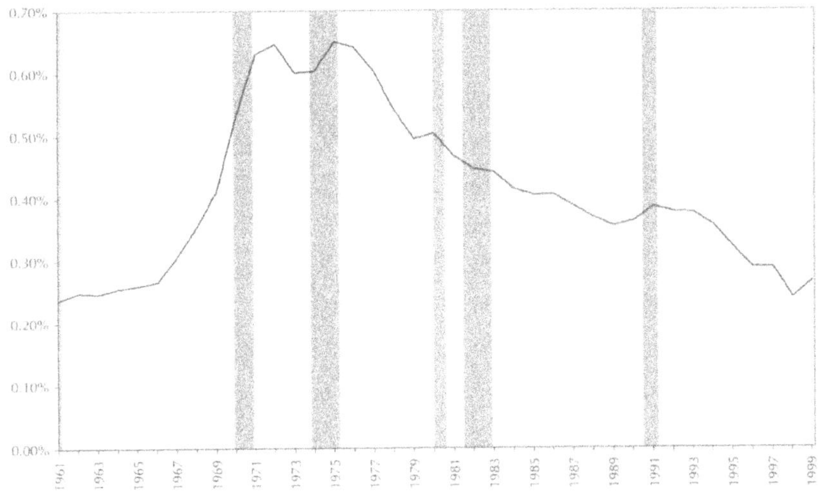

Figure 2 Total federal and state expenditures for TANF and AFDC as a percentage of GDP, 1961 to 1999

prior to the advent of the TANF block grants, welfare's role as a countercyclical measure was waning. The block grants take this effect even further by leaving states responsible for coming up with additional welfare funds during a recession.

The Minimum Wage

The minimum wage was established during the Great Depression. With so many people out of work, downward pressure on wages was severe. Minimum wages were designed to preserve some purchasing power (effective demand) during a time when workers are likely to sell their labor at ever declining prices. The minimum wage puts a floor on that income erosion, and thus helps stabilize the economy during recessions.

As Figure 3 shows, the real value of the minimum wage has fallen markedly since 1968. Today's minimum wage provides a real-wage floor at the same level as existed in 1955. That means its ability to prop up the bottom of the labor market has eroded considerably in recent decades—only a severe recession is likely to find the current minimum-wage floor binding.

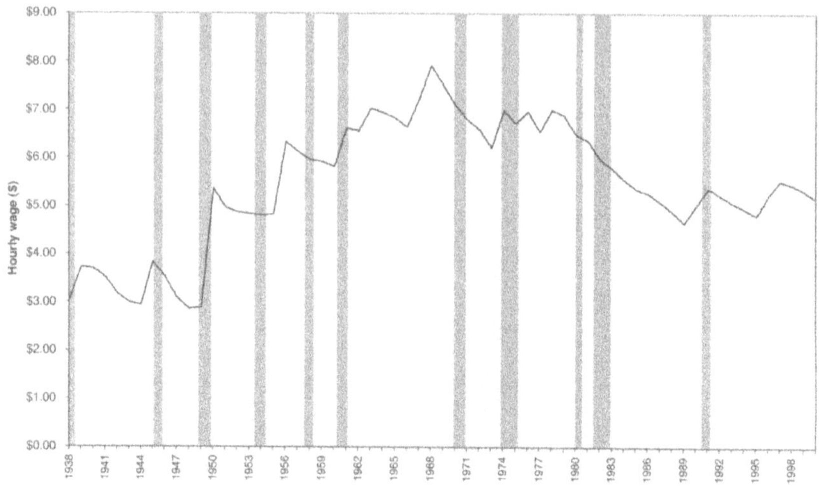

Figure 3 Real value of the federal minimum wage, 1938–2000 ($, year 2000)

MAKING THE SYSTEM MORE STABLE

Structuring the economy to best handle future expansions and contractions requires shoring up fiscal stabilizers. The tax system should be structured so revenues are sensitive to, and move inversely with, changes in income and prices. The need to incorporate stabilizing elements into the economy "argues for having a progression of tax brackets and rates over incomes in the middle ranges," wrote Minsky (1986, 308). In contrast, the yet-to-be-phased-in tax cuts of 2001 pull the system in the opposite direction.

Unemployment insurance needs to be reformed so the program reaches more people and provides more adequate benefits. Among the needed reforms: A state's extended-benefits program should start when its insured unemployment rate reaches 4 percent, as was the case before 1981. Also, workers laid off from part-time jobs should be eligible for jobless benefits.

Welfare and the minimum wage also require adjustment. The country's current welfare spending program, TANF, needs changes that will trigger more federal spending during recessions, and that will encourage states to create "rainy day" funds. Similarly, welfare time limits should be extended for individuals when macroeconomic contractions occur (Peterson 2002, 436–37). The minimum wage needs to be raised and automatically adjusted for inflation.

Another way to add stability to the economy is to establish the government as employer of last resort (ELR). Policymakers and academics have discussed this idea at least since the Great Depression, but Minsky was one of its strongest advocates in the 1980s and early 1990s. More recently, L. Randall Wray and Mathew Forstater have been at the forefront of efforts to develop the intellectual foundation and policy framework for guaranteeing a public-sector job to anyone not able to find private-sector work (Wray 1998; Forstater 1998).

The ELR notion is similar to New Deal jobs programs such as the Works Progress Administration and Civilian Conservation Corps, but ELR would be permanent. As Minsky wrote, this program would be "operating at a base level during good times and expanding during recession" (Minsky 1986, 308). ELR allows the government to establish a "buffer stock of labor," one that can counteract both unemployment and inflation (Wray 1998, 543).

Finally, there is one idea that could destroy government's ability to make use of automatic stabilizers: the notion that there should be a balanced-budget amendment to the U.S. Constitution. Such an amendment has often gained much popular and political support—and it may again receive attention in the next few years, as legislators in both parties try to stop a return to deficits "as far as the eye can see." But this amendment would force tax increases or spending cuts in the midst of a contraction—moves that would worsen the downturn. And there would not be an increase in government debt as needed to provide the portfolio benefits described earlier. These dangers should to be kept in mind by those interested in making the economic system more stable.

THE SURPRISE ECONOMY?

If the built-in stabilizers of the U.S. economy have eroded in recent decades, why has the latest downturn not been much more severe? Many media commentators have suggested that the recession that began in March 2001, as determined by the National Bureau of Economic Research (NBER), has been rather mild. But that is not entirely true. And there was an unusual combination of policy actions and economic conditions that kept the contraction from getting worse during much of 2002.

Not So Mild

In many respects, the downturn that ended the 1990s boom has indeed been consequential. Consider the following.

The economy experienced a dramatic change in direction between late 1999 and early 2001. After growing at an annual rate of over 7 percent in the last quarter of 1999, and still expanding at nearly 5 percent in mid-2000, GDP contracted in the first three quarters of 2001 (U.S. Department of Commerce 2002).

The stock market suffered severe losses in both the year before and the year after September 11, 2001. In the twelve months prior to the terrorist attacks on

New York and Washington, DC, the Standard & Poor's 500 (S&P) lost more than 25 percent of its value, the Dow Jones Industrials dropped 15 percent, and the NASDAQ fell over 55 percent. In the twelve months following the attacks, the S&P and Dow again lost roughly the same amount, while the NASDAQ fell 27 percent ("Figures of the Week" 2001–2002).

Capital spending, which fueled the 1990s expansion, collapsed in late 2000—along with the revenue of many telecommunications and information-technology companies. Business spending on capital equipment grew by 15 percent a year, on average, from 1997 to mid-2000. Then it contracted for six quarters in a row, starting with the fourth quarter of 2000.

Profits took a similar path. In the last quarter of 2000 and the first quarter of 2001, earnings for the 900 companies in *BusinessWeek's* Corporate Scoreboard took double-digit tumbles from a year earlier. The Scoreboard then posted record-breaking profit declines in each of the next four quarters, culminating in a stunning 56 percent fall in the first quarter of 2002 ("Corporate Scoreboard" 2001–2002).

Even labor market performance has been weaker than surface appearances might suggest. As of this writing, the recession's unemployment rate has not exceeded 6 percent. But a larger fraction of private-sector jobs were lost between October 2000 and June 2002 than in the same number of months at the outset of the early 1980s period of rising unemployment and recession, according to the Economic Policy Institute (2002).

The official unemployment rate also hides another fact: The labor force has been growing more slowly than in the 1990s. In January 2002, for example, the economy experienced a net loss of jobs, but the unemployment rate fell "as more people stopped looking for work and thus did not count as unemployed" (Leonhardt and Altman 2002). Without the decline in labor force growth, unemployment would have been considerably higher in this recession:

> Had the labor force continued to grow at the rate that prevailed before the slowdown, and if instead of leaving or not joining the labor force half of these missing job seekers had unsuccessfully sought work over this period, then the unemployment rate would have been 6.6 percent in June 2002 instead of 5.9 percent. (Economic Policy Institute 2002)

Quick Action

The recession that started in 2001 could have been worse, but that year also brought a rare combination of aggressive interest-rate cutting and rapid action on expansionary fiscal-policy initiatives. That combination, along with low inflation, zero-percent-financing offers on new cars, and sustained productivity growth, kept consumer spending strong and prevented business earnings from falling further.

Federal Reserve easing of monetary policy began well before the NBER declared an end to the 1990s expansion. The federal funds rate was 6.5 percent in May 2000; starting in January 2001, the Fed put in place a series of rate cuts. Those cuts brought the funds rate to 1.75 percent by mid-December 2001, the lowest rate since August 1958.

Policymakers in the nation's capital enacted tax cuts and spending increases with exceptional speed in 2001. Tax cuts came quickly because President George W. Bush had advocated a huge package of cuts during the 2000 presidential campaign. The initial Bush goal was to make fiscal changes consistent with his philosophy of government, not to stimulate the economy. The economic decline helped him get the congressional votes needed to pass his package—and more. In particular, tax rebates that were not part of the initial Bush plan served as a powerful economic stimulus by putting cash directly into the hands of consumers. In addition, the government responded to September 11, 2001, by increasing spending on national security, and by providing aid to troubled industries, especially the airlines. (Even more economic assistance came in early 2002, in the form of new, generous write-offs for business depreciation, and an extension of unemployment benefits timed to aid those who lost work in the wake of the terror attacks.)

No Surprise

By mid-March 2002, *BusinessWeek's* cover announced that the economic tide seemed to have turned. The magazine's economic writers called it "The Surprise Economy" (Cooper and Madigan 2002).

Minsky probably would not have been very surprised, however. It is more likely that he would have applauded the Fed for its swift action, and then argued that the fiscal stimulus validated his notion of government as an economic stabilizer. It is also likely that he would have stressed that it took extraordinary circumstances to get fiscal action—and that it would be preferable, and much better for business and consumer confidence, to rely on automatic fiscal stabilizers.

Speedy fiscal-policy action spurred sizable growth in government and consumer spending in the fourth quarter of 2001. In that quarter, personal consumption expenditure rose at a seasonally adjusted, annualized rate of 6.0 percent, and government spending (government consumption expenditures and gross investment) rose 10.5 percent. Together, these sectors offset falling private investment—and helped enable investment to post an increase in the first quarter of 2002 (U.S. Department of Commerce 2002).

Moreover, the tax cuts of 2001 were politically possible due to federal budget surpluses. Those surpluses were not exactly the type that Minsky had in mind for booms, because they were due at least as much to belt-tightening in the realm of discretionary policies (motivated by a desire to contain the federal debt) as to automatic stabilizers. The magnitude of the surpluses, however, was entirely consistent with what he thought to be appropriate for a period of robust economic expansion (Minsky 1986, 303–4).

CONCLUSION: FIX THE ROOF BEFORE THE RAIN BEGINS

The major economic lessons of the twentieth century should have been that capitalism is inherently unstable, that it can be structured in ways that contain instability, and that instability is best contained by Big Government and accommodative monetary policy (which includes using the central bank as lender of last resort). Big Government, meanwhile, is defined as a fiscal structure that contains built-in stabilizers. Yet this article has demonstrated that the U.S. economy's stabilizers have been eroded in the past few decades.

Unusually swift and aggressive monetary and fiscal actions, along with low inflation and other favorable conditions, have helped contain the most recent downturn. But we may not be so fortunate the next time—and consumer indebtedness is now so great that a widespread effort to lower that debt burden would only worsen a serious downturn. That means it is prudent to act on the lessons provided by U.S. economic history. It makes sense to shore up the economy's fiscal stabilizers. Better to fix the roof before the rain begins.

Besides, a double-dip recession remains a distinct possibility. Indeed, "five of the past seven recessions were interrupted by brief periods of growth followed by a continued slump" (Coy 2002, 36–37).

There are a number of reasons to be concerned that a double dip may happen. As this article goes to the publisher, investors remain skittish due to recent scandals involving brokerage "research" and corporate accounting tricks. And most economy watchers are unsettled by even more recent developments, including: release of data that suggest sagging consumer expectations; business reports of softer-than-expected retail sales; and news about anxiety among the nation's purchasing managers. There are also jitters over the possibility that the United States will attack Iraq. Meanwhile, much of the stimulus effect of past discretionary fiscal initiatives is wearing off.

When it comes to fashioning a more stable economic structure, there may be no time to lose.

REFERENCES

Blank, Rebecca M. 2001. "Welfare and the Economy." *Welfare Reform & Beyond Policy Brief No.* 7. Washington, DC: Brookings Institution.

Chimerine, Lawrence, Theodore S. Black, and Lester Coffey. 1999. "Unemployment Insurance as an Automatic Stabilizer: Evidence of Effectiveness Over Three Decades." *Unemployment Insurance Occasional Paper 99–8.* Washington, DC: U.S. Department of Labor.

Cooper, James C., and Kathleen Madigan. 2002. "The Party Spreads to the Factory Floor" and "The Surprise Economy." *BusinessWeek* (March 18): 29–37.

"Corporate Scoreboard." 2001–2002. *BusinessWeek.* Various issues.

Coy, Peter. 2002. "Why the Bears Aren't Backing Down." *BusinessWeek* (March 18): 36–37.

Economic Policy Institute. 2002. "Executive Summary to *The State of Working America,* 2002–2003." www.epinet.org.

Fazzari, Steve, and Hyman Minsky. 1984. "Domestic Monetary Policy: If Not Monetarism, What?" *Journal of Economic Issues* 18 (March): 101–16.

"Figures of the Week." 2001–2002. *BusinessWeek,* September 23, 2001, p. 138, and September 16, 2002, p. 92.

Forstater, Mathew. 1998. "Flexible Full Employment: Structural Implications of Discretionary Public Sector Employment." *Journal of Economic Issues* 32 (June): 557–63.

Keynes, John Maynard. 1937. "The General Theory of Employment." *Quarterly Journal of Economics* 51 (February): 209–23.

Leonhardt, David, and Daniel Altman. 2002. "Economy Shows Healing Signs as Recession Is Still Wheezing." *New York Times,* February 2.

Minsky, Hyman P. 1982. *Can "It" Happen Again? Essays on Instability and Finance.* Armonk, NY: M.E. Sharpe.

———. 1986. *Stabilizing an Unstable Economy.* New Haven: Yale University Press.

———. 1996. Foreword to *Political Economy for the 21st Century*, ed. Charles J. Whalen. Armonk, NY: M.E. Sharpe.

Peterson, Janice. 2002. "The TANF Reauthorization Debate: Key Welfare Reform Issues and Concerns." *Journal of Economic Issues* 36 (June): 431–39.

Spring, Frances. 1994. "Hyman P. Minsky: The Success of Big Government Capitalism." Jerome Levy Economics Institute *Report* (December): 13–14.

U.S. Department of Commerce. 2002. "National Accounts Data." Bureau of Economic Analysis, various tables (www.bea.doc.gov/bea/dnl.html), September 7.

Vroman, Wayne. 1990. "The Aggregate Performance of UI, 1980–1985." In *Unemployment Insurance: The Second Half-Century*, ed. W. Lee Hansen and James F. Byers. Madison: University of Wisconsin Press.

Weaver, R. Kent. 2002. "The Structure of the TANF Block Grant." *Welfare Reform & Beyond, Policy Brief No.* 22. Washington, DC: Brookings Institute.

Woodbury, Stephen A., and Murray A. Rubin. 1997. "The Duration of Benefits." In *Unemployment Insurance in the United States: Analysis of Policy Issues*, ed. Christopher J. O'Leary and Stephen A. Wandner. Kalamazoo, MI: W.E. Upjohn Institute for Employment Research.

Wray, L. Randall. 1998. "Zero Unemployment and Stable Prices." *Journal of Economic Issues* 32 (June): 539–45.

17. Money manager capitalism and the end of shared prosperity

Hyman Minsky often stated that there are "as many varieties of capitalism as Heinz has pickles." The capitalism in place in America at the end of World War II produced nearly a quarter-century of economic growth, relative stability, and shared prosperity. Today's capitalism, however—what Minsky called "money-manager" capitalism—is different in both character and outcomes. This article traces the development of Minsky's ideas on postwar structural change, outlines his conception of the current era, and discusses the connection between the rise of the present period and the end of shared prosperity.

MINSKY ON STRUCTURAL CHANGE

Business cycles are the primary focus of a large portion of Minsky's writings and of the professional literature that his works have spawned. While standard economic theory attributes cyclical macroeconomic fluctuations to government activism or other forces that constitute an exogenous disturbance to decentralized markets, Minsky traced instability to an endogenous source—capitalist finance. Minsky also understood that observed patterns of cyclical behavior are heavily influenced by the existing, yet always evolving, institutional structure. As he wrote in 1957, this means "the next financial crisis will never be just like the last one" [Minsky 1982a, 175].

Minsky's perspective leads to a recognition that "monetary economics cannot escape being institutional economics" [Minsky 1982a, 280]. Both theory and policy must be grounded in an understanding of the actual nature and evolution of real-world markets [Ferri and Minsky 1989, 124]. From the outset of his career, Minsky was motivated by this attitude to write about observed changes in money and financial markets [see, for example, Minsky 1982a, 162–191]. By 1963, his deep familiarity with such changes had already led Minsky to the conclusion that the rather steady growth of the early postwar economy was threatened by signs of increased financial fragility [Minsky 1982a, 3–13].

Reprinted with permission from *Journal of Economic Issues* 31 (2), June 1997, 517–525.

Although most of Minsky's energies between 1963 and 1980 were directed toward development of his "Wall Street paradigm" and its implications for short-term fluctuations, one still finds a number of references to what he saw as destabilizing financial trends in America [see, for example, Minsky 1964, 335; 1982a, 62, 69, 113–114]. As explained in an article appearing in this journal in 1980, Minsky's view was as follows: (1) the U.S. economy had undergone a secular transition from early postwar tranquility to growing (yet contained) turbulence; (2) the "credit crunch" of 1966 signaled the end of the old financial regime; (3) the new regime of fragility was caused by innovations in the financing of capital assets; (4) such innovations, motivated by perceived profit opportunities, are a normal occurrence, as Henry Simons recognized decades earlier; and (5) policymakers operating with the standard monetary and fiscal levers of the era confronted an "unappetizing" trade-off between a serious debt deflation and accelerating inflation [reprinted in Minsky 1982a, 71–89].

The elements just described constitute what might be considered the secular dimension of Minsky's "financial instability" hypothesis (FIH). This dimension of his FIH was further developed in a number of writings in the early and mid-1980s, including his *Stabilizing an Unstable Economy* [Minsky 1986a]. In identifying the institutional roots of the era's stagflation, these writings focus not just on the financial system and conventional economic policies, but also on wage and price determination. While government policy is identified as the "engine of inflation" [Minsky 1986a, 270], Minsky gives a supporting role to an administered pricing structure that raises corporate markups not only to accommodate rising overhead costs, but also to maintain profits in the face of downturns.[1] Although wage growth in excess of productivity growth is also mentioned as a contributing factor, Minsky stresses that trade union contributions to inflation have been overblown [Minsky 1982b, 1983, 1986a; Minsky and Ferri 1984].

Minsky's work on structural economic change outgrew the FIH in the late 1980s and early 1990s. The FIH was useful in accounting for economic changes from 1945 to 1966, but Minsky seems to have been searching for a broader historical analysis to help explain subsequent developments. The "further evolution of the financial structure" was clearly on his mind in 1986 [Minsky 1986b]. Perhaps it is merely a coincidence, but this was also the year that saw the first in a series of Minsky's essays that reflect upon the ideas of his former Harvard University professor, Joseph Schumpeter.[2] In that initial essay, Minsky writes: "The task confronting economics today may be characterized as a need to integrate Schumpeter's vision of a resilient intertemporal capitalist process with Keynes's hard insights into the fragility introduced into the capitalist accumulation process by some inescapable properties of capitalist financial structures" [Minsky 1986c, 121].

Minsky found three valuable elements in Schumpeter's vision: (1) that profit seeking leads not only to new products and processes, but also to new financing relations and financial institutions;[3] (2) that credit (finance) is at the center of capitalist economic development; and (3) that all capitalist economies are not the same; "capitalism is resilient because it takes many particular forms" [Minsky 1990a, 65]. While these elements involve only a small departure from Minsky's own guiding vision as expressed prior to that time, Schumpeter seems to have served as a sufficient source of inspiration for Minsky. The result, presented initially in the second of his essays on Schumpeter, was a new Minsky analysis—a historical account that traces capitalist development through a number of distinct stages [Minsky 1990a, 65–720].[4]

Minsky's historical analysis focuses on the changing relations between finance and business. But the impact of these stages of capitalist financial development is believed to reverberate throughout the entire economic system, "for the endogenous evolutionary dynamics of capitalist economies change the relations between financial and real economic variables which, in turn, change the dynamic patterns of the economy" [Minsky 1990a, 66]. The earliest statements of this theory identify four regimes—"commercial capitalism," "finance capitalism," "managerial capitalism," and "money-manager capitalism" [Minsky 1990a; 1992b; 1993a].[5] In two later essays, the second stage ("finance capitalism") is divided into two eras, "industrial capitalism" and "financial capitalism" [Minsky 1996; Minsky and Whalen 1996–97].

FROM COMMERCIAL CAPITALISM TO MONEY-MANAGER CAPITALISM

The first stage of American capitalism identified by Minsky is the *commercial* period. During commercial capitalism, external finance was used primarily to facilitate commerce by financing goods in transit or in process. Minsky writes:

> In the pure commercial capitalism regime, the financing of expensive and long-lived capital assets falls outside the domain of the banks and organized financial markets. Proprietorships, partnerships, and governments provide the funds for the capital assets of such an economy. Pure commercial capitalism did not survive the introduction of capital-intensive transportation, modern utilities, or factory manufacturing. Raw material export economies were typically characterized by banking structures that specialized in commercial credit; such banking structures are ill-suited for financing the capital development of their community [Minsky 1990a, 67].

While commercial capitalism was a period of both dispersed economic power and production dominated by labor and tools, *finance* capitalism, which emerged in a number of countries during the century leading up to World War

I, was an era dominated by powerful banks and the machinery of industrial production. The early phase of this period is what Minsky called *industrial* capitalism, a period during which the corporate form of organizing business became recognized as most appropriate for an economy with expensive and durable capital assets. In the United States and England, vast resources required for mills, railroads, and other projects were financed during this era by the rise of investment banks. Minsky writes: "This was the era of the houses of Rothschild and Morgan" [Minsky 1990a, 67].[6]

Industrial capitalism was also a period of booms and depressions. In response to these cycles, some investment banks sought to protect the cash flows of their clients by encouraging and financing the formation of trusts, cartels, and monopolies. This new financing direction, pursued by bankers since at least the 1880s, is the central element in what Minsky calls *financial* capitalism—a largely unregulated era that came to an end with the economic contraction and eventual financial-system collapse in the period 1929–33.

The *managerial* era was ushered in by the economic policies and reforms of the New Deal. Important aspects of the managerial period's financial system included:

1. Countercyclical fiscal policy, which sustained profits when the economy faltered.[7]
2. Low interest rates and interventions by the Federal Reserve unconstrained by gold-standard considerations.
3. Deposit insurance for banks and thrifts.
4. Infusion of government equity into transportation, industry, and finance through the Reconstruction Finance Corporation.
5. Restrictions on competition (including geographic barriers to market entry, compartmentalization of financial institutions by function, and interest-rate regulation).
6. Interventions by specialized organizations (such as the Agricultural Adjustment Administration and the Federal Housing Administration) created to address sectoral concerns.

Another important aspect of the managerial period was the nature of indebtedness. From 1933 through the end of World War II, government represented the main source of external financing for the economy. By 1946, a broad set of households owned financial assets mainly in the form of government debt or as interests in insurance policies and bank deposits, which were in turn largely offset by government debts. Business and household indebtedness were minimal; many of the great corporations had large net positions in government debts and bank deposits—and many working-class households held substantially larger net financial asset positions than hitherto.

Money-manager capitalism emerged out of this initial post-World War II position. In part it is the result of the evolution of financial practices toward more speculative endeavors—the secular aspect of Minsky's FIH. This aspect of the FIH can be restated as follows.

Economic activity in the early postwar setting began with a cautious use of debt. As the period of economic prosperity began to lengthen, margins of safety in indebtedness decreased and the system evolved not only toward a greater reliance on debt relative to internal finance, but also toward short-term financing and the increased use of debt to acquire existing assets. There was also an explosion of activity by finance companies and other non-bank financial institutions—as well as a steady stream of bank innovations such as the securitization of loans and the creative use of off-balance sheet commitments. As a result, the once robust financial system became increasingly fragile.[8]

But money-manager capitalism is also partly a product of institutional innovations that dramatically altered the control of corporate equities and bonds: as the label "money-manager" capitalism suggests, central to this new stage are institutions that manage large portfolios of financial instruments. In the current era, the largest proportion of the liabilities of corporations are held either by financial institutions, such as bank trust departments and insurance companies, or by pension or mutual funds that are restricted in their holdings only by contract.[9] The stated aim of these money managers, and the sole criterion by which they are judged, is the maximization of the value of the investments made by the fund holders.[10] Money-manager capitalism introduces a new layer of intermediation into the financial structure.

A consequence of the rise of institutional investors is that business leaders have become increasingly sensitive to the stock market valuation of their firm. In the early postwar period, corporate managers were allowed some freedom from stockholder influence due to widespread caution in finance, America's dominance in the global economy, and less financial intermediation. Today, however, corporations are often subject to relentless shareholder pressure via these funds.

Another consequence of the rise of money managers is an environment conducive to mergers, acquisitions, breakups, leveraged buyouts, and stock buybacks. Fund managers have a powerful incentive to support all takeovers and buybacks that will boost near-term portfolio value. Their funds often provide the resources that raiders need to secure corporate control.[11]

Finally, Minsky observed that money-manager capitalism is international. Today's money funds are global both in terms of contributions received and assets held; and looking ahead, Minsky could see only a drive toward further global financial integration. He also recognized the trend toward further internationalization of trade and production. Minsky stressed that the development of worldwide capitalism would soon demand increasing attention from policy-making bodies throughout the globe [Minsky 1995; 1990a, 71; 1990b].[12]

THE END OF SHARED PROSPERITY

When one considers the pressures on U.S. business executives from both the rapidly evolving financial system and the internationalization of production and trade, it is no surprise that economic inequality is on the rise and that work force insecurity is pervasive. With the end of the managerial era of the early postwar period, stability in U.S. industrial relations has also ended. Workers at nearly all levels are insecure, as entire divisions are bought and sold and as corporate boards exhibit a chronic need to downsize overhead and to seek out the least expensive set of variable inputs. A similar pressure is being felt in the public sector, where privatization and outsourcing have become widespread.

While the mid-1990s have seen record gains on Wall Street and relatively low unemployment and inflation rates, most working families are having trouble distinguishing recovery from recession. As Stephen Roach, chief economist at Morgan Stanley, writes: "Recovery or not, the 1990s are still all about downsizing, longer workdays, white-collar shock and relatively limited opportunities for new employment" [Roach 1995]. Beneath the misleading macroeconomic surface are numerous signs of the end of shared prosperity—from divergent trends in family incomes to wage stagnation, falling levels of health and pension coverage, longer employment searches and other increases in the cost of job loss, and an explosive growth in (involuntary) part-time and contingent work [Whalen 1996].

According to the editors of *Fortune* magazine, returns on shareholder equity are, by any number of measures, at record levels. But driving the current expansion is corporate restructuring, which is precisely what is contributing to increased economic insecurity for large numbers of Americans. In fact, employment at the largest U.S. firms has fallen 22 percent since 1978. Yet there is still more to the story. As *Fortune* explained to its readers, behind much of the drive to increase corporate performance is the pressure of mutual funds—pressure fueled not just by the demands of the wealthy, but also by ordinary citizens who invest their retirement money in search of the highest possible short-term return [Editors 1996, 259–276].

The *long-term* economic, social, and political costs of today's trends, however, could be staggering. The toll of income stagnation and employment insecurity has already been tremendous on many; a dangerous and uncivilized "fortress capitalism," a system with declining fortunes for all but a minority who seek protection behind walled and gated communities, is the likely product of current developments. Additional long-term concerns include the following: (1) current corporate returns cannot be sustained forever; (2) continued economic growth is threatened by the inequality it now breeds; (3) welfare reform may soon add thousands of workers to labor markets such as New York and Philadelphia, which have been experiencing huge net job losses during the latest economic expansion; and (4) today's capitalism may be ineffective in the financing of major innovations and capital development projects that require multiple-year time horizons [Thurow 1995; Editors 1996, 272; Bernstein 1994; Minsky 1990a, 72; 1992b, 32; 1992c, 21–22].

DIRECTIONS FOR THE FUTURE

Conventional economists are hesitant to offer policy suggestions to address America's current problems and disturbing trends. But Minsky recognized long ago that such economists operate from a theoretical framework that misspecifies the nature of our economy and is rooted in an assumption that cannot be proven by either theory or history: that market forces alone enable an economy to achieve and sustain the best possible outcomes for all. The economy is a time-dependent, institutionally determined social system, not a natural system or automatic mechanism.

According to Minsky, capitalism evolves and so, too, must the legislated institutional structure. The institutions of the private sector are primarily market driven—their evolution is driven by agents acting in their own interest. This evolution can undermine the barriers to instability, dynamic inefficiency, intolerable insecurity, and inhumane outcomes. Such undermining has to be offset from time to time by collective action.

Minsky believed deeply in the possibility of reducing present-day economic insecurity without sacrificing economic progress. There could be no better Minsky legacy than a profession that works to stop the drift toward fortress capitalism and instead seeks to establish a new age of shared prosperity.[13]

NOTES

1. By validating existing liability structures and stabilizing profits, government is both "a blessing and a curse," according to Minsky. It is a blessing because it prevents another deep depression; but it is a curse because traditional fiscal and monetary policies have sustained and even accelerated inflation surges. For discussions about the sort of government that is particularly inflationary—one with expenditures weighted heavily toward transfers and defense rather than toward direct resource creation—see Minsky [1986a]. For more on the supporting inflationary role of an industrial structure dominated by large units with market power, see Fazzari and Minsky [1984].
2. For the essays on Schumpeter, see Minsky [1986c; 1990a; 1992a; 1993a].
3. Minsky writes:

> Schumpeterian creation and destruction occurs in finance as well as in products and processes. The essential point of Schumpeter's view of money and

banks is that new combinations in production and in products could not appear without being financed: finance and development are in a symbiotic relation. Restricting the Schumpeterian vision to technology or even industrial organization misses the essentially integrated character of Schumpeter's vision [Minsky 1990a, 61].

4. In 1990, Minsky wrote, "Our great ancestors, such as Schumpeter, are useful as they help us to understand the problems with which we struggle" [Minsky 1990a, 51]. In retrospect, it seems only logical that Minsky moved a bit away from Keynes and toward Schumpeter as he turned from struggling with business cycles to confronting longer-term issues of structural change. While Keynes is certainly a formidable figure in the realm of macroeconomic cycles, Schumpeter is unquestionably a "giant" in the literature on long-term capitalist development.
5. A discussion of money-manager capitalism can also be found in Minsky [1990b]. The next section of the present article, "From Commercial Capitalism to Money-Manager Capitalism," draws on that essay and the other works mentioned in the paragraph (above) within which this endnote is located.
6. In contrast, Germany saw the rise of universal banking structures [see Minsky 1990a, 67; 1991].
7. For a discussion of how the National Labor Relations ("Wagner") Act was also designed to contribute to macroeconomic stabilization, see Kaufman [1996].
8. Other factors contributing to increased fragility include the deregulation and globalization of financial markets [Minsky 1992c, 23–24; 1986d].
9. Between 1950 and 1990, money managers saw the fraction of U.S. corporate equities under their control grow from 8 percent to 60 percent [Porter 1992, 69]. Over the same period, pension funds increased their share of total business equities from less than 1 percent to almost 39 percent, while their fraction of corporate debt rose from 13 percent to 50 percent [Ghilarducci 1992, 117]. Money-manager capitalism is therefore partly a consequence of the emergence of private pension funds that supplement the Social Security system. For more on institutional investors, see Useem [1996].
10. The value of a fund-holder's investment is measured by the total return on assets: the combination of dividends and interest paid out and the appreciation in per-share value.
11. These funds have also contributed to financial-system evolution by providing a ready pool of buyers for securitized loans, the commercial paper of finance companies, and other innovations.
12. For more on his view of international economic issues, see Minsky [1985; 1986d; 1986e].
13. For Minsky's views on the institutional prerequisites for successful capitalism, see Minsky and Whalen [1996–97] and Minsky [1992c, 23–30; 1993b, 23–25; 1996].

REFERENCES

Bernstein, Aaron. "How the Gap Between Rich and Poor Hurts the Economy." *Business Week* no. 3385 (August 15, 1994): 78–82.

Editors. "The Fortune 500." *Fortune* 133 (April 29, 1996): 260–276.

Fazzari, Steve, and Hyman P. Minsky. "Domestic Monetary Policy: If Not Monetarism, What?" *Journal of Economic Issues* 18 (March 1984): 101–116.

Ferri, Piero, and Hyman P. Minsky. "The Breakdown of the IS-LM Synthesis: Implications for Post-Keynesian Economic Theory." *Review of Political Economy* l, no. 1 (1989): 125–143.

Ghilarducci, Teresa. *Labor's Capital: The Economics and Politics of Private Pensions.* Cambridge, Mass.: MIT Press, 1992.

Kaufman, Bruce E. "Why the Wagner Act?" In *Advances in Industrial and Labor Relations,* edited by David Lewin, Bruce Kaufman, and Donna Sockell. Greenwich, Conn.: JAI Press, 1996.

Minsky, Hyman P. "Longer Waves in Financial Relations: Financial Factors in the More Severe Depressions." *American Economic Review* 54 (May 1964): 324–335.

———. *Can "It" Happen Again?* Armonk, N.Y.: M.E. Sharpe, 1982a.

———. "Debt Deflation Processes in Today's Institutional Environment." *Banca Nazionale Del Lavoro Quarterly Review* 35 (December 1982b): 375–393.

———. "Institutional Roots of American Inflation." In *Inflation Through the Ages,* edited by Nathan Schmukler and Edward Marcus. New York: Brooklyn College Press, 1983.

———. "Money and the Lender of Last Resort." *Challenge* 28 (March–April 1985): 12–18.

———. *Stabilizing an Unstable Economy.* New Haven, Conn.: Yale University Press, 1986a.

———. "The Evolution of Financial Institutions and the Performance of the Economy." *Journal of Economic Issues* 20 (June 1986b): 345–354.

———. "Money and Crisis in Schumpeter and Keynes." In *The Economic Law of Motion of Modern Society,* edited by H. J. Wagener and J. W. Drukker. Cambridge: Cambridge University Press, 1986c.

———. "Global Consequences of Financial Deregulation." *Marcus Wallenberg Papers on International Finance* 2, no. 1 (1986d): 1–19.

———. "Conflict and Interdependence in a Multipolar World." *Studies in Banking and Finance* 4 (1986e): 3–22.

———. "Schumpeter: Finance and Evolution." In *Evolving Technology and Market Structure,* edited by Arnold Heertje and Mark Perlman. Ann Arbor: University of Michigan Press, 1990a.

———. "Money Manager Capitalism, Fiscal Independence and International Monetary Reconstruction." In The *Future of the Global Economic and Monetary System,* edited by M. Szabo-Pelsoczi. Budapest, Hungary: Institute for World Economics, 1990b.

———. "The Transition to a Market Economy: Financial Options." Working Paper no. 66. Annandale-on-Hudson, N.Y.: Jerome Levy Economics Institute, 1991.

———. "Commentary." In *Entrepreneurship, Technological Innovation and Economic Growth,* edited by Frederic M. Sherer and Mark Perlman. Ann Arbor: University of Michigan Press, 1992a.

———. "Reconstituting the U.S. Financial Structure." Working Paper no. 69. Annandale-on-Hudson, N.Y.: Jerome Levy Economics Institute, 1992b.

———. "The Capital Development of the Economy and the Structure of Financial Institutions." Working Paper no.72. Annandale-on-Hudson, N.Y.: Jerome Levy Economics Institute, 1992c.

———. "Schumpeter and Finance." In *Market and Institutions in Economic Development,* edited by Salvatore Biasco, Alessandro Roncaglia, and Michele Salvati. New York: St. Martin's Press, 1993a.

———. "Finance and Stability: The Limits of Capitalism." Working Paper no. 93. Annandale-on-Hudson, N.Y.: Jerome Levy Economics Institute, 1993b.

———. "Longer Waves in Financial Relations: Financial Factors in the More Severe Depressions II." *Journal of Economic Issues* 29 (March 1995): 83–96.

———. "Uncertainty and the Institutional Structure of Capitalist Economies." *Journal of Economic Issues* 30 (June 1996): 357–368.

Minsky, Hyman P., and Piero Ferri. "Prices, Employment and Profits." *Journal of Post Keynesian Economics* 6 (Summer 1984): 489–499.

Minsky, Hyman P., and Charles J. Whalen. "Economic Insecurity and the Institutional Prerequisites for Successful Capitalism." *Journal of Post Keynesian Economics* 19 (Winter 1996–97): 155–170.

Porter, Michael E. "Capital Disadvantage: America's Failing Capital Investment System." *Harvard Business Review* 70 (September–October 1992): 65–82.

Thurow, Lester. "Why Their World Might Crumble." *The New York Times Magazine* (November 19, 1995): 78–79.

Useem, Michael. *Investor Capitalism: How Money Managers are Changing the Face of Corporate America.* New York: Basic Books, 1996.

Whalen, Charles J. "The Age of Anxiety." *USA Today* [magazine] 125 (September 1996): 14–16.

18. Integrating Schumpeter and Keynes: Hyman Minsky's theory of capitalist development

In a number of books and articles, Hyman P. Minsky influenced many of today's institutional and Post Keynesian economists. In fact, Minsky often chose the pages of this journal as the place to present and extend his Wall Street paradigm, financial theory of investment, and investment theory of business cycles, the latter of which is often called the financial instability hypothesis (FIH). Those contributions have all received significant attention in recent years, along with Minsky's writings on what might be called the secular (multi-cycle) dimension of the FIH.[1] What has gone almost entirely unnoticed, however, is that during the last decade of his life Minsky adopted, and sought to develop and explore, an even more historical approach to economic analysis—a theory of capitalist development.

This article seeks to prompt professional consideration of Minsky's theory of capitalist development by explaining and presenting it. The article begins by describing Minsky's interest in such a theory. The theory is then outlined, both in terms of its essential elements and as it applies to the US economy. Directions for future research are also identified.

Because Minsky's theory centers on the economy's evolving institutional structure, it should be of particular interest to evolutionary economists—especially now, an era in which even mainstream economists are beginning to ask whether the economy has changed in fundamental ways. Both Thorstein Veblen and John R. Commons saw the need for a theory of capitalist development. In many respects, Minsky's work provides an extension of their forays into this realm. Minsky's theory is also a valuable complement to the more recent institutionalist literature on American economic structure, a fact capable of injecting additional strength into what is already an impressive research tradition.

Reprinted with permission from *Journal of Economic Issues* 35 (4), December 2001, 805–823.

THE NEED FOR THEORY

Minsky considered economics serious business. Many post-World War II economists have demonstrated little interest in contributing to the resolution of social problems. But Minsky's aim was always a more humane economy as a first step toward a better society. In his view, practical problem solving—not abstract puzzle solving—was the fundamental purpose of economic scholarship.

Minsky also believed that economics provides no easy answers. He knew that neither history nor theory offers strong evidence that markets alone can produce widespread prosperity and economic stability. Making Minsky's search for practical answers even more difficult was the US economics profession's infatuation with neoclassical theory—an approach he rejected as an inadequate starting point for economic analysis. Indeed, reflecting on the fact that neoclassicalism was thoroughly entrenched in the nation's advisory and policy-making circles, he once wrote, "Nobody 'up there' understands American capitalism" (Minsky 1982a, 202).[2]

But Minsky's problem-solving orientation and rejection of neoclassical economics did not lead to an atheoretical outlook. Rather, he sought theories that would enable "economists and policymakers to do better" (Minsky 1982a, xii). In fact, Minsky saw a number of reasons to engage in a theoretical examination of capitalism's development.

Minsky believed that effective policy making requires an understanding of the dynamics of an accumulating capitalist economy. Since such dynamics include short-term macroeconomic fluctuations and longer term economic evolution, he saw the need to develop theories that improve our understanding of both. According to Minsky, fashioning and updating such theories should be the primary mission of modern economic theory (Ferri and Minsky 1992, 89; Ferri and Minsky 1989, 124; Minsky 1993a).

Beyond the perennial need for useful theories to guide policy, Minsky saw a growing immediate need for historically grounded theory in the 1980s. This need was mandated by decades of financial innovation and economic change (Minsky 1986a). By the early 1990s, Minsky had become thoroughly convinced that institutional reform was essential within both the financial system and the broader economy. As he wrote in 1991, "To create a worthy successor to the financial system that served us so well between the 1930s and 1980s requires a deeper look at our institutions than we have taken so far" (1991a, 16). Since Minsky saw the need for nothing less than a thorough re-examination of "our current model of capitalism," he found the most effective way to obtain this "deeper look" was to focus on long-term capitalist development rather than business cycles (Minsky 1993b, 1; Ferri and Minsky 1992; Minsky 1993a, 113; Minsky 1996a).

Another reason for devising and utilizing such an alternative to neoclassical theory in the early 1990s was Minsky's desire to stress the flawed nature of unregulated macroeconomic activity. In the two years leading to the Republican takeover of the US House of Representatives, there was a growing dismissal of counter-cyclical macroeconomic management within academic and policy circles. And that sentiment became even stronger after the 1994 election. In this period, Minsky thought it was essential to combat the dominant trend with analyses grounded in history and institutional reality. In a series of essays and public presentations, he focused on the decades before and after the New Deal and stressed that unregulated markets are inherently unstable and can produce an intolerable distribution of income (Minsky 1993b; Levy Institute 1994, 13–14; Minsky 1995a; Minsky 1996b).

Minsky's exploration of capitalist development was also designed to stress that capitalism comes in many varieties—varieties with varying implications for stability, efficiency, and the distribution of market power. This fact was seen as an essential starting point not only for US economic reconstruction but also for societies that sought to move from planned to market economies (Minsky 1991b; Minsky 1992). As Minsky argued, "Whereas all capitalisms are flawed, not all capitalisms are equally flawed" (Minsky 1986b, 295).

Finally, Minsky's broad examination of capitalist development provided an opportunity to consider the important links between various contemporary economic issues. While much of his work focused on the financial system, his analyses also explored the challenge of resource creation, economic insecurity, and tax reform. The message was unmistakable: specific policy areas should not be addressed in isolation—economists must be able to provide policymakers with a conception of the economy as an interrelated system (Ferri and Minsky 1992, 83; Minsky 1991a, 15–16; Minsky 1993b; Minsky 1996a; Minsky and Whalen 1996–97).

ESSENTIAL ELEMENTS

Minsky argued there was merit to standing on the shoulders of an intellectual giant. Writing on business cycles, Minsky made considerable use of the prior work of John Maynard Keynes. In the mid 1980s, though, he became convinced that the structure of the US economy had so fundamentally changed that an analysis of structural evolution was essential. It was at this point that Minsky turned to the insights of Joseph A. Schumpeter, his Harvard dissertation advisor. In a 1986 essay, Minsky wrote: "The task confronting economics today may be characterized as a need to integrate Schumpeter's vision of a resilient intertemporal capitalist process with Keynes's hard insights into the fragility introduced into the capitalist accumulation process by some inescapable properties of capitalist financial structures" (Minsky 1986c, 121).

Minsky thought such an integration was possible because Schumpeter and Keynes (along with Marx and the institutionalists) had a common perception of the task of economics: "They each define the problem that economic theory must explain as the path of development of an accumulating capitalist economy through historical time" (Minsky 1986b, 285). From this perspective, the economy is a complex, time-dependent system. Society is an "evolutionary beast," changing in response to endogenous factors, not an equilibrium-seeking and -sustaining system (Ferri and Minsky 1992; Minsky 1993a, 104).

If the first element in Minsky's theory is the focus on economic activity as a process in time, then the second element is that capitalist dynamics can take many forms. The path of the economy through time can be progressive, stagnant, or deteriorating—and tranquil or turbulent. In fact, it may be highly irregular—even chaotic.[3]

A fundamental determinant of the particular path of capitalist development is the economy's institutional structure. It is this structure that facilitates, influences, regulates, and constrains economic activity. In recognition of the range of structures found throughout history, Minsky often stated that "capitalism comes in as many varieties as Heinz has pickles."[4] Moreover, given the notion of the economy as an evolving system, Minsky also stressed the dynamic nature of the institutional structure.

While standard economic theory emphasizes exchange, Minsky's recognition of historical time caused him to emphasize that production precedes exchange—and that finance precedes production. Thus, credit and finance are at the center of capitalist development. Moreover, "[b]ecause credit is essential to the process of development, a theory of economic development needs to integrate money into its basic formulation." The result is an approach inconsistent with Walrasian theory: "Monetary factors cannot be added on after a prior or dominant model has determined the basic output and relative price variables" (Minsky 1990a, 55).

So far it has been suggested that "the in-place financial structure is a central determinant of the behavior of a capitalist economy" (Minsky 1993a, 106). Yet another essential element in Minsky's theory is the driving force of the profit motive. This motive was an essential element in Minsky's writings throughout his career. He had long argued that present and prospective profits influence economic activity within the context of a given institutional structure—and that the structure itself changes in response to profit seeking. As Minsky gave increasing attention to capitalist development, profit-driven structural change took on increasing importance in his writings (Minsky 1986c; Ferri and Minsky 1989, 135; Minsky 1993a).

Scholars have long recognized Schumpeterian forces of creation and destruction in products and manufacturing processes. But Minsky emphasized that Schumpeter also gave attention to changes in financial systems. As a result, Minsky's theory stresses that financial markets evolve not only in response to profit-driven demands of business leaders and individual investors but also as a result of the profit-seeking entrepreneurialism of financial firms (Minsky 1986b; Minsky 1990a; Minsky 1993a). In fact, Minsky wrote: "Nowhere is evolution, change and Schumpeterian entrepreneurship more evident than in banking and finance and nowhere is the drive for profits more clearly the factor making for change" (1993a, 106). In short, financial innovation is another essential element in Minsky's theory—indeed, such innovation is a crucial determinant of institutional evolution.[5]

To summarize, capitalist development is shaped by the institutional structure, but this structure is always evolving in response to profit-seeking activity. The financial system takes on special importance in this theory not only because finance exerts a strong influence on business activity but also because this system is particularly prone to innovation. Since finance and industrial development are in a symbiotic relation, financial evolution plays a crucial role in the dynamic patterns of the economy.

There is, however, one more essential element of Minsky's theory: public policy. Government action is an inescapable determinant of capitalist economic development. Its decisions shape the institutional framework that conditions economic activity.

As US economic experience has shown since 1933, discretionary policy interventions and institutional containing mechanisms can both be utilized to promote economic stability. Counter-cyclical fiscal policy (achieved by what Minsky called "Big Government") and lender-of-last-resort central-bank initiatives have been among the most potent stabilizers employed in the past half century.[6] But financial- and labor-market regulations have also played contributing roles. As Minsky indicated in *Stabilizing an Unstable Economy*, "Policy influences both the details and overall character of the economy." Thus, economists and policymakers "must be concerned with the design of institutions as well as with operation within a set of institutions" (Minsky 1986a, 7, 293; Ferri and Minsky 1992; Delli Gatti, Gallegati, and Minsky 1996; Minsky 1996a).

Since the economy evolves endogenously, no policy regime will provide a "once and for all solution" to economic difficulties. In time, policies that once worked well may no longer be adequate, due to innovations in finance and business or to the emergence of new problems (Minsky 1986a, 293). While Minsky recognized it is neither possible nor desirable for policy makers to engage constantly in institutional reform, he stressed that such change becomes essential when inadequate economic performance becomes widely evident and deemed serious by the public and its representatives.[7]

US CAPITALIST DEVELOPMENT

The history of economic thought contains a variety of theories of capitalist development. Some recent theories are efficiency driven. Others focus on technology, product innovation, or class struggle. Minsky's theory is finance driven, and the relations between finance and business are at its core. Key questions to be asked at each stage are, What is being financed? What is the pivotal source of external financing?[8] and What is the balance of economic power between those in business and banking?

A consideration of Minsky's theory as it applies to US economic history provides evidence that capitalism does indeed come in many varieties. At least five stages can be identified—and we might now be on the verge of creating a sixth. The five stages can be labeled as follows: merchant capitalism (1607–1813), industrial capitalism (1813–1890), banker capitalism (1890–1933), managerial capitalism (1933–1982), and money-manager capitalism (1982–present).[9] (See Table 1.)

Merchant capitalism emerged from European feudal society and took root in America with the establishment of British colonies in the 1600s. From the outset, there were joint-stock corporations in America: Virginia and Massachusetts were both products of joint-stock ventures. Still, merchants dominated the economic scene until approximately 1813, when the Boston Manufacturing Company (organized by Francis Lowell) began operating the first integrated cotton textile factory in the United States.[10]

The dominant source of finance in this initial era provided funds for goods in process, stock (inventories), or transit. The financing was provided by merchant banking—"vouching for the legitimacy of distant trade partners" and financing goods in transit—and by commercial banking (Minsky 1990a, 67; 1992, 30–31). According to Minsky (1990a, 67), private economic power in this period was "fragmented and dispersed."

Merchant capitalism was characterized by owner-managed enterprises—sometimes involving a partnership among relatives—with few employees and often a small number of transactions per day (Heilbroner and Singer 1994, 62). To a large extent, the US economy was a raw-material export economy in this era. Production was by labor and tools, rather than by machinery and labor.

A growing population and the arrival of the industrial revolution helped undermine merchant capitalism. But Minsky is correct in drawing our attention to the profit motive, for profit was the driving force for individuals whose names have become synonymous with the arrival and expansion of industrial capitalism (Francis Lowell, Eli Whitney, Cyrus McCormick, Cornelius Vanderbilt, and Andrew Carnegie, for example). Moreover, innovation in finance was a prerequisite—for the banking structures of merchant capitalism were ill suited to finance the capital development of the economy.

Table 1 Stages of capitalist development

	Merchant capitalism (1607–1813)	Industrial capitalism (1813–1890)	Banker capitalism (1890–1933)	Managerial capitalism (1933–1982)	Money-manager capitalism (1982–present)
What distinctive activity is financed?	Transportation of goods; acquisition of inventories; goods production	Industrial expansion (Acquisition of factories and machines)	Industrial consolidation (Trusts and mergers)	Macroeconomic growth and stability	Increase of stock-market values and corporate profits (Often involves merger, buyout or break-up)
What is the pivotal source of external financing?	Commercial or merchant bank (Also important: internal finance)	Investment bank	Investment bank	Central bank (Internal finance important again)	Institutional investment funds (Pension and mutual funds)
What is the fundamental enterprise or entity financed?	Proprietorship and partnership	Industrial corporation	Combined corporation	Private sector (Financed through the banking system; conglomerate form dominates in business)	International corporation
What group holds the greatest economic power?	Power is dispersed (Merchants and bankers)	Investment bankers	Investment bankers	Corporate managers (Assumes government macroeconomic stabilization)	Money-fund managers
What is the distinctive input?	Labor	Machinery	Management (Coordination of the industry and the firm)	Macroeconomic stabilization by government; microeconomic coordination by business managers	Expertise in finance and accounting

Industrial capitalism was characterized by emergence of financial organizations that could mobilize the resources needed for factory manufacturing, capital-intensive transportation, mills, and mines. This era saw organization of the New York Stock Exchange and the rise of investment banking houses such as that of J. P. Morgan.[11] The partnership gave way to the corporation, and home production was supplanted by factory production.

Industrial capitalism was also a period characterized by numerous rounds of cutthroat price competition. By threatening the financial health of industrial firms, this competition jeopardized the ability of corporations to fulfill their payment commitments. Also threatened was the security of investments. Thus, many business leaders and bankers "began to abhor competitive markets" (Minsky 1993a, 109). Morgan, for example, is reported to have said, "I like a little competition; but I like combination better" (Heilbroner and Singer 1994, 206). Others were even less generous toward the invisible forces of the marketplace.

Banker capitalism was the new era established when investment bankers responded to cutthroat competition in the 1880s and 1890s. Its arrival was characterized by investment bankers turning their attention toward the financing of industrial combinations (cartels, trusts, and mergers), a trend not at all altered by the Sherman Anti-Trust Act. Indeed, there was a merger wave in its aftermath.[12] "By 1904, one or two giant firms—usually put together by merger—controlled at least half the output in seventy-eight different industries" (Heilbroner and Singer 1994, 208).

In the evolution from merchant capitalism to banker capitalism, private economic power became greatly concentrated. While the law of supply and demand was not repealed, private-sector financiers and managers exerted their own formidable force during banker capitalism—at the enterprise and the industry level. At the enterprise level, "scientific" techniques devised or inspired by Frederick Winslow Taylor combined with assembly line production, enabling managers to generate significant increases in factory output. At the industry level, meanwhile, investment bankers acquired a controlling position in the economy not only by arranging mergers but also by securing large ownership shares and seats on the boards of directors of newly combined corporations.

Minsky's writings say little about the speculative boom and collapse that brought about both the Great Depression and the end of banker capitalism.[13] Evidence exists, however, that is consistent with the essential elements of his analysis (and with his extensive writings on business cycles and secular—or multi-cycle—fragility). It is said that the financial panic of 1907–08 was brought to an end when Morgan stepped in to minimize the economic losses. But his firm was not able to repeat the achievement in 1929 (Galbraith 1961, 103–132). According to Guilio Pontecorvo's landmark study of the 1920s, investment banking firms had become victims of their own success (Pontecorvo 1958).

Although the years between 1908 and 1929 were not recession free, they were depression free and generally prosperous—a sharp contrast with the American experience from 1866 through 1908. Because the US capital market was without significant policy constraints prior to 1933, any regulation had to come from within the financial community. But the relative stability and prosperity attracted not only new investors but also new investment bankers to the industry (many commercial banks, for example, formed investment banking affiliates in the 1920s). While the older firms were more conservative in their practices, the new firms were "aggressively engaged in expansion of their business." Moreover, close ties between some investment companies and speculative interests meant that their policies contributed more to market instability than to stability (Pontecorvo 1958, 171).

Pontecorvo wrote that the effect of entry into investment banking in the 1920s "was to reduce the relative importance and the leadership role of the original firms. Furthermore, the industry developed a large competitive fringe. This fringe of highly competitive firms had a considerable effect on the behavior of the industry." He concluded: "The overall impact of these changes was the elimination of any internal controls that may have been present in the earlier period. The instability in the structure created by the rise of new firms was a factor in the security inflation that followed" (Pontecorvo 1958, 170). In classic Minskian fashion, success bred daring—and when the speculative bubble burst, then not even the nation's great investment banking houses could contain the collapse.

The depression made manifest the need for public action to stabilize economic activity in the face of business downturns. Due to the divergence between individual and collective rationality, it was nearly impossible for individual bankers, business leaders, and farmers to do anything except cut loans, slash prices, reduce employment, and increase agricultural yields—all of which made matters worse in the aggregate. Franklin Roosevelt's answer was the New Deal, a series of policies and reforms that ushered in the next stage of US capitalist development.

Managerial capitalism began with bold government action in the realm of monetary policy and banking. Through the Emergency Banking Act and other initiatives, Americans were provided with an accommodative Federal Reserve, bank reorganizations, and institutional reform including deposit insurance, securities regulation, and compartmentalization of financial institutions. Combined with counter-cyclical fiscal policy, farm policies, and labor-market regulations, this government action helped set the stage for an unprecedented period of stability and prosperity after World War II.

The postwar economic environment—characterized by oligopolistic markets, insignificant foreign competition, and government macroeconomic management[14]—enabled US corporate managers a high degree of independence from banker and stockholder pressures. Unfortunately, as managers emphasized stability, many neglected adaptation—preferring, instead, bigness through conglomeration. The result was complacency that produced considerable economic upheaval when inflation and intense foreign competition both appeared on the scene in the 1970s.

Another trend after World War II was the secular evolution of a more fragile financial system, as postwar prosperity and lender-of-last-resort monetary interventions by the Fed encouraged reductions in margins of safety, greater reliance on debt financing, and a turn toward short-term financing. In time, there was also an explosion of activity by finance companies and other non-bank financial institutions—as well as a steady stream of bank innovations such as the securitization of loans and the creative use of off-balance-sheet commitments.[15]

One major innovation in the financial system during the postwar period was the rise of managed-money funds—pension funds, mutual funds, bank trust funds, and the like. Part of this growth was due to the spread of private pensions as a feature of the US labor market. Over time, such funds accumulated vast sums. Inflation's damaging effect upon bank deposits also contributed to the increase in managed-money funds. As the postwar era progressed, "individual wealth holdings increasingly took the form of ownership of the liabilities of managed funds rather than the holding of a portfolio of the liabilities of individual businesses" (Minsky 1993a, 110–111).

Money-manager capitalism became a reality in the 1980s as institutional investors, holders of the largest share of corporate stocks and bonds by the end of that decade, began to exert their influence on financial markets and business enterprises.[16] The aim of money managers, and the sole criterion by which they are judged, is the maximization of the value of investments made by fund holders. As a result, business leaders became increasingly sensitive to short-term profits and the stock-market valuation of their firm. In the era of managerial capitalism, corporate managers "were the masters of the private economy" (Minsky 1993a, 110). During the long expansion that began in 1982, it became increasingly clear that money managers were the masters.

The rise of institutional investors encouraged continued financial-system evolution by providing a ready pool of buyers for securitized loans, the commercial paper of finance companies, and other innovations. It also fueled the trend toward mergers, acquisitions, corporate breakups, leveraged buyouts, and stock buybacks—since fund managers have a strong incentive to support whatever initiatives promise to boost near-term portfolio value. Their managed-money funds often provided the resources that raiders needed to secure corporate control.

Money manager pressures—often in combination with the force exerted by growing international competition and by rapid technological and product-market changes—also encouraged corporate downsizing and re-engineering. While such changes sometimes gave remaining employees greater individual autonomy than they had under scientific management, organizational restructuring and management re-engineering also generated worker insecurity. In addition to job insecurity, employees (including professional workers and managers) faced a workplace in which productivity pressures and contingent work were on the rise—while many intra-organizational job ladders and employer-provided training opportunities were being eliminated. As the Wharton School's Peter Cappelli and a research team of distinguished US scholars concluded in 1997, employment relations under money-manager capitalism involved a rush toward treating human resources as a cost to be minimized (Cappelli et al. 1997). Labor was seen increasingly as just another "spot market" commodity.

Throughout this period, government has continued to provide lender-of-last-resort assistance to stabilize the overall economy. But it has also provided its own encouragement to the evolution of the financial system by removing many regulations imposed during the New Deal. Tax law changes have also encouraged takeovers, buyouts, and other types of corporate restructuring (Wolfson 1994, 111–112).

A decade ago, Minsky observed that money-manager capitalism is global and that further international economic integration would take place in the years ahead. Here is a sampling of his comments on these matters:

- "Managed money capitalism is international in both the funds and the assets of the funds. It has rendered obsolete the view that trade patterns determine the short-run movement of exchange rates" (Minsky 1990a, 71).
- "As the countries that are involved in managed money capitalism increase, an international division of responsibility for maintaining global aggregate gross profits will be necessary" (Minsky 1990a, 71).
- "Global financial integration is likely to characterize the next era of expansive capitalism. The problem of finance that will emerge is whether the financial and fiscal control and support institutions of national governments can contain both the consequences of global financial fragility and an international debt deflation" (Minsky 1995b, 93).[17]

This presentation of Minsky's theory of US capitalist development began with the suggestion that a sixth economic stage might now be emerging. This suggestion comes from the fact that national and international entities not only contained the recent Asia-centered global financial crisis but also acknowledged the need to prevent similar crises from appearing in the future (see, for example, Council of Economic Advisors 1999, ch. 7). If the international financial architecture is indeed reformed with an eye to preventing and containing future crises, it may soon be possible to speak of a new era of coordinated policies and institutions that might be called "global finance capitalism."

FUTURE RESEARCH DIRECTIONS

Minsky's theory of capitalist development provides today's economists with a number of directions for future research. One is to more thoroughly develop his theory as it relates to the US economy. Minsky made it clear that for each stage we should ask, What is the distinctive activity being financed? What is the pivotal source of financing? and What is the balance of economic power between those in business and banking/finance? He also suggested that we strive to identify the essential financial, business, and policy institutions of each era. Today, there is still much room for scholarship on these topics—and on the inter-relations of finance and business within each stage.

Developing Minsky's theory more thoroughly might also involve explorations that begin by dividing each stage into three periods: financial exploration and experimentation; institutionalization and diffusion of new practices; and erosion. Providing insight into the transition from one stage to another is an important aspect of any valuable theory of capitalist development. A deeper understanding of the economy is likely to be achieved by fleshing out his theory in this manner.

Minsky's theory will also require updating. Minsky did not live to see the emergence of venture capitalists as central players in the financing of US innovation. Responsibility for incorporating that emergence and other recent developments into his framework falls on those who share his vision of economics as an evolutionary science.[18]

Another possible research direction is to consider how the essential elements of his theory can be applied to other nations. Minsky's writings offer only a few suggestions on this (see, for example, Minsky 1990a; 1991a). There is plenty of room for fruitful research here—research with the potential not only to further our understanding of economic activity but also to help shape the continued evolution of market economies. Indeed, transitional economies may find such scholarship particularly useful as they prepare to continue on the path from planning to markets.

The aforementioned research avenues offer room for rigorous analyses and hypothesis testing. But there is also room for those who are even more inclined to mathematical and conceptual explorations. A starting point for such work is an article in which Domenico Delli Gatti, Mauro Gallegati, and Minsky employed a macroeconomic model to explore how different institutional constraints can affect economic performance through time (1996).

Yet another research possibility involves taking Minsky's theory of the US economy as a point of departure for an inquiry into one or more specific questions with contemporary policy significance. For example:

- How can technological dynamism be sustained in the era of money-manager capitalism (or its successor, if recent trends indeed warrant us to think in terms of a successor)? Can the private sector alone promote advanced technology? If not, what should be the role for government (Minsky 1990a, 72)?[19]
- How can policy makers promote a level of private (and public) resource creation consistent with full employment and reasonable economic growth (Minsky 1986b, 294)? (In part, answering this question requires considering whether the economy is better served by financial institutions that are centralized or decentralized, and are broad or compartmentalized (Minsky 1992, 37).)
- What are the likely effects of alternative policies on inflation, macroeconomic stability, efficiency, and economic security (Minsky 1986b, 295)?[20]
- Does the pension fund system—and the wider social security, retirement, and tax systems—need to be overhauled? Can/should open-ended IRAs attenuate the power of pension funds? Should the income tax be transformed into a spending tax (Minsky 1992, 34–35)?
- How can the business need for profits be balanced with both the household's need for security through time and the economy's need for capital development (Minsky 1991a, 16; Minsky 1996a)?[21]
- How should the global financial system be structured to promote growth and contain instability (Minsky 1995b, 93; Minsky 1990b)?

In short, Minsky's theory of capitalist development provides the foundation for a comprehensive research program. Minsky started with a commonsense suggestion—that policy would be more apt if it reflected an understanding of the economy as an evolving entity. From this he constructed a formidable alternative to the neoclassical paradigm.

CONCLUSION: MINSKY AND THE INSTITUTIONALISTS

Given recent attention to the question of whether the US economy has changed in important ways from the economy of the past few decades, Minsky's theory of capitalist development deserves widespread consideration. But it is likely to be of special interest to evolutionary economists—institutionalists—who find inspiration in the writings of Veblen, Commons, and their intellectual descendants. In many ways, Minsky's theory is a logical extension of the historical analyses provided by Veblen and Commons. And by emphasizing financial markets, Minsky provides a valuable complement to the long and distinguished institutionalist tradition of examining America's economic structure.

Veblen's *The Theory of Business Enterprise* is a masterful examination of the stage that Minsky calls industrial capitalism. Although published in 1904, early in the era described above as banker capitalism, Veblen's central purpose was to distinguish the form of US capitalism that had become clearly discernable by the 1870s from the earlier era of commerce that dominated America and England in the eighteen century. Veblen captured the essence of the industrial era by focusing on the organization of corporations that produced goods and services through extensive use of mechanical processes.

Veblen emphasized that industrial firms operated in a "credit" economy, not the mere "money" economy of the earlier era of handicrafts and trade. "Trading under the old regime was a traffic in goods; under the new regime there is added, as the dominant and characteristic trait, trading in capital" (1904, 151). Credit extensions in the industrial era still could come in the form of old-fashioned loans, Veblen explained. But the capital market of industrial capitalism made additional credit instruments available in the form of stocks and bonds. Indeed, these instruments provide the crucial link between what Veblen identified as the two "characteristic features" of the economic system he was describing: "the machine process and investment for profit."

Regardless of whether Veblen would have approved of Minsky's distinction between industrial capitalism and the later stage of banker capitalism, it is clear Veblen was attuned to the emergence of business coalitions in the early twentieth century. In fact, Veblen's discussion of business cycles in *The Theory of Business Enterprise* identifies the core elements of the transition Minsky described: cutthroat competition and the possibility that business coalitions might stabilize industrial output. And in his later work, *Absentee Ownership and Business Enterprise in Recent Times*, Veblen appeared to give additional support to Minsky's distinction by noting that the "Captains of Industry" mentioned in both volumes have "made the passage from industrial adventurer to corporation financier" (1923, 112).

Commons, meanwhile, would have certainly accepted the first three stages as presented by Minsky. Indeed, they are compatible with the intertwined industrial and economic stages that Commons presented in *Institutional Economics* (1934, 763–805).[22] In particular, Commons saw the US economy as having evolved as follows: from merchant capitalism and an era characterized by scarcity; through employer capitalism, which used industrial power to create an era of abundance; and into the period of banker capitalism, a time when stabilization of industry was the central thrust of the era.[23] Moreover, it is likely that Commons would have approved of Minsky's focus on the financial system. Although Commons saw the expansion of markets and technological developments as important contributors to capitalism's dynamism, his use of the term "banker capitalism" was meant to acknowledge "the prevalence of the credit system" in the economy of his day (1934, 766).[24]

To be sure, Minsky's theory is not the only possible extension of the analyses of Veblen and Commons. But as indicated by this brief discussion, there is more that unites the approaches of these three scholars than their view that capitalism is "an evolutionary concept," not "a single or static concept" (Commons 1934, 766). There are, in fact, numerous similarities between the early stages contained in Minsky's theory and the analyses of Veblen and Commons. There are also shared beliefs, including the notions that financial gain is the system's driving force and that the financial system is an important determinant of business structures and practices.

Finally, Minsky's attention to the financial system makes his work an important complement to institutionalist writings on the structure of the American economy. The institutionalist tradition of producing path-breaking work on the US economic structure is nearly as old as evolutionary economics itself. Indeed, Adolf Berle and Gardner Means caught the attention of the entire economics profession with a volume on this subject in the 1930s (Berle and Means 1933).[25] In the post-World War II era, institutionalists including Robert Averitt (1968), John Kenneth Galbraith (1973), and John Munkirs (1985) have continued to advance our understanding of the economic structure.[26] But as Averitt wrote in the late 1980s, institutionalist analyses could still do a better job of reflecting the fact that "money and the financial system are at the heart of a modern economy" (1987, 799). Minsky's theory of capitalist development may hold just the ingredient needed to inject a greater financial element into contemporary institutionalist explorations of the economy's structure and operations.

NOTES

1. Minsky argued that at the heart of neoclassical economics is the notion of a barter economy, one where the essential question is how the price system can best allocate existing goods and services. As an alternative, he offered a "Wall Street paradigm": the underlying image is of a world shaped largely by corporate and banking decisions regarding investments and financial portfolios. That alternative enabled Minsky to focus on how individuals and organizations manage cash flows and debt in a world in which production takes time and where the future is uncertain.

   The Wall Street paradigm is the foundation of Minsky's financial theory of investment and his investment theory of business cycles. His theory of investment emphasizes three factors: the price of capital assets, the price of current output, and the financial-market conditions that affect the availability of external financing (i.e., institutional realities and the climate of expectations). In his theory of cycles, investment during a recovery contributes to expanding prosperity. And that affluence causes the evolution of a more and more fragile financial structure—one that must eventually break down, usually because of Federal Reserve attempts to curb inflation or because an inability to meet debt-payment commitments somewhere in the system causes a quick and widespread market revaluation of assets.

Minsky's cycle theory is often called the financial instability hypothesis, but that hypothesis also has a secular (multi-cycle) dimension. In particular, he argued that the post–World War II era saw the evolution of an increasingly fragile financial structure in the United States. See, for example, Minsky 1980 and 1986d in this journal.

2. During Minsky's last public lecture, he stated: "In the neoclassical school, even in its most modern forms, it is not clear that the economy under analysis is capitalist" (1996a, 362).
3. Chaotic behavior involves a complex, nonlinear time path (Ferri and Minsky 1992, 82).
4. This is a reference to the Heinz slogan, "57 varieties."
5. On financial innovation, Minsky wrote: "To understand the short-term dynamics of the business cycle and the longer-term evolution of economies it is necessary to understand the financing relations that rule, and how the profit-seeking activities of businessmen, bankers, and portfolio managers lead to the evolution of financial structures. ... Consumer sovereignty is subordinated to the vision of entrepreneurs and the critical analysis of bankers in determining the path of the economy" (1993a, 106–107).
6. Drawing on Schumpeter, Minsky (1990a, 56) noted that if the banker/financier is the "ephor" (controlling figure) of a market economy, then the central bank is the ephor of the ephor. On the fiscal policy role played by "Big Government," the other key stabilizer of the economy since the Great Depression, see note 14 below.
7. Since policy interventions in the economy are the product of political processes, Minsky stressed that the path through time of an economy is a "political economy phenomenon" (Ferri and Minsky 1989, 138).
8. While this discussion focuses on external financing, a driving force behind both capitalist evolution and the emergence of economic instability, it should be noted that internal financing was important in merchant capitalism—and again in managerial capitalism (Minsky 1990a, 67; 1993a, 110).
9. Minsky called merchant capitalism and banker capitalism "commercial capitalism" and "financial capitalism," respectively. For me, the former labels—borrowed from John R. Commons—are slightly more descriptive. For Minsky's most detailed discussions of these stages, see Minsky 1990a, 1992, and 1993a. Elements of this analysis are also discussed in Minsky 1990b, 1991a, and 1996a and in Minsky and Whalen 1996–97; see also Whalen 1997. The present section (US Capitalist Development) is based on these references.
10. Lowell's factory was "integrated" in that "the plant both spun cotton and thread and wove it into cloth by machine" (Heilbroner and Singer 1994, 109).
11. Investment banking houses, working in securities markets, were the dominant financial institutions of this era (industrial capitalism). Investment bankers "acted as brokers when they facilitated trade in existing [stock and bond] issues and as dealers when they underwrote new issues" (Minsky 1993a, 108–109).

12. Between 1892 and 1902, for example, J. P. Morgan played an instrumental role in arranging mergers that created General Electric, American Telephone and Telegraph, International Harvester, and United States Steel Corporation (Heilbroner and Singer 1994, 206).
13. For some attention to the Great Depression, see Minsky 1975, 60, 64, 142–144; 1982b; and 1986a, 172–173.
14. Minsky argued that "Big Government" was an essential ingredient of successful macroeconomic management. By "Big Government," Minsky meant government "big enough to ensure that swings in private investment lead to sufficient offsetting swings in the government's deficit so that profits are stabilized" (Minsky 1986a, 296–297).
15. The reader will note it is here that the secular dimension of Minsky's FIH connects with his theory of capitalist development. For related discussions of the evolution of financial practices in the postwar period, see Niggle 1986, 1988, and 1990 and Wray 1990, 193–241.
16. Between 1950 and 1990, money managers saw the fraction of US corporate equities under their control grow from 8 percent to 60 percent (Porter 1992, 69). Over the same period, pension funds increased their share of total business equities from less than 1 percent to almost 39 percent, while their fraction of corporate debt rose from 13 percent to 50 percent (Ghilarducci 1992, 117). For more on the rise of money managers, see Useem (1996).
17. In contrast, neoclassical economists did not foresee the Asian financial crisis and had little to offer when it occurred. As Paul Krugman wrote on the Asian crisis in October 1998 (23), "Suppose that you were to buy a copy of the best-selling textbook on international economics. What would it tell you about how to cope with such a sudden loss of confidence by international investors? Well, not much." He then added: "Trust me—I'm the co-author of that textbook."
18. See Rima (2001) for more on the need to consider venture capital from Minsky's perspective.
19. Minsky was concerned that "the emergence of money-manager capitalism means that the financing of the capital development of the economy has taken a back seat to the quest for short-run total returns" (Minsky 1992, 32; see also Minsky 1993a, 113). He was particularly concerned that the capital needs of advanced technology development would be passed over by the private sector (Minsky 1990a, 72). While some would argue that venture capitalists have done a surprisingly fine job of financing innovation in recent years, others—such as Bluestone and Harrison (1999)—have argued that Minsky's fear may indeed have been warranted.
20. Two notes are warranted—on fiscal policy and monetary policy, respectively. Minsky believed better coordination is needed between the macroeconomic impact of government spending, which promotes the conditions that sustain profit flows, and the microeconomic impact of such spending, "which creates the conditions conducive to private resource creation and progressive enterprise" (Minsky 1992, 36). Niggle (1990; 1991), meanwhile, has shown how understanding the evolution of money and banking—an element of the Minsky analysis—is essential to understanding monetary policy.
21. One way to link the business need for profits with the household need for security might be through a policy that makes government the employer of last resort. This idea was often mentioned by Minsky (see, for example, 1986a, 308–313) and has recently been developed by Wray (1998).

22. Since Commons's volume was published in 1934, it is not possible to know how he would have treated the end of the stage of banker capitalism. Still, the elements he used to characterize that particular stage are compatible with those of Minsky. Moreover, Commons clearly saw macroeconomic stabilization—the key to Minsky's managerial era—as the central issue facing economics at the time his volume was published (Commons 1934).
23. In a 1925 essay, Keynes (1932) adopted Commons's three-stage analysis as the foundation for his discussion of government's role in the economy. Minsky's work, therefore, helps restore a crucial link between the economics of Keynes and the institutionalists. For an early statement of Commons's analysis, see Commons (1925); for a detailed exploration of the institutional foundation of Keynes's methodology, see Crotty (1990).
24. American institutionalists, of course, were not the only scholars who recognized key differences between industrial capitalism and banker (finance) capitalism. See, for example, Hilferding (1981).
25. In *The Modern Corporation and Private Property*, Berle and Means (1933) demonstrated how corporate stock ownership transformed the economy by separating business ownership from control—and by centralizing control in fewer directors' hands.
26. While Averitt (1968), Galbraith (1973), and Munkirs (1985) each gave some attention to economic evolution, their primary contributions serve to update our understanding of the economy's structure.

REFERENCES

Averitt, Robert T. *The Dual Economy: The Dynamics of American Industry Structure.* New York: W. W. Norton, 1968.

———. "The Dual Economy Twenty Years Later." *Journal of Economic Issues* 21 (June 1987): 795–802. Berle, Adolf A. M., and Gardiner C. Means. *The Modern Corporation and Private Property.* New York: Macmillan, 1933.

Bluestone, Barry, and Bennett Harrison. *Growing Prosperity.* Boston: Houghton Mifflin, 1999.

Cappelli, Peter, and Lauri Bassi, Harry Katz, David Knoke, Paul Osterman, and Michael Useem. *Change at Work.* New York: Oxford University Press, 1997.

Commons, John R. "Marx Today: Capitalism and Socialism." *The Atlantic Monthly* 136 (November 1925): 682–693.

———. *Institutional Economics: Its Place in Political Economy.* New York: Macmillan, 1934.

Council of Economic Advisers. *Economic Report of the President.* Washington, DC: United States Government Printing Office, 1999.

Crotty, James R. "Keynes on the Stages of Development of the Capitalist Economy: The Institutional Foundation of Keynes's Methodology." *Journal of Economic Issues* 24 (September 1990): 761–811.

Delli Gatti, Domenico, Mauro Gallegati, and Hyman P. Minsky. "Financial Institutions, Economic Policy, and the Dynamic Behavior of the Economy." In *Behavioral Norms, Technological Progress, and Economic Dynamics: Studies in Schumpeterian Economics*, edited by Ernst Helmstadter and Mark Perlman. Ann Arbor: University of Michigan Press, 1996.

Ferri, Piero, and Hyman P. Minsky. "The Breakdown of the IS-LM Synthesis: Implications for Post-Keynesian Economic Theory." *Review of Political Economy* 1 (July 1989): 123–143.

———. "Market Processes and Thwarting Systems." *Structural Change and Economic Dynamics* 3, no. 1 (1992): 79–91.

Galbraith, John Kenneth. *The Great Crash 1929.* Boston: Houghton Mifflin, 1961.

———. *Economics and the Public Purpose.* Boston: Houghton Mifflin, 1973.

Ghilarducci, Teresa. *Labor's Capital: The Economics and Politics of Private Pensions.* Cambridge, Mass.: MIT Press, 1992.

Heilbroner, Robert, and Aaron Singer. *The Economic Transformation of America: 1600 to the Present.* New York: Harcourt Brace, 1994.

Hilferding, Rudolf. *Finance Capital.* 1910. Reprint, edited by Tom Bottomore. London: Routledge & Kegan Paul, 1981.

Keynes, John Maynard. "Am I a Liberal?" 1925 lecture. In *Essays in Persuasion.* New York: Harcourt, Brace and Company, 1932, 323–338.

Krugman, Paul. "The Confidence Game." *The New Republic* 219 (October 5, 1998): 23–25.

Levy Institute. "Hyman P. Minsky: The Success of Big Government Capitalism." *Levy Institute Report* 4 (December 1994): 13–14.

Minsky, Hyman P. *John Maynard Keynes.* New York: Columbia University Press, 1975.

———. "Capitalist Financial Processes and the Instability of Capitalism." *Journal of Economic Issues* 14 (June 1980): 505–523.

———. *Can "It" Happen Again? Essays on Instability and Finance.* Armonk, N.Y.: M. E. Sharpe, 1982a.

———. "Debt Deflation Processes in Today's Institutional Environment." *Banca Nazionale Del Lavoro Quarterly Review* 35 (December 1982b): 375–393.

———. *Stabilizing an Unstable Economy.* New Haven: Yale University Press, 1986a.

———. "The Crises of 1983 and the Prospects for Advanced Capitalist Economies." In *Marx, Schumpeter and Keynes: A Centenary Celebration of Dissent*, edited by Suzanne W. Helburn and David F. Bramhall. Armonk, N.Y.: M. E. Sharpe, 1986b.

———. "Money and Crisis in Schumpeter and Keynes." In *The Economic Law of Motion of Modern Society: A Marx-Keynes-Schumpeter Centennial,* edited by H. J. Wagener and J. W. Drukker. Cambridge, UK: Cambridge University Press, 1986c.

———. "The Evolution of Financial Institutions and the Performance of the Economy." *Journal of Economic Issues* 20 (June 1986d): 345–353.

———. "Schumpeter: Finance and Evolution." In *Evolving Technology and Market Structure: Studies in Schumpeterian Economics*, edited by Arnold Heertje and Mark Perlman. Ann Arbor: The University of Michigan Press, 1990a.

———. "Money Manager Capitalism, Fiscal Independence, and International Monetary Reconstruction." In *The Future of the Global Economic and Monetary System,* edited by M. Szabo-Pelsoczi. Budapest: Institute for World Economics, Hungarian Academy of Sciences, 1990b.

———. "The Rationale for the Conference: An Agenda for the Good Financial Economy." Remarks prepared for delivery at the Jerome Levy Economics Institute, November 21, 1991a. Photocopy.

———. "The Transition to a Market Economy: Financial Options." Jerome Levy Economics Institute Working Papers No. 66, November 1991b.

———. "Reconstituting the United States' Financial Structure: Some Fundamental Issues." Jerome Levy Economics Institute Working Papers No. 69, January 1992.

———. "Schumpeter and Finance." In *Market and Institutions in Economic Development: Essays in Honor of Paulo Sylos Labini*, edited by Salvatore Biasco, Alessandro Roncaglia, and Michele Salvati. New York: St. Martin's Press, 1993a.

———. "Finance and Stability: The Limits of Capitalism." Jerome Levy Economics Institute Working Papers No. 93, May 1993b.

———. "A Positive Program for Successful Capitalism." Draft paper, distributed by Minsky to his colleagues at the Jerome Levy Economics Institute, 1995a. Photocopy.

———. "Longer Waves in Financial Relations: Financial Factors in the More Severe Depressions II." *Journal of Economic Issues* 29 (March 1995b): 83–95.

———. "Uncertainty and the Institutional Structure of Capitalist Economies." *Journal of Economic Issues* 30 (June 1996a): 357–368.

———. "Foreword." In *Political Economy for the 21st Century: Contemporary Views on the Trend of Economics*, edited by Charles J. Whalen. Armonk, N.Y.: M. E. Sharpe, 1996b.

Minsky, Hyman P., and Charles J. Whalen. "Economic Insecurity and the Institutional Prerequisites for Successful Capitalism." *Journal of Post Keynesian Economics* 19 (winter 1996–97): 155–170.

Munkirs, John R. *The Transformation of American Capitalism.* Armonk, N.Y.: M. E. Sharpe, 1985.

Niggle, Christopher J. "Financial Innovation and the Distinction between Financial and Industrial Capital." *Journal of Economic Issues* 20 (June 1986): 375–382.

———. "The Increasing Importance of Financial Capital in the U.S. Economy." *Journal of Economic Issues* 22 (June 1988): 581–588.

———. "The Evolution of Money, Financial Institutions, and Monetary Economics." *Journal of Economic Issues* 24 (June 1990): 443–450.

———. "The Endogenous Money Supply Theory: An Institutionalist Appraisal." *Journal of Economic Issues* 25 (March 1991): 137–151.

Pontecorvo, Guilio. "Investment Banking and Security Speculation in the Late 1920s." *Business History Review* 34 (summer 1958): 166–191.

Porter, Michael E. "Capital Disadvantage: America's Failing Capital Investment System." *Harvard Business Review* 70 (September–October 1992): 65–82.

Rima, Ingrid H. "Venture Capitalist Financing: Extending Minsky's "Wall Street" Perspective, with Some Casual Empiricism." Paper presented at the annual meeting of the Eastern Economic Association, New York City, February 24, 2001.

Useem, Michael. *Investor Capitalism: How Money Managers are Changing the Face of Corporate America.* New York: Basic Books, 1996.

Veblen, Thorstein. *The Theory of Business Enterprise.* New York: Charles Scribners Sons, 1904.

———. *Absentee Ownership and Business Enterprise in Recent Times.* New York: B. W. Huebsch, 1923.

Whalen, Charles J. "Money-Manager Capitalism and the End of Shared Prosperity." *Journal of Economic Issues* 31 (June 1997): 517–525.

Wolfson, Martin H. *Financial Crises: Understanding the Postwar U.S. Experience.* Armonk, N.Y.: M. E. Sharpe, 1994.

Wray, L. Randall. *Money and Credit in Capitalist Economies: The Endogenous Approach.* Aldershot, UK: Edward Elgar, 1990.

———. *Understanding Modern Money: The Key to Full Employment and Price Stability.* Cheltenham, UK: Edward Elgar, 1998.

19. Money manager capitalism: still here, but not quite as expected

Hyman Minsky is well known for books and essays on the cyclical instability of capitalism. In the last dozen or so years of his life, however, Minsky often looked beyond business cycles and focused instead on the structural evolution of economic systems over long periods of time. He believed that the US economy of the 1980s and 1990s was profoundly different from the economy of the 1950s and 1960s—and that an appreciation of the key differences was essential to understanding and managing economic activity at the end of the twentieth century.

Minsky explained the post-World War II changes in the US economy by presenting a theory of capitalist development. That theory, influenced by his association with Joseph Schumpeter, emphasizes financial-market innovations and their impact on the broader economy. In particular, Minsky argued that the US economy evolved through three stages prior to the 1980s—commercial capitalism, finance capitalism, and managerial capitalism—and that it entered a new stage, *money manager capitalism,* in the 1980s (Minsky 1990; 1993; Whalen 1997; 2001).

If imitation is the highest form of praise, then the notion of money manager capitalism (MMC) has received considerable acclaim. Michal Useem, of the Wharton School, published a book in 1996 entitled *Investor Capitalism* (1996). In 2000, James Hawley and Andrew Williams, of Saint Mary's College of California, published *The Rise of Fiduciary Capitalism* (2000). Like Minsky's writings, both works stress how money managers—institutional investors, especially those who oversee pension and mutual funds—can have a profound effect on business and the economy.

The core insights that Minsky offered in the 1980s and 1990s remain relevant today. Institutional investors wield great power in the US economy and have forced corporations to intensify their attention to the growth of stockholder value. Yet much has happened since Minsky first wrote about the growing importance of pension and mutual fund managers in 1983.[1] MMC is still here, but its effects on the economy have not always been what he anticipated.

Reprinted with permission from *Journal of Economic Issues* 36 (2), June 2002, 401–406.

WHAT MINSKY HAD RIGHT

Minsky was correct when he proposed that money managers had become major players in the economy. Between 1950 and 1990, money managers saw the fraction of US corporate equities under their control grow from 8 percent to 60 percent (Porter 1992, 69).[2] Over the same period, pension funds increased their share of total business equities from less than 1 percent to almost 39 percent—while their fraction of corporate debt rose from 13 percent to 50 percent (Ghilarducci 1992, 117). Institutional investor assets tripled in the 1990s (Conference Board 2000).[3]

Mutual funds have seen especially explosive growth. From the start of 1998 to the end of 2001, total mutual fund assets rose from $4.8 trillion to $6.9 trillion. And 2001 was the first year in which the majority of US households (52 percent) owned such funds (Investment Company Institute 1998–2001; 2001).

Minsky was also right when he wrote that money managers, obliged to maximize the value of their assets over each short period, would pressure corporate managers to take steps that raise stock prices. Business executives enjoyed considerable independence from bankers and stockholders in the early postwar years—a period that Minsky called "managerial capitalism." The situation has been very different since the early 1980s.

One source of institutional pressure on an enterprise is obvious: Fund managers can sell company stock. Minsky explained how "block trading" developed to accommodate purchases and sales by billion dollar funds. The stock market crash of October 1987 showed that uneasy block traders can have a profound impact not only on individual companies but also on the entire market (Minsky 1990, 70).

Institutional investors promote greater corporate attention to stock prices in another way as well—by fueling acquisitions and buyouts. Fund managers have a strong incentive to support whatever organizational changes promise to boost near-term value, Minsky wrote, and that opens the door to both friendly and unfriendly challenges to corporate control (Minsky 1990, 70). Useem agrees: "During the mid-1980s, institutional holders ... rendered shares to would-be acquirers; they invested funds in takeover and buyout funds, and they gave votes to strategic block investors. These developments help explain why mergers and acquisitions of publicly traded companies more than doubled between 1980 and 1988, and leveraged buyouts rose by a factor of 10" (Useem 1996, 25–26). Although companies have since found many ways to resist hostile takeovers, corporate consolidation and the financial restructuring of enterprises continues with help from money managers.

Still another undeniable feature of MMC is that it encourages downsizing, outsourcing, and business re-engineering. In 1996, Minsky observed that companies had "an almost chronic need" to downsize and to cut labor costs

(Minsky 1996, 363). In many parts of the economy, that trend continued even as the overall unemployment rate fell in the late 1990s and 2000—in part due to an explosion in the worldwide outsourcing of production and services (Engardio 2000). According to Peter Cappelli of the University of Pennsylvania, employment security, workplace training, and internal labor markets have all been jettisoned in a drive to treat labor as a "spot market" commodity (Mehring 2001).

SOME UNEXPECTED DEVELOPMENTS

Not everything about MMC has continued as Minsky expected. He believed that institutional investors would hold stock for short periods rather than for the long term. The emphasis, he wrote, is on "the quick turn of the speculator"—and likened the actions of fund managers to casino gambling (Minsky 1993, 111).[4] Some institutional investors still engage in frequent trading. In the 1990s, however, many funds began to adopt other strategies.

The common element in these other approaches is that they change corporations from within. "Rather than immediately disposing of a corporate position at the first sign of bad weather, investors seek other means for responding to adverse conditions, including pressing managers for changes in strategies or directors for changes in management," wrote Useem, whose entire book explores this trend (Useem 1996, 33). As William Van Lear indicated in a recent article in *Challenge*, MMC has come to be characterized by long-term commitment of funds and an integration of ownership and (managerial) control (2001)—not at all what Minsky anticipated.[5]

Minsky also did not anticipate that the late 1990s would see an investment-led boom. Perhaps his biggest concern about the rise of MMC was that it would restrain investment—by intensifying corporate attention on the short term and by forcing financial maneuvers that would leave many firms too highly leveraged to invest heavily. The worry was greatest with respect to investment in new technologies: "Capitalism may require intervention to remain technologically dynamic in an era of managed money capitalism." In particular, financing of truly innovative technologies may need to "become a state responsibility," Minsky wrote (1990, 72).

But the United States did get an investment boom—a long one. And it was driven by new technologies, most of them related to computers and telecommunications.[6]

A possible reason for this unexpected outcome is the new, close relationship between owners and managers. "A certain uniformity in attitude and recognition of common financial interests by firms and their financiers have produced financial institutions that are committed long-run backers of large businesses that account for much of the economy's investment," wrote Van Lear (2001, 110–111). Existence of such "long-run" backers promotes investment and may even boost corporate entrepreneurialism. Moreover, the "uniformity in attitude" that Van Lear mentioned would fuel the already self-reinforcing movement from prosperity to boom, a process that Minsky often described.[7]

Part of the investment boom was also a result of the explosive growth in venture capital financing. Venture capital firms never invested more than $5 billion per year in the 1980s. They distributed funds at a rate of more than $100 billion per year in the first quarter of 2000. Even after the tech boom went bust, venture capitalists invested at an annual rate of $26 billion in the third quarter of 2001, the most recent period for which data are available (Mandel 2000, 18; PricewaterhouseCoopers 2001).[8]

Venture capital bears watching. In 1990, Minsky acknowledged that such firms would help spur innovation. But he expected that they would not be a powerful enough force to ensure technological progress for the entire economy (Minsky 1990, 72). What Minsky may not have counted on, however, is that large amounts of managed-money resources would find their way into the venture-capital world. According to Michael Mandel of *BusinessWeek,* "About 40% of the money put up for venture capital funds in the 1990s came from public and private pension funds, with another 15% coming from college endowments, foundations, and similar organizations" (2000, 21).

Barry Bluestone and the late Bennett Harrison have offered yet another part of the reason why the United States experienced technology-driven growth at the end of the twentieth century. They have argued this boom was the "long-awaited" information revolution, one that got its initiative—"and a good part of the funds that underwrote it"—from the government (Bluestone and Harrison 2000, 17–18). In particular, Bluestone and Harrison have pointed to defense-related investments and research support that the government used to promote the development of computers, microprocessors, software, and the Internet. They also have argued that this source of economic growth is nothing new: Public investment has always been an important complement to private investment, and "it typically takes decades" for public investments to yield applications that spread throughout the economy (Bluestone and Harrison 2000, 18).

According to the argument of Bluestone and Harrison, MMC has not been the development of the past two decades that has most threatened the prospect for long-term technological advancement. Rather, the biggest threat to future innovation and growth has come from the government's neglect of infrastructure, education, and scientific research. Minsky could always be counted on to make a strong pitch for macroeconomic stabilization and full employment. He said far less about the government's centuries-old role in promoting technological change through public investment.

A QUICK RECAP—AND A WORD ON GLOBALIZATION

Minsky may not have correctly anticipated all the economic implications of MMC. He did, however, identify some of the essential developments that shaped the US economy of the last two decades—developments that continue to shape the economy today. Events and changes that he did not fully anticipate, meanwhile, are intriguing ones that warrant further research.[9]

Another topic deserving further attention is the question of how MMC relates to an increasingly global economy. Minsky fully expected that MMC would extend well beyond the United States. As a result, he stressed the need for institutions to promote international economic stability (Minsky 1995, 93; 1990, 71). He probably would have been encouraged by efforts—often discussed in the wake of the Asian-centered financial crisis—to reform the international financial architecture with an eye to preventing, or at least containing, future economic crises (Council of Economic Advisers 1999, ch. 7). In contrast, Minsky probably would have been discouraged to see the Bush administration and the International Monetary Fund allow Argentina's economy to collapse at the end of 2001 (Rohter 2001).

NOTES

1. The first essay in which Minsky emphasized the influence of professionally managed money was written for a 1983 conference on Marx, Schumpeter, and Keynes (Minsky 1986). Beginning in 1990, MMC is presented as the latest phase in the long history of capitalist development (see, for example, Minsky 1990).
2. Michael Useem offered slightly different numbers on institutional holdings, though the general trend is the same. He wrote that stock holdings by institutional investors rose from 16 percent in 1965 to 46 percent in 1990 (Useem 1996, 25).
3. Minsky argued the seeds of MMC were planted when corporations established pension plans for their employees. Inflation also encouraged the growth of managed-money funds by encouraging personal savings to migrate from savings accounts to managed portfolios (Minsky 1990, 69).
4. "The professionalization of money management has made enterprise finance ever more the by-product of the activities of the casino" (Minsky 1986, 291).
5. Minsky saw US capitalism as having evolved from a stage during which ownership and control were united (commercial capitalism) to stages in which ownership and control became increasingly separated. In particular, he argued that MMC "involves the intrusion of a new layer of intermediation" (pension and mutual funds) into the financial structure (Minsky 1996, 363).
6. In contrast, Minsky wrote the following just a few years before the start of the 1990s boom: "The financial evolution of the past decade may well have been retrograde [with respect to its implications for future investment]" (Minsky 1993, 113). (The article was written at the end of the 1980s.)

7. It's also important to recall that much spending during the recent investment boom was designed to boost business productivity—a direct outgrowth of the pressure to raise corporate profits and stock market values.
8. It should be noted that recent venture-capital investments are not just keeping struggling firms afloat. Looking at third-quarter data for 2001, the latest available, Michael Mandel wrote: "Venture-capital investors have funded more companies at the startup and seed stages than ever before—including the boom years of 1999 and 2000" (2001).
9. An attempt to account for Minsky's incorrect predictions points today's economist in a constructive research direction. Minsky's readers would have far less to work with had he employed an ahistorical and institutionally empty theory (such as is offered by neoclassical economics).

REFERENCES

Bluestone, Barry, and Bennett Harrison. *Growing Prosperity.* Boston: Houghton Mifflin, 2000.

Conference Board. "Institutional Investor Assets Reach $18.6 Trillion." News release, December 5, 2000. Council of Economic Advisers. Economic *Report of the President.* Washington, DC: United States Government Printing Office, 1999.

Engardio, Pete. "The Barons of Outsourcing." *BusinessWeek* (August 28, 2000): 177–178.

Ghilarducci, Tersa. *Labor's Capital: The Economics and Politics of Private Pensions.* Cambridge, Mass.: MIT Press, 1992.

Hawley, James P., and Andrew T. Williams. *The Rise of Fiduciary Capitalism: How Institutional Investors Can Make Corporate America More Democratic.* Philadelphia: University of Pennsylvania Press, 2000.

Investment Company Institute. "Trends in Mutual Fund Investing." Various monthly reports, 1998–2001.

———. "Majority of US Households Own Mutual Funds." News release, October 3, 2001.

Mandel, Michael J. *The Coming Internet Depression.* New York: Basic Books, 2000.

———. "The Slow Road to Recovery." *BusinessWeek* (December 10, 2001): 30–32. Mehring, James M. "Flexibility Is No Key to Stability." *BusinessWeek* (March 5, 2001): 30.

Minsky, Hyman P. "The Crises of 1983 and the Prospects for Advanced Capitalist Economies." In *Marx, Schumpeter and Keynes: A Centenary Celebration of Dissent,* edited by Suzanne W. Helburn and David F. Bramhall. Armonk, N.Y.: M. E. Sharpe, 1986.

———. "Schumpeter: Finance and Evolution." In *Evolving Technology and Market Structure: Studies in Schumpeterian Economics,* edited by Arnold Heertje and Mark Perlman. Ann Arbor: The University of Michigan Press, 1990.

———. "Schumpeter and Finance." In *Market and Institutions in Economic Development: Essays in Honor of Sylos Labini,* edited by Salvatore Biasco, Alessandro Roncaglia, and Michele Salvati. New York: St. Martin's Press, 1993.

———. "Longer Waves in Financial Relations: Financial Factors in the More Severe Depressions II." *Journal of Economic Issues* 29 (March 1995): 83–95.

———. "Uncertainty and the Institutional Structure of Capitalist Economies." *Journal of Economic Issues* 30 (June 1996): 357–368.

Porter, Michael E. "Capital Disadvantage: America's Failing Capital Investment System." *Harvard Business Review* 70 (September–October 1992): 65–82.

PricewaterhouseCoopers. "MoneyTree Survey Results, Q3, 2001." Internet: PricewaterhouseCoopers, <http://www.pwcmonetree.com>.

Rohter, Larry. "Consequences for the United States in Argentina's Collapse." *The New York Times* (December 25, 2001). Internet: *The New York Times,* <http://www.nytimes.com>.

Useem, Michael. *Investor Capitalism: How Money Managers Are Changing the Face of Corporate America.* New York: Basic Books, 1996.

Van Lear, William. "Macroeconomic Implications of Institutional Equity Ownership." *Challenge* 44 (July–August 2001): 108–117.

Whalen, Charles J. "Money Manager Capitalism and the End of Shared Prosperity." *Journal of* Economic *Issues* 31 (June 1997): 517–525.

———. "Integrating Schumpeter and Keynes: Hyman Minsky's Theory of Capitalist Development." *Journal of Economic Issues* 35 (December 2001): 805–823.

20. A Minsky perspective on the global recession of 2009

INTRODUCTION

On 18 August 2007, a front-page story in *The Wall Street Journal* highlighted the ideas of economist Hyman Minsky. With the US economy in the midst of a worsening credit crunch, reporter Justin Lahart observed that although Minsky died in 1996, his views were 'reverberating from New York to Hong Kong as economists and traders are trying to understand what's happening in the markets' (Lahart, 2007: p. 1).

Since 2007, attention to Minsky's ideas has increased as global economic conditions have deteriorated (see, for example, Cassidy, 2008; Pollin, 2008). As an economist who has long appreciated Minsky's insights, I am happy to see this flurry of interest. Yet I fear that many observers have missed the full significance of his contributions.

Many of those now on the Minsky bandwagon treat his ideas as relevant to understanding a single economic event. Market analysts and traders even refer to that event as a 'Minsky moment', which arrives 'when overindebted investors are forced to sell even their solid investments to make good on their loans' (Lahart, 2007: p. 1). If the trouble were to become so widespread that it threatened the banking system at the national or international level, then some would replace the word 'moment' with 'meltdown' (Magnus, 2008). However, the focus is still on a single incident, not on the evolutionary path of economic activity.

Others exposed to Minsky's ideas acknowledge that his work was grounded in a dynamic conception of the economy. For most in this group, though, Minsky's place in economics rests on what he called the 'financial-instability hypothesis'. According to Minsky, capitalist financial systems tend to endogenous cycles – moving from a conservative state of affairs called 'hedge financing',

Reprinted with permission from D. Tavasci and J. Toporowski (eds.), *Minsky, Crisis and Development* (Palgrave Macmillan [Springer Nature], 2010), 106–126.

to a more risky form called 'speculative financing', to an unsustainable form called 'Ponzi financing', and then back to 'hedge financing' for another round. This pattern of economic activity generates a series of booms and recessions, and the severity of the latter depends largely on the effectiveness of government regulation and stabilisation policies (Minsky, 1982, 1992a).

A full appreciation of Minsky's insights, however, must recognise that about the last dozen years of his life were devoted largely to synthesising the financial-instability hypothesis and an understanding of long-term capitalist development. Indeed, in an essay written for the hundredth anniversary of the birth of John Maynard Keynes and Joseph Schumpeter, Minsky wrote: 'The task confronting economics today may be characterised as a need to integrate Schumpeter's vision of a resilient inter-temporal capitalist process with Keynes's hard insights into the fragility introduced into the capitalist accumulation process by some inescapable properties of capitalist financial structures' (Minsky, 1986a: p. 121). A key conclusion of Minsky's pursuit of such a synthesis is that although the 'basic path' of real-world capitalism is cyclical (Minsky, 1975: p. 9), the 'money-manager capitalism' characteristic of recent decades differs substantially from the 'managerial capitalism' found in the United States immediately after Second World War (Minsky, 1990a, 1993a). A successful economic policy for the present era must be built upon recognition of the institutional features of this stage of capitalist development (Minsky and Whalen, 1996–1997).

This chapter offers a Minsky perspective on the global recession of 2009 by drawing on the insights Minsky gained from both Keynes and Schumpeter. While the Keynesian and Schumpeterian dimensions of Minsky's viewpoint are intertwined in the real world, the cyclical and structural aspects of the current crisis are highlighted separately in the analysis that follows. After examining the nature and causes of the global downturn from those two lenses, Minsky's policy proposals are compared with recent policy steps taken by the US government.

CYCLICAL DYNAMICS

Minsky's financial-instability hypothesis can be seen as an alternative to the 'efficient-market hypothesis' of conventional economics. According to that conventional view, investors, lenders and other financial-market participants are not, as a group, predisposed to overconfidence or other biases (Shefrin, 2000: p. 4). In contrast, the financial-instability hypothesis treats overconfidence and panic as regular features of the economic landscape.

Minsky traces this aspect of his perspective to Keynes, especially to the latter's 1937 article in *The Quarterly Journal of Economics*, 'The General Theory of Employment' (Keynes, 1937; Minsky, 1975: pp. 64–67). In that essay,

Keynes describes his departure from the mainstream economics of his time, which he called 'classical economic theory', as the departure from a focus on long-period equilibrium (Keynes, 1937: pp. 213–214). Behind both the classical theory of Keynes's time and the efficient-market hypothesis of our own is an assumption that the future can be treated as a matter involving risk (reducible to the calculation of probabilities), not uncertainty. Keynes, however, dismisses this substitution of risk for uncertainty in the case of most economic analyses:

> The whole object of the accumulation of wealth is to produce results, or potential results, at a comparatively distant, and sometimes at an *indefinitely* distant, date. Thus the fact that our knowledge of the future is fluctuating, vague and uncertain renders wealth a peculiarly unsuitable subject for the methods of classical economic theory. This theory might work very well in a world in which economic goods were necessarily consumed within a short interval of their being produced. But it requires, I suggest, considerable amendment if it is to be applied to a world in which the accumulation of wealth for an indefinitely postponed future is an important factor; and the greater the proportionate part played by such wealth-accumulation the more essential does such amendment become. (Keynes, 1937: p. 213)

According to Minsky, the financial structure of our economy becomes more and more fragile over a period of prosperity. In the early stages of prosperity, enterprises in highly profitable segments of the economy are rewarded for taking on increasing amounts of debt. And their success encourages other firms to engage in similar behaviour.

This pattern was certainly evident in the high-tech sector during the late 1990s and in the housing sector during the early- and mid-2000s. In fact, construction companies and contractors were not the only ones taking on more debt in the 2000s. Homebuyers were also doing so as the housing market began heating up, in part because interest rates were low and the stock market had become less attractive in the wake of the dotcom boom and bust. While it had long been customary for US homebuyers to make a 20 per cent down payment on a home, 42 per cent of first-time home purchasers and 13 per cent of buyers who were not first-time purchasers put no money down to acquire homes in the mid-2000s (Irwin, 2005; Max, 2005; Baker, 2009a).[1]

In retrospect, it seems that enterprises and homebuyers should have resisted the impulse towards increasing indebtedness, but the incentives at the time were just too great. As Gary Dymski and Robert Pollin explain in a 1992 essay, nobody in a robust sector of the economy wants to be left behind due to underinvestment:

> Even if market participants did have full knowledge of the Minsky model, and were aware that financial crises will occur at some point, that would still not enable them to predict when the financial crisis will occur. In the meantime, aggressive firm managers and bank loan officers will be rewarded for pursuing profitable opportunities and gaining competitive advantages. Cautious managers, operating from the understanding that boom conditions will end at some uncertain point, will be penalised when their more aggressive competitors surpass their short-run performance. (Dymski and Pollin, 1992: p. 45)[2]

As the preceding quote indicates, lenders as well as borrowers fuel the tendency towards greater indebtedness in an expansion. The same climate of expectations that encourages borrowers to acquire more risky financial liability structures also eases lenders' worries that new loans might go unpaid (Minsky, 1975). Moreover, it is not just that borrowing and lending expand in the boom. There is also financial innovation. In fact, in a 1992 essay, Minsky wrote that bankers and other financial intermediaries are 'merchants of debt, who strive to innovate with regard to both the assets they acquire and the liabilities they market' (Minsky, 1992a: p. 6).

The boom cannot continue forever, however; we eventually arrive at what some have called the 'Minsky moment' (Lahart, 2007: p. 1). In other words, it eventually becomes clear that some borrowers have become overextended and need to sell assets (or secure a government bailout) to make their payments. In the current crisis, early high-profile cases involved the mortgage broker Countrywide, the British bank Northern Rock and two hedge funds run by Bear Stearns (Foley, 2007; Larsen and Giles, 2007; Reckard et al., 2007; Stempel, 2007; Mildenberg, 2008).[3]

Then the problem spreads. Since bankers and investors hold subjective views about acceptable debt levels, once a shortfall of cash and a forced selling of assets materialise somewhere in the economy, it can lead to a widespread reassessment of how much debt or lending is appropriate. Moreover, the build-up can go on for years, but when anything goes wrong the revaluation can be sudden (Minsky, 1982: p. 67).

When banks decide to rein in their lending, we find ourselves in a credit crunch. It is easy to think of the present economic crisis as something that began with the world-wide stock-market downturn in the autumn of 2008. In fact, though, the difficulties of 2008 were preceded by a credit crunch that began in the summer of 2007, and signs of trouble – traceable in large part to the 'subprime' mortgage market – were evident as early as March 2007 (Foley, 2007; Magnus, 2007; Timeline, 2009).

Once a credit crunch emerges, financial difficulties are no longer confined to one sector. In fact, a crunch threatens not only business investment, but also household spending. This means that when a sectoral bubble bursts – in the high-tech sector nearly a decade ago or in the housing sector more recently – the collapse threatens to trigger an economy-wide recession.

And that sort of recession is what the United States and much of the world now experiences. Moreover, it is pretty clear the situation has gone beyond a 'Minsky moment' and is more akin to an economic 'meltdown', at least with respect to US housing, banking and stocks. The Dow Jones industrial average, for example, fell 37 per cent between 1 April 2007 and 1 April 2009 (Yahoo Finance, 2009). Meanwhile, the US unemployment rate rose from 4.4 per cent in March 2007 to 8.5 per cent in March 2009 (the latest monthly data available at the time of writing), and is widely expected to continue rising through 2009 (US Department of Labor, 2009; Obama's economic aide sees rising U.S. unemployment, 2009).

STRUCTURAL EVOLUTION

In a pair of articles designed to integrate key contributions of Keynes and Schumpeter, Minsky mentions that Keynes and institutionalist Wesley C. Mitchell had a common perspective on business cycles (Minsky, 1993a, 1990a). Bringing Mitchell into the picture helps underscore the sort of synthesis towards which Minsky was aiming: Mitchell had long ago written that 'each new cycle presents idiosyncrasies. Business history repeats itself, but always with a difference' (Mitchell, 1941: p. ix). In the 1990s, Minsky still believed that the US economy moves along a cyclical path, but he also believed that the system had recently entered a new stage of capitalist development. The managerial era that matured in the immediate aftermath of Second World War had, during the 1980s, given way to a stage characterised by emergence of money managers as the nation's dominant economic decision-makers (Minsky, 1990a, 1993a, 1996; see also Whalen, 2001, 2002).

While Keynes offered insights into cyclical fluctuations, Schumpeter (Minsky's dissertation advisor at Harvard until the relationship was cut short by Schumpeter's untimely death) provided Minsky with insights into structural economic evolution over a series of cycles. In fact, Minsky underscored an aspect of Schumpeterian 'creative destruction' that few others recognised: 'Nowhere are evolution, change and Schumpeterian entrepreneurship more evident than in banking and finance and nowhere is the drive for profits more clearly the factor making for change' (Minsky, 1993a: p. 106). Thus, four institutional features of money-manager capitalism emerge to play a role in explaining the economic difficulties of the past few years. The origin of the current global crisis can be traced in large part to the following financial-sector innovations: unconventional mortgages, securitisation, the rise of hedge funds and the globalisation of finance.

At the heart of the current financial crisis are home mortgages that deviate from the traditional US home-loan arrangement, which involves a long-term loan on fixed-rate terms. Many of these unconventional – some have even called them 'exotic' – mortgages have adjustable interest rates and/or payments that balloon over time. Federal law allowed banks to issue adjustable-rate mortgages since 1982, but their use and complexity have exploded in the past decade. For example, industry experts estimate that a variant called the 'option adjustable rate mortgage' (option ARM), which offers a low 'teaser' rate and later resets so that minimum payments skyrocket, accounted for about 0.5 per cent of all US mortgages written in 2003, but close to 15 per cent (and up to 33 per cent in many US communities) in 2006. More precise figures are unavailable because banks have not been required to report how many option ARMs they originate (Der Hovanesian, 2006).

Many of these mortgages were created to target less-creditworthy customers, including those in what the banking industry calls the subprime market (Baker, 2009a). Others were marketed to people who wanted to speculate in the booming housing market, people who intended to buy and then quickly resell property. However, many unconventional loans were marketed to ordinary working families who could have handled conventional mortgages (Marks, 2008).

Unfortunately, it was clear from the outset that many of these exotic mortgages could never be repaid. (For an eye-opening look at the aggressive marketing of unconventional mortgages, see Morgenson (2007).) But why did this happen? Why did the mortgage market evolve in this dangerous direction?

This is where securitisation comes into the picture. Securitisation is simply the bundling of loans – which can include auto loans, student loans, accounts receivable and, of course, mortgages – and the subsequent selling of bundle shares to investors. In the mid-1980s, Minsky returned home from a conference sponsored by the Federal Reserve Bank of Chicago and wrote that securitisation was emerging as a key, new financial innovation. 'That which can be securitised, will be securitised', he wrote (Minsky, 1990a: p. 64). He was right, but way ahead of his time. Securitisation of mortgages exploded onto the scene in the past decade.

After the dotcom bubble burst in 2001, housing in the United States looked like a safer and more attractive investment than ever to many Americans, especially with low interest rates in place due to Federal Reserve policy. Still, returns on conventional mortgages were too mundane to satisfy the aims of most money managers. As a result, what Minsky and Schumpeter might have called the 'financial-innovation machine' turned its attention to housing and shifted into high gear.

Securitisation of mortgages meant that home loan originators could be less concerned about the creditworthiness of borrowers than in the past. Thus, they had an incentive to steer customers towards the most profitable types of mortgages, even if they were the riskiest (which, of course, they were) (Der

Hovanesian, 2006). The result was the explosive growth in option ARMs and in 'no money down' and 'no documentation (of income)' loans. Minsky warned of all this in 1992, when he observed that securitisation means mortgage originators are rewarded as long as they avoid 'obvious fraud' (Minsky, 1992b: p. 22–23).[4]

Securitisation worked like magic upon risky mortgages. Instead of 'garbage in, garbage out', risky loans went into the process, but out came bundles that received high credit ratings from agencies like Standard and Poors. According to Christopher Huhne, a member of the British Parliament and former rating-agency economist, part of the challenge of rating the bundles was 'that financial markets fall in love with new things, with innovations, and the [important] thing about new things is that it is very difficult to assess the real riskiness of them because you don't have a history by definition' (Huhne, 2007).

Another problem is that the rating agencies do not verify the information provided by mortgage issuers. Instead, they base their decisions on information received from intermediaries that, as Minsky put it, 'do not hazard any of their wealth on the long term viability of the underlying [loans]' (Minsky, 1992b: p. 23).

Moreover, there are so many middlemen in the mortgage securitisation game, including a number permitted to operate in a largely unregulated manner, that no one person or organisation can be easily assigned blame in the event of default. The chain between the borrower and the investor includes realtors, home appraisers, mortgage brokers, mortgage originators, investment banks that bundled the mortgages, agencies that rated the bundles and even companies (like American International Group) that insured many of the bundles (Whalen, 2008a: p. 235).[5]

Trillions of dollars worth of mortgage-backed securities were bundled and sold as shares to investors. In late 2008, Fannie Mae and Freddie Mac alone held $4.1 trillion (Lanman and Kopecki, 2008). Moreover, the private market in credit default swaps – used as a hedge against (mortgage-backed) securities losses, as a way to speculate that other companies will experience a loss, or as an arbitrage instrument – reached $45 trillion by late 2007 (O'Hara, 2009: p. 14).

Many of the mortgages underlying mortgage-backed securities are now in foreclosure or are headed there. In 2008, 2.3 million US homes went into foreclosure, up 81 per cent from 2007 and 225 per cent from 2006 (RealtyTrac, 2009a). There were another 803,489 filings in the first quarter of 2009 (the most recent period for which data are available at the time of writing), up 9 per cent from the previous quarter (RealtyTrac, 2009b).

Mortgage delinquencies are also up sharply. In February 2009, 7 per cent of US homeowners with mortgages were at least 30 days late on their loans, an increase of more than 50 per cent from a year earlier. Among subprime borrowers, that month's delinquency rate was 39.8 per cent (Chernikoff, 2009).[6] (Again, these are the latest available figures at the time of writing.)

There has been much public discussion over the past year or so in the United States about reckless homebuyers, but mortgage seekers could not and did not bring the economy to its knees on their own. Exotic home loans and mortgage securitisation are products of money-manager capitalism. As Minsky stressed at a pair of professional conferences in the late 1980s and early 1990s, there is a symbiotic relationship 'between the growth of securitisation and managed money.' Fund managers, he argued, 'have outgrown the orthodox high quality stock and bond portfolios of fiduciaries' (Minsky, 1990a: p. 71; 1992c: p. 32).

From a Minsky perspective, the economic participants most responsible for bringing down the economy are hedge funds and other investment funds, investment banks and other financial institutions. Looking at hedge funds offers a glimpse at what happened. Although the following discussion focuses on hedge funds because they are a relative newcomer to the scene and have become infamous for operating beyond the reach of much government regulation, the investment banks and other institutions played a similar role (and since 1999, US banking has operated without the Glass-Steagall firewall that separated commercial and investment banking for over a half century).

Some of the biggest purchasers of securitised mortgages have been hedge funds. The earliest of these funds were established in the first few decades after Second World War for the purpose of seeking absolute returns (rather than beating a benchmark stock-market index). They were indeed 'hedged' funds, which sought to protect principal from financial loss by hedging investments through short selling or other means. The number of hedge funds and the assets under their management expanded in the 1990s and grew even more rapidly in the 2000s. At the same time, these assets became increasingly concentrated at the top ten firms and funds became more diverse in terms of the strategies their managers employed. In mid-2008, the Alternative Investment Management Association estimated that the world's hedge funds (based primarily in the United States) were managing \$2.5 trillion, though it acknowledged that other estimates were as high as \$4 trillion (Ineichen and Silberstein, 2008: p. 16).

The total value of assets under hedge-fund management is uncertain because such funds are typically restricted to wealthy individuals and institutional investors, which exempts them from most financial-sector reporting requirements and regulation. Taking advantage of their largely unregulated status, managers of hedge funds used their mortgage-backed securities as collateral to take out highly leveraged loans. They then purchased an assortment of financial instruments, including still more mortgage bundles. As a result, the world's hedge funds used securitised mortgages to lay an inherently flimsy foundation for a financial 'house of cards' (Freeman, 2009; Holt, 2009).

The current crisis is unmistakably global. It is having economic and political ramifications on all continents (Timeline, 2009; Whalen, 2009). The trouble is even affecting unexpected places like rural China: factories in cities along that nation's coast are laying-off workers and sending them back to their villages (Lee, 2009).

The global nature of the current situation would not have surprised Minsky, who stressed early on that money-manager capitalism 'is international in both the funds and the assets in funds' (Minsky, 1990a: p. 71). Looking ahead to the current crisis, Minsky wrote: 'The problem of finance that will emerge is whether the ... institutions of national governments can contain both the consequences of global financial fragility and an international debt deflation' (Minsky, 1995: p. 93). He worried that the United States would be unable to serve as 'the guardian angel for stability in the world economy' and stressed the need for 'an international division of responsibility for maintaining global aggregate gross profits' (Minsky, 1986b: p. 15; 1990a: p. 71).

In short, the global economy is now reeling from the consequences of a classic Minsky crisis. Its origins are in a housing boom fuelled by rising expectations, expanding debt and financial innovation. Then the bubble burst, creating first a credit crunch, then a broader banking and stock-market crisis and now a recession.

The consequences have been staggering. In the housing sector, an unprecedented one in nine US homes (14 million) sits vacant, while another 9.4 million are for sale (El Nasser, 2009). The US stock market lost an unprecedented $1.2 trillion of value in just a single day in late September 2008 (measured by the Wilshire 5000), and for 2008 overall the Dow Jones industrial average had its worst year since 1931 (Blaine, 2008; Twin, 2008). Unemployment may soon hit double digits in the United States and has already reached double digits in some parts of Europe (Eurostat, 2009).

Since 2007, the global banking industry has seen an unprecedented shakeout (Timeline, 2009), but there is still uncertainty about how much more difficulty lies ahead. As the Bank for International Settlements indicated in a report released in June 2007:

> Assuming that the big banks have managed to distribute more widely the risks inherent in the loans they have made, who now holds these risks, and can they manage them adequately? The honest answer is that we do not know. Much of the risk is embodied in various forms of asset-backed securities of growing complexity and opacity. They have been purchased by a wide range of smaller banks, pension funds, insurance companies, hedge funds, other funds and even individuals, who have been encouraged to invest by the generally high ratings given to these instruments. (Bank for International Settlements, 2007: p. 145)

Warren Buffett made the point more vividly: 'You only learn who has been swimming naked when the tide goes out' (Buffett, 2008: p. 3). Although the risks are now being laid bare, it will still be some time before the world learns the full extent of the financial exposure.

PUBLIC POLICY

The current global economic situation requires a two-pronged economic-policy strategy: recovery and reform. Beyond stabilising the troubled financial sector and preventing the current downturn from becoming more severe, the overarching policy objective should be greater macroeconomic stability and broadly shared prosperity in the United States and abroad (Minsky, 1986c; Minsky and Whalen, 1996–1997). This section highlights some of the most important policy issues by comparing Minsky's recommendations with recent US government action.[7]

Recovery

A government strategy for recovery must have at least three components: fiscal policy, monetary policy and financial-market policy. Each is considered in turn.

The foundation of Minsky's strategy for avoiding another Great Depression is what he calls 'Big Government' (Minsky, 1986c: pp. 292–308). At the heart of Big Government is a federal budget that tends towards surpluses in inflationary periods and that produces deficits large enough to stabilise aggregate profits in recessionary periods. Minsky stressed that such countercyclical spending should be a 'built-in' feature of the budget structure, but he also recognised that discretionary action would be needed on occasion (Minsky, 1986c: pp. 132, 292).

Since the mid-1970s, however, policymakers have allowed the automatic stabilising features of the US federal budget to erode. As a colleague and I demonstrated in late 2002, income taxes, unemployment insurance, welfare expenditures and the minimum wage have all lost much of their ability to serve as countercyclical mechanisms. We concluded: 'It makes sense to shore up the economy's fiscal stabilisers. Better to fix the roof before the rain begins' (Whalen and Wenger, 2002: p. 91). By the time the storm finally hit, however, little had changed.

The erosion of automatic stabilisers has forced discretionary measures to do all the heavy lifting. In the current downturn, fiscal policy in the United States has moved in the right direction, but the initiatives have been too timid. The first stimulus attempt, passed in early 2008, included $100 billion in tax rebates and provided a modest boost to consumer spending (Broda and Parker, 2008), but the bill also included tens of billions in less stimulative business tax cuts. More recently, President Barack Obama signed into law a stimulus package totalling $787 billion over 2 years. However, Paul Krugman was probably correct when he suggested the package should have been twice as big and even more tilted towards spending (as opposed to tax cuts), especially since recent data revisions show that fourth-quarter US gross domestic product fell by 6.3 per cent, not 4 per cent as reported originally (Earnshaw, 2009; Krugman, 2009a).[8]

Beyond giving a major role to the fiscal policy of Big Government, Minsky stressed that the central bank must intervene as lender-of-last-resort in response to the threat of a serious credit crisis and economic contraction. 'Central banks are the institutions responsible for containing and offsetting financial instability', he wrote in *Stabilising an Unstable Economy*, published in 1986 (Minsky, 1986c: p. 322). In that same year, Minsky also contributed an article emphasising the globalisation of finance and the need for international central-bank coordination to prepare for the next big financial crisis (Minsky, 1986b).

From a Minsky perspective, monetary policy has largely been on the right track since the credit crunch hit in mid-2007. In an effort to stabilise the financial sector and overall economy, the Federal Reserve has aggressively cut interest rates, allowed banks to borrow from it at nominal rates and given banks cash in exchange for risky assets (promising to take on the risk if those assets prove worthless).[9] The Fed has also engineered bank mergers and worked with other central banks to increase the supply of dollars world-wide. In a very short time, Fed chairman Ben Bernanke has moved a long way from the days when he was known as a champion of inflation targeting.[10]

In contrast, financial-market policy at the US Treasury Department has been woefully inadequate from a Minsky vantage point. The Troubled Asset Relief Program, more commonly known as the $700 billion Wall Street Bailout, seemed designed to clean up bank balance sheets by purchasing their bad assets. Instead, the Treasury was soon writing banks cheques and buying large quantities of bank stocks. The underlying problem of the 'toxic' assets remained unresolved, banks remained reluctant to lend and much of the added liquidity was transformed into bank stock dividends.

The Treasury's latest plan, a 'public–private partnership' that creates a market for troubled assets with government loans and guarantees, is not much better. The plan offers what Joseph E. Stiglitz calls a 'win-win-lose proposal: the banks win, investors win – and taxpayers lose.' He argues the plan encourages investors to bid high in that newly created market and socialises the losses that are likely to follow. In attempting to account for this proposal, Stiglitz writes: 'Perhaps it's the kind of Rube Goldberg device that Wall Street loves – clever, complex and nontransparent, allowing huge transfers of wealth to the financial markets' (Stiglitz, 2009: p. 1).

A different approach would likely have been endorsed by Minsky, who admired how the administration of President Franklin D. Roosevelt closed insolvent banks and assisted solvent ones during the Great Depression. Minsky would have almost certainly called for a more hands-on sorting-out of the current financial mess by means of bank restructuring.

Today, Krugman (2009b, 2009c), Dean Baker (2009b) and James K. Galbraith (2009) call for similar action. For example, Galbraith writes: 'If the subprime securities are truly trash, most of the big banks are troubled and some are insolvent. The FDIC should put them through receivership, get clean audits, install new management, and begin the necessary shrinkage of the banking system with the big guys, not the small ones' (Galbraith, 2009). The Obama administration recently ordered federal regulators to conduct 'stress tests' to gauge the condition of the nation's banks. As a next step, the receivership approach makes more sense than creation of a government-subsidised market for toxic assets.

Another aspect of financial-market policy that currently needs attention involves home mortgages. Throughout 2008, the United States largely avoided addressing the unaffordable mortgages that are at the heart of the current problem (Marks, 2008). The Obama administration has been encouraging the financial industry to voluntarily restructure those loans, but industry pressure has made many in the nation's capital reluctant to require it. For example, federal legislators have so far refused to let bankruptcy judges insist on home loan restructuring, despite the fact that judges can demand a restructuring of all loans except the mortgage on a homeowner's residence (legislation is stalled in the US Senate as of this writing). Although Minsky did not address this problem directly, his interest in social justice and a humane economy suggest he would have insisted that this problem be resolved by mortgage restructuring and would have been incensed that the problem has been unresolved for so long (Minsky, 1986c, 1993b).

Reform

Looking beyond the current downturn, a reform agenda must include stricter regulation and supervision of the financial system, a national commitment to the challenges facing America's working families and US participation in efforts that promote international economic stability and job creation.

Minsky believed that those responsible for government regulation and supervision of the financial system were in a 'never-ending struggle' with financial markets (Minsky, quoted in Phillips, 1997: p. 512). As he wrote in *Stabilising an Unstable Economy*, 'After an initial interval, the basic disequilibrating tendencies of capitalist finance will once again push the financial structure to the brink of fragility.' Still, he believed it was necessary for the Federal Reserve and regulators to continue the struggle: 'The evolution of financial practices must be guided to reduce the likelihood that fragile situations conducive to financial instability will develop' (Minsky, 1986c: pp. 322, 333).

Today, those adopting a Minsky perspective would hold the same view. Greater industry transparency, more rigorous bank examinations and broader regulatory oversight would be a good place to start. If policymakers had better information about the extent to which financial institutions were making use of option ARMs and other exotic instruments, perhaps at least a few would have more aggressively sought to address the mounting problem. It also seems appropriate to revive Minsky's notion of a cash-flow approach to bank examinations, which 'would use the examination process to generate information on not only the liquidity and solvency of particular institutions, but also on threats, if any, to the stability of financial markets' (Minsky, quoted in Phillips, 1997: p. 513). Similarly, mortgage brokers, hedge funds and other institutions that have gained increasing importance in the past decade deserve greater scrutiny from financial-system regulators.[11] In light of the current economic crisis, stricter oversight of securitisation and other recent financial innovations are clearly overdue, but the additional need is for regulators to be on the lookout for future innovations in an effort to head-off potential crises before they occur.

At the very least, the US government should not block state efforts designed to protect their citizens from gaps in federal law. Today, most Americans know about the 2008 Valentine's Day in Washington that cost former New York Governor Eliot Spitzer his job, but of greater national importance was his guest column that appeared in *The Washington Post* that day. It described how the federal government stopped states from cracking down on predatory lending practices. As Spitzer's essay documents, 'Not only did the Bush administration do nothing to protect consumers, it embarked on an aggressive and unprecedented campaign to prevent states from protecting their residents from the very problems to which the federal government was turning a blind eye. The tale is still unfolding, but when the dust settles, [the Bush administration] will be judged as a willing accomplice to the lenders who went to any lengths in their quest for profits' (Spitzer, 2008).

In the age of managerial capitalism (approximately 1935–1982), it may have been sufficient to focus on full employment, low inflation and steady economic growth. In the age of money-manager capitalism (since 1982), these goals are still important, but the challenges facing America's working families require more direct attention as well. Americans, like citizens elsewhere around the world, want the opportunity to develop and utilise their talents and to increase their standard of living in the process. They also want the prospect of an even better life for their children.

Unfortunately, rising worker insecurity is the flipside of money-manager capitalism. Under pressure from money managers, corporate executives have largely put aside the employer–employee social contract of the New Deal and the early decades following Second World War. Employers have moved increasingly towards treating labour as just another 'spot market' commodity (Minsky, 1996; Minsky and Whalen, 1996–1997; Whalen, 1997; Zalewski, 2002; Whalen, 2008b).

Thus, the economic challenges facing the United States extend far beyond stabilising the financial system and preventing a long and deep recession, as Minsky and I discussed in an article written shortly before his death (Minsky and Whalen, 1996–1997). The nation needs to spur the growth of domestic jobs that pay family-supporting wages and to ensure that Americans have access to the education and training such jobs require (Glover and King, 2010; Marshall, 2010). It needs to find a way to promote partnerships between workers and managers, so companies can compete on the basis of innovation, quality and customer service, rather than by outsourcing jobs or slashing wages and benefits. It needs to provide adjustment assistance to workers displaced by international trade (including service workers excluded from some existing benefits programs) and public-service employment to those unable to find private-sector work. And it needs health-care reform, retirement-system reform and labour-law reform to address medical insecurity, retirement insecurity and the insecurity of workers who seek to exercise their legal right to engage in union organising and collective bargaining (Whalen, 2008b, 2008c).[12]

To address the challenges facing America's working families, the Obama administration has created a Middle Class Task Force, headed by Vice President Joe Biden. Its goals suggest an awareness of the issues just mentioned (About the Task Force, 2009). Yet, only time will tell whether the administration devotes much attention and resources to these issues.

Finally, pursuit of greater economic stability and broadly shared prosperity cannot end at the borders of the United States. Indeed, as suggested above, Minsky recognised that money-manager capitalism is worldwide in scope and that stabilisation and development challenges must be addressed at a global level. From a Minsky perspective, Americans must help fashion international institutions that not only contain global financial instability, but also enhance labour rights and promote job growth (Minsky, 1995, 1993a, 1990b, 1986b; Palley, 1999: p. 55).

The world's key policymakers, however, have been reluctant to move in this direction.[13] Indeed, international economic policy has been dominated by a different outlook, as Stiglitz indicated after serving at the World Bank:

> During my three years as chief economist of the World Bank, labour market issues were looked at through the lens of neoclassical economics. 'Wage rigidities' – often the fruits of hard-fought bargaining – were thought part of the problem facing many countries. A standard message was to increase labour market flexibility. The not-so-subtle subtext was to lower wages and lay off unneeded workers. (Stiglitz, quoted in Komisar, 2000)

Stiglitz concluded, 'They had a strategy for job destruction. They had no strategy for job creation' (Stiglitz, quoted in Komisar, 2000). Economists who see the world from a Minsky perspective need to collaborate to develop that missing strategy.

CONCLUSION: STANDING ON THE SHOULDERS OF MINSKY

Minsky used to say we should stand on the shoulders of giants to better understand the economy. Just as he stood on the shoulders of Keynes and Schumpeter, we can now stand on his shoulders to understand and address the current global recession. From a Minsky perspective, an explanation of this recession must include cyclical and structural dimensions, while a policy strategy requires attention to both recovery and reform.

The recent attention to Minsky's ideas, both outside and within the academy, is encouraging. Yet we do ourselves and his memory a disservice when Minsky's insights are reduced to an analysis of a single event or even of financial instability. Standing squarely on the shoulders of Minsky means understanding the latest business cycle within the context of money-manager capitalism, and it means seeking to guide the further development of the system in a more humane direction.

NOTES

1. Homeowners were also able to fuel a consumption boom by taking on even more debt. That is because rising home prices encouraged banks to increase customers' credit-card limits and to heavily promote home-equity loans (Chu and Acohido, 2008; Story, 2008).
2. Dymski and Pollin add: 'When boom conditions do end, aggressive managers will already have been promoted, while cautious managers will have been demoted, if not dismissed. Moreover, during the slump, all aggressive managers will fail together, so no single individual will be singled out for blame. This is in contrast to the boom, where the miscalculating cautious will have been isolated' (Dymski and Pollin, 1992: p. 45).
3. Of course, Bear Stearns itself was to be a casualty of the crisis in early 2008.
4. Here are some figures that indicate the magnitude of US mortgage securitisation: in early 2007, about 65 per cent of mortgages were being turned into bonds via securitisation, up from 40 per cent in 1990; and, in the years 2004–2006, nearly $100 billion per year in option ARMs were sold to investors (Der Hovanesian, 2006; Pittman, 2007).
5. Mortgage brokers, who operate without much government regulation, accounted for 80 per cent of all US mortgage originations in 2006, double their share a decade earlier (Der Hovanesian, 2006).
6. According to the Federal Housing Finance Agency, mortgage delinquencies among the most creditworthy homeowners (prime borrowers) holding loans owned or

guaranteed by Fannie Mae and Freddie Mac rose 50 per cent from December 2008 to January 2009 (from 497,131 to 743,686) 'as borrowers said drops in income or too much debt caused them to fall behind' (Kopecki, 2009).

7. The primary focus of this discussion is on the United States, not merely because this is where most of the recent economic trouble originated, but also because it is the main focus of Minsky's analyses.
8. Another reason for suggesting the 2009 stimulus was too timid is that the first-year tax-cut multipliers estimated by Christina Romer and Jared Bernstein were considerably below 1.0 (Romer and Bernstein, 2009: p. 12). Thus, modifying the package in the direction of tax cuts (to ensure passage) seemed ill advised from a macroeconomic perspective.
9. It is interesting to observe the Federal Reserve's use of the discount window as a means of influencing the banking system during the current crisis. Minsky recommended that the Fed increase reliance on this mechanism throughout the business cycle, but he thought it was especially important to use this channel in a fragile financial environment (Minsky, 1986c: pp. 322–328).
10. For an unconventional look at Bernanke, including the suggestion of a surprising link between Minsky and Princeton University financial-market research convened by Bernanke, see Lahart (2008).
11. The use of leverage by hedge funds and the writing of no documentation home loans are among the practices in greatest need of regulatory attention. There is also a need to address the problem created by firms deemed 'too big to fail,' which is yet another issue Minsky (1986c) anticipated long ago.
12. Health-care reform was enacted as this chapter was being prepared for publication (March 2010).
13. The challenge of getting global leaders to cooperate for the purpose of establishing a foundation for greater stability and more widespread global economic well-being can be seen even in the current economic climate; see Zalewski and Whalen (2009: pp. 17–18).

REFERENCES

'About the task force,' The White House Blog (30 January 2009), http://www.whitehouse.gov/blog_post/about_the_task_force_1/ (accessed 13 April 2009).

Baker, D. (2009a), 'The economic crisis: how we got here,' PowerPoint Presentation. Labor and Employment Relations Association Annual Meeting. 3 January. San Francisco, California.

Baker, D. (2009b), 'Geithner's plan will tax Main Street to make Wall Street richer,' *The Huffington Post* (30 March), http://www.huffingtonpost.com/dean-baker/geithners-plan-will-tax-m_b_181021.html (accessed 13 April 2009).

Bank for International Settlements (2007), 77th Annual Report. Basel, Switzerland: Bank for International Settlements Press and Communications.

Blaine, C. (2008), 'Wall Street says 'good riddance!' to 2008,' MSN Money (31 December), http://articles.moneycentral.msn.com/Investing/Dispatch/worst-year-since-1931-123108.aspx (accessed 13 April 2009).

Broda, C. and J. Parker (2008), 'The impact of the 2008 tax rebates on consumer spending: Preliminary evidence.' University of Chicago Graduate School of Business, 29

July, available at http://faculty.chicagobooth.edu/christian.broda/website/research/unrestricted/Research.htm (accessed 13 April 2009).

Buffett, W.E. (2008), Letter to shareholders, Berkshire Hathaway Inc., 2007 Annual Report.

Cassidy, J. (2008), 'The Minsky Moment?' *The New Yorker* (4 February), http://www.newyorker.com/talk/comment/2008/02/04/080204taco_talk_cassidy (accessed 28 April 2009).

Chernikoff, H. (2009), 'U.S. mortgage delinquencies up 50 percent,' Reuters UK, http://uk.reuters.com/article/economyNews/idUKTRE5374LT20090408 (accessed 13 April 2009).

Chu, K. and B. Acohido (2008), 'How rising home values, easy credit put your finances at risk,' USA Today (15 December), http://www.usatoday.com/money/perfi/credit/2008-06-17-credit-card-trap_N.htm (accessed 13 April 2009).

Der Hovanesian, M. (2006), 'Nightmare mortgages,' *BusinessWeek* (11 September), http://www.businessweek.com/magazine/content/06_37/b4000001.htm (accessed 13 April 2009).

Dymski, G. and R. Pollin (1992), 'Minsky as hedgehog: the power of the Wall Street paradigm,' in S. Fazzari and D.B. Papadimitriou (eds), *Financial Conditions and Macroeconomic Performance: Essays in Honor of Hyman P. Minsky* (Armonk, New York: M.E. Sharpe).

Earnshaw, A. (2009), 'Krugman: stimulus needs to be twice as big,' *Portland Business Journal* (2 February), http://www.bizjournals.com/portland/stories/2009/01/26/daily68.html (accessed 13 April 2009).

El Nasser, H. (2009), 'Open house anyone? 1 in 9 homes sit empty,' *USA Today*, http://www.usatoday.com/money/economy/housing/2009-04-09-vacanthomes_N.htm (accessed 13 April 2009).

Eurostat (2009), 'Euro area unemployment up to 8.5 percent,' News Release, Eurostat Euroindicators (1 April), downloaded from http://ec.europa.eu/eurostat/euroindicators (accessed 13 April 2009).

Foley, S. (2007), Anatomy of a credit crunch,' *The Independent* (London, 27 July), http://findarticles.com/p/articles/mi_qn4158/is_20070727/ai_n19447440/?tag=content;col1 (accessed 13 April 2009).

Freeman, J. (2009), 'How the money vanished,' *The Wall Street Journal* (6 March), http://online.wsj.com/article/SB123630340388147387.html (accessed 13 April 2009).

Galbraith, J. K. (2009), 'The Geithner plan won't work,' *The Daily Beast* (24 March), http://www.thedailybeast.com/blogs-and-stories/2009-03-24/the-geithner-plan-wont-work/full/ (accessed 13 April 2009).

Glover, R.W. and C.T. King (2010), 'Sectoral approaches to workforce development: toward an effective U.S. labor market policy,' in C.J. Whalen (ed.), *Human Resource Economics and Public Policy: Essays in Honor of Vernon M. Briggs*, Jr. Kalamazoo, Michigan: W.E. Upjohn Institute for Employment Research, pp. 215–252.

Holt, C. (2009), 'A graphical look at hedge fund leverage,' Seeking Alpha (8 March), http://seekingalpha.com/article/124783-a-graphical-look-at-hedge-fund- leverage

Huhne, C. (2007) 'Comments on credit rating agencies and the U.S. credit crunch.' *World Business Review*, BBC World Service (1 September).

Ineichen, A. and K. Silberstein (2008), *AIMA's Roadman to Hedge Funds* (London: The Alternative Investment Management Association).

Irwin, G. (2005), 'No money down gains more buyers,' *Akron Beacon Journal* (31 July), http://www.policymattersohio.org/media/

ABJ_No_money_down_gains_more_buyers_2005_0731.htm (accessed 13 April 2009).

Keynes, J.M. (1937), 'The general theory of employment,' *The Quarterly Journal of Economics*, vol. 51.

Komisar, L. (2000), 'Interview with Joseph Stiglitz,' *The Progressive* (June), http://www.progressive.org/0901/intv0600.html (accessed 13 April 2009).

Kopecki, D. (2009), 'Fannie, freddie defaults rise as borrowers cite lower income,' Bloomberg.com (21 April), http://www.bloomberg.com/apps/news?pid=20601087&sid=aw4.u4ryoAq0&refer=home (accessed 26 April 2009).

Krugman, P. (2009a), 'Stimulus arithmetic (wonkish but important),' *The New York Times* (6 January), http://krugman.blogs.nytimes.com/2009/01/06/stimulus-arithmetic-wonkish-but-important/ (accessed 13 April 2009).

Krugman, P. (2009b), 'Despair over financial policy,' *The New York Times* (21 March), http://krugman.blogs.nytimes.com/2009/03/21/despair-over-financial-policy/ (accessed 13 April 2009).

Krugman, P. (2009c), 'Geithner plan arithmetic,' *The New York Times* (23 March), http://krugman.blogs.nytimes.com/2009/03/23/geithner-plan-arithmetic/ (accessed 13 April 2009).

Lahart, J. (2007), 'In time of tumult, obscure economist gains currency,' *The Wall Street Journal* (8 August).

Lahart, J. (2008), 'Bernanke's bubble laboratory,' *The Wall Street Journal* (16 May), 1; http://online.wsj.com/public/article_print/SB121089412378097011.html (accessed 28 April 2009).

Lanman, S. and D. Kopecki (2008), 'Fed commits $800 billion more to unfreeze lending,' Bloomberg.com (25 November), http://www.bloomberg.com/apps/news?pid 20601103&refer=us&sid=a.IQxmdJnJMc (accessed 13 April 2009).

Larsen Thal, P. and C. Giles (2007), 'Bank of England to bail out Northern Rock,' *Financial Times* (14 September 2007), http://www.ft.com/cms/s/0/c6de12c8-6258-11dc-bdf6-0000779fd2ac.html (accessed 28 April 2009).

Lee, D. (2009), 'Migrant factory workers at a loss as China's economy slumps,' *Los Angeles Times* (23 January), http://articles.latimes.com/2009/jan/23/business/fi-chinamigrant23 (accessed 13 April 2009).

Magnus, G. (2007), 'The credit cycle and liquidity: have we arrived at a Minsky moment?' Economic insights – By George, *UBS Investment Research, London* (March).

Magnus, G. (2008), 'Is there time to avert a Minsky meltdown?' *The Financial Times* (14 October).

Marks, B. (2008), 'Bailout must address the foreclosure crisis,' *The Boston Globe* (24 September), http://www.boston.com/bostonglobe/editorial_opinion/oped/articles/2008/09/24/bailout_must_address_the_foreclosure_crisis/ (accessed 13 April 2009).

Marshall, R. (2010), 'Learning systems for a globalised economy: do Americans face tough choices or tough times?' in Charles J. Whalen (ed.), *Human Resource Economics and Public Policy: Essays in Honor of Vernon M. Briggs Jr.* (Kalamazoo, Michigan: W.E. Upjohn Institute for Employment Research), pp. 187–214.

Max, S. (2005), 'Risky real estate moves,' CNNMoney.com (4 April), http://money.cnn.com/2005/03/07/real_estate/financing/riskyloans/index.htm (accessed 13 April 2009).

Mildenberg, D. (2008), 'Bank of America to acquire Countrywide for $4 billion,' Bloomberg.com (11 January), http://www.bloomberg.com/apps/news?pid=20601087&refer=home&sid=aCbUSVliDIKQ (accessed 13 April 2009).
Minsky, H.P. (1975), *John Maynard Keynes* (New York: Columbia University Press).
Minsky, H.P. (1982), *Can 'It' Happen Again? Essays on Instability and Finance* (Armonk, New York: M.E. Sharpe).
Minsky, H.P. (1986a), 'Money and crisis in Schumpeter and Keynes,' in Hans-Jurgen Wagener and Jan W. Drukker (eds), *The Economic Law of Motion of Modern Society: A Marx-Keynes-Schumpeter Centennial* (Cambridge, UK: Cambridge University Press).
Minsky, H.P. (1986b), 'Global consequences of financial deregulation,' *The Marcus Wallenberg Papers on International Finance*, vol. 2, no. 1.
Minsky, H.P. (1986c), *Stabilising an Unstable Economy* (New Haven: Yale University Press).
Minsky, H.P. (1990a), 'Schumpeter: finance and evolution,' in Arnold Heertje and Mark Perlman (eds), *Evolving Market Technology and Market Structure: Studies in Schumpeterian Economics* (Ann Arbor: The University of Michigan Press).
Minsky, H.P. (1990b), 'Money manager capitalism, fiscal independence, and international monetary reconstruction,' in Miklos Szabo-Pelsoczi (ed.), *The Future of the Global Economic and Monetary System* (Budapest, Hungary: Institute for World Economics of the Hungarian Academy of Sciences).
Minsky, H.P. (1992a), 'The financial instability hypothesis,' *Working Paper Number 74, The Levy Economics Institute of Bard College.*
Minsky, H.P. (1992b), 'The capital development of the economy and the structure of financial institutions,' *Working Paper Number 72, The Levy Economics Institute of Bard College.*
Minsky, H.P. (1992c), 'Reconstituting the United States' financial structure: some fundamental issues,' *Working Paper Number 69, The Levy Economics Institute of Bard College.*
Minsky, H.P. (1993a), 'Schumpeter and finance,' in Salvatore Biasco, Alessandro Roncaglia, and Michele Salvati (eds), *Market and Institutions in Economic Development: Essays in Honour of Paulo Sylos Labini* (New York: St. Martin's Press).
Minsky, H.P. (1993b), 'Community development banks: an idea in search of substance,' *Challenge*, vol. 36, no. 2.
Minsky, H.P. (1995), 'Longer waves in financial relations: financial factors in the more severe depressions II,' *Journal of Economic Issues*, vol. 29, no. 1.
Minsky, H.P. (1996), 'Uncertainty and the institutional structure of capitalist economies,' *Journal of Economic Issues*, vol. 30, no. 2.
Minsky, H.P. and C.J. Whalen (1996–1997), 'Economic insecurity and the institutional prerequisites for successful capitalism,' *Journal of Post Keynesian Economics*, vol. 19, no. 2.
'Minsky's moment' (2009), Economist.com (2 April), http://www.economist.com/finance/displaystory.cfm?story_id=13415233 (accessed 28 April 2009).
Mitchell, W.C. (1941), *Business Cycles and Their Causes* (Berkeley, California: University of California Press).
Morgenson, G. (2007), 'Inside the countrywide lending spree,' *The New York Times* (26 August), http://www.nytimes.com/2007/08/26/business/yourmoney/26country.html?hp (accessed 13 April 2009).

'Obama's economic aide sees rising U.S. unemployment,' AFP [Agence France-Presse] (9 April 2009), http://www.google.com/hostednews/afp/article/ALeqM5g2urt_Wnm7T-ePnhznr5dLcBYY1w (accessed 13 April 2009).

O'Hara, P.A. (2009), 'The global securitised subprime market crisis,' paper prepared for the *Association for Institutional Thought Annual Meeting*, Albuquerque, New Mexico (17 April).

Palley, T.I. (1999), 'International finance and problems of capital account governance,' in Lynndee Kemmet, Karl Widerquist, and Ajit Zacharias (eds), *Conference Proceedings: Ninth Annual Hyman P. Minsky Conference on Financial Structure*, Annandale-on-Hudson, New York: The Jerome Levy Economics Institute of Bard College.

Phillips, R.J. (1997), 'Rethinking bank examinations: a Minsky approach,' *Journal of Economic Issues*, vol. 31, no. 2.

Pittman, M. (2007), 'Subprime bondholders may lose $75 billion from slump,' Bloomberg.com (24 April), http://www.bloomberg.com/apps/news?pid=20601087&sid=aq3flDbwBCbk&refer=home (accessed 13 April 2009).

Pollin, R. (2008), 'We're all Minskyites now,' *The Nation* (17 November).

RealtyTrac, S. (2009a), 'Foreclosure activity increases 81 percent in 2008,' RealtyTrac.com (15 January), http://www.realtytrac.com/ContentManagement/pressrelease.aspx?ChannelID=9&ItemID= 5681 (accessed 13 April 2009).

RealtyTrac, S. (2009b), 'Foreclosure activity increases 9 percent in first quarter,' RealtyTrac.com (16 April), http://www.realtytrac.com//ContentManagement/PressRelease.aspx?channelid=9&ItemID=6180 (accessed 25 April 2009).

Reckard, E.S., E. Douglass and T. Petruno (2007), 'BofA invests $2 billion in Countrywide,' *Los Angeles Times* (23 August), C1, http://articles.latimes.com/2007/aug/23/business/fi-mortgage23 (accessed 13 April 2009).

Romer, C. and J. Bernstein (2009), *The Job Impact of the American Recovery and Reinvestment Plan*. (Washington, DC: Presidential Transition Team) 9 January.

Shefrin, H. (2000), *Beyond Greed and Fear: Understanding Behavioral Finance and the Psychology of Investing* (Boston: Harvard Business School Press).

Spitzer, E. (2008), 'Predatory lenders' partner in crime,' *The Washington Post*, http://www.washingtonpost.com/wp-dyn/content/article/2008/02/13/AR2008021302783.html (accessed 13 April 2009).

Stempel, J. (2007), 'Countrywide uses $11.5B credit line to pay for loans,' *USA Today* (16 August), http://www.usatoday.com/money/economy/housing/2007-08-15-countrywide-stock_N.htm (accessed 13 April 2009).

Stiglitz, J.E. (2009), 'Obama's ersatz capitalism,' *The New York Times* (31 March) http://www.nytimes.com/2009/04/01/opinion/01stiglitz.html (accessed 13 April 2009).

Story, L. (2008), 'Home equity frenzy was a bank ad come true,' *The New York Times* (15 August), http://www.nytimes.com/2008/08/15/business/15sell.html (accessed 13 April 2009).

'Timeline: credit crunch to downturn,' *BBC News* (3 April 2009), http://news.bbc.co.uk/2/hi/business/7521250.stm (accessed 13 April 2009).

Twin, A. (2008), 'Stocks crushed,' CNNMoney.com (29 September), http://money.cnn.com/2008/09/29/markets/markets_newyork/index.htm?cnn=yes (accessed 13 April 2009).

U.S. Department of Labor (2009), 'Employment situation summary.' Economic News Release, Bureau of Labor Statistics, http://www.bls.gov/news.release/empsit.nr0.htm (accessed 13 April 2009).

Whalen, C.J. (1997), 'Money manager capitalism and the end of shared prosperity,' *Journal of Economic Issues*, vol. 31, no. 2.

Whalen, C.J. (2001), 'Integrating Schumpeter and Keynes: Hyman Minsky's theory of capitalist development,' *Journal of Economic Issues*, vol. 35, no. 4.

Whalen, C.J. (2002), 'Money manager capitalism: still here, but not quite as expected,' *Journal of Economic Issues*, vol. 36, no. 2.

Whalen, C.J. (2008a), 'The credit crunch: A Minsky moment,' *Studi e Note Di Economia*, vol. 13, no. 1.

Whalen, C.J. (2008b), 'Post-Keynesian institutionalism and the anxious society,' in S.S. Batie and N. Mercuro (eds), *Alternative Economic Structures: Evolution and Impact* (London: Routledge).

Whalen, C.J. (2008c), 'A labor agenda filled with hope and change,' LERA Commons (18 December), http://lerablog.org/2009/03/18/a-labor-agenda-brimming-with-hope-and-change-by-charles-whalen/ (accessed 13 April 2009).

Whalen, C.J. (2009), 'The financial crisis: causes and consequences,' PowerPoint Presentation to the Finger Lakes Forum (19 January) Geneva, New York.

Whalen, C.J. and J. Wenger (2002), 'Destabilising an unstable economy,' *Challenge*, vol. 45, no. 6.

Yahoo Finance (2009), Dow Jones Industrial Average: Historical Prices, http://finance.yahoo.com (accessed 13 April 2009).

Zalewski, D.A. (2002), 'Retirement insecurity in the age of money-manager capitalism,' *Journal of Economic Issues*, vol. 36, no. 2.

Zalewski, D.A. and C.J. Whalen (2009), 'Financialisation and income inequality: a post Keynesian institutionalist analysis,' paper prepared for the *Association for Evolutionary Economics Annual Meeting* in San Francisco, California (revised 24 April).

21. Economic policy for the real world

INTRODUCTION: ECONOMIC REALITY

I recently received an e-mail from one of my former students, a young woman who graduated in May of this year. "I've applied to job after job after job, and am not getting anywhere," she wrote of her attempt to find work related to her academic field of study.

This woman is no slacker. As a Utica College graduate, she holds a Syracuse University degree, well respected across New York State.[1] Aware of the upward trend in aging within the United States, she majored in health care management, with the expectation that it would offer robust employment opportunities. And, she got a jump start on the job search by visiting the campus career center well before graduation, and by seeking work through formal and informal channels. "I just took a job at Macy's," she continued, "because I'm absolutely desperate for money!" I understand her situation. She's from a rural community, her family is not wealthy, and the tuition alone at Utica is nearly $27,000 per year. Making the investment in college was not easy—and now there was no return on the horizon.

On the same day, I received an e-mail from James K. Galbraith mentioning a *New York Times* opinion piece presenting his and other economists' views on unemployment and job creation.[2] One of those economists was Heather Boushey, of the Center for American Progress. In her commentary, Boushey cites research on the labor-market impact of graduating from college in a recession. The consequences—for graduates like my former student and her peers—are "large, negative and persistent" (Boushey 2010).

Boushey also mentions recent research on dislocated workers. The data show that experienced workers who lose their jobs suffer an average income loss of 20 percent upon reemployment—and that the income losses persist over time.

Reading her comments, I experienced déjà vu. At first, I thought it was because I had met Boushey through my affiliation with the Levy Institute in

Reprinted with permission from the Levy Economics Institute, *Policy Note* No. 2010–1, July 2010, 1–5.

the mid-1990s; in fact, she participated in the Eastern Economic Association (EEA) conference session at which Hy Minsky and I presented a paper on money-manager capitalism in 1996.[3] But then it hit me. Digging through my files from that era, I located my own essays on worker insecurity. Sure enough, one of the dimensions addressed was the cost of employment dislocation for experienced workers—and the average and persistent income losses were of the same magnitude as indicated by Boushey (Whalen 1996).

In addition to my student and Jamie Galbraith, a friend contacted me recently from Massachusetts. He is nearly 50 years old and also holds a Syracuse degree—in engineering. His son enters college in the fall; two other children are in high school.

My friend understands quite a bit about dislocated workers. He has a temporary position that will end in a few weeks. Except for a few short-term project assignments, he's been unemployed since the current recession began. Over his career, he has been in multiple jobs—often with well-known companies like IBM—that have moved offshore. He is persistent and has tried the entrepreneurial, small-business path, but the economic insecurity endures.

Retirees are also struggling in the current downturn. For example, my parents have seen their medical insurance premium increase more than 6 percent this year. Their experience is consistent with research that shows health care has become a large and rapidly growing expense for retirees—a trend not likely to be reversed by recent federal health care reform (Jewel 2010).

Years ago, my father expected that his employer, Polaroid Corp., would be paying his health care expenses following retirement. Then the company made unilateral benefits changes. Actually, that was just one in a string of job-related bumps in his road to retirement. Before the company reneged on retirement benefits for him and other former employees, my dad was part of a wave of downsizing. And before that, he and fellow workers were assigned to help relocate Polaroid machinery to a factory overseas. Today, even more companies are turning their sights on retiree benefits and other labor costs as a way to cope with the global downturn (Karvounis 2008).

A SILENT DEPRESSION

The reminiscences above illustrate the fact that what we now face in the United States is not simply a *cyclical* crisis. Indeed, it is not merely an *employment* crisis. Rather, it is a standard-of-living-and-economic-opportunity crisis. In fact, what we are currently experiencing is just the latest phase in a decades-long "silent depression" (Peterson 1994).

The 1990s dot-com boom—and to some extent, the more recent housing boom—masked this long-simmering problem. But signs of worker insecurity appeared even then. Contingent work was on the rise, pension and health care benefits continued to erode, and job "off-shoring" remained persistent.[4]

If we are truly going to resolve the current crisis, then our policy response must reflect that we are dealing with a deep-seated structural problem, one rooted in the evolution of U.S. economic development. And interestingly, that was precisely the point Minsky and I sought to make in our 1996 paper. This also explains what I found so compelling about Minsky's work on money manager capitalism: I was studying the mounting challenges facing working families, and Minsky's analysis helped explain what was happening.

ECONOMIC POLICY

What needs to be done? The short answer is that there must be an agenda of recovery and reform.

At present, the *recovery* policy agenda requires another fiscal stimulus, including a major assistance package for state and local governments—entities that cannot easily engage in deficit spending and that are now counteracting the federal stimulus by laying off workers and raising taxes. Advocates of a larger federal stimulus in early 2009 warned that states required more help, and that mounting concerns about rising deficits would make a second stimulus bill more difficult to enact.[5] They were right.

There is also a need for more relief for the unemployed, and for those who are facing foreclosure on their homes. As of this writing, however, the U.S. Senate is blocking an extension of unemployment benefits, as well as legislation that would allow bankruptcy judges to mandate the restructuring of a residential mortgage. While the federal Troubled Assets Relief Program propped up financial institutions, there has been extraordinarily little assistance provided to borrowers saddled with the underlying "nightmare" mortgages (see Hall 2010, AP 2010).

In the realm of *reform*, there is, of course, a need for change in the financial sector. This legislation must include tougher supervision of a broad array of financial institutions, not just "banks." It must also provide supervisors the authority needed to contain innovations that threaten financial stability. Such reform should also address the "too big to fail" problem.[6]

There is also a need for fiscal reform, especially in the form of stronger automatic stabilizers.[7] This should include public service employment, which would enable the government to serve as employer of last resort.[8] Some economists worry that public service employment would be hard to administer and ineffective, but research by Vernon M. Briggs Jr., of Cornell University, and others shows that such employment in the 1970s directly targeted the unemployed, boosted aggregate spending more quickly than tax cuts, and did not substitute federal dollars for local funds (Whalen 2010, 102).

A third area warranting reform involves innovation policy. The United States needs a vigorous commitment to technological development and associated education. Singapore, China, and Denmark are among the nations that have made such a commitment, but the United States lags behind (see Kao 2007, Bradsher 2010). For example, while public universities are slashing jobs in New York State, the tiny island of Macau—with help from the Chinese government—is moving ahead with construction of a new university campus that will cost nearly a billion dollars and is designed to help transform the Pearl River Delta into a hub of technological development and scientific research (see *Macau News* 2009). Moreover, if green jobs are the focus of U.S. industrial policy, then it does little good for government incentives to spur domestic demand for wind turbines manufactured abroad (Schumer 2009).

A fourth, broad area involves issues that directly affect working families. In fact, attention to the concerns of working families must be at the top of the national economic agenda—not deficit reduction or vague notions of "fiscal responsibility," or even a focus on economic growth, price stability, and overall employment. As a guiding principle, policymakers must concentrate on fostering economic opportunities, especially as they relate to the development and utilization of the nation's human resources and the improvement of living standards. In the process, they must acknowledge—indeed, address—challenges of resource depletion and environmental sustainability.

Once the economy recovers, a key component of policy reform aimed at the well-being of working families must be a commitment to keeping aggregate demand high and the economy running hot. A retired United Auto Workers leader tells me that jobs were so plentiful in Buffalo during the 1950s and 1960s that workers could change employers simply by crossing the street; in fact, for a while he held two full-time jobs because the opportunities were too good to pass up.[9] Can we replicate the hot labor market of that earlier era? I'm not certain, but what the Nobel-winning economist William S. Vickrey called "chock-full" employment should surely be our goal (Warner, Forstater, and Rosen 2000).

Another component of this agenda should be the strengthening of retirement security. Providing older Americans with a secure retirement is good for individuals, the economy, and society. In his commentary in the *New York Times*, Galbraith (2010) suggests reducing the eligibility age for Medicare to 55 because it would "allow older workers to opt into early retirement." This makes sense, especially in the current labor market because it would make room for new workers. Another sensible policy reform would be to encourage a return to defined-benefit pension plans—in conjunction with a system that facilitates pension portability—and away from the defined-contribution plans that currently dominate the benefits world.

The U.S. Treasury has recently lobbied hard for an increase in the value of China's currency. But even with such a change, there will still be huge disparities between employment in the United States and employment in many nations overseas. Exchange-rate adjustments are not enough: a level international playing field for workers also requires an elevation of worker standards according to International Labor Organization conventions, the United Nations' Universal Declaration of Human Rights, and other international agreements.[10]

Of course, the United States is no worker heaven either. Employers frequently violate federal wage and hour laws, and workers often suffer reprisals for exercising their right to form a union (Orley 2007, Compa 2000). Thus, we need to better enforce worker rights and labor standards here at home. In addition, we need labor law reform that gives workers a more realistic chance to organize and bargain collectively—and an opportunity to have meaningful input when workplace decisions are made.[11]

CONCLUSION: THE ROAD AHEAD

The nation's economic challenges are daunting. Restoring robust American prosperity and widespread economic opportunity will not be easy. But, as Minsky stressed, "Economic systems are not natural systems. Policy can change both the details and the overall character of the economy" (2008, 7). It's time to design an effective economic policy for the real world, and we must begin by recognizing the deep roots of the problems we now face.

NOTES

1. Utica College was founded in 1946 as "Utica College of Syracuse University," a name it retained until beginning a recent transition toward institutional independence. At present, undergraduate degrees for Utica College students continue to be issued jointly by the college and the university.
2. See http://roomfordebate.blogs.nytimes.com/2010/06/24/can-obama-create-more-jobs-soon.
3. The session, titled "The Employment Act: Fifty Years Later," was organized as part of the EEA Annual Meeting, held in Boston on March 15, 1996; see Minsky and Whalen 1997.
4. For evidence that companies continued to press for workforce flexibility during the dot-com boom, see Mehring 2001, 30.
5. For a by-the-numbers analysis, see Krugman 2009.
6. Much of the policy discussion found in Minsky's 1986 book *Stabilizing an Unstable Economy* remains relevant to contemporary discussions of financial reform.

7. For a discussion of the erosion of automatic stabilizers prior to the Great Recession, see Whalen and Wenger 2002.
8. For Minsky's discussion of an employment strategy, see Minsky 2008 (1986), 343–49. For more on the notion of an employer of last resort, see Kaboub 2007, 495–502.
9. For more on the experience of that worker and on union efforts to improve the economy of western New York, see Whalen 2000, 22E4–E6.
10. For discussions of workers' rights in China, see Munro 2004, Chan 2004, and Brown 2004. For another view of the struggle for workers' rights, this time in Mexico, see Compa 2003.
11. For an overview of U.S. labor law, see Gould 2008, 110–22. For an examination of proposals for labor law reform, see Gould 2009, 1–46. For a discussion of ways to enhance the voice of workers in business organizations and society, see Kochan 2005.

REFERENCES

Associated Press (AP). 2010. "Mortgage Relief Dropouts Could Stall Recovery." June 21.

Boushey, H. 2010. "Keep the Money Flowing." Room for Debate Blog, comment posted June 24, http://roomfordebate. blogs.nytimes.com/2010/06/24/can-obama-create-more-jobs-soon/.

Bradsher, K. 2010. "China Leading Global Race to Make Clean Energy." *The New York Times,* January 30.

Brown, E. V. 2004. "Legal Aid, Labor Law Remedies, and Industrial Relations in China." *Perspectives on Work: Online Companion* (Fall).

Chan, A. 2004. "Exploitation of Migrant Workers in China's Export Manufacturing Sector." *Perspectives on Work: Online Companion* (Fall).

Compa, L. 2000. *Unfair Advantage: Workers' Freedom of Association in the United States under International Human Rights Standards.* New York: Human Rights Watch.

———. 2003. *Justice for All: The Struggle for Worker Rights in Mexico, A Report by the Solidarity Center.* Washington, D.C.: American Center for International Labor Solidarity.

Galbraith, J. K. 2010. "Shrink the Labor Force." Room for Debate Blog, comment posted June 24, http://roomfordebate. blogs.nytimes.com/2010/06/24/can-obama-create-more-jobs-soon/.

Gould, W. B., IV. 2008. "Industrial Relations and the Law." In C. J. Whalen, ed., *New Directions in the Study of Work and Employment: Revitalizing Industrial Relations as an Academic Enterprise.* Cheltenham, UK, and Northampton, Mass.: Edward Elgar.

———. 2009. "New Labor Law Reform Variations on an Old Theme: Is the Employee Free Choice Act the Answer?" *Louisiana Law Review* 70, no. 1 (Fall): 1–46.

Hall, K. G. 2010. "Mortgage Relief Efforts Lagging, Obama to Shift Gears." *McClatchy,* March 25.

Jewel, M. 2010. "For Retired Couples, Health Costs Will Only Go Up." *Mail Tribune* (Medford, Ore.), April 4.

Kaboub, F. 2007. "Institutional Adjustment Planning for Full Employment." *Journal of Economic Issues* 41, no. 2 (June): 495–502.
Kao, J. J. 2007. *Innovation Nation: How America Is Losing Its Innovative Edge, Why It Matters, and What We Can Do to Get It Back.* New York: Free Press.
Karvounis, N. 2008. "Retiree Health Benefits in the Recession." Taking Note: A Century Foundation Group Blog, comment posted December 17, http://takingnote.tcf.org/2008/ 12/retiree-health-benefits-in-the-recession.html.
Kochan, T. A. 2005. *Restoring the American Dream: A Working Families' Agenda for America.* Cambridge, Mass.: The MIT Press.
Krugman, P. 2009. "Stimulus Arithmetic (Wonkish but Important)." The Conscience of a Liberal Blog, comment posted January 6, http://krugman.blogs.nytimes.com/2009/01/06/stimulus-arithmetic-wonkish-but-important/.
Macau News. 2009. "Macau to Pay $150M for Land in Zhuhai to Build University of Macau New Campus." September 30.
Mehring, J. M. 2001. "Flexibility Is No Key to Stability" *BusinessWeek,* March 5.
Minsky, H. P. 2008 [1986]. *Stabilizing an Unstable Economy.* New York: McGraw-Hill.
Minsky, H. P., and C. J. Whalen. 1997. "Economic Insecurity and the Institutional Prerequisites for Successful Capitalism." *Journal of Post Keynesian Economics* 19, no. 2 (Winter 1996–97): 155–70.
Munro, R. 2004. "Labor Unrest and Denial of the Right to Organize in China." *Perspectives on Work: Online Companion* (Fall).
Orley, M. 2007. "Wage Wars." *BusinessWeek*, October 1. Peterson, W. C. 1994. *Silent Depression: The Fate of the American Dream.* New York: W. W. Norton.
Schumer, U.S. Senator C. E. 2009. "Schumer Urges Obama Administration to Block $450M in Stimulus Funds Sought by Wind Farm Project with Parts Built in China." Press release, November 5.
Warner, A. W., M. Forstater, and S. M. Rosen, eds. 2000. *Commitment to Full Employment: The Economics and Social Policy of William S. Vickrey*. Armonk, N.Y.: M. E. Sharpe.
Whalen, C. 2010. "The Human Resource Economics of Vernon Briggs." *Challenge* 53, no. 3 (May–June): 97–120.
Whalen, C., and J. Wenger. 2002. "Destabilizing an Unstable Economy." *Challenge* 45, no. 6 (November–December): 70–92.
Whalen, C. J. 1996. "Economics Must Change: Workforce Insecurity and the Need for a New Political Economy." *Bard Journal of Social Sciences* 5, no. 1–2: 34–40.
———. 2000. "Can Teamwork Rescue a Rust-belt City?" *BusinessWeek,* December 4.

22. Minsky goes to Buffalo—and takes on the economics establishment

In the past few years, much attention has been given to the economics of Hyman Minsky. His influence was particularly evident at a recent (October 2009) international gathering of post-Keynesian economists. Indeed, it would be no exaggeration to say the spirit of Minsky animated the entire conference.

I was privileged to participate in the opening session of that conference, which convened on the campus of Buffalo State College. What follows is a summary of my remarks. They do not rehash the details of the paper I prepared and distributed (Whalen 2009). Instead, they focus on the significance of Buffalo, New York, as the site for such a gathering; summarize essential elements of a Minsky perspective on the current economic situation in the United States; and challenge the image of Minsky recently presented to the public by mainstream economists and journalists. Special attention is given to Paul Krugman's Robbins Memorial Lecture, "The Night They Reread Minsky" (Krugman 2009a).

BUFFALO

New York's "Queen City" may not rank near the top of U.S. convention destinations, but Buffalo struck me as an especially appropriate place for post-Keynesians to gather. The location was also significant personally as well as professionally.

In the 1980s, when Buffalo and the United States had many more family-supporting manufacturing jobs than at present, the Brookings Institution's Charles Schultze insisted that America was not experiencing deindustrialization. Schultze maintained that our economic difficulties were unrelated to any deep-seated structural transformation. In his view, there was nothing going on that couldn't be cured by conventional macroeconomic policies (Schultze 1983).[1]

Indeed, in the 1980s, most economists claimed they really didn't understand all the fuss about deindustrialization. But I had lived in the Rust Belt, and was raised in the congressional district that produced John F. Kennedy, so my

Reprinted with permission from *Forum for Social Economics* 40 (2), July 2011, 273–280.

response to those who denied deindustrialization would have been: "Let them come to Buffalo."

In retrospect, that really was my response; it just took 250 pages for me to say it formally (Whalen 1988). My doctoral thesis involved fieldwork conducted partly in Buffalo. It was also steeped in the institutionalist and post-Keynesian traditions, drawing most heavily on John R. Commons and Minsky. And there was no mistaking where I stood. An early chapter bears the title, "What's Wrong with Neoclassical Economics?" and begins with a quote from Philip Klein: "In economics, the paradigm is not the solution—it is the problem" (Klein 1980: 880).

My economic research in the 1980s led to Buffalo and Minsky for the same reason: to better understand unemployment and rising U.S. economic insecurity in the post-World War II era. And, at least with respect to the study of Minsky's ideas, the timing was fortuitous. Although Minsky's research had long been associated with understanding cyclical unemployment, his work in the 1980s began to shift toward an analysis of structural economic change. In fact, two of his earliest references to "money-manager capitalism" can be found in papers first delivered in 1988 (Minsky 1990a, b). As Minsky and I (separately and jointly) subsequently explained, rising worker insecurity and deindustrialization in places like Buffalo were not merely correlated with the emergence of money-manager capitalism; these trends and this new capitalist era are, in fact, two sides of the same coin (Minsky 1996; Minsky and Whalen 1996–1997; Whalen 1997).

Since the 1980s, I've spent a number of years in Buffalo. Much of that time has been devoted to fostering cooperative labor-management relations within enterprises and across the community. A good portion of my work took place at a century-old brass factory just down the road from Buffalo State. Michael Moore once said he planned to use Buffalo as the location for a film about capitalism, and it's easy to see why; the story of U.S. capitalist development could be told quite effectively by examining that city.

A MINSKY PERSPECTIVE

Fast-forwarding to the present, we find a worldwide recession precipitated by a global financial crisis. A Minsky perspective on the current situation in the United States would recognize that the crisis resulted from a confluence of cyclical dynamics and structural evolution.

The cyclical dynamics are rooted in Minsky's "financial-instability hypothesis," which treats overconfidence and panics as regular features of the economic landscape. The financial-instability hypothesis is Minsky's alternative to the "efficient-market hypothesis" that has long dominated the field of finance.

Like Wesley Mitchell's examinations of business cycles decades earlier, Minsky's discussions of financial instability usually began with a state of economic recovery. From there, Minsky would explain how recovery generates a boom due to growing indebtedness, decreasing margins of safety in lending and borrowing, and increasingly fragile liability structures. Then he would describe how the boom eventually unravels, often threatening the entire macroeconomy in the process; this is where his theory of financial markets links most vividly to a broader theory of business cycles.

Minsky argued that the financial-instability hypothesis is rooted in John Maynard Keynes, but financial instability and cyclical dynamics are not the whole story. As Minsky wrote in 1986, "The task confronting economics today may be characterized as the need to integrate [Joseph] Schumpeter's vision of a resilient intertemporal capitalist process with Keynes's hard insights into the fragility introduced into the capitalist accumulation process by some inescapable properties of capitalist financial structures" (Minsky 1986a: 121). In other words, the basic path of a capitalist economy is cyclical, but business cycles are not simply fluctuations within a fixed economic structure; cycles represent both a cause and consequence of changes to the economic structure.

The paper I distributed in Buffalo focuses on four financial-sector innovations contributing to the current crisis: unconventional mortgages, securitization, hedge funds (and other institutional investors), and the globalization of finance (Whalen 2009). I also mentioned that financial-market deregulation, associated with all of the above, could be added to the list as an additional element.

The unconventional or "exotic" mortgages of recent years would not have been possible without deregulation and securitization. L. Randall Wray has recently contributed significantly to post-Keynesian scholarship by drawing attention to insights Minsky offered on securitization while at Washington University in 1987 (Minsky 2008). But, alas, Wray's impact suggests partly that few readers have ventured beyond Minsky's three books (Minsky 1975, 1982, 1986b).

For example, Minsky's warnings about the emergence, shortcomings and dangers of securitization can be found in an article published in 1986 and in an essay delivered at a conference in 1988 and then published in 1990 (Minsky 1986c, 1990b). In fact, Minsky gave special attention to mortgage securitization in 1992, in a paper where he pointed out that all a loan originator must do to profit from securitization is avoid "obvious fraud" (Minsky 1992: 23).

In those and other articles, Minsky described "a symbiotic relation between the growth of securitization and of managed money" (1990b: 71). He also wrote that securitized instruments have become international assets, which led him to conclude, "The growth of securitization means that, even as the power and authority of [financial market] regulators are attenuated, the scope and dimensions of their task increase." Minsky was particularly concerned that the Federal Reserve could not handle the crisis he saw on the horizon: "It is no longer clear that the United States can act as the guardian angel for stability in the world economy" (Minsky 1986c: 14–15).

By integrating Keynes's attention to booms and busts with Schumpeter's attention to structural evolution, Minsky was implicitly continuing the institutionalist cycle-theory tradition of Mitchell. According to Mitchell, "Business history repeats itself, but always with a difference. Each new cycle presents idiosyncrasies" (1941: ix). In short, cyclical and structural elements are always intertwined.[2]

MINSKY AND THE MAINSTREAM

A Minsky analysis of the recent economic crisis leads to a two-part policy response: one part aimed at recovery and the other at reform. Washington has managed to put in place many of the elements needed for a recovery, but the shape of reform is still up for grabs (Whalen 2009). The economics establishment, however, seems not to have fared as well in its attempt to come to grips with Minsky's insights.

First, there is all the attention to a "Minsky moment." Despite following the literature by and on Minsky for a quarter of a century, the first time I came across the notion of a Minsky moment was when reading a story in *The Wall Street Journal* during the early days of the recent credit crunch (Lahart 2007).

To be sure, it is wonderful that Minsky's ideas are receiving attention. Yet, as I suggested in *Challenge* in early 2008, the profession and the wider public are ill-served when Minsky's insights are reduced to the analysis of a single event—or even to an exploration of financial instability (Whalen 2008a). And it is one thing for journalists to reduce Minsky contributions in this way; it's another for Krugman to do it at the London School of Economics (LSE) during the prestigious Robbins Lecture (Krugman 2009a).

Minsky is about much more than a "moment" or even a "meltdown." His insights challenge the widespread belief in the inherent efficiency of markets and a laissez-faire stance toward economic policy. But they also challenge the notion that you can turn to Keynesian macroeconomic policies during a crisis and then let Keynes—and Minsky—fall back into obscurity when the crisis dissipates. That is because, in the end, Minsky draws attention to the value of evolutionary and institutionally focused thinking about the economy.

Minsky offers a paradigmatic break from conventional economics. While standard theory is built on a village-fair (barter) paradigm, Minsky's perspective is rooted in a "speculative-financial" paradigm—the starting point is a banker making deals on Wall Street, not a craftsman trading in a bazaar

(Minsky 1975, 57–58). In other words, Minsky's economics recognizes that finance precedes production and production precedes exchange. The result is a monetary theory of production, which explains why his work helps integrate the institutionalist and post-Keynesian traditions (Dillard 1987). Of course, Minsky's approach appears to many economists as too much of a deviation from mainstream concepts and theories, but Minsky without a monetary theory of production and an analysis of economic performance through time is, to borrow one of his own lines, like *Hamlet* without the Prince.

Second, I want to dispute the notion, suggested most recently in *The Boston Globe*, that Minsky's vision was "dark," "pessimistic," and "even tragic" (Mihm 2009). Yes, Minsky argued the "major flaw of our type of economy is that it is unstable." Yet, in the same paragraph, he also wrote, "We can, so to speak, stabilize instability" (Minsky 1986b: 9–10). Indeed, that belief was reflected in the title of his 1986 book, *Stabilizing an Unstable Economy.*

Of course, we have to understand the realities of capitalist dynamics. And those realities are worlds away from the vision most economists have gleaned from Adam Smith. But Minsky's goal was always optimistic, constantly pointing toward a "successful program" of change and economic reform—indeed, toward "a more humane economy as a first step toward a humane society" (Minsky 1986b: 3, 293).

Third, I reject the contention in the *Globe* article that Minsky spent his career "in professional isolation," and that while some of his views "may limit the extent to which Minsky becomes part of any new orthodoxy... that's probably how he would have preferred it" (Mihm 2009).

Minsky's ideas might have been out of the mainstream, but he was still a graduate of Chicago and Harvard, with longstanding personal ties to James Tobin and others at the top tier of the profession in the United States and United Kingdom. In Italy, meanwhile, the economics department in Bergamo was named after him in 1988.

Minsky was also deeply integrated into the U.S. banking community. And, at least in his later years, he nurtured an ever-expanding circle of younger colleagues. When he was ill, there were calls and visitors from around the world.

Anyone who thinks Minsky preferred to be on the outside of the profession needs to re-read his final public lecture, published in the *Journal of Economic Issues* (Minsky 1996). One of my first trips to the Levy Economics Institute involved participating in a workshop Minsky organized in the summer of 1991. Describing what he had in mind for the gathering, Minsky wrote, "The perspective that underlies the work of this workshop is that to move policy it is necessary to move the discipline. To move the discipline, we have to communicate with the dominant practitioners, even as we change the agenda" (Minsky 1991). That same spirit drives Minsky's 1996 essay. In fact, Minsky praised Tom Sargent's *Bounded Rationality in Macroeconomics*, expressing optimism that it meant "differences have narrowed" to the point where "a partial convergence between the economics of Keynes and the new classical economics has occurred" and "a fruitful discourse may now be possible" (Minsky 1996: 362).

Finally, I must address Krugman's LSE lecture, "The Night They Reread Minsky." Let us gloss over the fact that Krugman says "economists win their spurs by doing difficult stuff," yet when he eventually gets around to Minsky in his lecture he says, "Minsky is—it's actually interesting to think about—Minsky's work is—is—is not easily readable." We will also skim over the part where Krugman says, "Who's going to plow through [Minsky's heterodoxy] to get to the really good insights in one chapter about—about um—and it's interesting because Keynes was a total insider" (Krugman 2009a).

In fact, let's bypass the entire lecture and get to his response to a question about Friedrich von Hayek and business cycle theory. Krugman says that cycle theorists, including Schumpeter, missed an opportunity to integrate Keynes into the business cycle. Yet, it seems a little digging through some moderately "difficult stuff" should have led Krugman to discover—and acknowledge—that Minsky did just that.

In a recent *New York Times* article based on his lecture, Krugman writes that what economists must do today is question the efficient-market view of the financial sector and "do their best to incorporate the realities of finance into macroeconomics" (Krugman 2009b). Now, it is one thing to marginalize Minsky, but it is nothing short of the age-old definition of chutzpah to pretty much bury Minsky and then claim economists need—and couldn't predict the current crisis because they currently don't have—precisely what Minsky offered during most of his career.

BUFFALO REVISITED

But there's even more in Minsky than what Krugman seeks. And telling the rest of the story brings us back to Buffalo and other communities grappling not just with a cyclical downturn, but also with a more fundamental economic transformation. The era of managerial capitalism that brought broadly shared prosperity to the United States is long gone. The fight ahead is over the future of what Minsky called money-manager capitalism—and over the accompanying economic insecurity for working families in places like Buffalo (Whalen 2008b).

As Jack Kennedy might have said, "All progressive economists, wherever they may live, are citizens of Buffalo." And, therefore, as a post-Keynesian institutionalist, I take pride in the words "Ich bin ein Buffalonian."

NOTES

1. In 1980, there were 132,876 manufacturing jobs in the Buffalo-Niagara Metropolitan Statistical Area and 18.7 million in the United States overall (New York State Department of Labor undated; U.S. Bureau of Labor Statistics 2009a). By late 2009, the Buffalo-Niagara number had fallen to 53,400 and the U.S. figure had fallen to 11.7 million (U.S. Bureau of Labor Statistics 2009b, c).
2. For further evidence of how cyclical and structural elements are intertwined in the Great Recession, see Kregel (2008). He explains that the recent U.S. subprime mortgage crisis is traceable in large part to insufficient margins of safety built into many of the mortgages generated by the new "originate and distribute" financial system. Kregel also distinguishes between the evolutionary erosion of margins of safety in Minsky's financial-instability hypothesis (FIH) and the inadequate safety cushions inherent in the structure of securitized, subprime mortgages, but, as indicated above, Minsky offered more than the FIH: he also anticipated the key structural changes we now confront.

REFERENCES

Dillard, D. (1987). Money as an institution of capitalism. *Journal of Economic Issues, 21*(4), 1623–1647.

Klein, P. A. (1980). Confronting power in economics: a pragmatic evaluation. *Journal of Economic Issues, 14*(4), 871–896.

Kregel, J. (2008). *Minsky's cushions of safety: Systemic risk and the crisis in the U.S. subprime mortgage market. Public policy brief, No. 93.* Annandale-on-Hudson: Levy Economics Institute.

Krugman, P. (2009a). The night they re-read Minsky. June 10, London School of Economics. http://www2.lse.ac.uk/newsAndmedia/videoAndAudio/publicEventsVideos/LSELive_previous.aspx. Accessed 1 December 2009.

Krugman, P. (2009b). How did economists get it so wrong? *The New York Times* (2 September) http://www.nytimes.com/2009/09/06/magazine/06Economic-t.html. Accessed 1 December 2009.

Lahart, J. (2007). In time of tumult, obscure economist gains currency. *The Wall Street Journal* (18 August), 1.

Mihm, S. (2009). Why capitalism fails. *The Boston Globe* (13 September). http://www.boston.com/bostonglobe/ideas/articles/2009/09/13/why_capitalism_fails. Accessed 1 December 2009.

Minsky, H. (1975). *John Maynard Keynes*. New York: Columbia University Press.

Minsky, H. (1982). *Can "it" happen again? Essays on instability and finance*. Armonk: M.E. Sharpe.

Minsky, H. (1986a). Money and crisis in Schumpeter and Keynes. In H. J. Wagener & J. W. Drukker (Eds.), *The economic law of motion of modern society: A Marx-Keynes-Schumpeter centennial* (pp. 112–122). Cambridge: Cambridge University Press.

Minsky, H. (1986b). *Stabilizing an unstable economy*. New Haven: Yale University Press.

Minsky, H. (1986c). Global consequences of financial deregulation. *The Marcus Wallenberg Papers on International Finance, 2*(1), 1–19.

Minsky, H. (1990a). The future of the global economic and monetary system. In M. Szabo-Pelsoczi (Ed.), *The relationship between international economic activity and international monetary reconstruction* (pp. 209–218). Budapest: Institute for World Economics of the Hungarian Academy of Sciences.

Minsky, H. (1990b). Schumpeter: Finance and evolution. In A. Heertje & M. Perlman (Eds.), *Evolving technology and market structure: Studies in Schumpeterian economics* (pp. 51–74). Ann Arbor: University of Michigan Press.

Minsky, H. (1991). Summer workshop introductory remarks. Jerome Levy Economics Institute.

Minsky, H. (1992). The capital development of the economy and the structure of financial institutions. Working Paper No. 72, The Jerome Levy Economics Institute of Bard College.

Minsky, H. (1996). Uncertainty and the institutional structure of capitalist economies. *Journal of Economic Issues, 30*(3), 357–368.

Minsky, H. (2008). Securitization. Levy Economics Institute *Policy Note*, No. 2008-2. With Preface and Afterword by L. R. Wray.

Minsky, H., & Whalen, C. (1996–1997). Economic insecurity and the institutional prerequisites for successful capitalism. *Journal of Post Keynesian Economics, 19*(2), 155–170.

Mitchell, W. C. (1941). *Business cycles and their causes*. Berkeley: University of California Press.

New York State Department of Labor. (Undated). Employment and earnings trends in the Buffalo-Niagara MSA, 1980–1999. http://www.amherst.ny.us/archive/pdf/compplan/inventory_analysis/table%206-1.pdf. Accessed 1 December 2009.

Schultze, C. L. (1983). Industrial policy: a dissent. *The Brookings Review, 2*, 3–12.

U.S. Bureau of Labor Statistics. (2009a). Employment, hours, and earnings from the Current Employment Statistics Survey. http://www.bls.gov/ces/cesbtabs.htm. Accessed 1 December 2009.

U.S. Bureau of Labor Statistics. (2009b). Selected BLS economic indicators: Buffalo-Niagara Falls, 30 October update. http://www.bls.gov/ro2/buffalo.pdf. Accessed 1 December 2009.

U.S. Bureau of Labor Statistics. (2009c). Employment situation summary. October 2009. http://www.bls. gov/news.release/empsit.nr0.htm. Accessed 1 December 2009.

Whalen, C. J. (1988). *Beyond Neoclassical thought: Economics from the perspective of Institutionalists and Post Keynesians*. Ph.D. dissertation, The University of Texas at Austin.

Whalen, C. J. (1997). Money-manager capitalism and the end of shared prosperity. *Journal of Economic Issues, 31*(2), 517–525.

Whalen, C. J. (2008a). Understanding the credit crunch as a Minsky moment. *Challenge, 51*(1), 91–109.

Whalen, C. J. (2008b). Post-Keynesian Institutionalism and the anxious society. In S. Batie & N. Mercuro (Eds.), *Alternative institutional structures: Evolution and impact* (pp. 273–299). London: Routledge.

Whalen, C. J. (2009). A Minsky perspective on the global recession. The fourth bi-annual cross-border Post Keynesian conference; available at http://faculty.buffalostate.edu/joth/pk2009/Site/program.html. Accessed 1 December 2009. An updated version of this paper appears in D. Tavasci and J. Toporowski (Eds.), *Minsky, crisis and development*. Basingstoke, UK: Palgrave Macmillan (2010), chapter six.

PART V

Integrating institutional and post-Keynesian economics

23. Post-Keynesian institutionalism: past, present, and future

> As capitalism evolves, so too should economic theory and policy.
>
> Hyman Minsky (1996a)

INTRODUCTION

Delivering his presidential address to the Association for Evolutionary Economics (AFEE) in the 1960s, Gruchy (1969: 5) reported meeting a graduate student a few years earlier: "This young student said he was happy to shake my hand as he understood that I was the last of the institutionalists." Gruchy dismissed the cheeky remark as a reflection of the view of many distinguished economists. After all, he noted, Kenneth Boulding had said more than a decade earlier that institutionalism's days had passed and it deserved to be placed in a museum.

A half-century after Gruchy's address, it was my turn to serve as AFEE's president. Institutionalism—by which I mean the intellectual tradition known as original institutional economics, which originated in the work of economists such as Thorstein B. Veblen, John R. Commons, and Wesley C. Mitchell, and was central to the founding of AFEE—remains alive; and its work remains as important as ever.[1] In my experience, post-Keynesian institutionalism (PKI), a branch of the institutionalist tradition that draws heavily on common ground shared by many institutionalists and post-Keynesians, is an important reason for the tradition's continued vitality.

This article contributes as a survey of PKI as follows. The first section examines PKI by reviewing its origins and development. That section ends with a definition of PKI and a summary of core ideas. Then the article highlights existing PKI contributions in the course of outlining directions for future research. A concluding section includes reflections on how post-Keynesian economics

Reprinted with permission from *Evolutionary and Institutional Economics Review* 17 (1), January 2020, 71–92.

has helped energize the institutionalist tradition, an acknowledgment of the article's limitations, and an expression of hope for international participation in the further shaping of PKI.

A BRIEF HISTORY

PKI emerged as a branch of institutional economics in the 1980s, but that emergence was foreshadowed between the world wars of the last century by the work of Commons and John Maynard Keynes. For example, Atkinson and Oleson (1998: 1019) demonstrate that Commons and Keynes shared "an interest in applying their research to the practical issues of the day" as well as a "skeptical attitude" toward deterministic economic models. For both Commons and Keynes, any useful economic theory must recognize that economic activity and outcomes are shaped by history, institutions, and expectations about an uncertain future.

Commons and Keynes also rejected socialism and laissez-faire capitalism. They considered the former incompatible with human freedom and unable to match the creativity of capitalism, and they saw capitalism as too deeply flawed to be unmanaged. Thus, they aimed to develop the "institutions necessary to save capitalism," especially from the high unemployment (which tends to be self-reinforcing, not self-correcting) and other harmful consequences of macroeconomic fluctuations (Atkinson and Oleson 1998: 1019). Corresponding with Commons about economic policy in 1927, Keynes wrote: "There seems to me to be no other economist with whose general way of thinking I feel myself in such genuine accord" (Atkinson and Oleson 1998: 1019).[2]

After Keynes's *General Theory*

Despite the common ground that existed in the work of Commons and Keynes, development of PKI was not foreordained. Many institutionalists were indifferent or even hostile to Keynes's ideas in the wake of publication of *The General Theory of Employment, Interest, and Money* (Keynes 1936) and in the period after World War II when the neoclassical version of Keynesianism rose to prominence in academic and policy circles.[3] Some institutionalists even kept their distance from post-Keynesianism when it coalesced in the 1970s through the work of economists such as Joan Robinson, Sidney Weintraub, Alfred Eichner, and Paul Davidson, who highlighted aspects of Keynes not easily accommodated in conventional Keynesianism. For example, Gruchy (1987: 147–159) argued to the end of his career that institutionalists and post-Keynesians do not have enough in common to form a united front against economic orthodoxy and must, therefore, remain independent movements.

However, many institutionalist attitudes began to change toward the end of the 1970s. A watershed moment was when Peterson (1977) devoted his AFEE presidential address to core ideas that he saw as the foundation of both post-Keynesianism—which he called the "economics of Keynes"—and institutionalism, and concluded that economists of both traditions would be best able to understand and address real-world problems by building a shared analytical framework. In particular, Peterson's presentation focused on the following shared ideas: (1) uncertainty is an inescapable part of the backdrop of economic life; (2) institutions and power relations influence human behavior and economic performance, and underscore the need for economists to give serious attention to income distribution; (3) money and finance are capitalism's key institutions; (4) economies change continuously and organically (in irreversible, historical time), and advanced capitalist economies are inherently prone to cyclical instability[4]; and (5) public action is recognized as essential to addressing excessive concentrations and abuses of private power, even as private power is acknowledged to often have a grip on public power. Peterson identified a number of economists who paved the way for such an interpretation of Keynes—including Robinson, Weintraub, and Davidson—and gave special attention to Hyman Minsky, who he called "one of the architects" of the new economics of Keynes (Petersons 1977: 217).

A few years later, Dillard (1980) took a path similar to that of Peterson. Dillard's presidential address to AFEE explored how Keynes and the institutionalists give special attention to financial institutions and profit expectations as factors explaining production, employment, unemployment, and business cycles. Dillard described that common focus as a monetary theory of production, and concluded with a call for integrating institutionalism and the economics of Keynes into a new macroeconomic theory. According to Dillard (1980: 271), that (business cycle oriented) macroeconomics could be infused with considerable institutionalist insight into technological change and modern corporations, resulting in a powerful alternative to neoclassical theory.

By the early 1980s, the time for PKI had arrived. Brazelton (1981) highlighted the common interest that institutionalists and post-Keynesians had in real-world wage and price determination, including the institutional determinants of wages and the macroeconomic significance of markup pricing.[5] Keller (1983) echoed Peterson by underscoring institutionalist and post-Keynesian compatibility with respect to the economic significance of time, money, and power, and then added that the traditions were complementary because institutionalism offered a deeper consideration of the constructive role of government in the economy, while post-Keynesianism offered a more developed analysis of problems such as stagflation.[6] In the same year, Marshall (1983)—after observing that the US economy had just experienced extraordinarily high inflation and was confronting the worst downturn since the Great Depression— surveyed the landscape of discredited economic theories (including monetarism and supply-side economics) and called on institutionalists and post-Keynesians to seize the opportunity and form a synthesis that would provide a superior economic analysis.[7]

Post-Keynesian Institutionalism

As if on cue, Wilber and Jameson (1983) published *An Inquiry into the Poverty of Economics*. It explicitly offers PKI as an alternative to conventional economics and other economic paradigms. According to Wilber and Jameson, PKI aims to understand and resolve real-world problems from a vantage point that sees the economy as not only constantly evolving, but also holistic and systemic. In other words, from the perspective of PKI, the economy is not neatly separable from other social spheres: interdependencies are pervasive, and society's various institutions shape economic life. The book builds on institutionalist John Kenneth Galbraith's analysis of the "bimodal economy," which described the nature and functioning of a US economy with about a thousand large corporations at its core and many thousands of small firms on its periphery. In particular, the authors integrate that analysis with other institutionalist and post-Keynesian insights to address the problem of stagflation.[8]

Although their PKI foundation was well constructed, Wilber and Jameson failed to receive much attention because their book focused heavily on inflation at a time when it was being beaten down. As a result, PKI needed a new focus if it was to survive the 1980s. The economics of Minsky—which centered on economic instability and gave particular attention to the interaction of finance and macroeconomics (see, for example, Minsky 1982, 1986)—provided that focus.

In the mid 1980s, Minsky's ideas featured prominently in two special issues of the institutionalist *Journal of Economic Issues*. In 1984, Minsky and colleague Steven Fazzari drew upon the post-Keynesian perspective, especially the notion that capitalism is inherently unstable, to critically examine monetarism and outline an alternative to conventional economic theory and policy (Fazzari and Minsky 1984). A few years later, Dillard (1987b: 1642) identified Minsky's analysis of financial instability as a "major contribution" to understanding money as an institution of capitalism; and Peterson (1987: 1613) highlighted Minsky's work as "a promising and imaginative start" toward incorporating the key institutions of modern capitalism into macroeconomics.

Minsky, who years earlier had written that monetary economics "cannot help being institutional economics" (Minsky 1969: 225), was well suited to the task of helping to bring together institutionalism and post-Keynesianism. Although widely recognized as an important contributor to post-Keynesianism—owing in large part to authoring a book that stressed non-neoclassical aspects of Keynes's scholarship (Minsky 1975)—Minsky cast a wide net when seeking to understand economic problems. Minsky's university studies exposed him to a broad spectrum of economic ideas, including those of Henry Simons, Oscar Lange, Frank Knight, Paul Douglas, Joseph Schumpeter, Alvin Hansen, and Wassily Leontief. He also conducted statistical reporting on human resources for David Saposs, a student of Commons, while serving with the US Army in Berlin at the end of World War II. According to Minsky (1985: 211–212): "The experience in Germany—and the interactions with Saposs—impressed upon me the importance of the specific institutions and historical circumstances upon what happens in the world".[9]

After Minsky

By the time Minsky died in 1996, two of his analytical contributions garnered the attention of post-Keynesians and institutionalists. One was the previously mentioned work on financial instability, with its central insight that financial system fragility is endogenously generated during periods of economic growth, leading to credit crunches and possibly to severe economic downturns (Minsky 1982, 1986). The other was his analysis of the emergence of money manager capitalism, a term he coined to highlight the dominant position that institutional investors came to hold in the US economy beginning in the 1980s (see, for example, Minsky 1993). Because Minsky was equally at home among institutionalists and post-Keynesians, and attracted economists from both camps, his work on instability and money manager capitalism soon became key components of the emerging PKI. Minsky (1996b) encouraged that emergence shortly before his death by using the occasion of his receipt of AFEE's Veblen-Commons Award to stress not only the affinity between Keynes and Commons, but also the continuing relevance of that affinity.

During the Internet boom and crash, a period roughly from 1995 through 2002, PKI attracted considerable attention among heterodox economists. That is partly because Minsky's Veblen-Commons Award and subsequent death prompted tributes and research that focused on the intersection of the economics of Keynes and institutionalism (see, for example, Papadimitriou and Wray 1997; Whalen 1997). As a result, many economists recognized that the 1990s expansion and subsequent contraction were broadly consistent with Minsky's financial instability analysis (see, for example, Rima 2002). But PKI also attracted economists because greater awareness of Minsky's work on money manager capitalism coincided with growing public attention to what business journalists were calling the New Economy (see, for example, Zalewski 2002). Consistent with Minsky's money manager analysis, those journalists argued that much of the 1990s expansion was being driven by corporate restructuring—and that the pressure for such restructuring was coming from institutional investors (Whalen 2008b: 287).

PKI received even wider attention as a result of the global financial crisis that began in late 2007 and lasted into 2009. In fact, when the crisis hit, Minsky's ideas were featured on the front page of *The Wall Street Journal* (Lahart 2007). Asked to explain why mainstream economists did not see the crisis coming, Lawrence Summers (2011) stressed that conventional economics is particularly weak at the intersection of macroeconomics and finance: "I think economics knows a fair amount. But I also think economics has forgotten a fair amount that's relevant—and it has been distracted by an enormous amount".

Definition and Core Elements

As indicated above, I view PKI as a branch of the institutionalist tradition that draws heavily on common ground shared by many institutionalists and post-Keynesians. However, the terms "institutionalist" and "post-Keynesian" can cover much territory, so let me clarify the terrain I have in mind.

When it comes to institutionalism, my attention is (as mentioned in the article's introduction) on work done in the tradition of original institutional economics. At the time that PKI was emerging, Galbraith was among the most prominent scholars associated with such institutionalism (see for example, Galbraith 1977). He wrote on a wide range of topics, including corporations, the structure of industry, inflation, financial instability, economic power, and the role of government. Galbraith often drew upon Veblen, but also the institutionalism of Berle and Means (1932), and the economics of Keynes.[10]

With regard to post-Keynesianism, I have in mind the variety that Hamouda and Harcourt (1988) associated most closely with the ideas of Keynes, a camp often considered the *Keynes* strand. This is also known as the *American* strand of post-Keynesianism because most of its original contributors—Weintraub, Davidson, and Minsky, for example—were based or originated in the USA.[11] Lavoie (2014: 38) summarizes this strand's focus as follows: "The main concerns of these authors are the descriptions of a monetized production economy, the fragility and instability of the financial system, questions tied to liquidity preference, and fundamental uncertainty." The other two strands of post-Keynesianism identified by Hamouda and Harcourt are rooted primarily in the work of Michael Kalecki and in Piero Sraffa. Research associated with those two strands has never played a large role in the literature that I refer to as PKI.[12]

The relevance of the Keynes strand to PKI can be traced to the addresses by Peterson and Dillard that were discussed above. But, of course, those addresses, and the related essays by Brazelton and Keller, merely highlighted the pre-analytic perspectives and research interests that such institutionalists and post-Keynesians already held in common. The overlap was so considerable and apparent that even in the late 1970s some economists, including

Galbraith, Eichner, and Dillard, considered themselves both institutionalists and post-Keynesians.

Since the 1980s, the roster of economists working at the intersection of institutionalism and post-Keynesianism has grown steadily, and many call themselves post-Keynesian institutionalists.[13] Recognizing this overlap, Lavoie (2014: 40–41) views the intermingling of institutionalist and post-Keynesian research (on a range of microeconomic and macroeconomic topics) as one of five strands of today's post-Keynesian economics.[14] He mentions Galbraith (an early financial supporter of the *Journal of Post Keynesian Economics*), Eichner, and Dillard as important sources of inspiration for that strand, and Fred Lee, John Harvey, James Galbraith, and Charles Whalen as among the more recent contributors.[15] Lavoie also acknowledges that Minsky's work can be seen as cutting across the Keynes and institutionalist strands. What follows is a brief summary of what I see as core elements of today's PKI.[16]

According to Dugger (1996), institutionalists define economics as the study of ever-evolving, real-world processes of social provisioning, and that definition provides their economics tradition with its underpinnings. PKI builds on the same perspective. The following are some implications of that foundation: (1) PKI theorists are more interested in analyses built on realistic assumptions (recognizing, of course, that all theories are an abstraction from reality) than on construction of formal models; (2) people act in a world of uncertainty: they rely heavily on habits and social conventions; lessons are learned through experience (which often involves unmet expectations); and ends and means are subject to constant reconsideration; and (3) PKI sees institutions, not impersonal forces or universal laws of nature, as the balancing wheel of the economy.

Because PKI is the product of scholars in market-oriented economies aiming to better understand the problems surrounding them, its research centers on the study of economic life under capitalism—recognizing that, as Commons (1934: 766) writes: "Capitalism is not a static or single concept." PKI accepts that the price system may exhibit equilibrating tendencies, but market dynamics can also involve cumulative causation, path dependence, and hysteresis; as a result, real-world markets may not rapidly or fully correct themselves, particularly in a downturn. In PKI, rational decision-making about an uncertain future can lead to booms, severe downturns, and economies that stall at far below potential for extended periods. Moreover, economic change occurs even when the economy is stuck in a slump.

In addition to an institutionalist foundation and a focus on capitalist evolution, PKI begins with a Wall Street paradigm. Conventional economics is constructed around a barter paradigm: money, finance, capital assets, and production can all be added, but the paradigm assumes that the central features of capitalism can be grasped without them. In contrast, the Wall Street paradigm—described most fully by Minsky (1975), but also implicit in institutionalism and in Keynes—is rooted in recognition that capitalism is driven by pursuit of financial gain, that production precedes exchange, and that finance precedes production.[17]

PKI also approaches macroeconomics from a perspective that treats the endogenous generation of business cycles as "a basic characteristic" of contemporary capitalism (Minsky 1975: 164). PKI does not offer a single explanation for all cycles, but it does aim to explain the transition from one phase in a cycle to another in a coherent fashion. To that end, PKI follows Minsky (1975) in giving particular attention to the interplay of two features of the economy that have become nearly synonymous with modern capitalism: (1) expensive and durable capital assets; and (2) institutions of finance that allow short-term financing and position-taking.[18]

In addition, PKI incorporates the "financial instability hypothesis" (FIH) into its analyses (see, for example, Minsky 1986: 173). That hypothesis—which accommodates herd behavior and sudden changes in expectations—represents an alternative to the efficient market hypothesis of financial markets. In addition, it includes a theory of the business cycle that emphasizes not just aggregate demand (as is customary in the economics of Keynes), but also evolution of the financial structure over time. While the FIH is rooted in the work of Minsky (1982), many analysts have applied it to help explain more recent economic developments (see, for example, Barbera 2009; Lewitt 2010)—and post-Keynesian institutionalists have recently made fruitful extensions by combining consumer spending and inequality into their analyses (see for example, Kaboub et al. 2010).

PKI also builds on the Schumpeter–Minsky theory of capitalist development. The money manager capitalism that Minsky highlighted in the 1990s is the latest stage in a finance-driven theory of capitalist development that Minsky acquired while studying with Schumpeter at Harvard.[19] According to that theory, capitalism in the USA passed through four stages—commercial capitalism, industrial capitalism, financial capitalism, and managerial capitalism—before money manager capitalism emerged in the early 1980s (Minsky 1990, 1993, 1996b). In addition to the strong influence of institutional investors upon economic decision-making, money manager capitalism is characterized by a fast pace of financial innovation as well as by increased worker insecurity and rising income inequality (Whalen 2017).

The inevitable and creative role of government in economic life rounds out our summary of PKI's core elements. Conventional economics maintains that the proper role of government is to serve as a corrective entity—that is, to correct for market failures such as the existence of externalities. In contrast, PKI views the government as deeply and unavoidably involved in shaping the economy by making and enforcing rules that are always evolving. PKI also recognizes that government's creative effort can be directed toward different conceptions of efficiency, and that public policy is often shaped by other considerations (such as a concern for social justice).[20]

CONTRIBUTIONS AND DIRECTIONS FOR FUTURE RESEARCH

In January 2019, more than 10,000 economists gathered in Atlanta, Georgia, for the annual meeting of the Allied Social Sciences Association, an umbrella group including the American Economic Association, AFEE, and other economists' organizations. Only a small fraction would consider themselves post-Keynesian institutionalists. In fact, it is likely that many attendees were never introduced to institutionalism or post-Keynesianism. Moreover, it has been a decade since the Great Recession and global financial crisis; most of the economics profession appears content to have moved beyond the days when real-world turmoil challenged conventional economic theory and policy.

Meanwhile, an intrepid band of economists have continued to contribute research that builds upon or helps integrate institutionalist and post-Keynesian insight. Like Commons and Keynes, their work aims to address the practical socioeconomic issues of the day by understanding the institutions and evolution of economic life. In the course of suggesting directions for future research, this section highlights some of their contributions.[21]

Foundations and Methods

Any serious economic paradigm needs secure pre-analytic foundations, and all scholars need useful methods and tools. Institutional economists have long given attention to their foundational preconceptions (about reality, the economy, society, values, and science) and methods—and Wilber and Jameson (1983) incorporated that insight into their PKI. In contrast, most post-Keynesians initially devoted the bulk of their attention to analyzing problems, and not so much to reflecting on foundations and methods (Keller 1983). Over the years, however, methodology (foundations and methods) has become a more integral part of the work of post-Keynesians (see, for example, Dow 2001). Staying on top of methodological developments in post-Keynesianism as well as institutionalism must be one aspect of the future work undertaken by economists within PKI.

Of course, keeping abreast is not enough: Advancing PKI requires assimilating, in ways that fortify its own methodology, the insights of institutionalism, post-Keynesianism, and beyond. That is already happening. Examples include the work of Tauheed (2011), Fernández-Huerga (2008), and Brazelton (2011). Tauheed (2011) proposes an innovative approach to policy deliberation that combines elements from post-Keynesian system dynamics with a heuristic framework of analysis from institutionalism.[22] Fernández-Huerga (2008) draws on neurosciences and psychology to highlight the influence of habits and social institutions upon human cognition, reasoning, and decision-making, and to outline a PKI model of human economic behavior that is more realistic than the model implicit in conventional economics.[23] Brazelton (2011), motivated by an interest in how PKI can shed more light on financial crises, looks at sociological research on how memories are determined and finds that societal influences shape our recollections, which, in turn, affect how we respond to economic events.[24] PKI can and should continue to learn from other traditions and disciplines in the years ahead.

Financial Instability

PKI must continue to apply the financial instability hypothesis. As discussed previously, economists interested in PKI have given attention to Minsky's contributions on financial instability since the mid 1980s, and attention to those contributions has been especially strong during periods of financial-market turmoil. Focusing on the USA, examples of such research include Wray (2002, 2008) and Whalen (2007). Others, such as McClintock (1996) and Wolfson (2002), have taken an international perspective. Still others, including Kregel (2000), Levy-Orlik (in Tavasci and Toporowski 2010: 155–167), and Girón (2018), have applied this approach to other countries and regions. The Minsky analysis has proven its usefulness and offers a stark contrast to the efficient-markets approach of the economics mainstream, which is incapable of exploring financial panics and crises (see Buiter 2009).

One direction for future research is to further incorporate households and income inequality into analyses of financial instability. Such work is suggested by Todorova (2009a), who integrates households into the post-Keynesian and institutionalist monetary theory of production, and is undertaken by Brown (2008) in an analysis of the US household debt surge prior to the Great Recession. In addition, Kaboub et al. (2010) stress that although mortgage-related debt played a major role in the Great Recession, the downturn was worsened by significant US income inequality and high levels of other forms of consumer indebtedness (such as credit card debt), both of which can be traced in large part to decades of wage stagnation. Scott and Pressman (2019) are currently pursuing important research in this direction by building on the FIH to explore changes in household financial instability since the 1980s. It is hoped that others will also bring the household sector—and rising inequality across households—into the instability picture.[25]

Examinations of financial instability that do not rely on Minsky's framework should also be encouraged. Jameson (2004), for example, studies Ecuador's dollarization decision by giving attention to institutional evolution, economic power, and other concepts drawn from the foundations of PKI. Similarly, Harvey (2006; 2012) highlights the psychological and institutional forces influencing exchange rates and then builds on that work to explore exchange rate behavior during the Great Recession, demonstrating that currency swings made matters worse. Such PKI research does not merely advance economic understanding; it also can inspire other innovative analyses of instability.

Money Manager Capitalism

Prior to Minsky's address upon receipt of AFEE's Veblen-Commons Award, few people were aware of his theory of capitalist development, which had been presented mostly in book chapters and working papers. But that address and an article published posthumously (Minsky and Whalen 1996–1997) drew attention to the theory, as did a flurry of publications including:

- Whalen (1997), which focuses on how money manager capitalism and the spread of worker insecurity—the end of "shared prosperity"—are two sides of the same coin;
- Whalen (2001), which fleshes out the theory's stages and their evolution;
- Van Lear (2001), which finds that widespread institutional equity ownership inhibits economic growth;
- Van Lear (2002), which argues that the economic evolution outlined by Minsky is incompatible with fundamental American principles such as a commitment to liberty, representation, and enterprise;
- Whalen (2002), which examines the technology-driven boom that preceded the dot-com collapse;
- Zalewski (2002), which explores retirement security in the age of money manager capitalism; and
- Whalen (2008b), which updates the interaction between money manager capitalism and worker insecurity in the USA up to the eve of the global financial crisis.

Since the financial crisis that triggered the Great Recession, Minsky's theory of capitalist development—especially its discussion of money manager capitalism—has provided an important PKI framework. Of course, the theory has been used to analyze that crisis in the USA (see, for example, Wray 2009; Whalen 2008c, 2010). But there have been other interesting US-focused analyses as well, including an examination by Cardwell and Todorova (2016) of household agency over stages of US capitalism, and an exploration by Van Lear and Sisk (2010) of similarities between money manager capitalism and the economic stage that preceded the Great Depression.

Economists have also used Minsky's stages of analysis to examine issues beyond the USA. This includes the following: (1) looking across countries (such as Zalewski and Whalen 2010, which investigates inequality and financialization); (2) examining relations among countries (such as Liang 2011, which discusses international capital flows and development in emerging economies); (3) focusing on certain types of countries (such as Ventimiglia and Tavasci, in Tavasci and Toporowski 2010: 168–187, which studies primary commodity-dependent countries), and (4) analyzing problems within geographic regions (such as Correa 2014, which focuses on financial crises in Latin America). The global applicability of Minsky's analysis shows the power of his perceptiveness; and the ability of PKI to incorporate his insight into its framework is a key reason why Correa (2014: 323) writes: "To understand what really happens during financial crises and the changes in overall economic activity that they produce, a post-Keynesian institutionalist theoretical approach is essential." Looking at various parts of the world (and at the dynamic interplay among countries) through the lens provided by this element of PKI will certainly offer a vibrant research direction for years to come.

Since societies are "evolutionary beasts" (Minsky 1993: 104), Minsky's analysis of stages will always need updating and reevaluating. Such work should probably give special attention to the evolution of finance (for illustrative starting points, see Rima 2002; Nesvetailova 2015; Baranes and Hake 2018) and intangible property (see Atkinson 2010). Economists working with this aspect of the PKI tradition should also explore research on financialization, now being conducted by social scientists in various fields (Palley 2007). It is clear that scholarship on financialization dovetails with the study of money manager capitalism and that the two terms can in many cases be used interchangeably (Whalen 2017; Jo and Henry 2015).[26]

Labor Markets and Pricing

As mentioned above, Brazelton (1981) helped motivate the creation of PKI by pointing out that institutionalists and post-Keynesians shared an interest in real-world wage and price determination. Eichner (1985, 1987) was an important contributor to the study of labor markets and pricing at the intersection of institutionalism and post-Keynesianism, but in the wake of Eichner's death in 1988 attention to macroeconomic issues have often overshadowed further development of PKI in these areas. Since Eichner, there has been some work on labor markets and pricing, but more must be done going forward.

In the realm of labor markets, Seccareccia (1991) draws on Eichner and others (including important contributions found in Piore 1979) to outline an explicitly post-Keynesian institutionalist perspective. The result is a view highlighting the segmented and stratified nature of real-world labor markets.

Seccareccia (1991:47–48) also stresses that workers are "molded by their social and institutional environments," and that social norms and customary practices play critical roles in wage determination.

A view similar to that of Seccareccia is presented by Prasch (2004: 151), who points additionally to the significance of "job clusters" and "wage contours," concepts developed many decades ago by labor economists associated with the interdisciplinary field of industrial relations. Over the past few decades, however, employers have increasingly treated labor as a spot-market commodity—a trend explored by Cappelli et al. (1997) and other industrial-relations scholars.[27] Still, by looking toward researchers associated with industrial relations, Prasch was on the right track. In the years ahead, PKI must stay in touch with industrial-relations scholars and others conducting interdisciplinary research on employment relations. An important place to start is Weller (2015), which looks at the growing role of finance in labor relations—an examination that, in large part, represents an exploration of financialization (money manager capitalism) and its connection to the spread of worker insecurity.[28]

Turning to pricing, we find that Fred Lee built on Eichner's work to produce what Lee (1996) called an empirically grounded pricing model. He saw the model as broadly consistent with elements of post-Keynesian and institutional economics, but also aimed to advance the literature. Rather than focus on a single pricing procedure, Lee emphasized that firms use a variety of types of administered pricing methods, including markup, normal cost, and target rate of return pricing (Lee 1996: 88). The actual procedures (and the size of any associated profit markups) depend on enterprise goals, which, in turn, depend on social values. Thus, Lee argued that the evolution of capitalism in the twenty-first century will reflect the outcome of the clash of those values, especially across nations. The picture that emerges from Lee's work is that it is not just labor markets that are "social" markets—so too are product markets. This is a key insight of PKI, and will remain crucial to future work.

In addition to the work of Lee, economists interested in advancing pricing from the perspective of PKI will want to look at Nichols et al. (2006) and Jo (2016). Nichols and his colleagues build on PKI to fashion an economic model incorporating the circular and cumulative nature of administrative pricing structures. Jo, delivering the AFEE presidential address in place of Lee (who died before fulfilling that obligation himself), stresses that price and quantity decisions are made separately within enterprises before goods are sold. As a result, the role of the price mechanism "is not to coordinate supply and demand, but to reproduce the going concern by generating monetary profits" (Jo 2016: 340). Pricing is still important as a strategic business decision (along with decisions about investment, finance, and production), but that is different from seeing prices as the economy's coordinating mechanism or balancing wheel. Institutions—a broad array of them—play that role.[29]

Public Policy

Research related to public policy, is, of course central to the work of PKI. In the 1990s, Minsky and Whalen (1996–1997) offered a policy agenda that they envisioned as providing the institutional prerequisites for successful capitalism in the age of money managers. But, as mentioned at the outset of this article, policy must evolve with an ever-changing economy. "There is no magic economic bullet; no single program or particular reform that will set things right forever" (Minsky 1986: 293).

In response to the Great Recession, a number of economists have drawn on key elements of PKI to address economic policy issues.[30] For example, Wray (2008) and Whalen (in Tavasci and Toporowski 2010) outlined agendas for sustained recovery and reform; Tymoigne (2007, 2011) stressed the need for supervision and regulation of financial institutions; Todorova (2009b) explored what makes government bailouts of financial institutions acceptable as well as what might make such bailouts obsolete; Zalewski (2012) looked at the US foreclosure crisis as a failure of the federal government to fulfill its role of lender of last resort; and Kaboub (2011) highlighted the need for government to serve as employer of last resort. More recently, Zalewski (2018) called for policies that promote greater economic security as a means of addressing economic inequality and growing middle-class anxiety; and Tcherneva (2018) outlined the contours of a job guarantee proposal for the USA.[31]

Looking ahead, there will certainly be unforeseen challenges demanding policy research. There will also be a perennial need for PKI to detect financial fragility and find ways to regulate finance in pursuit of more broadly shared prosperity. In addition, there will be the related need to conduct policy research and analysis on the ongoing problems of inequality and worker insecurity. Indeed, these are global problems, warranting the attention of economists worldwide (International Labour Organization 2019a, b; Alvaredo et al. 2018). Moreover, scholars in all fields must find ways to help address the serious threat of global warming (United Nations 2018).[32]

CONCLUSION: "STILL IT MOVES"

PKI has existed only since the 1980s. When considered against the backdrop of centuries of economic thought, it is a new paradigm. Its adherents and contributors usually operate with extraordinarily limited resources and mostly on the margins of the economics profession.

Nevertheless, post-Keynesian institutionalists have a solid methodological foundation, powerful analytical elements, a strong record of constructive work on theory and policy, and a full research agenda for the years ahead.

Their foundation is rooted in a century of institutionalist scholarship, supplemented increasingly by overlapping methodological research conducted by post-Keynesians, and, more recently, by those who identify as post-Keynesian institutionalists. Their economic analyses draw not only on a monetary theory of production, extensive studies of labor market institutions, and an empirically grounded approach to administered prices, but also on tools and theories for analyzing endogenously generated business cycles, financial instability, and capitalist development. While conventional economists were unprepared for the global financial crisis of 2007, it was foreshadowed in the work of post-Keynesian institutionalists, who were quick to offer constructive policy recommendations aimed at recovery and reform, as well as a policy agenda for addressing the longer-term problems of increasing economic inequality and worker insecurity.

The post-Keynesian institutionalist research agenda outlined in this article calls for further work on methodology, microeconomics, macroeconomics, and global issues. PKI is a branch of institutional economics that has always aimed to be "relevant to the problems of the times" (Hamilton 1919: 318). New problems will always emerge, requiring new analyses, new institutional adjustments, and new public policies. After all, what Galileo said of the Earth, PKI says about the economy, "Still it moves."

In the past half-century, institutional economists' engagement with post-Keynesianism has helped energize the institutionalist tradition. In the early 1980s, original institutionalism was in decline.[33] The bulk of the economics profession ignored the work of institutionalists, and the number of graduate programs offering courses with original institutionalist content was small and decreasing rapidly. Even worse, students determined to study institutionalism found arcane vocabulary, deep factional divides, and interminable internal debates centering most often on matters of economic methodology.[34] Peterson, Dillard, Eichner, Minsky, and others exploring the common ground of institutionalism and post-Keynesianism offered a different focus: one centered much more directly on pressing real-world problems such as economic instability, inflation, and unemployment.

Those intensely problem-oriented economists inspired a generation of economists (including, for example, Lee, Harvey, Phillips, Prasch, Whalen, and Wray) to become comfortable with institutionalism and post-Keynesianism. As a result, by the end of the 1990s, work involving financial instability and other research at the crossroads of institutionalism and post-Keynesianism had become widely recognized as major features of contemporary institutional economics (O'Hara and Waller 1999). Moreover, that generation's scholarship has, in turn, inspired many others (such as Kaboub, Liang, Tcherneva, and Todorova) to become economists and contribute to PKI, and the study of money manager capitalism (financialization) has become an important element of that scholarship and institutionalism overall. While institutionalism remains a small part of the economics profession, PKI has given the institutionalist tradition renewed vigor.

To be sure, some define institutional economics differently than I have in this article. At one extreme is Gruchy (1987), who viewed institutionalism in such a narrow manner that he insisted it must remain independent from post-Keynesianism. At the other extreme is Chavance (2009), who identifies a range of "families" of institutional economics including original institutionalism, Austrian economics and "ordoliberalism," new institutional economics, regulation theory, and the economics of conventions.[35] Between those extremes is the definition of institutionalism used in this article: a definition that reflects my understanding of institutionalism as practiced, primarily in the USA, by most economists associated with AFEE. It is beyond the scope of the present essay to present a comparative evaluation of different types of institutionalism.[36]

It is also beyond the scope of this article to assess PKI relative to other types of scholarship produced under the post-Keynesian label. As indicated above, post-Keynesianism is recognized as having various strands. Moreover, economists disagree on how to best draw from those strands to engage in constructive economic analyses (Lavoie 2014: 41–47; King 2002). The modest aim of this article has been to report on the sort of work that economists calling themselves post-Keynesian institutionalists have either built upon or produced. It remains for others to select the yardstick of their choice and appraise PKI relative to other types of post-Keynesianism. However, the present essay should make such assessments easier by having provided an outline of PKI.[37]

Finally, readers are invited to take this essay as the starting point for a dialog on PKI's contours and content. I hope especially for international participation in the further shaping of PKI. Although the tradition began primarily as a movement within the USA, it has shown itself to have much wider relevance. But PKI also has much to learn; and various intellectual traditions that originated outside the USA (such as critical realism and regulation theory) or have become well established internationally (such as industrial ecology) feature important elements that should be better understood by post-Keynesian institutionalists. Given that markets and enterprises are global in scope, national economies are globally interconnected, and humanity's greatest threats are worldwide, it is clear that PKI must also be robustly international.

NOTES

1. For a brief introduction to original institutional economics, see Mayhew (2018).
2. For more on Commons and Keynes, see Whalen (2008a). For elements in Keynes and the pioneering institutionalism of Veblen and Mitchell that also foreshadow emergence of PKI, see Dillard (1987a).

3. Reaction of institutionalists to *The General Theory* should be viewed in the context of their own macroeconomic research, which anticipated elements of the book (such as the multiplier analysis), but also highlighted matters that Keynes excluded (Rutherford and Desroches 2008).
4. Attention to historical time (in contrast with the logical time in neoclassical economics) highlights the fact that "past events influence current outcomes" (Setterfield 2001, 97) and provides room for considering phenomena such as path dependence, hysteresis, and cumulative causation.
5. The post-Keynesians that Brazelton (1981: 541, n. 1) had in mind were economists such as "Keynes, Weintraub, Minsky, Davidson, and (Daniel R.) Fusfeld, [who] stress uncertainty and [economic] instability".
6. According to Keller (1983, 1089), "[Post-Keynesians] have interpreted and expanded upon Keynes's revolutionary new way of analyzing real world economic problems. The group of post-Keynesians whose analysis is most compatible with institutionalism corresponds to what Paul Davidson calls center and center-left Keynesianism. The representatives of this group include P. Davidson, A. Eichner, J. Kregel, H. Minsky, J. Robinson, G. Shackle, S. Weintraub, and P. Wells".
7. Marshall (1983) did not elaborate on his call to action, except to suggest that achieving and sustaining prosperity require institutions to supplement and channel market behavior.
8. Wilber and Jameson (1983: 151) write that they chose the label "Post-Keynesian Institutionalism" because the roots of their approach "are in Keynes and in the American Institutionalists." They also explain that they find "the key to Keynes" in his belief that the economy is inherently prone to booms and busts (Wilber and Jameson 1983: 273, n. 11). Eichner and Robinson are among the post-Keynesians cited most often in *An Inquiry into the Poverty of Economics*.
9. Another economist who could—and did—bring together institutionalists and post-Keynesians in the 1980s was Alfred Eichner (1985). In fact, when he died suddenly in 1988, Eichner was attempting to forge a synthesis of institutionalism and post-Keynesianism in the realms of both microeconomics and macroeconomics. If Eichner had been able to continue his research agenda, it is likely he would have become a leading contributor to PKI.
10. Some other prominent institutionalist contributors of that era, such as Peterson and Dillard, have already been mentioned above.
11. A prominent non-American contributor to this strand was Robinson, especially by means of work produced late in her career; see, for example, Robinson (1980).
12. One possible reason for the limited influence of these two strands on PKI is that they have not been as well known in the USA, where PKI first emerged.
13. In this section and the one that follows, I discuss the research of various economists working at that intersection. Where possible, I will highlight distinctly post-Keynesian or institutionalist contributions and their complementarities, but because the traditions overlap so heavily (as Niggle (2006) also recognized) most of the research discussed has been done by economists comfortable with both labels or with just PKI.
14. In addition to the strands identified by Hamouda and Harcourt, Lavoie (2014: 41) adds the institutionalist strand and another strand rooted in the work of Nicholas Kaldor. Like the Kaleckian and Sraffian strands, the Kaldorian strand has not played a large role in PKI.
15. For the full list of contributors and sources of inspiration, see Lavoie (2014, 43).

16. This section draws on Whalen (2013), which offers more detail on each of the elements discussed here.
17. At the heart of the Wall Street paradigm is the monetary theory of production (mentioned above) that Dillard highlighted in his research.
18. Veblen, Commons, and Mitchell had cycle views similar to that of Minsky; see, for example, Dillard (1987b) and Whalen (1993).
19. Commons had a similar analysis of capitalist development; see Atkinson and Whalen (2011).
20. This perspective on the role of government has been central to institutionalism from its inception (for an excellent statement, see Samuels 1989); overlapping post-Keynesian views have been expressed on numerous occasions (see, for example, Eichner 1979: 165–184; Pressman 2001).
21. Nearly all of the authors cited below consider themselves post-Keynesian institutionalists or are comfortable in both the institutionalist and post-Keynesian camps.
22. Tauheed also mentions the usefulness of "stock-flow consistent modeling," an approach associated with post-Keynesian Wynne Godley, but traceable to institutionalist Morris Copeland's flow-of-funds analysis. For more on such modeling, see Lavoie and Zezza (2012).
23. In a more recent work, Fernández-Huerga (2013) builds on his human behavior research to produce a post-Keynesian institutionalist alternative to the neoclassical conception of the market.
24. See also Brazleton (2005). In addition, Brazelton and Whalen (2011) find insight relevant to PKI in psychology and behavioral economics.
25. For additional PKI explorations of inequality, consumer and household indebtedness, economic insecurity, and financial instability, see Tymoigne (2007), Weller and Sabatini (2007); Galbraith (2012); and Wunder (2012). Also, see Todorova (2014, 2016) for examinations of gender and other culturally constructed categories as they relate to consumption and production.
26. Analyses of PKI should also strive to better integrate Minsky's approaches to financial instability and capitalist development, thereby pushing such research still further in the direction (mentioned earlier) envisioned by Dillard (1980, 271).
27. It should come as no surprise that such scholars, at least in the USA, often trace their scholarship to Commons, a pioneer in the study of labor and industrial relations.
28. Economists interested in the labor market from the vantage point of PKI should also look at Fernández-Huerga et al. (2017).
29. Commenting on a draft of this article, one reader observed the absence of a discussion of others who have worked on pricing, including Kalecki, Marc Lavoie, Adrian Wood, and Geoffrey Harcourt. Unfortunately, such scholarship—tied most closely to strands of post-Keynesianism beyond the Keynes camp— is yet to be incorporated into most PKI, although it is reflected in Lee's research. Lavoie (2001, 2014) provides a logical starting point for post-Keynesian institutionalists and others seeking to further explore that wider literature.
30. This is not to suggest that such work did not precede the Great Recession; see, for example, Phillips (1997) on the need to rethink bank examinations; Whalen and Wenger (2002) on the need to shore up automatic stabilizers; Zalewski (2003) on using tax incentives to maximize social equity, and Kaboub (2007) on planning for full employment.
31. See also Tcherneva (2011) and, for discussions of policy beyond the USA, see, for example, Tavasci and Toporowski (2010).

32. Of course, the preceding is by no means an exhaustive research agenda. For example, some other issues worth examining in the years ahead are: (1) the role that functional finance should play in PKI (for one view, see Todorova 2013); (2) the relationship between PKI and "modern monetary theory" (Nesiba 2013); and (3) the concern raised by Galbraith (2008) that the dominant feature of contemporary American capitalism is predation, not competition, class struggle, or middle-class striving—and that agents of a "predator class" now control the US government.
33. In fact, according to Rutherford (2001), that decline began in the 1940s.
34. As a graduate student in that period, I recall reading an essay by Piore (1983) that criticized Marxist scholarship for involving too many quarrels that seemed far removed from important contemporary issues. According to Piore (1983: 253), even more frustrating was that "to know where one stood [regarding these quarrels], to know even whether one cares about them in the first place, one would have to resolve the intellectual puzzles which one wants the paradigm and its theoretical constructs for in the first place". Piore's words about Marxism matched how I often felt about institutionalism.
35. Chavance's new institutional economics encompasses not just scholarship in the tradition of Oliver Williamson and Douglass North, but also the work, based in game theory, of Masahiko Aoki and Avner Greif. Also, the ordoliberalism he examines is a German tradition that views the state as the guardian of competitive order, while the economics of conventions is a French tradition on the border of economics and sociology.
36. Scholars identifying with original institutionalism have written much on its relationship to the new institutionalism. For a recent contribution, see Spithoven (2019).
37. I also leave it for others to engage in a thorough comparison of what I call post-Keynesian institutionalism and what Hodgson (1989) and Philip Arestis (1996) describe as post-Keynesianism. All three of us envision some fusion of institutionalism and post-Keynesianism, but our aims are distinct. Mine has been to trace an existing institutionalist research tradition that has for decades drawn mainly on the common ground of institutionalism and Keynes. Hodgson aimed to identify some ideas long associated with institutionalism (including habits, norms, conventions, and cumulative causation) that he thought economists could use to construct a foundation for post-Keynesian theory. Arestis pursued the ambitious aim of providing "a comprehensive survey of post-Keynesian economics" (Arestis 1996: 111)—on methodology, theory, and policy—drawing on three traditions: (1) Alfred Marshall and Keynes; (2) Robinson and Kalecki; and (3) Veblen and other original institutionalists.

REFERENCES

Alvaredo F, Chancel L, Piketty T, Saez, E, Zucman G (2018) World inequality report 2018. World Inequality Lab. http://www.wid.world. Accessed 14 Oct 2019

Arestis P (1996) Post-Keynesian economics: towards coherence. Camb J Econ 20:111–135 Atkinson G (2010) The legal foundations of financial capitalism. J Econ Issue 44:289–299

Atkinson G, Oleson T (1998) Commons and Keynes: their assault on laissez faire. J Econ Issue 32:1019–1030

Atkinson G, Whalen CJ (2011) Futurity: cornerstone of post-Keynesian institutionalism. In: Whalen CJ (ed) Financial instability and economic security after the Great Recession. Edward Elgar, Cheltenham, pp 53–74
Baranes AI, Hake ER (2018) The institutionalist theory of capital in the modern business enterprise: appropriation and financialization. J Econ Issue 52(2):430–437
Barbera R (2009) The cost of capitalism. McGraw Hill, New York
Berle AA, Means GC (1932) The modern corporation and private property. Macmillan, New York
Brazelton WR (1981) Post Keynesian economics: an institutional compatibility? J Econ Issue 15:531–542
Brazelton WR (2011) Neuroscience, psychology, sociology with relevance to economic analysis. In: University of Missouri, Kansas City, Working paper, prepared for Association for Institutional Thought annual meeting
Brazelton WR, Whalen CJ (2011) Towards a synthesis of institutional and post Keynesian economics. In: Whalen CJ (ed) Financial instability and economic security after the Great Recession. Edward Elgar, Cheltenham, pp 28–52
Brazleton WR (2005) Selected theories of the business cycle in terms of "econsochology". J Econ Issue 39:527–533
Brown C (2008) Inequality, consumer spending and the saving puzzle. Edward Elgar, Cheltenham
Buiter W (2009) The unfortunate uselessness of most "state of the art" academic monetary economics. http://www.voxeu.org/index.php?q=node/3210 (6 March). Accessed 17 Feb 2019
Cappelli P, Bassi L, Katz H, Knoke D, Osterman P, Useem M (1997) Change at work. Oxford University Press, New York
Cardwell L, Todorova Z (2016) Evolution of US household agency over stages of capitalism. J Econ Issue 50:542–548
Chavance B (2009) Institutional economics. Routledge, New York
Commons JR (1934) Institutional economics: its place in political economy. Macmillan, New York
Correa E (2014) Institutional changes in financial crises: lessons from Latin America. J Econ Issue 48:323–330
Dillard D (1980) A monetary theory of production: Keynes and the institutionalists. J Econ Issue 14:255–273
Dillard D (1987a) The evolutionary economics of a monetary economy. J Econ Issue 21:575–585
Dillard D (1987b) Money as an institution of capitalism. J Econ Issue 21:1623–1647
Dow S (2001) Post Keynesian methodology. In: Holt RPF, Pressman S (eds) A new guide to post keynesian economics. Routledge, New York, pp 11–20
Dugger WM (1996) Redefining economics: from market allocation to social provisioning. In: Whalen CJ (ed) Political economy for the 21st century: contemporary views on the trend of economics. ME Sharpe, Armonk, pp 31–43
Eichner AS (1979) A guide to post Keynesian economics. M.E. Sharpe, White Plains
Eichner AS (1985) Toward a new economics: essays in post-Keynesian and institutionalist theory. ME Sharpe, Armonk
Eichner AS (1987) Prices and pricing. J Econ Issue 21:1555–1584
Fazzari SM, Minsky HP (1984) Domestic monetary policy. J Econ Issue 18:101–116
Fernández-Huerga E (2008) The economic behavior of human beings: the institutional/post-Keynesian model. J Econ Issue 43:709–726

Fernández-Huerga E (2013) The market concept: a characterization from Institutional and post-Keynesian economics. Am J Econ Sociol 72:361–385

Fernández-Huerga E, García-Arias J, Salvador A (2017) Labor supply: toward the construction of an alternative conception from post Keynesian and institutional economics. J Post Keynesian Econ 40:576–599

Galbraith JK (1977) The bimodal image of the modern economy. J Econ Issue 11:189–200

Galbraith JK (2008) The predator state. Free Press, New York

Galbraith JK (2012) Inequality and instability. Oxford University Press, New York

Girón A (2018) Is China living a Minsky moment? J Econ Issue 52:445–454

Gruchy AG (1969) Neoinstitutionalism and the economics of dissent. J Econ Issues 3:3–17

Gruchy AG (1987) The reconstruction of economics. Greenwood Press, Westport

Hamilton WH (1919) The institutional approach to economic theory. Am Econ Rev 9:309–318

Hamouda OF, Harcourt GC (1988) Post Keynesianism: from confusion to coherence. Bull Econ Res 40:1–33

Harvey JT (2006) Psychological and institutional forces and the determination of exchange rates. J Econ Issue 40:153–170

Harvey JT (2012) Exchange rate behavior during the Great Recession. J Econ Issue 46:313–322

Hodgson G (1989) Post-Keynesianism and institutionalism: the missing link. In: Pheby J (ed) New directions in post-Keynesian economics. Edward Elgar, Aldershot, pp 94–123

International Labour Organization (2019a) Work for a brighter future. Global Commission on the Future of Work, ILO, Geneva

International Labour Organization (2019b) World employment social outlook: trends 2019. ILO, Geneva

Jameson KP (2004) Dollarization in Ecuador: a post-Keynesian institutionalist analysis. Department of Economics working paper, no. 2004-05, University of Utah

Jo TH (2016) What if there are no conventional price mechanisms? J Econ Issue 50:327–344

Jo TH, Henry JF (2015) The business enterprise in the age of money manager capitalism. J Econ Issue 49:23–46

Kaboub F (2007) Institutional adjustment planning for full employment. J Econ Issue 41:495–502

Kaboub F (2011) Understanding and preventing financial instability: post-Keynesian institutionalism and government as employer of last resort. In: Whalen CJ (ed) Financial instability and economic security after the Great Recession. Edward Elgar, Cheltenham, pp 73–90

Kaboub F, Todorova Z, Fernandez L (2010) Inequality-led financial instability: a Minskian structural analysis of the subprime crisis. Int J Pol Econ 39:3–27

Keller RR (1983) Keynesian and institutional economics: compatibility and complementarity? J Econ Issue 17:1087–1095

Keynes JM (1936) The general theory of employment, interest, and money. Macmillan, London

King JE (2002) A history of post Keynesian economics since 1936. Edward Elgar, Cheltenham

Kregel JA (2000) Yes "IT" happened again: the Minsky crisis in Asia. In: Bellofiore R, Piero F (eds) Financial Keynesianism and market instability. Edward Elgar, Cheltenham, pp 194–212
Lahart J (2007) In time of tumult, obscure economist gains currency. Wall St J 18:A1
Lavoie M (2001) Pricing. In: Holt RPF, Pressman S (eds) A new guide to post Keynesian economics. Routledge, London, pp 21–31
Lavoie M (2014) Post-Keynesian economics: new foundations. Edward Elgar, Cheltenham
Lavoie M, Zezza G (eds) (2012) The stock-flow consistent approach: selected writings of Wynne Godley. Palgrave Macmillan, Basingstoke
Lee FS (1996) Pricing and the business enterprise. In: Whalen CJ (ed) Political economy for the 21st century: contemporary views on the trend of economics. ME Sharpe, Armonk, pp 87–99
Lewitt ME (2010) The death of capital. Wiley, Hoboken
Liang Y (2011) Money-manager capitalism, capital flows, and development in emerging economies: a post-Keynesian institutionalist analysis. In: Whalen CJ (ed) Financial instability and economic security after the Great Recession. Edward Elgar, Cheltenham, pp 179–201
Marshall R (1983) Comments on the institutionalist view of Reaganomics. J Econ Issue 17:503–506
Mayhew A (2018) An introduction to institutional economics: tools for understanding evolving economies. Am Econ 63:3–17
McClintock B (1996) International financial instability and the financial derivatives market. J Econ Issue 30:13–33
Minsky HP (1969) Private sector asset management and the effectiveness of monetary policy: theory and practice. J Financ 24:223–228
Minsky HP (1975) John Maynard Keynes. Columbia University Press, New York
Minsky HP (1982) Can "It" Happen Again? essays in instability and finance. ME Sharpe, Armonk
Minsky HP (1985) Beginnings. Banca Nazionale Del Lavoro Quart Rev 38:211–221
Minsky HP (1986) Stabilizing an unstable economy. Yale University Press, New Haven
Minsky HP (1990) Schumpeter: finance and evolution. In: Heertje A, Perlman M (eds) Evolving technology and market structure. University of Michigan Press, Ann Arbor, pp 51–74
Minsky HP (1993) Schumpeter and finance. In: Biasco S, Roncaglia A, Salvati M (eds) Markets and institutions in economic development. St. Martin's, New York, pp 103–115
Minsky HP (1996a) Foreword. In: Whalen CJ (ed) Political economy for the 21st century: contemporary views on the trend of economics. ME Sharpe, Armonk, pp xi–xiii
Minsky HP (1996b) Uncertainty and the institutional structure of capitalist economies. J Econ Issue 30:357–368
Minsky HP, Whalen CJ (1996–1997) Economic insecurity and the institutional prerequisites of successful capitalism. J Post Keynesian Econ 19:155–170
Nesiba RF (2013) Do Institutionalists and post-Keynesians share a common approach to modern monetary theory? Eur J Econ Econ Policies Interv 10:44–60
Nesvetailova A (2015) A crisis of the overcrowded future: shadow banking and the political economy of financial innovation. New Pol Econ 20:431–453
Nichols M, Pavlov O, Radzicki MJ (2006) The circular and cumulative structure of administered pricing. J Econ Issue 40:517–526

Niggle C (2006) Evolutionary Keynesianism: a synthesis of institutionalist and post Keynesian macroeconomics. J Econ Issue 40:405–412
O'Hara PA, Waller W (1999) Institutional political economy: major contemporary themes. In: O'Hara PA (ed) Encyclopedia of political economy, vol 2. Routledge, New York, pp 528–532
Palley T (2007) Financialization: what it is and why it matters. Political Economy Research Institute working paper, no. 153, University of Massachusetts, Amherst
Papadimitriou DP, Wray LR (1997) The institutional prerequisites for successful capitalism. J Econ Issue 31:493–500
Peterson WC (1977) Institutionalism, Keynes and the real world. J Econ Issue 11:201–221
Peterson WC (1987) Macroeconomic theory and policy in an institutionalist perspective. J Econ Issue 21:1587–1621
Phillips RJ (1997) Rethinking bank examinations: a Minsky approach. J Econ Issue 31:509–516
Piore MJ (ed) (1979) Unemployment and inflation: institutionalist and structuralist views. ME Sharpe, White Plains
Piore MJ (1983) Labor market segmentation: to what paradigm does it belong? Am Econ Rev 73:249–253
Prasch R (2004) How is labor distinct from broccoli? Some unique characteristics of labor and their importance for economic analysis and policy. In: Champlin DP, Knoedler JT (eds) The institutionalist tradition in labor economics. ME Sharpe, Armonk, pp 146–158
Pressman S (2001) The role of the state and the state budget. In: Holt RPF, Pressman S (eds) A new guide to post Keynesian economics. Routledge, London, pp 102–113
Rima IH (2002) Venture capitalist financing: contemporary foundations for Minsky's "Wall Street" perspective. J Econ Issue 36:407–414
Robinson J (1980) Time in economic theory. Kyklos 33:219–229
Rutherford M (2001) Institutional economics: then and now. J Econ Perspect 15:173–194
Rutherford M, Desroches CT (2008) The institutionalist reaction to Keynesian economics. J Hist Econ Thought 30:29–48
Samuels WJ (1989) Some fundamentals of the economic role of government. In: Samuels WJ (ed) fundamentals of the economic role of government. Greenwood Press, Westport, pp 167–172
Scott RH, Pressman S (2019) Financially unstable households. J Econ Issue 53:523–531
Seccareccia M (1991) An alternative to labour-market orthodoxy: the post-Keynesian/institutionalist policy view. Rev Polit Econ 3:43–61
Setterfield M (2001) Macrodynamics. A new guide to post Keynesian economics. Routledge, London, pp 92–101
Spithoven A (2019) Similarities and dissimilarities between original institutional economics and new institutional economics. J Econ Issue 53:440–447
Summers LH (2011) Conversation on new economic thinking. http://ineteconomics.org/people/participants/larry-summers (4 April). Accessed 6 Apr 2012
Tauheed L (2011) A proposed methodological synthesis of post-Keynesian and institutional economics. J Econ Issue 45:819–838
Tavasci D, Toporowski J (2010) Minsky, crisis and development. Palgrave Macmillan, Basingstoke
Tcherneva PR (2011) The case for labor demand targeting. J Econ Issue 45:401–410
Tcherneva PR (2018) The job guarantee: design, jobs, and implementation. Levy Economics Institute of Bard College working paper, no. 902

Todorova Z (2009a) Money and households in a capitalist economy: a gendered post Keynesian—institutional analysis. Edward Elgar, Cheltenham
Todorova Z (2009b) What makes a bailout acceptable? J Econ Issue 43:319–325
Todorova Z (2013) Connecting social provisioning and functional finance in a post-Keynesian–institutional analysis of the public sector. Eur J Econ Econ Policies Interv 10:61–75
Todorova Z (2014) Consumption as a social process. J Econ Issue 48:663–678
Todorova Z (2016) A further Veblenian articulation of a monetary theory of production. In: Jo TH, Lee FS (eds) Marx, Veblen, and the foundations of heterodox economics: essays in honor of John F. Henry. Routledge, New York, pp 102–122
Tymoigne E (2007) A hard-nosed look at worsening US household finance. Challenge 50:88–111
Tymoigne (2011) Financial stability, regulator buffers and economic growth after the Great Recession. In: Whalen CJ (ed) Financial instability and economic security after the Great Recession. Edward Elgar, Cheltenham, pp 114–140
United Nations (2018) Global warming of 15° C: summary for policymakers. Intergovernmental Panel on Climate Change, Geneva
Van Lear W (2001) Macroeconomic implications of institutional equity ownership. Challenge 44:108–117
Van Lear W (2002) A populist challenge to corporate capitalism. World Scientific, Singapore
Van Lear W, Sisk J (2010) Financial crisis and economic stability: a comparison between finance capitalism and money manager capitalism. J Econ Issue 44:779–793
Weller CE (ed) (2015) Inequality, uncertainty, and opportunity: the varied and growing role of finance in labor relations. Labor and Employment Relations Association, Champaign
Weller CE, Sabatini K (2007) The financial vulnerability of families. Challenge 50:72–98
Whalen CJ (1993) Saving capitalism by making it good: the monetary economics of John R. Commons. J Econ Issue 27:1155–1179
Whalen CJ (1997) Money-manager capitalism and the end of shared prosperity. J Econ Issue 31:517–525
Whalen CJ (2001) Integrating Schumpeter and Keynes: Hyman Minsky's theory of capitalist development. J Econ Issue 35:805–823
Whalen CJ (2002) Money-manager capitalism: still here but not quite as expected. J Econ Issue 36:401–406
Whalen CJ (2007) The U.S. credit crunch of 2007: a Minsky moment. Public policy brief, no. 92, Levy Economics Institute of Bard College, Annandale-on-Hudson, New York
Whalen CJ (2008a) John R. Commons and John Maynard Keynes on economic history and policy: the 1920s and today. J Econ Issue 43:225–242
Whalen CJ (2008b) Post Keynesian institutionalism and the anxious society. In: Batie SS, Mercuro N (eds) Alternative institutional structures. Routledge, New York, pp 273–299
Whalen CJ (2008c) Understanding the credit crunch as a Minsky moment. Challenge 51:91–109
Whalen CJ (2010) An institutionalist perspective on the global financial crisis. In: Kates S (ed) Macroeconomic theory and its failings. Edward Elgar, Cheltenham, pp 235–259

Whalen CJ (2013) Post-Keynesian Institutionalism after the Great Recession. Eur J Econ Econ Policies Interv 10:12–27
Whalen CJ (2017) Understanding financialization: standing on the shoulders of Minsky. E-Finance 13:45–61
Whalen CJ, Wenger J (2002) Destabilizing an unstable economy. Challenge 45:70–92
Wilber CK, Jameson KP (1983) An inquiry into the poverty of economics. University of Notre Dame Press, Notre Dame
Wolfson MH (2002) Minsky's theory of financial crises in a global context. J Econ Issue 36:392–400
Wray LR (2002) What happened to Goldilocks? A Minskian framework. J Econ Issue 36:383–391
Wray LR (2008) Lessons from the subprime meltdown. Challenge 51:40–68
Wray LR (2009) The rise and fall of money manager capitalism: a Minskian approach. Camb J Econ 33:807–828
Wunder TA (2012) Income distribution and consumption driven growth: how consumption behaviors of the top two income quintiles help to explain the economy. J Econ Issue 46:173–191
Zalewski DA (2002) Retirement insecurity in the age of money manager capitalism. J Econ Issue 36:349–356
Zalewski DA (2003) Corporate objectives: maximizing social versus private equity. J Econ Issue 37:501–508
Zalewski DA (2012) Collective action failures and lenders of last resort: lessons from the US foreclosure crisis. J Econ Issue 46:333–342
Zalewski DA (2018) Uncertainty, control, and Karl Polanyi's protective response. J Econ Issue 52:483–489
Zalewski DA, Whalen CJ (2010) Financialization and income inequality: a post-Keynesian institutionalist analysis. J Econ Issue 44:757–777

24. The post-Keynesian institutionalism of Wallace Peterson

For nearly half a century, Wallace C. Peterson sought to help improve the human condition by analyzing economic institutions and working to advance public understanding of economic issues. In the process, he blazed a trail for post-Keynesian institutionalism (PKI), which builds on the economics of John Maynard Keynes and the institutionalists. I consider Peterson's contributions in three areas: (i) the foundations of economics; (ii) analyses of the U.S. economy; and (iii) discussions of public policy. Peterson's contributions in each area still merit attention and offer lessons for the study of current economic issues.[1]

FOUNDATIONS OF ECONOMICS

In the mid-1970s, Peterson's presidential address to the Association for Evolutionary Economics (AFEE) outlined the foundations of an economics science relevant to the policy challenges of the 1970s and beyond. His address emphasized the following issues: (i) the need to rebuild economics on the common ground shared by institutionalists and Keynes; (ii) the importance of money and finance in a market economy; and (iii) the value of incorporating a multifaceted conception of power into economic analyses (Peterson 1977). Today's PKI rests solidly on these points of emphasis, even as Peterson's attention to power remains worthy of further exploration and extension.

Keynes and Institutionalism

Confronted with the economic problems of the 1970s—high unemployment, high inflation, and increasing economic and financial instability—Peterson (1977) argued that a deeper understanding of the U.S. economy could be achieved by using institutionalism to broaden, rather than renounce, the economics of Keynes. In particular, he envisioned constructing an alternative to conventional Keynesianism on the following core notions:

Reprinted with permission from *Journal of Economic Issues* 50 (2), June 2016, 584–593.

- Uncertainty is an inescapable part of the backdrop of economic life.
- Institutions and power relationships influence human behavior and economic performance.
- Economies change continuously and organically.

From today's vantage point, Peterson's AFEE presidential address seems fairly innocuous, but at the time, it was bold. During the first few decades following the publication of *The General Theory*, many institutionalists took a skeptical view of Keynes and Keynesianism. Indeed, some founders of AFEE were among Keynes's most severe critics (Cavalieri and Almeida 2015). Peterson's address helped change that view and blazed a trail that many have subsequently followed (including Waller 2005 and Whalen 2011).[2]

Money and Finance

Peterson maintained that money and finance are the key institutions of modern capitalism. Their importance stems partly from being at the heart of what distinguishes capitalism from other economic systems. Making money is the central aim under capitalism, Peterson stressed, an objective that does not necessarily require producing goods and services. Sometimes, the surest path to making money involves merely controlling and maintaining the scarcity of things that command a price (Peterson 1977, 210–211).[3]

Moreover, when the path to making money *does* involve production, it can also generate business cycles (Peterson 1977, 211). Drawing on the work of Hyman P. Minsky, Peterson stressed that finance—which precedes production and investment—sets up cash-payment commitments that must be covered by the flow of future income. In the early stages of an economic expansion, those commitments are usually covered and investment expands. However, "when the flow falters, the economy falters" and downturns can be severe in the absence of fiscal and monetary policy intervention (Peterson 1987, 1613).

Power and Economics

Peterson often stressed the need for economics to recognize the important role of power in economic life. In fact, in addition to writing many articles on the subject (for example, Peterson 1974, 1976, 1980, 1989), he edited a research volume to draw attention to the matter in the late 1980s (Peterson 1988). In his works, Peterson consistently emphasized that power is a multifaceted concept, and that the struggle for it and the exercise of it are ubiquitous in economic life.

John Kenneth Galbraith provided the starting point for much of Peterson's thinking about economic power. Drawing on Galbraith, Peterson (1988, ix) argued that, while economists extoll the virtues of markets, people everywhere desire to use some form of power to escape from the "tyranny of the market" and to gain control over their incomes. Peterson also followed Galbraith (as well as Adolf Berle and Daniel Fusfeld) in emphasizing that economic power is made effective through institutions, especially large corporations. In fact, according to Peterson (1989, 381), the largest corporations "have power that in many cases rivals that of the state."[4] In addition, Peterson (1989, 382) assimilated Galbraith's observation that "the state is the prime object of economic power," which means that efforts to acquire economic and political power are intertwined.

Peterson (1980) argued that it was not easy to make generalizations about economic power because its exercise is a discretionary act tempered by (ever-changing) political, economic, cultural, and institutional considerations. Nevertheless, he believed that there was enough evidence for economists to reconsider how prices are determined in a world of large corporations. In particular, Peterson—drawing on the work of Gardiner Means and others—concluded that such corporations have the power to set ("administer") prices somewhat independently of market conditions, and that these firms usually set prices by means of a mark-up formula to achieve a target rate of return. As a result, the prices of goods and services sold by such firms may rise in an economic slump even as output and employment fall. In short, administered prices and target-return pricing are manifestations of market power (Peterson 1988, 168).

Peterson also maintained that corporate concentration was an important source of economic power. Observing both that a few hundred giant firms controlled the bulk of U.S. economic activity and that more than half of the production in almost any industry could be traced to its four largest firms, Peterson (1974, 1976) argued that this concentration was not essential for economic efficiency or for robust innovation. Rather, he concluded that increasing concentration harmed the economy and was a threat to the vitality of small businesses.

The Foundations Today

The foundational elements emphasized by Peterson serve as the basis for today's PKI. Analyses by post-Keynesian institutionalists are rooted in a pre-analytic framework that includes the core notions Peterson laid out in the 1970s (see, for example, Niggle 2006; Tauheed 2011; Whalen 2013). Those analyses also give special attention to money and finance, not only as important influences on spending, but also as key determinants of business cycles and longer-term patterns of economic growth and change (see, for example, Brown 2008; Whalen 2011). In addition, power that is acquired and exerted in the economic and political arenas is an important consideration in the research of post-Keynesian institutionalists (see, for example, Galbraith 2008; Zalewski and Whalen 2010).

In recent years, scholars in the PKI tradition have made considerable progress on synthesizing the methodological foundations of institutionalism and post-Keynesianism, and on tracing real-world monetary and financial developments. However, their progress on exploring power is more difficult to gauge. Peterson would not be surprised, as he recognized significant challenges associated with studying the role of power in economic life. At the same time, he demonstrated that understanding power is essential for understanding the economy. Thus, his attention to power continues to warrant further exploration and extension by today's post-Keynesian institutionalists. For example, PKI would benefit from a fresh look at corporate concentration and its significance in today's global economy.

ANALYSES OF THE U.S. ECONOMY

Peterson's effort to understand the U.S. economy focused on two topics: (i) the problem of stagflation (high inflation and high unemployment) that troubled the U.S. economy from the mid-1960s through the early 1980s and (ii) the silent depression faced by working families since the mid-1970s. While his work on both topics offers lessons for contemporary PKI, his attention to the silent depression remains particularly relevant.

Stagflation

Peterson wrote extensively on the problem of stagflation (see, for example, Peterson 1982, 1987). In particular, he argued that stagflation's inflationary momentum began with demand-pull inflation in the 1960s, but then continued into the 1970s in the form of cost-push inflation, owing in part to money wages rising faster than productivity growth. He also maintained that such momentum could not be broken without either a major recession or institutional changes in wage and price setting. At the same time, Peterson believed that much unemployment would be unaffected by the traditional tools of aggregate demand management and that tackling unemployment required more targeted labor market policies.

Peterson saw stagflation as a prime example of the need to broaden Keynesian economics by digging deep into *The General Theory* and combining Keynes's findings with insight from institutional economics. In Peterson's (1982, 1984) opinion, Keynes anticipated the nexus of money wages, productivity, and inflation in *The General Theory*, but there was more to the story of inflation in the 1970s. In particular, market power and expectations also played important roles. Peterson maintained that the high inflation that persisted until the severe recession of 1981–1982 was fueled by a number of factors: (i) by union power to press for wage gains in excess of productivity gains; (ii) by corporate power to increase prices during an economic downturn; and (iii) by widespread expectations of continued high inflation and rapidly increasing standards of living.

Peterson's analysis of stagflation illustrates how PKI can draw from Keynes and institutionalism to shed light on pressing economic problems. His analysis contributes to our understanding of the 1960s, 1970s, and early 1980s by probing more deeply into the functioning of economic institutions than did analyses offered by that era's competing paradigms (such as monetarism, neoclassical Keynesianism, and new classical economics). Peterson's analysis also underscores the need to appreciate economic change. The economy evolved in important ways throughout the era of stagflation, and Peterson's institutionalist orientation enabled him to examine how that evolution shaped the use of power and affected the inflation process.

Silent Depression

By the early 1990s, memories of stagflation and the deep recession of the early 1980s had begun to fade. But Peterson was troubled by the persistent and widespread stagnation of wages. Looking at various measures of real income for workers and families, he observed that most Americans had seen stagnant or declining earnings since 1973. He called it the silent depression (Peterson 1991, 1993, 1994).

Peterson blamed the silent depression on sagging productivity growth and the disappearance of well-paying manufacturing jobs. He attributed the slowdown of U.S. productivity growth to a long term slide in public infrastructure investment and the allocation of considerable scientific and engineering talent to defense industries during the Cold War. He ascribed the disappearance of manufacturing employment to widespread acceptance of a muddled vision of a post-industrial society, in which high paying service jobs would replace lower paying manufacturing jobs. "Since the end of the 1960s, nearly two million jobs have disappeared from manufacturing," Peterson reported. "Where did those workers go? Not to the high-tech, knowledge based industries where high incomes are the norm ... Lost jobs in manufacturing meant the end of a middle-class standard of life" (Peterson 1993, 5). As he explained in *Silent Depression*, a strong manufacturing sector is complementary to both high paying service employment and to overall economic strength and prosperity (Peterson 1994, 187–196).

Since Peterson's writings on the silent depression, post-Keynesian institutionalists have given considerable attention to wage stagnation and related aspects of economic distress faced by working families (see, for example, Whalen 2008, 2010; Zalewski 2002). Their work is rooted in Peterson's pioneering efforts, but his insight on the subject has been incorporated into a broader framework that draws on Minsky's analysis of capitalist development. This framework identifies widening wage stagnation and worker insecurity as the flipside of the emergence of money manager capitalism, an era in which institutional investors exert a strong influence on economic decision-making (Minsky and Whalen 1996–1997; Whalen 2012).

The silent depression is now widely recognized, even if the problem is not referred to by that name. In fact, wage stagnation and growing income inequality are widely discussed in academic and policy circles, as are concerns about economic insecurity, the precariousness of the middle class, and the erosion of the "American Dream." Thus, this aspect of Peterson's work remains highly relevant.

PUBLIC POLICY

Addressing public policy, Peterson stressed the need for action in three directions: (i) public investment to rebuild the nation's infrastructure; (ii) active labor-market policies to foster full employment; and (iii) tax reform aimed at a simpler and more progressive approach to taxation. All three currently generate considerable interest in policy circles and among the wider public.

Infrastructure Investment

Like most economists, Peterson devoted far more attention to economic analysis than to outlining policy recommendations. But a call for a substantial program of public infrastructure investment was a logical consequence of his analysis of the silent depression. In particular, Peterson argued that such investment would spur the economy by increasing employment, encouraging greater private investment, and revitalizing productivity growth.[5] In *Silent Depression*, Peterson (1994) suggested the goal of investing $100 billion per year for ten years, partly funded by defense reconversion in the aftermath of the Cold War and coordinated by a national development (infrastructure) bank.

Given the nation's current military threats, the notion of defense reconversion looks different today than it did shortly after the breakup of the Soviet Union. But the need for infrastructure investment continues to grow (Harrison 2015; Holtz-Eakin and Mandel 2015). As a consequence, the possibility of meeting those needs by means of new institutions, including a national infrastructure bank, remains a topic of lively debate in Washington (see, for example, Crebo-Rediker 2014; Jasinowski 2013). By focusing attention on real world institutions and problems, Peterson produced work that was ahead of its time not only on the problem of wage stagnation, but also on the matter of infrastructure investment.

Labor Market Policies

Peterson believed that a large scale infrastructure program would boost employment, but he also thought that more aggressive labor market policies were needed. In particular, Peterson an envisioned expanded use of apprenticeships and other training and worker-education programs, including initiatives that encourage employers to upgrade the knowledge and skill of their employees. He saw such programs as a way not only to counteract wage stagnation, but also to reduce a decades-long upward trend in the unemployment rate (Peterson 1994, 228–233; 1987, 1617).[6]

As a result of the Great Recession of 2007–2009 and the subsequent slow recovery, much has been written about the sort of labor market policies that Peterson advocated. In fact, a number of promising innovations were emerging in the field of workforce development even before the Great Recession. They include community-based sectoral approaches to workforce challenges and establishment of labor market intermediaries to bring together job-seekers, educational institutions, and employers (Benner, Leete and Pastor 2007; Glover and King 2010). The literature on such developments is compatible with the perspective of PKI and deserves attention from today's post-Keynesian institutionalists.

Tax Reform

Peterson saw the structure of the U.S. tax code as "absurd." Upon receipt of the Veblen-Commons Award for outstanding contributions to institutional economics, he recommended "a massive overhaul of the federal tax system" (1992, 346) that would close most loopholes and end most subsidies. Peterson added that:

> By simplification, by including all income, and by the judicious use of the principle of the negative income tax, we could simultaneously achieve simplicity and fairness, progression, reduction in poverty, and reform that uses a carrot, not a stick, to stimulate work incentives. There is a practical challenge here, one that ought to inspire institutionalists. The challenge is to work through the arithmetic and demonstrate that a practical reform can work. (Peterson 1992, 346)

It seems that much of the nation agrees with Peterson. For example, a recent report by the Pew Research Center indicates that 59 percent of Americans favor tax reform aimed at achieving greater simplicity and moderating income inequality (Cook 2015). This suggests that the time is ripe for economists to accept Peterson's challenge.

CONCLUSION

Wallace C. Peterson was an exemplary post-Keynesian institutionalist.[7] He wrote about the foundations of economics in a manner that paved the way for today's PKI. He analyzed the U.S. economy with a keenness that not only shed new light on the macroeconomic issues of his day, but also put him decades ahead of other economists on the problem of America's silent depression. Moreover, he identified policy issues—such as infrastructure investment, active labor-market policies, and tax reform—that continue to spark widespread public interest and discussion, as well as to provide opportunities for economists to engage in meaningful research.

Over the course of his career, Peterson watched with disappointment as Keynesianism and institutionalism fell out of favor in the economics profession. Yet, he remained undeterred in his effort to help improve the human condition by analyzing economic institutions and working to advance public understanding of economic issues. In 1987, Peterson stressed that history argues against the notion that a market economy is inherently stable. Then, presciently, he added: "In time, this will become apparent once again, even, perhaps, to a generation of economists trained to a narrow technical perfection" (Peterson 1987, 1618). The global financial crisis and Great Recession of 2007–2009 did indeed make capitalist instability painfully obvious, and the example of Peterson's scholarship continues to suggest a constructive way forward.

NOTES

1. A native of Omaha, Nebraska, Peterson served in WWII, and then studied and taught at the University of Nebraska, Lincoln. He chaired the university's economics department for a decade, advised policy-makers, ran twice in the Democratic primary for U.S. Senate, and won a national award for a newspaper column called "Money in America." Peterson served as president of the Association for Evolutionary Economics in the mid-1970s and received the association's highest honor, the Veblen-Commons Award, in 1992. He retired from teaching in 1990, but remained active as a scholar through 1999. He died in 2012. Peterson's publications include two university-level economics texts, several books accessible to wide audiences on the subjects of stagflation, wage stagnation, and Social Security, and dozens of scholarly articles.
2. Peterson certainly blazed a trail for my own work, which has focused primarily on integrating institutionalism and post-Keynesianism into a foundation for the study of wage stagnation and other economic challenges confronting working families.
3. Underscoring the divide between making goods and making money, Peterson (1997, 279–281) expressed concern in the 1990s that financial speculation in the United States had skyrocketed since the early 1970s.

4. Writing in the late 1980s, Peterson (1989, 381) added: "Some years ago it might have been accurate to suggest that the power of the giant corporation is partially offset by the power of the trade unions. No longer. Since the Reagan Administration, in part because of the deep recession of 1981–1982, the power of trade unions in this country has been drastically curtailed."
5. Peterson (1999) also thought that such growth would ease the nation's Social Security challenges.
6. In *Silent Depression*, Peterson (1994) discussed education policy and healthcare reforms, as well as labor market policies, all under the umbrella of "investing in the American people." Here I focus only on labor market policies, because of Peterson's decades-long attention to achieving and maintaining full employment and because the Affordable Care Act of 2010 altered the healthcare landscape.
7. Page constraints prevent a more detailed examination of Peterson's analyses, but such an examination might also be of limited added value. This is because Peterson focused primarily on the (ever evolving) institutional realities of his time, and that focus—even more than his attention to issues that remain relevant today—is what made him exemplary.

REFERENCES

Benner, Chris, Laura Leete and Manuel Pastor. *Staircases or Treadmills? Labor Market Intermediaries and Economic Opportunity in a Changing Economy*. New York, NY: Russell Sage Foundation, 2007.

Brown, Christopher. *Inequality, Consumer Credit, and the Saving Puzzle*. Cheltenham, UK: Edward Elgar, 2008.

Cavalieri, Marco and Felipe Almeida. "Institutionalists as Dissenters: Why Were Institutionalists So Dissatisfied with Economics During the Post-War Period?" *Journal of Economic Issues* 49, 2 (2015): 475–482.

Cook, Lindsey. "Is 2016 the Right Year for Tax Reform?" *U.S. News & World Report*, March 27, 2015. Available at http://tinyurl.com/ow464fy. Accessed December 26, 2015.

Crebo-Rediker, Heidi. "Infrastructure Finance: How We Get Smarter." Policy Innovation Memorandum No. 44. New York, NY: Council on Foreign Relations, 2014.

Galbraith, James K. *The Predator State*. New York, NY: Free Press, 2008.

Glover, Robert W. and Christopher T. King. "Sectoral Approaches to Workforce Development: Toward an Effective U.S. Labor-Market Policy." In *Human Resource Economics and Public Policy*, edited by Charles J. Whalen. pp. 215–252. Kalamazoo, MI: W.E. Upjohn Institute, 2010.

Harrison, David. "Nation's Crumbling Roads Put a Dent in Drivers' Wallets." *Wall Street Journal*, July 31, 2015. Available at http://tinyurl.com/okpl4ob. Accessed July 31, 2015.

Holtz-Eakin, Douglas and Michael Mandel. *Dynamic Scoring and Infrastructure Spending*. New York, NY: McGraw Hill, 2015. Available at http://tinyurl.com/n9agf3l. Accessed July 29, 2015.

Jasinowski, Jerry. "A National Infrastructure Bank." *Huffington Post*, March 25, 2013. Available at http://tinyurl.com/pz4jgmp. Accessed July 29, 2015.

Minsky, Hyman P. and Charles J. Whalen. "Economic Insecurity and the Institutional Prerequisites for Successful Capitalism." *Journal of Post Keynesian Economics* 19, 2 (1996–1997): 155–170.
Niggle, Christopher. "Evolutionary Keynesianism: A Synthesis of Institutionalist and Post-Keynesian Macroeconomics." *Journal of Economic Issues* 40, 2 (2006): 405–412.
Peterson, Wallace C. "The Corporate State, Economic Performance, and Social Policy." *Journal of Economic Issues* 8, 2 (1974): 483–507.
———. "Corporate Concentration, Small Business, and the Economy." *Nebraska Journal of Economics and Business* 15, 3 (1976): 25–40.
———. "Institutionalism, Keynes and the Real World." *Journal of Economic Issues* 11, 2 (1977): 201–221.
———. "Power and Economic Performance." *Journal of Economic Issues* 14, 4 (1980): 827–869.
———. *Our Overloaded Economy*. Armonk, NY: M.E. Sharpe, 1982.
———. "Economic Stabilization and Inflation." *Journal of Economic Issues* 18, 1 (1984): 69–100.
———. "Macroeconomic Theory and Policy in an Institutionalist Perspective." *Journal of Economic Issues* 21, 4 (1987): 1587–1621.
———, ed. *Market Power and the Economy*. Boston, MA: Kluwer, 1988.
———. "Market Power: The Missing Element in Keynesian Economics." *Journal of Economic Issues* 23, 2 (1989): 379–391.
———. "The Silent Depression." *Challenge* 34, 4 (1991): 29–34.
———. "What Is to Be Done? Remarks Upon Receipt of the Veblen-Commons Award." *Journal of Economic Issues* 26, 2 (1992): 337–348.
———. "America's Silent Depression: A Challenge to Social Economics." *Review of Social Economy* 51, 1 (1993): 2–13.
———. *Silent Depression*. New York, NY: W.W. Norton, 1994.
———. "Institutions and Institutionalism: Crisis and Opportunity." In *Borderlands of Economics*, edited by Nahid Aslanbeigui and Young Back Choi, pp. 269–285. New York, NY: Routledge, 1997.
———. *The Social Security Primer*. Armonk, NY: M.E. Sharpe, 1999.
Tauheed, Linwood F. "A Proposed Methodological Synthesis of Post-Keynesian and Institutional Economics." *Journal of Economic Issues* 45, 4 (2011): 819–838.
Waller, William. "Accidental Veblenian, Intentional Institutionalist, and Inevitable Feminist." *Journal of Economic Issues* 39, 2 (2005): 326–334.
Whalen, Charles J. "Post-Keynesian Institutionalism and the Anxious Society." In *Assessing the Evolution and Impact of Alternative Institutional Structures*, edited by Sandra Batie and Nicholas Mercuro, pp. 273–299. New York, NY: Routledge, 2008.
———. "Economic Policy for the Real World." *Policy Note* No. 2010-1. Levy Economics Institute of Bard College, July 2010.
———. *Financial Instability and Economic Security after the Great Recession*. Cheltenham, UK: Edward Elgar, 2011.
———. "Money Manager Capitalism." In *Handbook of Critical Issues in Finance*, edited by Jan Toporowski and Jo Michell, pp. 254–262. Cheltenham, UK: Edward Elgar, 2012.
———. "Post-Keynesian Institutionalism After the Great Recession." *European Journal of Economics and Economic Policies: Intervention* 10, 1 (2013): 12–27.

Zalewski, David A. "Retirement Insecurity in the Age of Money-Manager Capitalism." *Journal of Economic Issues* 36, 2 (2002): 349–356.
Zalewski, David A. and Charles J. Whalen. "Financialization and Income Inequality: A Post Keynesian Institutionalist Analysis." *Journal of Economic Issues* 36, 2 (2010): 349–356.

25. Financialization and income inequality: a post-Keynesian institutionalist analysis

Co-authored by David A. Zalewski

One of the most troubling developments in recent years has been the widening of income inequality, not only in the United States, but also in many other countries. Although after-tax annual income for the bottom fifth of U.S. households grew approximately 6% between 1979 and 2005, those in the top fifth realized gains of about 80% over this period (Congressional Budget Office 2007). The nation's highest earners fared even better: federal tax-return data compiled by Thomas Piketty and Emmanuel Saez (2008) show that the top 1% of families in the United States garnered 22.9% of all pre-tax income in 2006. That was more than double their share in 1976, and only slightly below a record high of 23.9% in 1928. Income disparities have also grown in countries as diverse as Germany, Norway, and Canada, although the gaps are not as striking as in America (Organization for Economic Co-operation and Development [OECD] 2008).

A significant body of research has attempted to explain this trend. Much of the literature examining the United States has focused on the role played by long-term changes in productivity and its determinants, especially educational attainment and technological change.[1] Although the studies provide evidence that these factors influence inequality, they do not adequately account for why it has widened during recent periods of U.S. economic expansion and productivity gains.

We argue that Post Keynesian Institutionalism (PKI) provides insight into the causes of increasing income inequality because it, unlike neoclassical theory, explicitly integrates the real and financial sectors of the economy.[2] A leading PKI scholar, Hyman Minsky (1990a), pointed out that financial innovation could be the catalyst behind the entrepreneurial process of economic development formulated by Joseph Schumpeter (1934); however, it also could inhibit economic progress by generating financial instability. What is important for our

Reprinted with permission from *Journal of Economic Issues* 44 (3), September 2010, 757–777.

study is how the gains generated by economic development and the losses from financial disturbances are shared across social groups.

The PKI perspective also provides a valuable framework for examining distributional issues because it emphasizes the importance of shifts in political and economic power in shaping economic outcomes (Minsky 1990a; Whalen 2008a). Here PKI dovetails with recent research on the impact of evolving financial systems on economic welfare that is commonly referred to as *financialization*. According to Thomas Palley (2007, 2), financialization is "a process whereby financial markets, financial institutions, and financial elites gain greater influence over economic policy and economic outcomes." The extent to which this process affects income inequality has been summarized by Michael Perelman (2008, 45): "Nothing has contributed to imbalances in the economy so much as the outlandish expansion of financialization, although the imbalances have also promoted financialization."

Our article's contribution is threefold. First, we explore the connection between the PKI emphasis on evolving economic structures and the financialization literature. Special attention is given to the PKI contributions of Minsky, who began drawing attention to structural changes in the financial sector as early as the mid-1980s (Minsky 1986a). We observe that PKI and the financialization literature are united in recognizing that a major structural shift has occurred in the United States and that an associated institutional evolution is still ongoing in this country and elsewhere. We also identify a subtle difference, which is that the relationship between institutional structure and economic outcomes seems more deterministic in the financialization literature than in PKI.

Second, we present and discuss data tracking changes in financial structure and income inequality for a sample of developed nations. We use the International Monetary Fund (IMF) Financial Index (FI), which gauges the extent to which an economy's financial transactions are characterized by traditional banking relationships (taking deposits and making loans), new financial intermediation (such as securitization, derivatives trading, and venture capital financing), or exchanges in securities (stock and bond) markets, and relate it to Gini coefficients for the mid-1990s and mid-2000s. Because basic banking involves earning fixed returns while managing credit, liquidity, and interest rate risk, its practitioners have traditionally been reluctant to speculate on market fluctuations or exercise power over others in pursuit of immediate financial gains. This is not the case, however, for the other types of financial transactions, which are conducted to maximize short-term profits. For this reason, we argue that because the IMF index captures the dominant mode of financial contracting in a nation, it can be used as a proxy for the financialization process described above by Palley. Moreover, consistent with his discussion of "conduits of financialization" (Palley 2007, 14–15), our findings show that the FI has increased in nearly all the countries sampled and that this increase has generally been accompanied by a rise in income inequality.[3]

Third, we find that the development of modern financial structures does not preclude an expansive welfare state and egalitarian public policies. This is especially evident when the United States is compared with Nordic countries, although, as we show later, inequality resulting from financialization has increased there as well. Our international comparison calls into question the strict relationship between economic structures, policy and outcomes found in the financialization literature. It instead yields results compatible with research that suggests the comparatively higher level of inequality in the United States does not stem solely from differences in financial systems, but also, as Glaeser (2005) observed, from differences in redistributionist policies that reflect variations in cultural and political values. This is congruent with Minsky's conception of PKI, which stressed both that "economic systems are not natural systems" and that capitalism comes in as many varieties as Heinz has of pickles (Minsky 1986b, 7; Minsky 1993a, 3, n. 3).

PKI AND RECENT EVOLUTION OF THE FINANCIAL SYSTEM

A central tenet of PKI is its emphasis on how the evolution of economic and social structures influence macroeconomic performance. This can be seen in an early PKI book by Charles Wilber and Kenneth Jameson (1983, 152), where they first stressed the need to "explain the dynamics of existing structures and institutions" and then traced how institutional changes of the early-1970s contributed to stagflation. Similarly, an essay by Minsky (1996) argued that economic theory deduced from a set of logical axioms is less relevant for explaining today's problems than approaches based on understanding the institutional structures of society and the forces that cause them to change.

In the 1990s, Minsky (1990a) stressed Schumpeter's "creative destruction" vision of economic progress and the central role that financial innovation plays in the economic development process. Minsky argued that although efficiency gains may arise from the transfer of resources from low-return, stagnant industries to dynamic, entrepreneurial ones, the co-evolution of financial arrangements and technological advances can also generate instabilities that impair economic performance. For example, Charles Kindleberger (2000) described how technological developments such as commercialization of the Internet could interact with financial innovation to create speculative bubbles, which eventually led to economic distress after they burst.

Minsky (1990a) also argued that because the relationship between industry and finance evolves over time, capitalist economies pass through various stages of development. Although he defined four stages of capitalist development in the United States, we will focus on the transformation from what Minsky called managerial capitalism – shaped by the experiences of the Great Depression and World War II – to the current system of managed-money capitalism (which he believed had emerged by the early 1980s).

During the period of managerial capitalism, the financial structure was conservative with low debt levels and attenuated speculative impulses. Many leading corporations exercised considerable market power, and because this enabled them to generate sufficient cash flows to self-finance capital accumulation, they were generally insulated from shareholder demands. Moreover, macroeconomic conditions were largely stable and, aside from an occasional mild recession, the United States avoided serious economic disruption. Collectively, these forces led to a substantial accumulation of wealth that was more equitably distributed throughout society than in earlier decades.[4]

It was this "shared prosperity" that helped create conditions from which managed-money capitalism arose. The confluence of greater wealth, accelerating inflation, deregulation, and financial and technological innovation in the 1970s led to disintermediation as funds flowed from bank deposit accounts to mutual funds and securities. As Minsky (1990a, 70) observed: "Managed-money capitalism is part of the trend toward an increase in the proportion of financing that takes place through markets rather than intermediaries."

FINANCIALIZATION AND FINANCIAL STRUCTURE

Greta Krippner (2005, 181) argued that because the term "financialization" has taken on several meanings, the literature on it "is at present a bit of a free-for-all, lacking a cohesive view of what is to be explained." Jonathan P. Goldstein's (2009, 453) remark that "a common definition of financialization has not emerged in the existing literature" suggests that the research agenda on this topic continues to be broad. For example, Gerald Epstein and Arjun Jayadev (2005) focused on how *rentiers* have increasingly exercised power to raise their incomes at the expense of others. In contrast, William Lazonick and Mary O'Sullivan (2000) emphasized the growing primacy of shareholder interests at the expense of other stakeholders.

However, a broad conception of financialization can be found that encompasses those just mentioned and many others: Palley's (2007) definition, quoted above, which stresses an evolution that shifts the center of economic influence from product markets to financial markets, from non-financial corporations to financial institutions, and from business elites to financial elites. According to Palley, financialization transforms economic systems and public policy, and shapes economic performance. "Its principle impacts are to (1) elevate the significance of the financial sector relative to the real sector, (2) transfer income from the real sector to the financial sector, and (3) increase income inequality and contribute to wage stagnation" (Palley 2007, 2).

The PKI and financialization research streams contain several common features. The most obvious is their recognition that the U.S. economy has moved from what Minsky called managerial capitalism to managed-money capitalism. There is also a shared understanding that, although this structural shift is most pronounced in the United States, a similar trend affects other industrialized economies (Palley 2007, 3; Minsky 1990b). There is also agreement that it appears the process of raising capital has been transformed across the globe: the more traditional reliance on bank lending has been giving way to the increasing use of financial markets for this purpose. Indeed, Kevin Phillips (2002, 140) places this decades-long transformation at the heart of the financialization process.

Despite these commonalities, the financialization literature and PKI also have an important difference. Contributors to the research on financialization assume a strong connection between economic structures, political processes and national outcomes. In contrast, the influence of Minsky (who drew attention to the varieties of capitalism long before it was fashionable) and a century of institutionalist scholarship leave PKI reluctant to accept any notion of economic determinism, especially without first considering economic performance across nations. There is much in the accounts of Palley, Perelman, Phillips and other financialization contributors that resonates with PKI scholars who have examined the U.S. experience, but a comparative analysis is required to determine whether that experience is universal. As Martin H. Wolfson (2001, 336) concluded: "Indeed, it seems to be the essence of the institutional method to compare similarities and differences among various case studies to develop a deeper understanding of the underlying processes involved."[5]

Since Phillips (2002) places the movement from a bank-based to a market-based finance system at the center of the financialization process, that transition in finance warrants being examined for evidence of a link between financial structure and the inequality-generating financialization process. Phillips's focus on the evolution of finance is also familiar territory to PKI because that evolution has been accompanied by important changes in the nature of transactions, which, according to John R. Commons, are the basic units of economic analysis (Whalen 2008a, 56).

Scholars generally define three types of social relationships in which financial transactions take place. The first is the traditional bank loan in which the lender and borrower possess private information about each other that has been obtained during their relationship. Accordingly, these transactions are known as *relational* (this could also be called the "lend and hold" model), and are useful for overcoming asymmetric information problems and reducing transaction costs. In addition, the lender is likely to negotiate with borrowers experiencing difficulties and try to reach an agreement that sometimes involves changing the terms of the loan.[6] Moreover, as Robert Pollin (1995) noted, bank-based systems are more amenable to expansionary macroeconomic policies than economies in which markets dominate.

In contrast, most transactions in financial markets are *arm's-length* arrangements between previously unrelated parties that are encoded in enforceable contracts based on publicly available information (IMF 2006, ch. 4). Mainstream economists argue that this type of financing promotes allocative efficiency since investors in liquid markets will "exit" rather than exercise "voice" to change corporate behavior when returns have been disappointing. This places downward pressure on securities prices, which managers interpret as a signal that adjustments are necessary. (Unlike bankers, money managers, for example, actively manage their portfolios and are always "in the market" [Minsky 1990a, 69].)

Other economists take the story further, however, and the result is far from an efficient outcome. Because managers have increasingly been compensated with stock options, they have an incentive to make decisions that boost equity values. As Minsky (1996; 1992) has observed, among the consequences of this process in the United States are lower real wages and increased employment insecurity for a large fraction of the workforce, and greater inequality and financial instability for the economy overall. More recently, Brown (2008) has contributed to institutionalism and post-Keynesianism by deepening our understanding of this causal chain and by drawing special attention to how financial elites promoted their own interests and propped up the economy with an unsustainable expansion of consumer credit.

Finally, between arm's-length and relational financing lies *"new" financial intermediation*, in which securitization plays a prominent role.[7] Although the initial loan transaction is similar to one in traditional banking, the difference is that the lender packages and sells loans to financial institutions, which raise funds for these purchases by selling securities (some call this the "originate and distribute" model). The lender then collects the loan payments and allocates them to the security holders. The benefits of securitization are increased risk sharing and the ability to access a global pool of funds, both of which can lower the cost of capital. The problem, however, is that lenders may become unconcerned about credit risk, and usually have little motivation or ability to renegotiate loan terms with troubled borrowers – as has been the case in the subprime mortgage crisis. Besides securitization, "new" banking has also involved an increasing reliance on "off-balance-sheet" activities to generate fees and speculative profits, the value of which are correlated with the amount of risk the bank is willing to assume (Minsky and Whalen 1996–1997, 158).

What types of financial systems are dominant in developed countries, and how have they changed over time? To help answer this question, economists at the IMF have developed a financial index that captures the degree to which national financial systems are relational or arm's length (IMF 2006, Ch. 4). The index values range between 0 and 1, with lower values indicating a greater dependence on financial intermediation.

The index is a simple average of three sub-indices that measure, respectively, the level of activity in traditional banking, new financial intermediation, and financial markets. The *traditional banking* sub-index contains data on the value of intermediated funds, the market power exercised by banks, and the amount of information about borrowers available to the public. The *new financial intermediation* measure gauges the involvement of traditional banks in fee-based activities, the value of non-bank lending, and the penetration of financial innovations such as the use of derivatives. Finally, the *financial market* sub-index is constructed using measures for variables such as stock-market turnover, the value of private bonds outstanding, access to financial markets, and the extent to which the legal system includes contract-enforcement mechanisms (IMF 2006, Ch. 4).

Table 1 reports the FI values for 18 nations in 1995 and 2004 and the percentage change in the value of the indices over this decade.[8] The average FI scores indicate there has been a trend away from relational financing, with some of the

Table 1 Financial Index for 18 nations, 1995 and 2004

Nation	1995 FI	2004 FI	% Change
Australia	0.49	0.55	+12.2
Austria	0.29	0.32	+10.3
Belgium	0.36	0.39	+ 8.3
Canada	0.44	0.53	+20.5
Denmark	0.43	0.46	+ 7.0
Finland	0.33	0.40	+21.2
France	0.35	0.41	+17.1
Germany	0.33	0.37	+12.1
Greece	0.30	0.29	− 3.3
Italy	0.31	0.43	+38.7
Japan	0.39	0.41	+ 5.1
Netherlands	0.48	0.54	+12.5
Norway	0.47	0.48	+ 2.1
Portugal	0.33	0.35	+ 6.1
Spain	0.35	0.42	+20.0
Sweden	0.40	0.44	+10.0
UK	0.50	0.56	+12.0
United States	0.64	0.74	+15.6
Average	0.41	0.46	+12.2

Source: IMF (2006).

largest increases having occurred in countries like the United States and Canada, which were already leaders in arm's-length financing.[9] It is notable, however, that several European countries – such as Finland, Italy, and Spain – have made significant movement away from a bank-dominant system, despite the fact that their financial structures remained quite different from those in the United States and Britain in 2004.

FINANCIAL STRUCTURE AND INCOME INEQUALITY: AN OVERVIEW

To explore the relationship between income inequality and financial structure, we use Gini coefficients that have been estimated by the Organization for Economic Co-operation and Development (OECD 2008) for the countries in our sample and compare them with the corresponding FI values. Table 2 reproduces the FI values from Table 1 and shows them alongside the Gini coefficients, which measure the distribution of disposable household income.[10] Overall, the movement toward a greater reliance on financial markets has been accompanied by an increase in inequality. The FI value for all countries has increased 12.2% and the increase in the Gini was 2.7% (Table 3). Despite these differences in the rates of increase, the correlation between the two values was stronger in the more recent period: + 0.254 versus + 0.184.[11]

Do the findings presented in Table 2 support the core hypothesis of the financialization literature, namely that the move toward arm's-length financing signals a shift toward the dominance of finance over industry, the shaping of public policy by financial elites, and the rise of income inequality? Although the general direction of the overall results is consistent with this theory, we must examine them more carefully by considering this process in the context of PKI theory to identify channels through which distribution can be affected.

Unfortunately, as Brown (2005, 915) observed, institutional economics lacks a unified theory of income distribution. Instead, what exists is "a hard-to-descry constellation of mutually consistent ideas distributed through a broad space of literature." What are some of the elements of this "constellation?" According to Brown (2005, 920), perhaps the most important is power: "As power is a decisive factor in accounting for disparities in material rewards, a theory of distribution should be indistinguishable from a theory of power." Further, the working rules and institutions of a society help determine how power affects the allocation of rewards and burdens from economic activity. For these reasons, we will conduct our detailed examination of the financialization hypothesis in the next section by organizing countries into groups that are defined by similarities in their basic institutions.

Table 2 Financial Index, Gini coefficient, and correlations, 1995 and 2004

	1995 FI	1995 Gini	2004 FI	2004 Gini
Anglo-American				
United States	0.64	0.361	0.74	0.381
UK	0.50	0.354	0.56	0.335
Australia	0.49	0.309	0.55	0.301
Canada	0.44	0.283	0.53	0.317
Average	0.51	0.327	0.60	0.334
Nordic				
Norway	0.47	0.256	0.48	0.276
Denmark	0.43	0.215	0.46	0.232
Sweden	0.40	0.211	0.44	0.234
Finland	0.33	0.228	0.40	0.269
Average	0.43	0.227	0.46	0.247
Continental				
Belgium	0.36	0.287	0.39	0.271
Portugal	0.33	0.359	0.35	0.385
Netherlands	0.48	0.282	0.54	0.271
Italy	0.31	0.348	0.43	0.352
Spain	0.35	0.343	0.42	0.319
France	0.35	0.270	0.41	0.270
Germany	0.33	0.272	0.37	0.298
Austria	0.29	0.238	0.32	0.265
Average	0.35	0.292	0.42	0.296
Other				
Greece	0.30	0.336	0.29	0.321
Japan	0.39	0.323	0.41	0.321
Average	0.35	0.325	0.35	0.321
Correlation Coefficients				
	FI-Gini, 1995		FI-Gini, 2004	
	+ 0.184		+ 0.254	

Sources: IMF (2006); OECD (2008).

Table 3 Financial Index and Gini coefficient percent changes from 1995 to 2004

	Change FI	Change Gini
Anglo-American	+17.6%	+2.6%
Nordic	+ 7.0%	+8.8%
Continental	+20.0%	+1.4%
All Nations	+12.2%	+2.7%

Sources: Authors' calculation, data from IMF (2006) and OECD (2008).

FINANCIAL STRUCTURE AND INCOME INEQUALITY: A CLOSER LOOK

As noted above and shown in Table 2, we divide countries into groups based on similar institutional characteristics. These are: (a) Anglo-American nations such as the United States and Britain in which financial markets are dominant, economic freedom is valued highly, and conservative leaders have headed governments in recent decades; (b) the "Nordic model" countries like Sweden and Denmark, which combine substantive welfare states with vibrant business sectors; and (c) Continental European states like France and Germany in which government, labor, and industry share the responsibility for economic decision-making.[12]

As expected, the Anglo-American countries have the highest FI values. In the case of Britain and the United States, deregulation played a major role in this transformation with the "Big Bang" of the mid-1980s in the former, and the wave of liberalization policies beginning in the Reagan administration in the latter. These countries also have the highest average level of income inequality in the two periods. Although the results have been skewed somewhat by the United States, which has the most market-oriented financial system and the highest level of inequality, the other countries in the Anglo-American group also score well above most of the other nations in both measures.

How has the movement toward a market-based financial system increased inequality in the Anglo-American countries? One way is through changes in the way the gains from economic activity are shared during normal (i.e., non-crisis) periods. As the OECD (2008, 16) noted in its report on inequality: "The only sustainable way to reduce inequality is to stop the underlying widening of wages and income from capital." Unfortunately, the opposite trend has developed in the United States. Lawrence Mishel, Jared Bernstein, and Sylvia Allegretto

(2006) reported that the share of capital income from corporate activity (about 75% of gross domestic product) rose from 19.5% in 1995 to 20.9% in 2005 – the second-highest level in 36 years. Moreover, the top 20% of households received 84.2% of total capital income in 2005, with 55.3% having gone to the top 1%. Meanwhile, average real wages have been stagnant in the United States since the early 1980s.

Although many factors underlie this widening divide, some of the most important relate to financialization. For example, managers may seek to increase profitability and workplace flexibility in ways that exacerbate inequality as well as worker insecurity, as Minsky (1996) observed in U.S. corporations in the era of managed-money capitalism. A major driving force during this period has been the increased role played by institutional investors in economic decision-making. Evidence of this influence lies in the fact that the share of U.S. corporate equities owned by financial institutions increased from 45.1% in 1995 to 54.4% in 2004 (calculated from Flow of Funds data provided by the Board of Governors of the Federal Reserve System [2009]), and that these investors have used this power not only to pressure corporate leaders to place investor concerns above those of other stakeholders, but have also lobbied political leaders to craft legislation and alter regulations in their favor.[13]

Other related sources of inequality have been the compensation earned by employees in the financial industry and changes in tax policies toward capital income. Kaplan and Rauh (2007) provide striking evidence of the earnings of some financial professionals by showing that the sum of the compensation for the top 25 hedge fund managers in 2004 exceeded that of all of the CEOs of the S&P 500 corporations combined. More generally, Philippon and Reshef (2007) found that U.S. financial sector earnings rose from 2.8% of total compensation in 1950 to 7.7% in 2005, with notable increases beginning in the 1980s as the U.S. economy has evolved from the traditional banking model. Reinforcing this trend have been changes in tax policy, which as Gerald E. Scorse (2008) summarized: "Over the last decade, nobody has gotten more love from Washington than investors." For example, President Bill Clinton lowered the tax rate on long-term capital gains from 28% to 20% in 1997, and President George W. Bush cut it again to 15% in 2003. In addition, the Bush administration decreased taxes on dividends and estates, and continued the practice of allowing hedge fund income to be taxed at favorable rates.

Consistent with this analysis are what Palley (2007) identifies as three "conduits of financialization," which explain how financial sector interests have contributed to inequality. One conduit operates directly through financial markets: a secular expansion of (business and consumer) debt, accompanying the changing financial structure, has increased inequality by transferring income "from high marginal propensity to spend debtors to lower marginal propensity to spend creditors." Another conduit is corporate behavior, which financial-market money managers have brought in line with their own interests – and in opposition to the interests of unions and wage earners. The third conduit is public policy, driven largely by the goals ("the effect of which is to box in workers") of small government, labor-market flexibility, globalization, and abandonment of full employment.[14]

Public policy can have a mitigating effect on inequality, however, as demonstrated in other countries with similar financial systems. Over the period examined, inequality declined slightly in Britain and Australia despite further movement from a bank-based economy in both countries.[15] Experts familiar with those economies attribute the movements in a more egalitarian direction (a 5.4% and 2.6% reduction in the Gini, respectively) to rising minimum-wage floors and the introduction of highly targeted tax cuts and transfers aimed at low-income families. Evidence of this comes from the OECD (2008, 116), which calculates that net cash transfers (cash transfers minus taxes paid) to people in the lowest quintile of the disposable income distribution in both countries are more than double that of the United States. The economists we consulted in each nation stress that income gaps would have widened in the absence of such policies, but the countervailing impact of the policies produced results inconsistent with the process described as financialization.[16]

Finally, financial instability and an economic crisis also can exacerbate inequality (Kuttner 2007; Wray 2007). The risk of instability may be most prevalent in market-based systems, but the current global financial crisis demonstrates that new financial intermediation has also been far from stable. Moreover, the burden of financial crises is likely to be shared unequally. Although the U.S. economy had shed approximately 5.1 million jobs from the start of the recession in December 2007 to March 31, 2009, and the unemployment rate reached 8.5% in March 2009 (eventually exceeding 10% in late 2009), financial elites – including some employed by firms like A.I.G. and Bank of America, which received U.S. government bailout funds – continued to receive outsized pay packages and "retention bonuses."

At the opposite end of the inequality spectrum are the Nordic countries. The data in Table 2 show that the average Nordic levels of income inequality are much lower than those in the Anglo-American countries and that Nordic financial systems are significantly more relational. Much of this difference can be explained by the expansive welfare states in Nordic countries along with effective collective bargaining. This comparison, however, ignores the fact that income inequality increased the most in the Nordic countries over the sample period.

Interestingly, the recent rise in Nordic inequality is largely due to financialization. According to the OECD (2008, 90–91), inequality associated with capital income has been most responsible. A case in point is Finland, where this trend has been the most pronounced. Marja Riihelä, Risto Sullström, and

Matti Tuomala (2005) found that the richest 1% of households in Finland derived 52% of their income from capital in 2002, an increase from 14% in 1990. Principally responsible for this trend has been a change in the tax code in 1993, which inaugurated a flat tax on capital income, with the top rate lower than the highest marginal tax rate on wage income.

It is also notable that income inequality in all four Nordic countries did not increase during the late 1980s and early 1990s, when the region suffered through a severe financial crisis and economic downturn. Rolf Aaberge et al. (2000) found that despite having reached levels of unemployment that approached those experienced during the 1930s, the values of the Gini coefficients remained remarkably stable. Although the researchers cited the generous unemployment compensation systems in these countries as a major reason for this result, they emphasized that other policies and social forces also helped restrain inequality.

The final group of countries in our sample is the Continental European nations. Although Table 2 shows that average Continental income inequality exceeds that of the Nordic nations, the Continental financial system is more relational. In fact, the change in these variables yields the opposite of what was found in the Nordic countries: in the Continental group, we find the highest levels of growth in the FI, but the smallest percentage increase in income inequality. One explanation for this difference is that unlike the Nordic nations, these countries are characterized more by parities in the wage bargaining process than by public programs that intend to reduce inequality after wages have been determined.

To summarize, this analysis suggests that both financialization and income inequality increased in nearly all of our sample countries during the ten-year period beginning in the mid-1990s. Except for Greece, all countries in the sample moved away from relational financing in the decade beginning in 1995.[17] To the degree that the FI serves as a proxy for financialization, the data for 2004 show that this process has been most pronounced in the Anglo-American group and less so in both the Nordic and Continental European countries. However, this development has been accompanied by rising inequality that is most pronounced in the Nordic countries. The question, which we address in the concluding section, is whether there is likely to be a neoliberal convergence, in which non-Anglo-American countries evolve toward this model, or movement toward more egalitarian regimes as a result of the recent global financial meltdown.

FINANCIALIZATION AND THE PROSPECTS FOR REFORM

There are several reasons for wanting to slow or reverse financialization. In addition to a market-based financial system's demonstrated ability to fuel inequality and worker insecurity, there is clear evidence that managed-money capitalism exacerbates financial instability.[18] Even after the recent global economic crisis, the present system in the United States retains its hazardous impulse to rely on consumer credit expansion to promote economic growth in the face of stagnant worker incomes (consistent with the analysis of Brown 2008). There are also questions about this form of capitalism's ability to adequately foster technological dynamism and long-term economic growth.[19] Thus, the key questions are whether structural change in the financial system is possible, and if so, will this reconstruction be sufficient to advance social progress?

There is no question that the recent financial crisis has provided both motive and opportunity for reforming the "new finance," which is broadly defined as the Anglo-American model. According to Zanny Beddoes (2008, 7): "Put crudely, the bright new finance is the highly leveraged, lightly regulated, market-based system of allocating capital dominated by Wall Street. It is the spivvy successor to 'traditional banking' in which regulated commercial banks lent money to trusted clients and held the debt on their books." By early 2009, however, this has changed as the investment banking industry has all but disappeared, securitization contracts have virtually dried-up, and officials from crisis-stricken nations have worked feverishly to enact rescue programs to stabilize the global financial system. Whether the product of these efforts will be a new financial structure that will generate egalitarian economic outcomes or just a response to the symptoms of the crisis remains to be seen. However, the outcome of the meeting of the Group of 20 nations held in Britain on April 2, 2009 – the first multilateral attempt to enact financial reform – gave few reasons to expect fundamental institutional change.

As John Burns and Landon Thomas (2009) reported, British Prime Minister Gordon Brown's plan – as official host of the meeting – was to initiate an overhaul of the Anglo-American financial system. Shortly before the conference, Brown made a speech in Strasbourg, France that not only linked finance and inequality, but also indicted the dominance of market-based contracting. Brown stated: "[R]iches are of value only when they enrich not just some communities, but all. As we have discovered to our cost, the problem of unbridled free markets in an unsupervised marketplace is that they can reduce all relationships to transactions, all motivation to self-interest, all sense of value to consumer choice and all sense of worth to a price tag." Brown's words were echoed by pro-U.S. French President Nicolas Sarkozy, who recommended that the "Anglo-Saxon presumption of dominance should be abandoned."

Unfortunately, the financial system reforms agreed to at the conference were weak, at best. The conferees pledged help to developing countries stricken by the crisis by pledging $750 billion to the IMF to increase its capacity to provide aid, and $250 billion in trade credits. The participating nations also promised to cooperate in expanding global trade. Finally, the countries adopted some financial regulation measures, but none that addressed the underlying causes of the crisis. As Harvard University economist Kenneth Rogoff concluded (quoted in Landler and Sanger 2009): "The rich countries are in denial about the depth of the problems remaining in the financial sectors. They want to congratulate themselves for taking all the right steps already, as if the only problem now is how to help emerging markets."

One reason for the inability to agree on meaningful reform is the significant cultural differences among developed countries. At the Group of 20 meeting, European leaders pressed for the development of a regulatory apparatus that would more closely monitor global financial markets – especially interbank holdings and transnational capital flows. This proposal, however, was rejected by the United States. Instead, officials agreed to form the Financial Stability Board – a reconstitution of the Financial Stability Forum, which promotes cooperation and transparency among financial regulators from G-20 countries. The effectiveness of this organization is questionable, however, since its members lack cross-border regulatory authority. U.S. and European officials also clashed over the adequacy of national fiscal stimulus programs, with President Barack Obama pressuring European leaders to increase spending. This strategy was unsuccessful as French and German leaders responded by claiming that their usual safety nets were sufficient to stabilize economic conditions.

These disagreements over the nature of reform should be unsurprising to heterodox economists, who recognize that markets are socially embedded. Palley and others define the financialization process as involving more than a change in the structure of finance, since it also encompasses public policy and other forms of social choice. The type of system prevalent in any country reflects the existing social order and the pressures for change brought upon it by political and economic forces. As a result, differences among the countries examined prevent us from making sweeping conclusions about the relationship between financial structure and inequality in developed nations or about how best to design policies to address the inequality problem. This conclusion is consistent with Minsky, who, as noted earlier, often referred to Heinz's "57 Varieties" slogan when making the point that capitalism comes in at least as many variations.

One of the fundamental differences among nations is how the costs and benefits related to the structure and function of financial systems are shared across society. The evidence presented in this article demonstrates that elite private interests in the United States disproportionately enjoy the gains – often at the expense of the prosperity and security of many others – while the losses are socialized by means of federal government intervention intended to prevent financial collapse. In contrast, in the more communitarian Nordic countries both economic gains and losses are socialized through a progressive tax system and an extensive welfare state without retarding either business activity or technical progress (Andersen et al. 2007).[20]

The benefits from a more cooperative approach to economic policy extend beyond sharing the benefits of prosperity, as can be seen by differences in responses to financial crises. Efforts by the U.S. Treasury Department and the Federal Reserve to stabilize the financial system throughout 2008 and 2009 have been cloaked in secrecy and complexity. Only after executives at A.I.G. and Bank of America paid large "retention bonuses" to key employees – despite having received enormous injections of public funds to help their firms survive – was there any significant public criticism of the bailout (Associated Press 2008). In contrast, the Swedish government quickly nationalized insolvent banks in the early 1990s, which not only stabilized the financial sector, but also minimized the public's share of the rescue program's cost. Stefan Ingves and Göran Lind (2008) argued that it was largely the cooperation between the central government and business leaders to resolve the crisis in a transparent manner that restored confidence and health to Sweden's financial sector.

Because cultural differences form the basis for allocating benefits and burdens, it is unlikely that the United States could emulate the Nordic model by changing the structure of its financial system. Torben Andersen and his colleagues argue that "Nordic sharing" is possible because of a strong sense of trust among the citizenry. Paul Zak (2008, 272) reported survey results on the degree of social trust within nations, and found that Norway, Sweden and Finland ranked numbers one, two, and four, respectively, out of a sample of forty-two countries. Like Andersen and his co-authors, Zak cited social homogeneity as a major source of this sentiment, but also noted that high-income levels and perceptions about contract enforcement explained the results. Because of that trust, the Nordic countries have been able to develop a modern financial system (sometimes even overcoming disastrous early attempts at financial liberalization, such as in the case of Sweden) while maintaining egalitarian public programs (Andersen et al. 2007). On the other hand, there is no social homogeneity in the United States to generate the sort of trust found in the Nordic countries. Instead, there is widespread suspicion toward public and private decision-makers that hovers over even well intentioned efforts to propose redistributive public policies.

Social welfare programs in Nordic nations are also more politically acceptable than in the United States because of underlying philosophical differences. Joakim Palme (2006) defined three types of public redistribution programs: (a) vertical programs that transfer resources from the well off to the disadvantaged; (b) horizontal programs, in which individuals reallocate their own wealth across their life cycles; and (c) risk-mitigation programs. He argued that Nordic welfare policies focus on horizontal approaches, and these – along with risk-reduction measures – apply to all citizens rather than just the needy. To focus on the extent to which these policies reflect the social homogeneity of the population is to miss the essential point: in Nordic nations, the role of the public sector in taming the excesses of capitalism is very different from that in the more laissez-faire United States.

The importance of an alternative conception of government suggests that all is not lost. In *Stabilizing an Unstable Economy* Minsky (1986b, 7) reminded us: "Economic systems are not natural systems;" an economy is a social organization that can be shaped by legislation. "Policy can change both the details and the overall character of the economy," he wrote. Thus, it is possible for the U.S. economy to be reshaped. And if that is to happen, then the United States must learn not only from Anglo-American nations who have achieved some success with efforts to attenuate inequality (such as the United Kingdom and Australia), but also from countries in the Nordic region, even though the institutions and policies such countries use to reduce inequality might need to be adapted to U.S. conditions.[21]

A unifying thread in PKI has always been the desire to ensure the survivability of capitalism by proposing policy interventions that offer citizens a reasonable level of economic security and that can foster shared prosperity. PKI scholars recognize that a nation cannot (and should not) radically change institutions on a regular basis. Yet there are times when major changes are needed. Since history has shown that Minsky was not only prescient on the emergence of managed-money capitalism, but also ahead of his time with analyses of its economic implications, it seems only fitting that we give him the last word on policy: "Only as the inadequate performance of an economic and social order becomes evident and serious does it become necessary to engage in thoroughgoing institutional reform. Such a time has arrived" (Minsky 1986b, 7).

NOTES

1. Aaron Steelman and John A. Weinberg (2005) provide a good overview of research on U.S. wage inequality, while in their recent book Claudia Goldin and Lawrence Katz (2008) explore the interaction between education and technology and its implications for U.S. inequality and economic growth.
2. For a description of Post Keynesian Institutionalism, see Whalen (2008a); see also Jameson (2004) and Whalen (2008b; 2008c, 251).
3. Viewed in conjunction with the complementary analysis of Christopher Brown (2008), our findings also reinforce Perelman's suggestion (indicated in the quote presented above) that there is cumulative causation between financialization and inequality. In particular, Brown's analysis highlights the ability of inequality to

fuel financialization, while our findings reinforce the view (shared by Minsky and Palley) that financialization can breed inequality.

4. Greenhouse (2008) provides a readable account of government, business, and labor relations during this period.
5. The process of gathering information and organizing it into similar or dissimilar sets is a key step in the process of investigation in institutional economics. See Atkinson and Oleson (1996), Ramstad (1986), and Wilber and Harrison (1978).
6. Although loan modifications can be helpful in stabilizing output and employment during economic downturns, this benefit may come at the cost of cronyism and the inability of "unconnected" borrowers to obtain credit. Indeed, while intermediaries are better at overcoming asymmetric information problems, financial markets are often believed to more successfully channel funds to entrepreneurs and to be more inclusive in providing access to finance (see Hanngsen [2006] and Rajan and Zingales [2004] for further discussion). However, there are also concerns about economic growth and technological development in an era of market-based financing (see note 19 below), and, of course, the movement away from relational financing appears to be a root cause of the current global economic crisis (Whalen 2008d).
7. Observing the new financial intermediation, Minsky (1990a, 71) wrote: "There is a symbiotic relation between the growth of securitization and of managed money."
8. While it would be useful to examine financial-system evolution over a longer time horizon, the IMF study provides data on only these two periods. The first of these two years (1995) provides a snapshot prior to the 1990s stock-market bubble, while the second (2004) comes before the start of the more recent global financial crisis. The authors of the IMF study cite data availability as the reason for limiting their sample to 18 advanced economies (IMF 2006, Ch. 4).
9. The IMF's FI score fell (by 3.3%) in only one of the 18 countries sampled, Greece. According to two Greek economists who have reviewed the index components (Theodosios Sampaniotis of EFG Eurobank Ergasias S.A. and Marica Frangakis of the National Bank of Greece), the index's movement toward bank financing is due primarily to privatization and deregulation of that country's banking system, which was largely state-owned (as a result of direct and indirect controls) until the early 1990s. The easing of state controls caused bank lending to increase rapidly in the period examined (Sampaniotis 2009; Frangakis 2009).
10. The Gini coefficients, which have a value between 0 (perfect equality) and 1 (perfect inequality), are from the OECD (2008). The data are computed using household after-tax cash incomes that were compiled from surveys – except in some Nordic countries, which use population registers. Although there are other common measures of inequality available, OECD economists found that these series are highly correlated with the Ginis used in this study.
11. Although the correlation data may imply that increasing reliance on market-based financing has widened inequality, which would be consistent with the financialization hypothesis, we submit the standard caveat that these values do not imply causation.
12. Since the nature of the systems in Japan and Greece do not fit the other groups, we place them in a separate category. However, although Andersen et al. (2007) claim that Norway could be excluded from the Nordic nations because of its dependence on oil exports, we consider that distinction irrelevant for this investigation.
13. The following are some of the methods that corporations in the era of managed-money capitalism have used to increase profitability and workplace flexibility and that exacerbate inequality and worker insecurity: refusing wage increases for

employees while awarding lucrative salary packages to executives; engaging in aggressive union avoidance strategies; scaling back employee benefits and opportunities for promotion; eliminating retiree pensions; and relying on part-time and outsourced work. For more on rising inequality and insecurity as the flipside to emergence of managed-money capitalism, see, for example, Brown (2008, 149–161); Cappelli et al. (1997); Minsky and Whalen (1996–1997); Weller (2006); Whalen (1997; 2008e); and Zalewski (2002; 2004). For an examination of how money managers have influenced corporations, see Useem (1996). For discussions of how financial interests have influenced government policies in the United States and the international arena, see Greider (1992; 1997) and Johnson (2009).

14. According to Palley (2007, 11–12):

> Economists have identified multiple factors behind the stagnation of wages and the growth of inequality. Those factors include the erosion of unions, the minimum wage, and labor market solidarity; globalization and trade; immigration; skill-biased technical change; and rising CEO pay supposedly driven by the logic of the economics of superstars. However, such an analysis tends to treat these factors as independent of each other. The financialization thesis maintains that many of these factors should be linked and interpreted as part of a new economic configuration that has been explicitly promoted by financial sector interests.

15. Within the Continental category, there are also countries that have seen inequality decline: Belgium, Netherlands, and Spain.
16. Scholars consulted include Peter Saunders (University of New South Wales), Ian Watson (Macquarie University), Bob Gregory (Australian National University), Andrew Leigh (Australian National University), John Buchanan (University of Sydney), Stephen Machin (University College London), Alastair Muriel (Institute for Fiscal Studies, United Kingdom), John Hills (London School of Economics), Peter Lawrence (Keele University), and Jan Toporowski (SOAS, University of London). For related discussions of inequality and policy in the United Kingdom and Australia, see Saunders and Bradbury (2006) and Sefton, Hills and Sutherland (2009). While these essays indicate that policy has helped attenuate inequality, they also indicate that more recent inequality measurements and data improvements suggest that the United Kingdom and Australia may have actually moved back in the direction of greater inequality. As John Hills said recently about the struggle for a more egalitarian society, "gains are possible through determined interventions, but they require intensive and continuous effort to be sustained" because the underlying economic trends are toward increasing inequality (quoted in Memon 2009).
17. The anomalous case of Greece is discussed in Note 9 above.
18. For evidence that the drift from relational financing exacerbates financial instability, see IMF (2006, Ch. 4; 2008, Ch. 4), Brown (2008), Minsky (1986), Whalen (2008d), and Wray (2008).
19. One concern is that money-manager capitalism diverts young talent from science and engineering to banking and finance. Another is that it may discourage risky investments that require a long gestation period. For a discussion of the attractive salaries of the financial world, see Andrew Sum et al. (2008). For expressions of concern about whether managed-money capitalism can foster technological dynamism, see Crotty (2005) and Minsky (1990a, 72; 1993b). Moreover, the investment-led boom of the 1990s does not refute the concerns of Crotty and Minsky;

according to Barry Bluestone and Bennett Harrison (2000, 17–18), the underlying source of that boom was public investment in prior decades, which is a view fully consistent with Minsky's analysis.

20. The OECD (2004) ranked member countries by the percentage of gross domestic product accounted for by research and development spending, and found that Sweden and Finland had the highest two ratios. Although Norway ranked low on the list, this can be explained by its reliance on natural resources.
21. In attempting to solve the U.S. banking crisis (but not the inequality problem), U.S. leaders have indeed recently looked toward the Nordic region; see Samuel (2009).

REFERENCES

Aaberge, Rolf, Anders Björklund, Markus Jäntti, Peder J. Pedersen, Nina Smith and Tom Wennemo. "Unemployment Shocks and Income Distribution: How Did the Nordic Countries Fare During their Crises?" *Scandinavian Journal of Economics* 102, 1 (2000): 77–99.

Andersen, Torben M., Bengt Holmström, Seppo Honkapohja, Sixten Korkman, Hans Tson Söderström and Juhana Vartiainen. *The Nordic Model: Embracing Globalization and Sharing Risks.* The Research Institute of the Finnish Economy (ETLA). Helsinki: Taloustieto Oy, 2007.

Associated Press. "1.6 Billion Went to Bailed-out Execs." MSNBC, 2008. http://www.msnbc.msn.com/id/28337800/. Accessed March 25, 2008.

Atkinson, Glen W. and Ted Oleson. "Institutional Inquiry: The Search for Similarities and Differences." *Journal of Economic Issues* 30, 3 (1996): 701–718.

Beddoes, Zanny Minton. "When Fortune Frowned: A Special Report on the World Economy." *Economist.* October 10, 2008: 3–33.

Bluestone, Barry and Bennett Harrison. *Growing Prosperity: The Battle for Growth with Equity in the 21st Century.* Boston: Houghton Mifflin, 2000.

Board of Governors of the Federal Reserve System. *Flow of Funds Accounts of the United States (Z1).* Washington, D.C., 2009.

Brown, Christopher. "Is There an Institutional Theory of Distribution?" *Journal of Economic Issues* 39, 4 (2005): 915–931.

———. *Inequality, Consumer Credit and the Saving Puzzle.* Cheltenham, UK: Edward Elgar, 2008.

Burns, John F. and Landon Thomas, Jr. "Anglo-American Capitalism on Trial." *New York Times.* March 29, 2009.

Cappelli, Peter, Laurie Bassi, Harry Katz, David Knote, Paul Osterman and Michael Useem. *Change at Work: Trends that are Transforming the Business of Business.* NPA Report Number 283. Washington, D.C.: National Policy Association, 1997.

Congressional Budget Office. *Historical Effective Federal Tax Rates, 1979–2005.* Washington, D.C.: CBO Printing Office, December 2007.

Crotty, James. "The Neoliberal Paradox: The Impact of Destructive Market Competition and 'Modern' Financial Markets on Nonfinancial Corporation Performance in the Neoliberal Era." In *Financialization and the World Economy*, edited by Gerald A. Epstein, pp. 77–110. Cheltenham, UK: Edward Elgar, 2005.

Epstein, Gerald A. and Arjun Jayadev. "The Rise of Rentier Incomes in OECD Countries: Financialization, Central Bank Policy and Labor Solidarity." In *Financialization and the World Economy* edited by Gerald A. Epstein, pp. 46–74. Cheltenham, UK: Edward Elgar, 2005.

Frangakis, Marica. E-mail correspondence with one of the authors. March 4, 2009.

Glaeser, Edward L. "Inequality." Discussion Paper Number 2078. Harvard Institute of Economic Research. July 2005. http://ssrn.com/abstract=756889. Accessed March 23, 2009.

Goldin, Claudia and Lawrence F. Katz. *The Race Between Technology and Education.* Cambridge, MA: Harvard University Press, 2008.

Goldstein, Jonathan P. "Introduction: The Political Economy of Financialization." *Review of Radical Political Economics* 41, 4 (Fall 2009): 453–457.

Greenhouse, Steven. *The Big Squeeze: Tough Times for the American Worker.* New York: Alfred A. Knopf, 2008.

Greider, William. *Who Will Tell the People? The Betrayal of American Democracy.* New York: Touchstone, 1992.

———. *One World, Ready or Not: The Manic Logic of Global Capitalism.* New York: Touchstone, 1997.

Hannsgen, Greg P. "Borrowing Alone: The Theory and Policy Implications of the Commodification of Finance." In *Ethics and the Market: Insights from Social Economics* edited by Betsy Jane Clary, Wilfred Dolfsma and Deborah M. Figart, pp. 41–54. London: Routledge, 2006.

Ingves, Stefan and Göran Lind. "Stockholm Solutions." *Finance and Development* 45, 4 (December 2008): 21–23.

International Monetary Fund. *World Economic Outlook: Financial Systems and Economic Cycles.* Washington, D.C.: International Monetary Fund, September 2006. http://www.imf.org/external/pubs/ft/weo/2006/02/index.htm. Accessed March 6, 2009.

———. *World Economic Outlook: Financial Stress, Downturns and Recoveries.* Washington, D.C.: International Monetary Fund, October 2008. http://www.imf.org/external/pubs/ft/weo/2008/02/index.htm. Accessed March 24, 2009.

Jameson, Kenneth P. 2004. "Dollarization in Ecuador: A Post-Keynesian Institutionalist Analysis." Working Paper No. 2004–5. Salt Lake City: University of Utah, Department of Economics, 2004. http://ideas.repec.org/p/uta/papers/2004_05.html. Accessed March 22, 2009.

Johnson, Simon. "The Quiet Coup." *Atlantic Monthly*, May 2009. http://www.theatlantic.com/doc/200905/imf-advice/. Accessed December 22, 2009.

Kaplan, Steven N. and Joshua Rauh. "Wall Street and Main Street: What Contributes to the Rise in the Highest Incomes?" Working Paper, Booth School of Business. Chicago: University of Chicago, 2007.

Kindleberger, Charles P. *Manias, Panics, and Crashes: A History of Financial Crises,* 4th ed. New York: John Wiley & Sons, 2000.

Krippner, Greta R. "The Financialization of the American Economy." *Socio-Economic Review* 3, 2 (May 2005): 173–208.

Kuttner, Robert. *The Squandering of America: How the Failure of Our Politics Undermines Our Prosperity.* New York: Alfred A. Knopf, 2007.

Landler, Mark and David E. Sanger. "World Leaders Pledge $1.1 Trillion for Crisis." *New York Times*, April 3, 2009.

Lazonick, William and Mary O'Sullivan. "Maximizing Shareholder Value: A New Ideology for Corporate Governance." *Economy and Society* 29, 1 (February 2000): 13–35.

Memon, Nasreen. "In-depth Assessment Delivers the Verdict on the Government's Promise of a More Equal Society." Joseph Rowntree Foundation. February 25, 2009. http://www.jrf.org.uk/node/4314. Accessed March 6, 2009.
Minsky, Hyman P. "Global Consequences of Financial Deregulation." *The Marcus Wallenberg Papers on International Finance* 2, 1 (October 1986a): 1–19.
———. *Stabilizing an Unstable Economy*. New Haven: Yale University Press, 1986b.
———. "Schumpeter: Finance and Evolution." In *Evolving Technology and Market Structure: Studies in Schumpeterian Economics*, edited by Arnold Heertje and Mark Perlman, pp. 51–73. Ann Arbor, MI: St. Martin's Press, 1990a.
———. "The Future of the Global Economic and Monetary System." In *The Relationship between International Economic Activity and International Monetary Reconstruction*, edited by Miklos Szabo-Pelsoczi, pp. 209–219. Budapest: Institute for World Economics of the Hungarian Academy of Sciences, 1990b.
———. "The Capital Development of the Economy and the Structure of Financial Institutions." Working Paper No. 72. Annandale-on-Hudson, NY: The Levy Economics Institute, January 1992.
———. "Finance and Stability: The Limits of Capitalism." Working Paper No. 93, Annandale-on-Hudson, NY: The Levy Economics Institute, May 1993a.
———. "Schumpeter and Finance." In *Markets and Institutions in Economic Development*, edited by Salvatore Biasco, Alessandro Roncaglia and Michele Salvati, pp. 103–115. New York: St. Martin's Press, 1993b.
———. "Uncertainty and the Institutional Structure of Capitalist Economies. *Journal of Economic Issues* 30, 2 (1996): 357–368.
Minsky, Hyman P. and Charles J. Whalen. "Employment Security and the Institutional Prerequisites for Successful Capitalism." *Journal of Post Keynesian Economics* 19, 2 (Winter 1996–1997): 155–170.
Mishel, Lawrence, Jared Bernstein and Sylvia Allegretto. *The State of Working America, 2006–2007.* Ithaca, NY: ILR Press, 2006.
Organization for Economic Co-operation and Development. *OECD Countries Spend More on Research and Development, Face New Challenges.* Paris: OECD Publications, December 23, 2004.
———. *Growing Unequal? Income Distribution and Poverty in OECD Countries*. Paris: OECD Publications, October 2008.
Palley, Thomas I. "Financialization: What It Is and Why It Matters." Working Paper No. 525. Annandale-on-Hudson, NY: The Levy Economics Institute, December 2007.
Palme, Joakim. "Income Distribution in Sweden." *Japanese Journal of Social Security Policy* 5, 1 (June 2006): 16–27.
Perelman, Michael. "The Corrosive Qualities of Inequality: The Roots of the Current Meltdown." *Challenge* 51, 5 (September/October 2008): 40–64.
Philippon, Thomas and Ariell Reshef. "Skill Based Financial Development: Education, Wages, and Occupations in the U.S. Financial Sector." Working Paper. New York: Stern School of Business, New York University, September 2007.
Phillips, Kevin. *Wealth and Democracy: A Political History of the American Rich.* New York: Broadway Books, 2002.
Piketty, Thomas and Emmanuel Saez. "Income Inequality in the United States, 1913–1998. *Quarterly Journal of Economics* 118, 1 (February 2003, with updated tables July 2008): 1–39. Updated tables at: http://elsa.berkeley.edu/~saez/. Accessed March 6, 2009.
Pollin, Robert. "Financial Structures and Egalitarian Economic Policy." *New Left Review* 214 (Nov./Dec. 1995): 26–61.

Rajan, Raghuram G. and Luigi Zingales. *Saving Capitalism from the Capitalists*. Princeton, NJ: Princeton University Press, 2004.

Ramstad, Yngve. "A Pragmatist's Quest for Holistic Knowledge: The Scientific Methodology of John R. Commons." *Journal of Economic Issues* 20, 4 (1986): 1067–1105.

Riihelä, Marja, Risto Sullström, and Matti Tuomala. "Trends in Top Income Shares in Finland." VATT Discussion Papers No. 371. Helsinki: Government Institute for Economic Research, June 2005.

Sampaniotis, Theodosios. E-mail correspondence with one of the authors. March 13, 2009.

Samuel, Henry. "U.S. Calls on Sweden's 'Mr. Fix It' Bo Lundgren." *Telegraph.co.uk*. March 20, 2009. http://www.telegraph.co.uk/finance/newsbysector/banksandfinance/5019186/US-calls-on-Mr-Fix-It.html. Accessed March 25, 2009.

Saunders, Peter and Bruce Bradbury. "Monitoring Trends in Poverty and Income Distribution: Data, Methodology and Measurement." *Economic Record* 82, 258 (September 2006): 341–364.

Schumpeter, Joseph A. *Theory of Economic Development*. Cambridge, MA: Harvard University Press, 1934.

Scorse, Gerald E. "Tax Policy Favors Investors Over Wage Earners." *Providence Journal Bulletin*. March 31, 2008, C5.

Sefton, Tom, John Hills and Holly Sutherland. "Poverty, Inequality and Redistribution." In *Towards a More Equal Society? Poverty, Inequality and Policy Since 1997*, edited by John Hills, Tom Sefton, and Kitty Stewart, pp. 21–45. Bristol, UK: Policy Press, 2009.

Steelman, Aaron and John A. Weinberg. "What's Driving Wage Inequality?" Federal Reserve Bank of Richmond *Economic Quarterly* 91, 3 (Summer 2005): 1–17.

Sum, Andrew and Paulo Tobar (with Joseph McLaughlin and Sheila Palma). "The Great Divergence: Real-Wage Growth of All Workers Versus Finance Workers." *Challenge* 51, 3 (May/June 2008): 57–79.

Useem, Michael. *Investor Capitalism: How Money Managers are Changing the Face of Corporate America*. New York: Basic Books, 1996.

Weller, Christian. "America Needs a More Balanced Economy." *Perspectives on Work* 10, 1 (Summer 2006): 14–16.

Whalen, Charles J. "Money-Manager Capitalism and the End of Shared Prosperity." *Journal of Economic Issues* 31, 2 (1997): 517–525.

———. "Toward 'Wisely Managed' Capitalism: Post-Keynesian Institutionalism and the Creative State." *Forum for Social Economics* 37, 1 (Spring 2008a): 43–60.

———. "John R. Commons and John Maynard Keynes on Economic History and Policy: The 1920s and Today." *Journal of Economic Issues* 42, 1 (March 2008b): 225–242.

———. "A Minsky Moment: Reflections on Hyman P. Minsky (1919–1996)." *Journal of Economic Issues* 42, 1 (2008c): 249–253.

———. "The Credit Crunch: A Minsky Moment." *Studie Note Di Economia* 13, 1 (2008d): 315–333.

———. "Post-Keynesian Institutionalism and the Anxious Society." In *Alternative Institutional Structures: Evolution and Impact*, edited by Sandra S. Batie and Nicholas Mercuro, pp. 273–299. New York: Routledge, 2008e.

Wilber, C. K. and Robert Harrison. "The Methodological Basis of Institutional Economics: Pattern Models, Storytelling, and Holism." *Journal of Economic Issues* 12, 1 (1978): 61–90.

Wilber, C.K. and K.P. Jameson. *An Inquiry into the Poverty of Economics.* Notre Dame, IN: University of Notre Dame Press, 1983.

Wolfson, Martin H. "Institutional Analysis of Financial Crises." In *Crossing the Mainstream: Ethical and Methodological Issues in Economics*, edited by Amitava K. Dutt and Kenneth P. Jameson, pp. 332–352. Notre Dame, IN: University of Notre Dame Press, 2001.

Wray, L. Randall. "Minsky's Approach to Employment Policy and Poverty: Employer of Last Resort and the War on Poverty." Working Paper No. 515. Annandale-on-Hudson, NY: The Levy Economics Institute of Bard College, September 2007.

———. "The Commodities Market Bubble: Money Manager Capitalism and the Financialization of Commodities." Public Policy Brief No. 96. Annandale-on-Hudson, NY: The Levy Economics Institute of Bard College, 2008.

Zak, Paul J. "Values and Value: Moral Economics." In *Moral Markets: The Critical Role of Values in the Economy*, edited by Paul J. Zak, pp. 259–279. Princeton, NJ: Princeton University Press, 2008.

Zalewski, David A. "Retirement Insecurity in the Age of Money Manager Capitalism." *Journal of Economic Issues* 36, 2 (2002): 349–356.

———. "Wealth and Power: Ethical Implications of Executive Compensation Since the 1980s." In *The Institutionalist Tradition in Labor Economics*, edited by Dell P. Champlin and Janet T. Knoedler, pp. 286–296. Armonk, NY: M.E. Sharpe, 2004.

26. Post-Keynesian institutionalism and the failure of neoliberalism

This article looks at the U.S. economy from the perspective of post-Keynesian institutionalism (PKI), a research tradition at the intersection of post-Keynesian and institutional economics. The article builds on two propositions offered by institutionalist John Watkins (2020): (1) addressing economic problems must begin by "recognizing the world as we find it," and (2) exploring "the failure of neoliberalism" is an important way to return realism to economics. By highlighting economic insecurity as the flip side of financialization, the latter of which is a key neoliberal aim, it underscores neoliberalism's failure as well as the promise of PKI, thereby helping to return realism to economics.

ECONOMIC INSECURITY

PKI has always been about starting with the reality of human experience and working to fashion a better world rooted in broadly shared prosperity (Whalen 2020). That requires looking beyond headline economic statistics. For example, in 2019, the final year of a decade-long economic expansion prior to the coronavirus (COVID-19) pandemic, the U.S. unemployment rate was 3.7 percent; the price index for personal consumption expenditures (the Federal Reserve's preferred inflation measure) increased at an annual rate of only 1.6 percent; real gross domestic product grew at 2.3 percent; and corporate profits and stock prices were at record-setting highs (Federal Reserve Bank of St. Louis 2020). Yet a national survey found that only 33 percent of Americans believed that "children today in our country" will eventually become better off financially than their parents (Pew Research Center 2019). Understanding why necessitates looking more closely at various dimensions of U.S. economic insecurity.[1]

Reprinted with permission from *Journal of Economic Issues* 55 (2), September 2021, 469–476.

Job Loss and Wage Stagnation

For most American families, stable jobs at good wages are the key to economic security. But permanent job loss has increasingly become a concern for U.S. workers over several decades. In the early decades after World War II, unemployed workers were often "laid off" with the expectation of being rehired at a later date. However, a growing trend since the mid-1970s has been toward losing a job permanently, which could be the result, for example, of downsizing, or, increasingly, because temporary work was completed (Valletta 2005).

As a result of the trend toward permanent job loss, the *duration* of unemployment at any stage in the business cycle has increased over time. For example, the average duration of an ongoing unemployment spell at the peak of the business cycle rose steadily from 7.9 weeks in 1969 to 21.7 weeks in 2019 (Federal Reserve Bank of St. Louis 2020). As Robert Valletta (2005, 1) writes, "Rising unemployment duration is linked to declining job security through the key contribution of rising permanent job loss." Moreover, offshoring and automation have increased the risk of job loss for U.S. workers: one study, for example, finds that a quarter of the nation's jobs and half of its low-skill positions are vulnerable to being offshored or automated within about a decade (Devaraj et al. 2017). In short, the reality and risk of permanent job loss combine to represent one dimension of economic insecurity that has increased over the past several decades.

Wage stagnation is another dimension of that insecurity. From the end of World War II until the 1970s, workers' wages increased broadly and robustly. But growth in average hourly wages, after adjusting for inflation, has stagnated since the mid-1970s. Those wages were only 10 percent higher in 2017 than in 1973, while productivity more than doubled over the same period (Shambaugh et al. 2017, i). Meanwhile, the ratio of CEO compensation to average worker compensation in the top 350 U.S. companies was 320-to-1 in 2019, up from 61-to-1 in 1989 and 21-to-1 in 1965 (Mishel and Kandra 2020).

Income Volatility and Thin Financial Cushions

Broadly experienced economic insecurity is also evident in income volatility and thin financial cushions. In the case of incomes, 34 percent of U.S. households experienced an income change of 25 percent or more between 2014 and 2015, according to one national survey. The median household experiencing an income loss over that period saw its income fall by 49 percent (Pew Charitable Trust 2017, 3–6). In contrast, looking at the overall economy in those years would show only economic expansion and modestly improving median household income.

Income volatility is not merely a phenomenon of the period following the Great Recession of 2007–2009. For example, Karen Dynan, Douglas Elmendorf, and Daniel Sichel (2012) find that household income "became noticeably more volatile between the early 1970s and the late 2000s," a trend they attribute to greater volatility in both earnings per hour and hours worked. They report: "The share of households experiencing a 50 percent plunge in income over a two-year period climbed from about 7 percent in the early 1970s to more than 12 percent in the early 2000s before retreating to 10 percent in the run-up to the Great Recession." According to the Aspen Institute (2016), labor market changes account for much of the increased volatility: "Disruptions [to income] seem to have become more common over time as employers increasingly demand flexible labor and as the 'on-demand' economy has grown."

While volatile incomes underscore the need for precautionary saving, household financial cushions are remarkably thin. Survey research conducted by the Federal Reserve in 2019 indicates that 37 percent of American adults were unprepared to cover an unexpected $400 expense (such as a car repair or medical bill) without selling something or borrowing money; that's actually a substantial improvement since 2013 (earlier in the post-Great-Recession expansion), when 52 percent were unable to cover such an expense (Federal Reserve 2020, 2014). The Federal Reserve (2020) also found that, in 2019, one out of four adults skipped medical care, such as a visit to a doctor or dentist, because they were unable to afford the cost, and, among non-retirees, that same fraction of respondents (25 percent) reported having no retirement savings.

According to economist Anqi Chen, households live paycheck to paycheck primarily because of indebtedness in a variety forms ranging from unpaid credit card balances and installment loans to student loans and mortgage payments (Nova 2019). Few long-term studies have tracked financial insecurity, but analyses of unexpected household expenses from 1986 through 2012 (Hacker et al. 2013) and financial cushions from 1988 through 2007 (Weller and Logan 2009) combine to suggest rising financial insecurity through 2010, followed by somewhat increased financial security during the subsequent long economic expansion.

Declining Mobility and the Shrinking Middle Class

At the heart of many conceptions of the American Dream are notions of upward economic mobility and a robust middle class. But widening inequality of income and wealth since the 1970s are eclipsing mobility and the middle class as key features of the U.S. economy. Because the overall inequality trends are well established and widely studied (see, for example, Saez and Zucman 2020), we focus here on what has happened to mobility and the middle class.

Upward mobility in the United States has been eroding for decades. For example, recent research suggests that only half of those born in the mid-1980s are projected to earn more than their parents, a fraction that has fallen markedly yet steadily since those born in the 1940s (Chetty et al. 2017). Moreover, according to Raj Chetty (2016, 37), if one views the American Dream as the case of being born to parents in the bottom fifth of the income distribution and reaching the top fifth, "Your chances of achieving the 'American Dream' are almost two times higher if you're growing up in Canada relative to the United States."

The middle class—and its share of aggregate household income—has been shrinking since the early 1970s. In research conducted in 2015, the Pew Research Center (2015) defined middle-class Americans as "adults whose annual household income is two-thirds to double the national median, about $42,000 to $126,000 annually in 2014 dollars for a household of three." Under that definition, "the middle class made up 50 percent of the U.S. adult population in 2015, down from 61 percent in 1971." To be sure, the study found that, over the period examined, the proportion of adults living in upper-income households grew slightly more than did the proportion of lower-income households. However, the Pew analysis also found that the share of aggregate household income held by middle-income households "plunged" from 62 percent in 1970 to 43 percent in 2014, and that the share held by lower-income households fell as well, resulting in 49 percent of all household income accruing to high-income households (Pew Research Center 2015, 4–5). In short, the U.S. economy appears to have polarized at the expense of the middle class, and those outside the upper-income tier must manage with a substantially smaller share of aggregate income than in the past.

Poverty and Despair

In 2018, poverty and despair were remarkably evident in the United States despite nearly a decade of macroeconomic expansion. In that year, a report by the United Nations Human Rights Council noted that the United States is "a land of stark contrasts"—one of the world's wealthiest societies, yet also characterized by the highest rate of income inequality among Western countries. The report found that about 40 million people (12.7 percent) live in poverty, 18.5 million in extreme poverty, and 5.3 million in "Third World conditions" of absolute poverty (Alston 2018, 3). It also found that the United States "has the highest youth poverty rate in the Organization for Economic Cooperation and Development (OECD), and the highest infant mortality rate among comparable OECD states. Its citizens live shorter and sicker lives compared to those living in all other rich democracies."

Although the United Nations report did not offer a historical perspective, the U.S. Department of Health and Human Services (HHS) provided a 50-year look at poverty in the United States in 2016. According to the HHS analysis, the U.S. poverty rate "fell precipitously" during the 1960s, reached a low of 11.1 percent in 1973, and then "remained within a fairly narrow range" (between 11.3 and 15.2 percent), rising with recessions and falling with economic expansions. The HHS analysis also shows that women, children, and people of color are often disproportionately affected by poverty, and that the poverty rate among workers has been close to 7 percent for three decades (Chaudry et al. 2016, 8, 23, 31).

The element of despair entered the picture in 2018 when the Centers for Disease Control reported three consecutive years of declining life expectancy in the United States; the last time that happened was in 1915–1918, owing to World War I and a flu pandemic (Brooks 2018). In the more recent instance, the nation's opioid epidemic was an important contributing factor, but Anne Case and Angus Deaton (2017) dug deeper and found that many deaths from drug abuse, alcoholism, and suicide are "deaths of despair," linked to decades of erosion of employment opportunities and economic conditions for workers, especially those without a college education.

Feeling Squeezed: Beyond the Numbers

The Pew survey cited at the start of this section suggests that most Americans were anxious about the ability of U.S. families to make continued economic gains even before the COVID-19 pandemic. The rest of the section has gone beyond the macroeconomic headlines to offer some of the reasons for that anxiety. But to fully understand U.S. economic insecurity requires going even further; it requires going beyond the numbers entirely.

Journalist Alissa Quart (2018) does just that in *Squeezed: Why Our Families Can't Afford America*. Quart weaves her own story in with those of others struggling to stay afloat in a sea of insecurity. For example, they include: a librarian overwhelmed by unexpected hospital expenses, retail workers holding down multiple jobs, an immigrant nanny who can't leave work early to make school visits with her son, adjunct professors living in poverty, a middle-aged engineer looking for work after corporate downsizing, teachers who drive for Uber at night, and a manager who routinely gets fired after completing a big project. Their stories show us that while economic insecurity centers mainly on work and pay, it also intersects with shortcomings in how society approaches matters including healthcare, childcare, education, and retirement. Quart isn't quite sure how to explain or fix the situation, but she does recognize that much of today's insecurity involves economic changes that have been occurring "since at least the Reagan era" (Quart 2018, 47).

INSECURITY, FINANCIALIZATION, AND NEOLIBERALISM

Post-Keynesian institutionalists, of course, have an explanation for today's insecurity. According to PKI, the spread and intensification of economic insecurity since the 1970s is attributable primarily to emergence of what Hyman Minsky called money manager capitalism. In other words, that insecurity is the flip side of what today is often called financialization. The insecurity also highlights the failure of neoliberalism.

Insecurity and Financialization

According to PKI, money manager capitalism is an era of U.S. capitalist development that began to take shape in the 1970s (with hints appearing even a bit earlier) and emerged in the early 1980s, replacing the managerial capitalism that was fashioned in response to the Great Depression (Whalen 2020). In the managerial era, corporate managers were the masters of the private-sector economy. In the managed-money era—which remains with us today—institutional investors emerged to exert their influence on financial markets and business enterprises, resulting in a focus on maximization of shareholder value (Minsky and Whalen 1996–1997).

Today, that focus is considered to be the heart of what many call financialization. A key common element in both post-Keynesian institutionalist research and the financialization literature is recognition that businesses' emphasis on shareholder value has led to a "hollowing" of corporations (by various means, including subcontracting, outsourcing, offshoring, and franchising) and an assault on unions and labor costs—indeed, an effort to treat labor (as much as possible) like a spot-market commodity (see, for example, Weil 2014; and Lazonick 2015). This outcome is especially true as private equity firms have played an increased role in the buying and selling of companies: cutting workers, reducing wages, and slashing benefits are all part of their business strategy (see, for example, Appelbaum and Batt 2014). In short, rising economic insecurity and financialization are two sides of the same coin.[2]

The Failure of Neoliberalism

The economic insecurity of the past several decades also demonstrates the failure of neoliberalism. According to John Watkins and James Seidelman (2019, 363), neoliberalism is a political and economic philosophy that originated in the 1960s and 1970s and espouses "economic freedom and laissez-faire policies as the best means of achieving economic prosperity." They also maintain that financialization is a key aim of neoliberalism (along with the complementary aims of free trade and economic deregulation). Gérard Duménil and Dominique Lévy (2005, 17) further underscore neoliberalism's connection to financialization, arguing that most analysts see neoliberalism as "the ideological expression of the reassertion of the power of finance." Instead of delivering broadly shared prosperity, neoliberalism tightened the grip of money managers on the economy and delivered growing insecurity for most others.

The presidential election of 2016 actually provides evidence of both the failure of neoliberalism and the entrenchment of financialization. As Watkins and Seidelman (2019, 364–365) note, many voters supported Donald Trump because he promised to provide jobs, end wage stagnation, and reverse "the decimation of working-class and middle-class standards of living." In short, those voters sought to end the economic insecurity produced by more than a generation of financialization and neoliberalism. But even as the election was largely a rejection of neoliberalism, Watkins and Seidelman also show that what emerged instead was a proto-fascist neoliberalism. Moreover, regardless of what Trump might have promised, we now know that he did not "reverse the shift from industrial capitalism to financial capitalism" (Watkins and Seidelman 2019, 364).

CONCLUSION: COVID-19 AND THE NEED FOR CHANGE

Two concluding observations are warranted. One is that, while the foregoing focused on the half-century preceding the COVID-19 pandemic, that pandemic has only intensified economic insecurity, especially for those most financially vulnerable (Mendez-Smith and Klee 2020). It also exposed other fundamental shortcomings of money manager capitalism, which have resulted in inadequate industrial capacity (leading to shortages of equipment needed to combat the pandemic), businesses ill-prepared to weather economic adversity (owing to heavy use of debt financing), and a dysfunctional public-sector safety net (traceable to the adverse influence of financialization on policymaking and public administration).[3]

The other observation is that the COVID-19 pandemic underscores the need for economic change—away from financialized (money manager) capitalism and toward more broadly shared and sustainable prosperity. Fortunately, contributors to PKI offer more than just theory and analyses. For years, they have proposed tax, regulatory, and other policy changes to bring corporate objectives and business practices closer in line with the interests of workers, communities, and the nation. They have also advocated labor law reform to restore workers' rights to organize and bargain collectively, stronger fiscal stabilizers and economic security policies to bolster economic well-being (including a job guarantee, living wages, retirement supports, and health care for all), and a technology-driven industrial policy to secure prosperity by focusing on "brainpower" industries, resilient infrastructure, and environmental sustainability (Whalen 2010; Zalewski 2003).[4] Neoliberalism has failed; by recognizing the world as we find it, PKI helps us fashion a more constructive way forward.

NOTES

1. To highlight the long-term trend toward U.S. economic insecurity, this article looks first at the economy prior to 2020 and then closes with a brief discussion of the economic consequences of the COVID-19 pandemic.
2. The app-driven "gig economy" is the latest phase of the era of money manager capitalism; it preys upon and fuels the spread of worker insecurity and contingent work.
3. For a look at the public sector's transformation in the era of money manager capitalism, see James Galbraith (2008).
4. For an overview with many references, see Whalen (2020); for a broad strategy that remains relevant, see Minsky and Whalen (1996–1997).

REFERENCES

Alston, Philip. 2018. "Report of the Special Rapporteur on Extreme poverty and Human Rights on His Mission to the United States of America." United Nations Human Rights Council. New York: United Nations General Assembly.

Appelbaum, Eileen, and Rosemary Batt. 2015. *Private Equity at Work*. Ithaca, NY: ILR Press.

Aspen Institute. 2016. "Income Volatility: A Primer." https://tinyurl.com/yy9qz9oy. Accessed November 12, 2020.

Brooks, David. 2018. "It's Not the Economy, Stupid." *New York Times*, November 29, 2018. https://tinyurl.com/y9mdo5vj. Accessed November 14, 2020.

Case, Ann, and Angus Deaton. 2017. "Mortality and Morbidity in the 21st Century." *Brookings Papers on Economic Activity* Spring 2017: 397–443.

Chaudry, Ajay, Christopher Wimer, Suzanne Macartney, Lauren Frohlich, Colin Campbell, Kendall Swenson, Don Oellerich, and Susan Hauan. 2016. *Poverty in the United States: 50-Year Trends and Safety Net Impacts March 2016*. Washington, DC: U.S. Department of Health and Human Services.

Chetty, Raj. 2016. "Improving Opportunities for Economic Mobility." In *Economic Mobility*, edited by the Federal Reserve Bank of St. Louis, 35–42. St. Louis, Missouri: Federal Reserve Bank of St. Louis.

Chetty, Raj, David Grusky, Maximilian Hell, Nathaniel Hendren, Robert Manduca, and Jimmy Narang. 2017. "The Fading American Dream." *Science* 356 (6336): 398–406.

Devaraj, Srikant, Michael J. Hicks, Emily J. Wornell, and Dagney Faulk. 2017. *How Vulnerable are American Communities to Automation, Trade, and Urbanization?* Muncie, IN: Center for Business and Economic Research, Ball State University.

Duménil, Gérard, and Dominique Lévy. 2005. "Costs and Benefits of Neoliberalism: A Class Analysis." In *Financialization in the World Economy*, edited by Gerald A. Epstein, 17–43. Cheltenham (UK): Edward Elgar.

Dynan, Karen, Douglas Elmendorf, and Daniel Sichel. 2012. "The Evolution of Household Income Volatility." *B.E. Journal of Economic Analysis and Policy* 12 (2): 1–42.

Federal Reserve. 2020. *Report of the Economic Well-Being of Households in 2019, May 2020*. Washington, DC: Board of Governors of the Federal Reserve System.

Federal Reserve. 2014. *Report on the Economic Well-Being of Households in 2013, July 2014*. Washington, DC: Board of Governors of the Federal Reserve System.

Federal Reserve Bank of St. Louis. 2020. U.S. Bureau of Economic Analysis and Bureau of Labor Statistics data retrieved from FRED (Federal Reserve Economic Data). https://fred.stlouisfed.org. Accessed November 11, 2020.

Galbraith, James K. 2008. *The Predator State*. New York: Free Press.

Hacker, Jacob, Gregory Huber, Austin Nichols, Philipp Rehm, and Stuart Craig. 2013. "ESI Update: Economic Security Continues to Improve; Big Strains Remain." Available at www.insecurityindex.org. Accessed November 12, 2020.

Lazonick, William. 2015. "Labor in the 21st Century." In *Inequality, Uncertainty, and Opportunity*, edited by Christian Weller, 143–196. Champaign, IL: Labor and Employment Relations Association.

Mendez-Smith, Brian, and Mark Klee. 2020. "Census Bureau's New Household Pulse Survey Shows Who Is Hit Hardest During COVID-19 Pandemic." Washington, DC: US Census Bureau. https://tinyurl.com/yyqrcbsf. Accessed November 15, 2020.

Minsky, Hyman P., and Charles J. Whalen. 1996–1997. "Economic Insecurity and the Institutional Prerequisites for Successful Capitalism." *Journal of Post Keynesian Economics* 19 (2): 155–170.

Mishel, Lawrence, and Jori Kandra. 2020. *CEO Compensation Surged 14 Percent in 2019 to $21.3 Million*. Washington, DC: Economic Policy Institute.

Nova, Annie. 2019. "Many Americans Who Can't Afford a $400 Emergency Blame Debt." CNBC. July 20, 2019. Available at https://tinyurl.com/y4bnrznf. Accessed November 12, 2020.

Pew Charitable Trust. 2017. "How Income Volatility Interacts with American Families' Financial Security." Available at https://tinyurl.com/y682o5lm. Accessed November 12, 2020.

Pew Research Center. 2015. *The American Middle Class is Losing Ground*. Washington, DC. December 9, 2015. Available at https://tinyurl.com/y4tmt5o7. Accessed November 13, 2020.

Pew Research Center. 2019. "Pessimism about Children's Future is Widespread in Most Economies." January 2, 2019. Available at https://tinyurl.com/y2f7vc7e. Accessed November 11, 2020.

Quart, Alissa. 2018. *Squeezed: Why Our Families Can't Afford America*. New York: Ecco.

Saez, Emmanuel, and Gabriel Zucman. 2020. "The Rise of Income and Wealth Inequality in America." *Journal of Economic Perspectives* 34 (4): 3–26.

Shambaugh, Jay. Ryan Nunn, Patrick Liu, and Greg Nantz. 2017. *Thirteen Facts about Wage Growth*. Washington, DC: The Hamilton Project.

Valletta, Robert. 2005. "Rising Unemployment Duration in the United States: Causes and Consequences." Federal Reserve Bank of San Francisco. Available at https://tinyurl.com/yxoofrjb. Accessed November 11, 2020.

Watkins, John P. 2020. "AFEE at ASSA 2021 Call for Papers." Available at https://tinyurl.com/y6x2g36n. Accessed November 7, 2020.

Watkins, John P., and James E. Seidelman. 2019. "The Last Gasp of Neoliberalism." *Journal of Economic Issues* 53 (2): 363–369.

Weil, David. 2014. *The Fissured Workplace*. Cambridge, MA: Harvard University Press.

Weller, Christian E., and Amanda M. Logan. 2009. "Measuring Middle Class Economic Security." *Journal of Economic Issues* 43 (2): 327–336.

Whalen, Charles J. 2010. "Economic Policy for the Real World." *Policy Note*, No. 2010–1. Annandale-on-Hudson, NY: Levy Economics Institute of Bard College.

Whalen, Charles J. 2020. "Post-Keynesian Institutionalism: Past, Present, and Future." *Evolutionary and Institutional Economic Review* 17 (1): 71–92.

Zalewski, David A. 2003. "Corporate Objectives—Maximizing Social versus Private Equity." *Journal of Economic Issues* 37 (2): 503–509.

Index